The Art of Talking with Children

The Simple Keys to Nurturing Kindness, Creativity, and Confidence in Kids

Rebecca Rolland, EdD

HarperOne

An Imprint of HarperCollinsPublishers

To Philippe, Sophie, and Paul

HarperCollins books may be purchased for educational, business, or sales promotional use. For information, please email the Special Markets Department at SPsales@harpercollins.com.

FIRST EDITION

Designed by Terry McGrath

Library of Congress Cataloging-in-Publication Data has been applied for.

ISBN 978-0-06-293888-6

22 23 24 25 26 LSC 10 9 8 7 6 5 4 3 2 1

Contents

Why Conversation Matters

I know we *did* a lot," I said to my husband, Philippe, after we'd finished putting our two kids to bed and cleaning up. "But what did we *talk* about?"

"I don't know." Philippe spoke with his usual straightforwardness. "The usual, I guess. Really, I don't remember."

We sat in our Boston apartment at the close of a busy weekend, planning the week's schedule as we usually did on Sundays. We had to get organized before Monday. Still, despite our best intentions, we usually forgot something. There was just so much to juggle. Our weeks passed, like those of many families, in a blur of activity; our weekends, too. We had little time to prioritize or reflect . . . and, I realized, little time to talk with each other, or with our kids.

That lack was especially ironic, given what I did for a living and what I was passionate about. For more than a decade, my work as a speech-language pathologist, lecturer, and researcher has centered on understanding and supporting children's language and literacy development. I've taught at Harvard Graduate School of Education and lectured at Harvard Medical School. During those years, I've worked with children from toddler age through graduate school. My work has brought me into contact with so many different children and families, from high-poverty preschools to Montessori schools, hospital clinics, and many places in between. I've met kids one-on-one, in small groups, and in classrooms, to assess their language and reading levels and teach them speaking, listening, reading, and writing skills. I've served as an academic learning specialist and taught kids with dyslexia, those on the autism spectrum, and those with major reading struggles. I've loved understanding these children's development, following them closely, talking with their parents, and figuring out strategies to help.

So that question I asked Philippe—minor as it seemed—mattered to me. Over the next days, it hung in my mind. In the rush of activity, what exactly *did* we talk about?

In talking to other parents, I realized our family wasn't alone. Nearly everyone *was* truly busy and didn't find time for much good conversation. "We hardly get home in time for dinner. Then it's a story and bedtime," one friend said. Another explained, "We know our son wants our attention at dinner, but when he's quiet, we use the time to check email." The frantic pace of family life didn't seem to allow for much beyond surface talk. Many parents I knew raised kids while working and caring for older relatives, part of the "sandwich generation."[1] Others worked night shifts or had to travel for work, or had long commutes and felt pressured to make the limited time with their kids count. Still others were exhausted by the demands of school, sports schedules, or college application deadlines.[2,3,4] And that wasn't even considering self-care.

When Conversations Happen

When I thought more carefully about our household conversations, I realized my daughter, Sophie, then five years old, and I *had* had many engaged, inspired conversations in the last weeks and months—but they hadn't been at the forefront of my mind. Several years back, I'd taken her to Boston's Museum of Fine Arts. She'd run around dim-lit hallways in the ancient Egyptian rooms, peering into each sarcophagus and asking question after question. Finally, she sat on a bench and grew quiet in the peace of the dark halls.

"Where did the mummies go?" she asked after a long pause.

"Sorry, what?" I sat beside her as she swung her legs.

"You said the mummies aren't here anymore. That their *bodies* are, but they aren't. So where did they go?"

"Hmm, good question." I considered myself spiritual, but not religious, and definitely didn't have an answer for that. So I hedged. "The Egyptians thought they'd travel to another world. That's why they worked so hard to mummify them."

"Okay." She sounded impatient. "But which part of them left? Their bodies are still here."

"Yes—but they're dead."

"Sure." A pause—then questions tumbled out. "But where did they *go*? And before they were born, where were they?" She met my gaze. "And where were *you* before you were born?"

"Wow—that's a tough one." I tried to buy time. "I don't remember. Do *you*?"

"Nope." Squinting, she shook her head.

"And if you had to guess?"

"I was an old man." She sounded surprisingly certain. "I got sick of being so old, so I turned into a baby again."

"I can see that." I put my arm around her.

"I'm starving." With a jolt, she stood and twirled around. "Let's have lunch."

On the way back, I couldn't help marveling at her insight and how easily she'd arrived at it. Somehow, at her age, she'd stumbled on the concept of reincarnation, or a version of it. And why had she brought it up, I wondered, precisely then? I thought back to her fascination with mummies, which had begun with a few Halloween picture books. Almost as soon as she could talk, she'd asked about them: whether they were real, if they could bite. Today's deeper question hadn't sprung out of nowhere. Instead, it had been building, bit by bit, starting with much simpler ones.

But what about *my* side of the conversation? I was struck by the fact that Sophie had seemed *more* engaged and interested in talking, precisely because I *didn't* have answers. Over the past weeks and months, I'd answered her dozens of questions as best as I could. This time, I admitted I didn't know. I didn't pretend to be an expert. Instead, I simply provided an opportunity and a willingness to dive in. As I'd later come to realize, these opportunities to talk abound if you open your mind to them. It's not about being perfect, having expertise, or even posing the right questions. It's definitely not about knowing exactly what to say. It has far more to do with an attitude of curious waiting: using talk to open a window and letting your child take it from there.

To be fair, this talk with Sophie was unusual. The fact that I still remember it so well, three years later, is testimony to how infrequently such conversations happen if we don't make an effort to cultivate them. But these conversations don't *have* to be unusual. Sure, having a quiet time and place to talk had made it easier for me to focus on Sophie and answer her questions. But talking like this doesn't require a special occasion. You don't even need to leave the house. A great conversation could have happened over a book or been inspired by the back of a cereal box.

But how should we make talk more of a priority? I wondered. Add "have quality conversation" to our weekly schedules? No one I knew had the mental energy or time, and surely no one needed the guilt. I had to think differently about talk in our house, and I imagined that other parents might be willing to also. Because what if talk with our kids wasn't another item on the to-do list, or yet another thing to worry about, but an opportunity?

In fact, you can make a difference in the quality of your conversations, and there's a method for doing it well that science supports. The opportunities are there, available at any time, anywhere, and to anyone. This book is designed to explore why these deeper, authentic conversations often go missing, and more important, how we can have more of them, in ways that help us raise curious, compassionate kids while enjoying ourselves.

With a few tweaks and key habits, you can have far more of these great conversations. They can become not more things to remember, or more stress or work, but engaging, fun additions to your lives. You can weave them throughout your days in ways that keep things interesting and, most important, that help your kids and your whole family thrive.

Before moving on, a short note on terms: in this book, I talk about parents for simplicity's sake. But, thank goodness, kids have many others who love, raise, and care for them: grandparents, cousins, aunts, neighbors, foster parents, and host families, as well as teachers, day-care staff, camp counselors, principals, babysitters, and nannies. It truly does take a village, and that goes for talk as well. If you find yourself interacting with kids on a regular basis, this book can help. Also, when I talk about kids, I'll be alternating "he" and "she" throughout this book.

The Great Conversation

When's the last time you had a great conversation with your child or children?

I don't mean a philosophical discussion, but one that intrigued or surprised you, that left you both wondering or curious. One that helped you understand each other better, brought you closer, or resolved an argument. One that you both engaged in, building on each other's ideas in a comfortable, back-and-forth flow. One that made you laugh out loud, or that seemed forgettable but that your child later reminded you of, showing he'd learned something or gained some insight. Or one that simply let you relax and enjoy each other's company.

I mean a conversation when you weren't talking about undone homework, clothes on the floor, the next day's school and sports schedules, who's picking whom up, or any number of other mundane logistical details. When you weren't rushing out for swim practice, or checking if your sixth-grader brought his violin, if you emailed the permission slip, or if your toddler put on his shoes. When you weren't asking "check-in" questions: How was the birthday party, did he enjoy the playdate, did the math test go well, or did he win the baseball game?

If you can think of one great conversation, try to come up with more. Remember them in detail. How recent were they? How often do they happen, as compared with the mundane ones?

If you struggled with that exercise, don't feel bad. You're far from the only one. Most of us talk with our kids every day. We listen if our kids are complaining or excitedly talking our ears off. We work to be patient. We're all trying our best. And yet our conversation is often trivial or mundane. We're distracted. We focus on getting points across but pay less attention to *how* we're talking, or how kids are hearing what we say. As a result, we miss out on chances for conversations that meet kids at their levels and evolve in a moment-by-moment way, as they have gradual insights or startling leaps. In fact, if we take the time to listen, there are so many opportunities right in front of us, not only to have kids follow directions or get answers right, but to help them stretch themselves: to make imaginative connections, empathize in new ways, or question what they thought they knew. That stretch is where the surprise happens, where kids feel challenged, where we feel intrigued or engaged, and where we often end up laughing out loud.

Instead, with the best of intentions, we're often focused on making sure our kids are successful in the short term. So many conversations revolve around scheduling rides, planning events, or asking about homework, birthday parties, sports outcomes, and grades. It's about getting things done for today and ready for tomorrow. It's about making sure balls aren't dropped and tasks are completed. There's little time to pause and discuss things (and prolong the dinner-making or homework-doing or cleaning up).

Yet, when we leave behind deeper conversations, we miss out on the chance to help kids truly relate and succeed, both now and in the long term. Success isn't the same thing as performance. Truer success comes not only in winning soccer games and scoring well on tests, but *also* in building skills like empathy and creativity that will serve kids in the moment, and for years to come. Really, if we want to raise thriving kids and build lasting bonds, it's those conversations we most need. What's more, those are often the conversations *kids* are longing for, even if they don't always say so. All kids, at every age, want to be heard and understood.

Why Does Conversation Matter?

A great conversation with your child offers a double promise. First, it helps you relate and connect in the moment in ways that almost nothing else can. Second, these conversations boost learning and well-being over the long term through building skills kids can use. See the figure on page 9 for how this double promise works.

The first promise is about the day-to-day. Great conversations aren't like broccoli—good for your kids, but unpleasant. Quite the opposite. Ideally, they're enjoyable and interesting, at best thought-provoking, even as they bond you over time.

In the moment, listening and talking in ways that let a child feel understood primes you to have a close, caring bond. When he feels respected, he is more likely to respect you. He asks deeper questions and shows more curiosity, since he feels you're on the journey alongside him. He's more willing to hear your side of an argument—even if he disagrees. And, afterward, you both have a better sense of where the other person is coming from, especially if you don't see things similarly.

When you offer this model of how to listen and talk in responsive ways, he's far more likely to learn those skills himself. He's also more likely to open up and share more of his real passions, interests, worries, and fears. That lets *you* understand better what he wants and needs and meet him at a "just-right" level. You might not give him everything he wants, but you understand his hopes and wants.

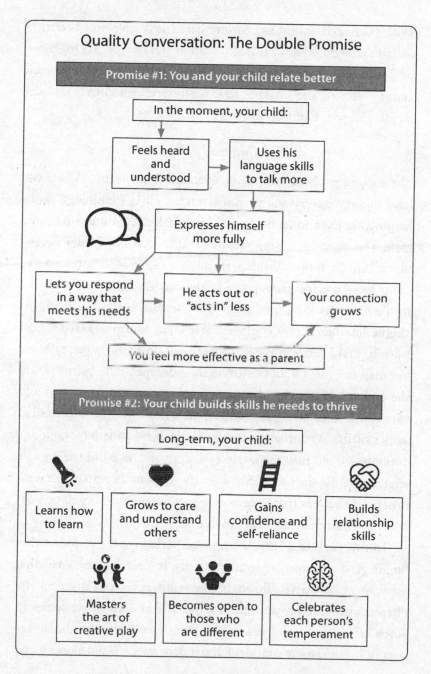

Quality Conversation: The Double Promise

Promise #1: You and your child relate better

In the moment, your child:

- Feels heard and understood
- Uses his language skills to talk more
- Expresses himself more fully
- Lets you respond in a way that meets his needs
- He acts out or "acts in" less
- Your connection grows
- You feel more effective as a parent

Promise #2: Your child builds skills he needs to thrive

Long-term, your child:

- Learns how to learn
- Grows to care and understand others
- Gains confidence and self-reliance
- Builds relationship skills
- Masters the art of creative play
- Becomes open to those who are different
- Celebrates each person's temperament

With your relationship as a strong base, he'll have an easier time socializing with others. He'll also tend to "act out" or "act in" less— he'll feel less anxious, depressed, overwhelmed, or simply irritable and stressed. As a result, your relationship feels smoother and more joyful, and your connection grows.

The Gateway to Skills

The second promise has to do with the long term. When you have quality conversations, you stretch a child's language skills, helping her expand on her initial ideas, ask deeper questions, and make the most surprising creative leaps. That builds her vocabulary, but far more. Talking through feelings and ideas makes them more precise: through talk, she clarifies to *herself* what she thinks, even as she learns to express herself. Back-and-forth dialogue lets her gently confront new ideas and perspectives and learn to make sense of them. In the most profound ways, talk lets her map her mental and emotional landscapes. She learns where she feels most proud and most vulnerable; where she shines and where she shies away; and where she's most and least confident in her skills. With that greater self-awareness, she has the foundation to go out into the world and strategically build the knowledge and skills she needs. She's also better able to empathize with others, as she sees that everyone is on a journey, and each person, adult or child, has his or her own unique gifts.

In my work as a speech-language pathologist, I've found that language is a gateway to so many skills, in precisely the areas that let your child thrive. Through conversation, as you'll see in the chapters that follow, your child will build skills and capacities in seven key areas. She'll learn how to learn. She'll learn to empathize deeply, become more confident and independent, build closer social bonds, and grow more playful and creative, more welcoming of differences among people, and more aware of her own and others' temperaments. Once developed, these skills let her become more compassionate, thoughtful, and understanding. She blossoms, becoming a better thinker and learner and a better friend. She learns to relate more easily, celebrate her own and others' quirks, and compromise in ways that meet everyone's needs. And she does so in a way that builds your bond. That bond strengthens through the process of working through arguments, making sense of disagreements, even noticing and responding to negative thoughts. It's not about perfection or constant happiness. It *is* about using dialogue to learn who each other is and appreciate each other—as your family dynamics evolve over time.

How Great Conversations Sound

The best part is that you can start early with these conversations. There are principles and conversational habits you can use from the time your child can talk, and even before, all the way through the young adult years. You won't use the same words or tone, and you may not even discuss the same topics, but the underlying principles stretch through the ages.

If all this sounds difficult or tedious, think again. More often than not, these conversations can be spur-of-the-moment, playful, and flowing. They let each person express his or her individuality in a way that celebrates uniqueness and quirks. Think less about one big talk, or even a series of them, and more about making the most of daily interactions—using what kids care about as springboards and jump starts.

But how? Over the course of writing this book, I interviewed dozens of researchers and scientists—linguists, psychologists, and neuroscientists—and spoke to countless parent colleagues, acquaintances, and friends to hear about their everyday experiences. I was inspired to see how many great conversations were happening, often under the radar. Many times, these conversations arose from irritating, awkward, or frustrating moments; the *last* places you'd think to look. For instance, a friend of mine finally managed to get her six-year-old daughter, Sasha, dressed and ready for a field trip, after going through the list of what they'd need. It had taken a long time, with Sasha constantly second-guessing every item. Afterward, on the car ride to school, Sasha kept grumbling. My friend asked her, "What six things would you take to the moon?" Sasha answered, then countered with, "What would *you* take, if you were traveling on a submarine?" Their car ride ended with laughter and a few creative lists, instead of their usual frustration. Sasha left for the field trip feeling happy and connected instead of stressed.

Or take my friend Debbie Blicher's discussion with her adopted daughter when her daughter was six years old. Sitting beside Debbie and her husband, her daughter said, "I feel so alone. I'm the only one in the family with red hair." Debbie responded, "Well, honey, I'm the only one who wears glasses." Her husband added, "And I'm the only one who's bald." Brightening, her daughter said, "And [my brother] is the only one who's really annoying!"

On the surface, these conversations might seem forgettable or even silly. But their power lies in their simplicity. There was no premeditation or sticking to a script. Instead, the parents noticed what their kids needed at the moment and let the dialogue flow. In the first, Sasha's mother broke open a tired routine by inviting Sasha to stretch her imagination. In the second, Debbie encouraged her daughter to see how each person in the family—adopted or not—was unique. Considering her daughter's age, she focused on the concrete, or aspects her daughter could see. And she left room for her daughter to express her frustration with her brother without feeling she'd be reprimanded. The shared humor bonded them and let her daughter realize it was okay to be different. In fact, it was normal. Her feelings didn't have to be perfect, either.

That's not to say being adopted is the same as wearing glasses, or that big worries can be resolved easily. In fact, Debbie told me this was only one in a long series of "adoption conversations" they'd had, many of them far more serious. But it *is* to say you can take on serious and important topics in lighthearted ways.

Certainly, these conversations aren't always possible to have. Sometimes, you or your child are in a hurry, or you're not in the mood. But these conversations are far less lofty than you might think. They don't have to take a long time. It's not about discussing philosophy or using big words. It's not about lecturing or making your point. It has far more to do with the back-and-forth, where you encourage your child's participation and say what you think. You leave room for twists and turns, let your child surprise you, and return to questions and ideas over days and weeks. You serve as a sounding board.

Of course a child will have many interactions and relationships with those around him—and each one changes him, in minor or major ways. We're far from the only ones to affect our kids. And yet, when they know we're there and that they can come back to us to reflect, they're far better able to navigate those other relationships. It's no accident that a study of kids who've bounced back from trauma found that each had at least one strong, stable relationship with a caring adult.[5] That groundbreaking study from the National Scientific Council on the Developing Child pointed to the power of "serve and return" conversations, in which there's a back-and-forth between adult and child, as especially powerful in building kids' resilience and even rewiring their brains.[6] To adapt to the challenges they'll face, kids need to have positive experiences and believe in themselves. They *also* need us as guides and mentors. Through checking in with them along the way, we can help them manage the lows and celebrate the highs.

The Power of Quality Conversation

Through my experiences as a researcher, lecturer, and mother, I've come to see how powerful high-quality conversation can be in raising thriving, successful kids. I've seen how these conversations can start early, with our interactions with babies. What's more, as I've seen in my clinical work and my talks with parents, quality conversation is a low-hanging fruit. It's freely available and doesn't require any advanced degree, training, or materials to harness it effectively.[7] You only need a bit of reflection, a few key habits, and small pockets of time.

Why can conversation do so much? It's because words aren't only entries in a dictionary. If conversation stopped at labeling, it would be horribly tedious. You never have a discussion where one person says, "Blue door," and you respond, "Open window." Kids never do, either. Even for young kids, many early words ("Hi," "bye-bye," "please") are all about managing relationships. As my Harvard colleague and well-known linguist Catherine Snow argues, words are concepts, ideas, and feelings; tools that let kids take on the world and relate. The more actively kids talk, and the more feedback they get, the bigger those toolboxes grow.[8,9]

Talking it out helps with far more than vocabulary. Kids who explain their learning strategies solve problems better and show more confidence.[10] Discussing and recognizing emotions helps kids show more empathy.[11] Those who talk through emotional stress have better coping skills.[12] And those who learn to describe themselves from multiple angles (for instance, as a brother, friend, and baseball player) show more creativity.[13] Quality conversation even links to greater happiness. College students who have more deep conversations tend to be happier than those who have fewer.[14] At the same time, conversation is a two-way street. It has as much to do with *how* kids are talking, and how engaged they are, as about the kinds of talk they hear.

This kind of engaged conversation is a fundamental gateway and an inborn need.[15,16,17] From infancy on, kids thirst to communicate, nearly as profoundly as they hunger for food. Even six-week-old babies communicate in back-and-forth exchanges, using eye gaze to respond when we talk.[18] These preverbal conversations help them notice what we're feeling and sense whether the outside world is safe or dangerous. Subconsciously, they match our emotions. When we interact with babies, even our heart rates sync up.[19,20]

On the flip side, kids suffer when they miss out on quality conversation. With the chain of communication broken or impaired, they can struggle to connect, at times in the most basic ways. Isolated, they may grow lonely, which in a vicious cycle further hurts their developing language skills. But even typically developing kids don't have a seamless language journey. All children have countless minor and major communication stumbles along the road to strong language skills. They all need regular opportunities to stretch their "talk muscles" and hone their listening abilities. For them—and for us as parents—conversation is a key way in.

The Goals of This Book

Here you'll find a new way to think about parenting: as a series of conversations. You'll find a new art—really, a blend of art and science—that lets you master the ways in which you talk to kids. I offer a model for quality conversation, which I call *rich* talk: conversations that help kids thrive more than any extracurricular class, team, or tutoring ever could. This talk, if you harness it well, lets you raise kids who are compassionate, creative, and curious, and who feel in control of their own happiness. This book unlocks the power of quality conversations in seven key areas of child development. Through mastering them, you'll build children's skills in learning, empathy, confidence and independence, relationships, play, openness to difference, and managing temperament. I've chosen these areas based on the science of child development, as well as interviews with dozens of researchers, parents, and caregivers. These areas are both critical for child development and open to change, based on children's talk and the talk they hear.

This book blends science with strategy, as I explore what works to enhance your conversations and why, for kids ranging from toddlers through teens. It's not about an overhaul, but about drawing on your family's unique strengths. When you reflect, you'll likely find you already have many habits that are working well. It's far more about *how* to have great conversations than precisely *what* to talk about. In this book, I encourage you to shore up your strengths, become conscious of trouble spots, and make small shifts to smooth the harder parts. To help, I introduce *conversational habits*, or easy, doable routines that act as gateways into big ideas. These routines are research-based and field-tested in my life and those of colleagues and friends. They're accessible, quick, and free. They support your child's development while helping your family feel more joyful, connected, and understanding, and less stressed.

While you may be naturally more social or happen upon these skills more easily, there's always room for enhancement. If you parent, care for, work with, or teach kids, you can benefit. Throughout, I'll also discuss what can happen when we don't make time for these habits. In our age of chatter and surface talk, our kids need these conversations more than ever. At the same time, each of us needs an approach tailored to our situations and to our kids. Think less about a perfectly orchestrated symphony and more about jazz. Your family is different from every other family, and there is no one right way to interact or talk. The only "right" way is the one that helps you and your family connect, reflect, and thrive.

As we go, I encourage you to keep an open mind about the strategies I suggest and try out the ones that seem interesting. As the Harvard psychologist Robert Kegan tells his students, think about "renting" these ideas, not buying them. Try them on and see how they fit. I fully expect that some strategies won't be useful or work well for you. That's normal. In fact, it's a good thing. If I— or anyone else—could prescribe ways of talking, we'd already be missing the point. Take my suggestions as jumping-off points, not scripts. The most important element is to notice your own family dynamics, pay attention to what helps or hurts, and make small shifts in response.

Already we invest a huge amount of time and passion caring for our kids. We give all our patience and love, even when we're exhausted or drained. But parenting is tough. Whether you're a single mom or surrounded by family, whether you have one child or four, whether you're raising preschoolers or preteens, there's a lot to keep track of and so many demands. Along with the fulfillment and joy of seeing kids grow up come countless everyday stresses—and the longer-term challenge of raising thriving, fulfilled adults. This book is designed to give you a powerful tool, often underappreciated and underused, that can help. I hope it makes your lives richer, bonds you more deeply, and lets you have more fun along the way.

CHAPTER 1

What Rich Talk Is,
and Why We're Missing Out

A real conversation always contains an invitation.
—DAVID WHYTE, POET[1]

It's a rainy Tuesday morning in November, and it's school-picture day. The Edwardses, a middle-class family living in a small town in the northeastern United States, are getting ready for work and school. The two teenage boys wake to their phone alarms. "Already?" the younger boy, Todd, moans. He'd stayed up late worrying over a math exam. At breakfast, he and his brother, Charles, sign on to their social media accounts to "like" their baseball team's win. "At least that's something," Charles says. Todd agrees, then gulps, remembering the homework he's left undone.

On the drive to school, both boys slump in the back, half-asleep. During the day, the parents work at office jobs: Jan, the boys' mother, as a hospital administrator, and Bill, her husband, as a marketing specialist. At school, the boys rush from science class to social studies, with both classes focused on test prep. In between, they text friends and scroll through videos but don't actually meet up with anyone.

At dinner, the family chats about Charles's upcoming college applications. "I can't believe there's only a month left," Jan says, flipping through forms. Soon the boys ask to be excused.

All in all, a standard day for a family raising two kids in a high-powered public school. They didn't talk much, but they didn't argue, either. Conversation came mostly in short blips. Even their media viewing involved customized, on-demand programming. Each child watched solo. There was no shared experience and no need to compromise.

In many ways, the family was lucky: they were all healthy, Bill and Jan had well-paying jobs, and the boys were getting decent grades. And yet, as Jan told me one evening, she sensed something was wrong. They were busy, but hardly seemed connected or even present in one another's lives. She certainly wasn't feeling a lot of joy. And yet, she convinced herself, that was normal. After all, she was raising teen boys, who weren't exactly known for being talkative.

Then came the phone calls. First from the school counselor, saying Charles was depressed and wanted to let Jan know but didn't feel he could tell her. Days later, Todd's soccer coach called, saying Todd was acting cruelly to his teammates. When confronted, Todd had apologized, saying he was stressed about school and had just broken up with his girlfriend.

Jan was stunned. Wouldn't Charles have come to her if he felt depressed? Wouldn't she have seen signs of Todd's aggression? She hadn't even *known* he'd had a girlfriend. Bill, when he heard the news, was equally dumbfounded.

"I'd thought we were all moving along just fine," Jan told me soon after. "Until we weren't." When she reflected, she realized they rarely took time to discuss hopes and plans or reflect on what worried or excited them. They often didn't even stop to talk through their days. Even as they were constantly connected to people online, they often passed by one another from day to day, living separate lives. They were functioning but not thriving, and getting increasingly unglued.

I bring up Jan's story not because it is so unusual or extreme. Her story echoes many others I've heard, in one flavor or another, over the years. We think we're managing—making it through minor and major bumps in the road—and don't take the time to notice or explore the cracks. If our lives are humming along, we don't tend to seek out dialogue about trouble spots. And the same goes for the positive side. We tend to emphasize external successes—trophies, prizes, or good grades—but not highlight the times a child learned something new, solved a problem creatively, empathized in a surprising way, or even resolved an argument well.

The Talk That Leaves Kids Stressed

As a result, while our kids are surrounded by chatter, they don't always spend as much time communicating in meaningful ways. They're not always supported to give voice to deeper thoughts or feelings or take the time to hear ours. Even with all their digital connections, they're increasingly isolated, fragile, perfectionistic, and often anxious, fearful, or depressed. In fact, stress and worry over performance have become an epidemic, as I've seen in my professional work and research, as well as in my talks with fellow parents.[2] According to the National Institute of Mental Health, nearly a third of teens will experience an anxiety disorder.[3] As college students, many are highly perfectionistic, in ways that feel toxic and harm their mental health.[4]

In the face of talk that emphasizes achievement over everything else, many kids end up self-critical. When they hear often about how successful others are—but not how they got there—they tend to feel at the mercy of their circumstances. When they think of learning as a game of "who gets the right answers fastest," they're less creative, empathetic, and open-minded than they could be. They might seem to be thriving when things come easily but get stuck when they hit roadblocks. Others, who've internalized the message of "fancy words mean you sound smarter," have large vocabularies but stunted skills in expressing or understanding feelings, leaving them disconnected from their families and friends. Others fear disappointing their parents and say they have no one who understands them, even as their parents say they're desperate to connect. So many parents I've talked to want to feel closer to their kids—but that closeness can feel hard to attain, with the pressure to help with homework or the guilt of making "quality time" count.[5]

In my own work, I've seen how much children are thirsting for the chance to process their thoughts and emotions through back-and-forth dialogue and to connect with others in ways that let their true selves be heard and seen. I've seen how they suffer when lacking such opportunities. When kids mostly hear us as nagging or pushing, managing or directing, they tend not to seek us out as much. We leave behind the chance to pursue questions more deeply—to explore what interests our kids and us—and to enjoy the time to talk that we do have.

If you're not paying attention, you might not notice the lack of deeper conversation. But you may see the aftereffects. College students, as a large review of more than 14,000 students over 30 years found, are less empathetic and community-oriented than in previous generations, with most of the decline seen after the year 2000.[6,7] Many kids, even young ones, fear the intellectual risk-taking that leads to creative thought. Over the years, I've seen kids who struggle to brainstorm or collaborate because they're overfocused on getting ahead; those who have trouble understanding how their friends feel; and those who don't take risks because they're terrified of mistakes. "I can't. I don't want to be wrong," I've heard kids respond when I've asked them to guess, or even estimate. Many of these kids also have trouble learning from others. When they see learning as a race to get answers, their talk turns to questions of who's best. They tend to focus on how well they're performing as compared with those around them. If they don't succeed at first, they're often hesitant to persevere, reflect on what happened, or try again.

In part, that's the fault of the world they're growing up in. We live in a society that prioritizes chatter over substance, quick updates over nuance, and on achievement seen in a narrow way. To help kids succeed, we're encouraged to focus on what's flashy, boosting their skills through the latest "build your brain" program, coding boot camp, or tutoring class. In doing so, we don't pay as much attention to our everyday talk, which filters through our lives and those of our kids. Such talk could help us relate and bond, but we don't always use it for that purpose. Instead, we often use talk to get us from here to there. But that leaves us in a language desert, where we have more words than ever—but less that brings us closer, delights us, or satisfies.

In my study of conversation, I've heard a message loud and clear: we and our kids are in desperate need of a reset from this childhood-turned-rat-race. Kids don't need encouragement to do more, faster. Instead, we need to step back and notice our talk. We need to become more intentional in focusing on what really matters for their development and well-being.

The Power of Time and Space to Talk

I was working at a high school for children with language and literacy disorders when I met Jenny, a ninth-grader with severe anxiety. Often, she felt so nervous in class that she ran out. Her teachers panicked. Someone had to search the school. Kids and teachers naturally got upset, and Jenny missed out on the chance to learn. Even worse were the fears for her safety, since no one knew where she'd gone. But with one teacher, Pamela—a soft-spoken woman who moonlighted as a yoga teacher—she stayed in class, and even lingered afterward. When I asked Pamela why, she simply smiled.

"I give her the time and space," she said, "to talk or to be quiet. Either way."

Most other teachers, it turned out, had grown frustrated and lectured Jenny, which only made her more flustered. But Pamela started out differently. Every day, she checked in and waited for Jenny to talk. Once Jenny described—often haltingly—how she was feeling, Pamela helped her explore how and why she was feeling that way. Whether Jenny felt excited or sad, Pamela listened equally. In the anxious times, Pamela counseled Jenny to take deep breaths, then use strategies to panic less. As a result, Jenny began taking hold of her anxiety. She also started taking ownership of how she felt. Through their talks, she grew to understand herself better, recognizing which strategies calmed her and evaluating her in-the-moment needs.

Back then, I simply thought Pamela was quiet, gentle, and understanding. And she was. But she wasn't always that way. One day, I heard her regaling a few students with jokes. With another student—a boy who complained daily about homework—she sounded surprisingly strict.

Looking back, I came to realize her true gift. She was a shapeshifter, able to change her talk based on what she heard each student needed. Instead of being only gentle or strict, she was *responsive*. That was her power: the ability to tailor her tone and talk depending on what she noticed about each child. She'd learned the art of having deep conversations, which started with making the space and time, and with being sensitive to a child's subtle cues. She noticed what Jenny was saying, and *how* she was saying it. And she did the same for the other kids.

Equally important, she noticed how *she* felt about each interaction. As a natural introvert, she found it easier to talk with Jenny than to manage kids who acted out. But her personality had many aspects, which she allowed herself to express. At times, she drew on her "louder" or funnier side. She reflected on which conversations left her energized versus frustrated, then sought out more of the energizing ones. While showing empathy to her students, she directed compassion at herself. Inevitably, she'd make a mistake or say something she shouldn't. Her students would, too. But her goal was connection, not perfection—and that's what her talk allowed.

Great Conversationalists Are Made, Not Born

As I later realized, Pamela wasn't unique. Over the years, as I met with parents, teachers, and caregivers from vastly different backgrounds, I was encouraged to see many others with similar skills. "Whenever kids talk with her, they're always laughing," I heard of one mother, who held weekly playdates at her house. Or, of a principal: "All the kids go to him to talk—especially when they're upset." Or I think back to Sophie's dentist, herself the mother of small kids, whom Sophie visited when she was six years old. We'd told Sophie she'd likely need to have a tooth pulled. Entering the office, she was practically shrieking. The dentist introduced herself calmly and asked about Sophie's favorite cartoons. After a few minutes discussing *PAW Patrol* and *Shimmer and Shine*, Sophie gradually relaxed—especially when the dentist said her daughter had liked the same shows. When Sophie asked about the cleaning tools, the dentist answered thoughtfully, seeming to sense Sophie's analytical nature and interest in how things worked.

After a few minutes, the conversation returned to the matter at hand, and Sophie went and had her X-rays done. But she came back with her jaw set tight.

"You're not going to pull my tooth," she said matter-of-factly. "I won't let you."

"I won't force you," the dentist said, and I sighed, fearing we'd have to return. Pulling out the X-rays, she passed them to Sophie. "Look." She pointed to one spot. "You have an infection under that tooth. See here? You might not feel it, but if you wait, the infection could get worse."

"I see it." Wide-eyed, Sophie leaned in.

"I'll give you a choice." The dentist put the X-rays away. "We can pull it now and get it over with, or wait and see. It might hurt more if you wait."

Sophie sighed and sat silent, lost in thought. Then a glimmer filled her eyes.

"Okay, fine." She opened her mouth wide. "Go ahead."

Without any force or artificial cheer, the dentist had recognized what Sophie needed to hear at that moment. Ever pragmatic, Sophie wanted the real story, which the dentist gave her—along with the X-rays. That satisfied her drive for information, in a concrete way, while letting her know we weren't trying to hurt her. Sophie wanted to feel she had some choice and that the situation was at least partially under her control. The dentist, in giving her options, allowed for that sense of control, while strongly suggesting that the "wait and see" approach wasn't the best.

In the moment, I found the dentist's approach a bit extreme. It was a matter of health and safety, after all. Wouldn't it be better just to tell Sophie, "The dentist has to pull it," and deal with the inevitable upset? Shouldn't we just have made her comply? But then I reflected. Forcing her wouldn't have felt good for her. She would have felt powerless, and probably even more stressed. And what about the *next* time she needed dental work? She'd have no reason to trust us if we said it would be no big deal. What's more, if this forceful approach became a pattern, it could erode our relationship longer-term. It wasn't only about the dentist, but about the way we related. Instead, a simple conversation became a great one. It responded to what Sophie needed and who she was. It put her in the driver's seat, letting her *choose* to do what needed to happen anyway.

For some kids, that approach wouldn't have made sense. But the dentist had talked to Sophie first. She'd built a connection and gotten a feel for Sophie's personality and style. She'd tested Sophie with the X-rays, seen her engagement, and only then offered the choice.

Taking it step by step, in a responsive way, made the dentist a great conversationalist. It wasn't any one phrase or strategy, or a combination. It wasn't her use of a script or recipe. Instead, it was her ability to sense what a child needed, tailor her response, then check in—and repeat the process, learning as she went.

To an outsider, these great conversationalists might seem born, not made. But in fact, having these conversations takes a specific set of skills, which can be practiced, learned, and tailored to each child in your family or at your school. The true measure of these conversations isn't how long they take or how impressive they sound. Instead, it has to do with what happens afterward. How close or distant do you and your kids feel? Did you and your child express what you needed or wanted to? Did they—or you—come away with more empathy, a satisfying resolution, or a new insight?

In daily life, we have many kinds of conversations, which are all valuable. We *do* need talk about who's doing the laundry or where the library book went. Even small talk—the "How are you?" and "How was your day?" questions—can be comforting, helping us relate to others and even enhancing our cognitive skills, well-being, and mental health.[8,9] Those social niceties can build empathy and perspective-taking skills, as we imagine how our conversational partners think and feel. But if we stop there, we're missing out on how much more conversations can do. This book is about nourishing those great conversations: prioritizing them and giving them room.

My Journey to Rich Talk

Arriving at these ideas has been, for me, a process of discovery. My training as a speech-language pathologist at the MGH Institute of Health Professions in Charlestown, Massachusetts, emphasized how tightly oral and written language—or speaking, listening, reading, and writing—are linked. I began to see how many kids who had trouble with writing, for example, also struggled to come up with ideas. I also saw how kids who talked through their ideas often had an easier time when it came time to write those ideas down.

With all this in mind, I began working at the school where I met Jenny and Pamela. I began to see how much interactions between teachers and kids counted, both to help them feel connected to each other and to help kids learn. It wasn't only what kids were reading and writing that mattered for their learning and development. The everyday talk in the classroom was key.

Soon, I decided to study these interactions. I enrolled in a doctoral program in education at Harvard and soon zeroed in on the idea of "classroom climate." That is, what aspects of teacher student relationships made the classroom feel positive and motivating? And did that positivity affect how well students learned or how motivated they felt?

Since no one seemed to have the answers, I decided to review all the studies I could find. I focused on older kids and on two aspects of classroom climate: the goals the classroom emphasized, and how much support the teachers gave. Most studies divided goals into types: mastery and performance.[10] With "mastery" goals, kids see mistakes as evidence of learning and failure as a necessary step to success. They feel comfortable trying new things. Learning is an end in itself, and errors are par for the course.[11] With "performance" goals, kids focus on getting answers right and avoiding mistakes. Often, they pit themselves against one another, in a competition to see who can finish fastest or be the best.

The goals that kids develop depend on the talk they hear. The responses their teachers encourage and the subtle messages they send play a part, as do the comments from their parents and friends. And this classroom talk, I soon found, mattered. Kids who felt their classrooms emphasized mastery got better grades, did better on standardized tests, and cared more about learning than kids whose classrooms emphasized performance.[12] In fact, the more kids felt their classrooms focused on performance, the *worse* their academic scores. When they felt they *had* to get the right answers, they did less well. The strongest link was for sixth-graders. Many kids at the start of middle school, I reasoned, pay lots of attention to how others view them. If they're worried about not being "good enough," a performance climate could make those fears worse.

Teacher support also mattered for children's learning and well-being. When children viewed their teachers as more supportive, they did better on standardized tests. They also had stronger senses of self-efficacy, or feelings that they could achieve their goals, and were more motivated, social, and caring. Their teachers' support, it seems, trickled down to how they felt about themselves.

I came away from that research with new questions and a sense of awe. We often assume learning is about academics and feelings aren't as important. But the way kids *felt* about their classrooms linked strongly to how engaged they were and how well they learned. Learning was about far more than the curriculum. Daily back-and-forth interactions played a key role in how well it went.

With that idea in mind, I began studying preschoolers, whose brains are still more plastic, and shifted my lens to the adults in their lives. If this everyday talk mattered so much, how could we enhance it? How would kids benefit?

The way we talk to kids, I reasoned, matters especially in times of high stress. But how did talk change in stressful circumstances? To find out, I began studying and interviewing teachers in a high-poverty preschool, as part of a team implementing a yearlong training to support those teachers' abilities to regulate their emotions and manage stress.[13] There, many kids and parents faced chronic stress, as did their teachers, whose full-time jobs often left them under the poverty line.[14,15,16] Over an academic year, as I observed and interviewed these teachers, I was impressed at how much tenderness, even love, they felt and showed for the kids they taught.[17] I was equally humbled to realize the severe stresses they faced and how hard they worked to keep an even keel.[18] How well they managed their stress, I found, affected how they talked, which changed how kids behaved. I recognized, in this work, how deeply factors such as poverty affect children's abilities to learn, develop, and thrive. Parents and teachers are in no way responsible for this cycle of poverty.[19,20]

But what about parents? Kids are in school, surprisingly, on average less than 15 percent of their waking hours.[21] The talk they hear and engage in at home sets the foundation for the rest of their lives. Soon, I began to wonder: How did "family climate," built on conversation, affect them, as much or even more than their "school climates" did?

While still in grad school, I started working as an oral and written language specialist, as part of an interdisciplinary team at a Boston hospital. As a group of psychologists, neuropsychologists, math specialists, and others, we diagnose children with language and learning disorders and make recommendations to their parents, teachers, and schools. The work is precise and in-depth. In our clinic, a child rotates among specialists for the better part of a day. Afterward, we spend an hour or more discussing each child's case as group. Collaboratively, we work to develop a learning profile of that child and make recommendations to help her learn and thrive long-term. The years of this work have given me insight into how complex a child's journey of learning and development can be, and how important it is to see him or her from all sides. I began to view the process of understanding children as detective work.

That detective work starts early on, with reading a child's file. Then, from the moment we meet, I observe everything I can about the ways he or she speaks and interacts. I always start with social conversation; for instance, asking how tired or awake she feels, whether she has plans for an upcoming vacation, or what she plans to do later in the day. This isn't idle chatter, but a key part of seeing how she interacts with a stranger. Later on, noticing one area of strength or challenge raises questions in my mind about what other areas might be relatively weak or strong. As I find the answers to some questions, new questions rise up. Hearing from my colleagues gives me new insight. Occasionally, it upends my understanding. For example, a neurologist may show that a child has attentional difficulties that affect his ability to listen or participate. As I go, I keep my mind open, listen carefully, and try to let my picture of a child evolve.

Those lessons are important ones for us as parents. As I've come to see, it's not only important to know a child's strengths and challenges, in order to help him or her thrive. It matters just as much to know how a child perceives her own challenges and strengths: where she feels pride or embarrassment, where the sore spots or points of shame lie. These aren't always the same as the sore spots *we* see. It's not because a child believes she's terrible in math that his teacher thinks so too, or because she feels she has no friends that she truly doesn't. But her feelings about her strengths and weaknesses matter more than her grades or scores. They affect how she behaves at home and in class, how she relates to others, and how she feels about herself. Those feelings, rather than any one test grade, are what will make or break her over the long term.

For example, I remember Michael, a child I worked with, who thought he was a poor reader. In part as a result, he didn't want to read out loud in class and told me he "wasn't a kid who reads." It turned out that he was reading right at grade level. It was just that many kids in his class were unusually high-achieving and reading *above* grade level. Understanding that situation helped Michael reframe his sense of himself. He might not be a superstar reader, but he could read just fine, and shouldn't need to feel stressed about keeping up with the rest of the class. At library time, he could check out the books he liked without worrying that they were "dumb."

It's through conversation that we're able to dive deeper into those feelings and thoughts. Over time, this helps kids become far more self-aware: more in tune with their values, more specific about their goals, and more compassionate toward others and themselves.

Through back-and-forth dialogue starting with a child's perceptions, we can help a child understand himself better. He can start to realize, for example, why he might be having negative thoughts. He can learn to reframe thoughts that are keeping him from trying new things. He can learn to make sense of where he's been, in terms of his own successes and challenges, and where he'd like to go. All this, over time, can change his learning and relationships with others, and even his life trajectory. And all this change starts with the smallest moments.

This experience was invaluable, but it also raised more questions. Especially after Sophie, my first child, was born, I began wondering: What specific conversational "moves" let us provide that help? How could our talk be a gateway of learning and connection? Which strategies could enrich our interactions and engage both ourselves and our kids?

Talk as a Parent's Way In

Inspired by those questions, I started paying more attention to the talk between parents and their children, everywhere I went. At times, I heard that talk going swimmingly. Parents and kids were (mostly) enjoying each other's company, and kids saw their parents as models, conversational partners, and sounding boards. But often, the picture I saw was far less bright. So many kids, I found, struggled to feel connected and accepted for who they were. Many were barely keeping their heads above water in the face of home and school demands. Some seemed anxious or depressed, others perfectionistic, and still others distracted, unmotivated, isolated, or simply exhausted. This was true for kids with challenges in language and literacy, but equally for those with average or above-average skills.

Ironically, it seemed that the parents *most* concerned about their children's development were also most struggling to relate in more satisfying ways. I found many instances of what Jennifer Senior describes in her 2014 book *All Joy and No Fun*: homework as "the new family dinner,"[22] consuming hours and often ending with arguments. Even parents who didn't overemphasize achievement often spoke of feeling distracted, rushed, or guilt-tripped over how much "quality time" they spent. They also felt disconnected from their kids, then anxious about that disconnection, in a vicious cycle.

But what could be done? To learn more, I delved into a pile of parenting books. Most focused on *behavior*: what we should or shouldn't allow, how loose or tight we should hold the reins. In 1980, Adele Faber and Elaine Mazlish published *How to Talk So Kids Will Listen & Listen So Kids Will Talk*.[23] This book, which became a major bestseller, provides a hugely helpful starting point for conversations. Instead of pushing away a child's negative feelings, the authors suggest, acknowledge and validate them. Notice and encourage cooperation. Describe what you see; for example, "There's a lot of water on the floor," rather than, "Why did you have to mess up the rug *again*?" Empower a child with choices. Praise wisely, in a way that encourages him to try again.

While I've recommended that book to many parents, I knew conversation could do still more. This book builds on and refines Faber and Mazlish's approach, from the perspective of a fellow parent with a professional background in speech and language. I take as a starting point many of their foundational principles. They have great insight into showing kids respect, helping them accept their feelings, and freeing them from playing "roles," such as the "whiny" or the "dawdling" kid. Like them, I also have the goal of helping you connect with your kids through effective communication. But in building on their work, I offer a more organic approach, focused far more on the back-and-forth that conversation allows. I'm proposing a framework where parents and kids can grow together, in dialogues that evolve over time. It's the exact opposite of a recipe or a script. Instead, I use my work as a clinician as a jumping-off point, showing you how kids can develop through dialogue that meets them where they are. I take you along my journey as a parent, and show you the journeys of other parents I've met. In doing so, I highlight what we all know intuitively: how complex and multifaceted kids are, and what a delight—and a challenge—it can be to get to know them, and let them know us, through the ways we listen and talk.

In this book, I bring your child and your relationship to the next level. I show you how to use conversation as a tool not only to help kids cooperate, but also as a means to inspire them. I delve deeply into the power of ongoing dialogue, which starts from a moment-by-moment understanding of what a child wants or needs—and what you do. In dialogue, there can be no recipes, and no "say this and not that." Your interactions are far too individualized and unique. Even what one child needs today, in one conversation, might not be what she needs tomorrow. The same goes for siblings. They might have far different conversational needs, depending on their personalities, the kind of day they've had, and even if they're together or alone. Sensing those needs, and shifting your response, is truly an art, not an exact science. At the same time, there are strategies to help.

What this book offers is a framework to master that art. It all starts with taking a compassionate look at your family's talking and listening habits, beginning with what's already working well. It gives you methods you can take into any conversation. And it shows how we all have our strong points in talking with kids, but also our weaknesses—especially if we're rushed, upset, tired, or stressed. Drawing from my own life, I show you times I've felt proud of my conversations, but also times I floundered, or when my contributions had the opposite effect of what I'd hoped. I talk about how important it is to flounder. *Not* knowing an answer is as important as knowing one. Showing that we're comfortable with struggling might feel hard, or embarrassing, but it lets kids grow comfortable with their own challenges. That lets them try more over time.

In this book, I give examples from parents I've met and worked with, as well as ideas backed by the scientific research on language development. And I show how powerful a tool conversation can be to connect us deeply and transform the relationships we have with our kids—if we can let go at times, listen deeply, and leave our own agendas behind.

These great conversations aren't possible all the time, certainly. Sometimes, they're the last things we have time for. But when we do make time for this talk, even in small moments, it can change how we see our kids and how they see us. It can profoundly enhance our relationship. We become more open to each other, and more understanding. We can even, in the best of times, feel inspired. What's more, creating this foundation means that hard times, later on, will feel less hard. With that strong base in place, your kids are more likely to come to you for support and comfort, not argument.

Conversation Giants

To understand the importance of these conversations, let's meet two key players who have influenced "talk about talk" for more than a century. The first is the twentieth-century Swiss psychologist Jean Piaget. His "stage theory" argues that children's thinking develops as they do, but it's not a steady climb. Instead, there are jagged leaps of insight, as kids engage with their environments, discovering as they go.[24] Kids learn through trial and error, as they have new experiences, then work to make sense of them. Your role is to provide new materials and opportunities and let them explore, while occasionally clarifying their ideas.[25,26] This is exactly where conversation comes in. Conversation is a constant chance to give and get feedback. Through close attention to what your kids are saying, and how they're saying it, you can learn so much about how they're thinking: where their errors lie, what they're excited or frustrated about, what tickles them, and especially how motivated or engaged they feel. As a result, your responses are far more likely to answer their real worries or questions, not the ones you assume they have. That's the key to helping them learn better—and just as important, to letting them feel they've truly been heard.

At the same time, another psychologist came to the stage who emphasized conversation far more. The Soviet psychologist Lev Vygotsky, born in the same year as Piaget, took a far more interactive approach.[27] Knowledge, he said, is built *through* the interaction between people. Through *scaffolding*, or feedback from an adult or older child, a child can reach insights far beyond those he could have on his own. Vygotsky's "Zone of Proximal Development" pinpoints the gap between what a child can do himself and where he can get with your help.[28,29,30] When you target that sweet spot, he's primed to make the most of what you have to say or teach. Your interaction is the key to helping him stretch. Over time, with your help, his zone gets bigger and bigger. He becomes more capable of doing more on his own. He learns more and learns *how* to learn. His capacity for feeling grows more deeply. His thinking becomes more nuanced and elaborate.

The following diagram shows how that stretch works:

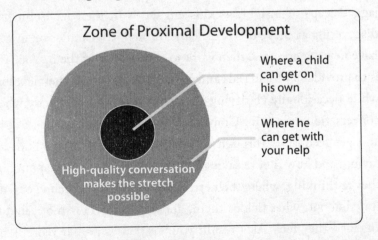

As Vygotsky argued, it's the scaffolding, or support and guidance received from an adult or older child, that helps a child reach his potential. But the stretch shouldn't be so big that it goes over her head or so small that it provides little challenge. Trust your intuition. It's not about what you read in a child development book—not even this one!

This book leans in Vygotsky's direction. Yes, kids *are* active and learn through exploring their worlds.[31] But, as decades of research have shown, your interactions are equally key to helping kids reach their potential.[32] Think about high-quality conversation as providing that stretch in the best way, *precisely* because it lets you learn what kids need and want at any one time.[33]

The Embodied Conversation

This book focuses on what's called *embodied face-to-face conversation*.[34] It's this kind of conversation that's especially powerful in enhancing your relationships and building kids' skills long-term. In these conversations, you're physically with each other. You're fully *present* in body and mind. You're paying attention to body language, facial expression, and other nonverbal cues, and encouraging your child to do the same. You're attending carefully, taking in *what* the other person says and *how* they're saying it.

Embodied conversation engages the five senses. In the blend of *what* each person says and *how* he or she says it, frowns and smiles and pauses help kids learn more deeply and engage. When you and your child sit close, you tend to mimic the other's actions and expressions, which forms a powerful social glue.[35] That's the foundation of empathy, since it gives your child a starting place from which to take your perspective. Watching your face offers hints about how you're feeling and thinking, in a way that goes beyond words.[36,37] In embodied conversation, you communicate warmth *while* you ask questions or tell stories. Your child learns *and* relates.

Simple greetings, such as "How are you?" and "Fine," aren't full conversations. The same for lecturing or giving lessons: you're communicating, but not really conversing. There's little room for your child to weigh in, or for the discussion to take an unexpected turn. Instead, when you talk *with* your child, not simply *at* him, he's far more likely to be engaged and to care than if you talk nonstop, even about something that interests him. He's also more likely to learn.[38,39]

Can you have conversations over email, video chat, or phone? Of course. When conversation isn't embodied, it's called *mediated*. In mediated conversation, you're not talking in person. You may be on the phone or chatting over text message, video chat, or email. I'm not knocking that conversation—it can be a great way to connect and keep in touch—but it doesn't provide the same opportunities for sensory information and feedback. It's important, and at times even necessary, but not enough.

Beyond Banning Phones

That's not to say mediated conversation is "bad" and embodied is "good." And it's certainly not to shame you or say that you shouldn't talk in mediated ways.[40] It's not a sign of bad parenting to multitask or respond to email while fixing dinner. At times, it's simply what our home and work lives demand. Focusing on talking with kids, then taking a break for social media, can let you have the best of both worlds. And if you have a work deadline or playdates to schedule, or a cousin asking to FaceTime, it's often not possible, or even advisable, to put the technology away.

Especially these days, mediated conversation has its place. At times, it can be a much more efficient way of operating than the embodied version. If you need to order plane tickets or contact customer service, it makes far more sense to pick up the phone or email than to physically go to each place. Within your family, texting and talking on the phone are often the easiest and best ways to know where everyone is, when you need to pick someone up, or even just say hi to a child who's not at home. And if you aren't living with your child, or if your partner or relative doesn't see him regularly, video chat can be a great alternative.

The same goes for social media. There's no question that *some* use does help kids—and us—connect in positive ways, whether sharing videos of weekend antics or planning a surprise party. Banning it isn't realistic and tends to make it a forbidden fruit. Still, social media—and mediated communication in general—has major limits, which we'll explore in the chapters to come. When we suggest that "it's all really the same," or "let's just move everything online," we miss out on the true power of embodied conversation, which gives our talk far more richness and nuance. Being present in person, with no devices in between us, sets us up to hear our kids more fully and to give more of ourselves. When we can do it, we should.

So how can you make the most of this conversation? Focus on what I call "rich talk": research-based principles that make quality dialogue more of a daily reality.

What Rich Talk Involves

In my study of the "moves" that make conversations great—including my talks with dozens of researchers and interviews with

parents—I've heard a few key themes over and over. I've been inspired by researchers in linguistics, child psychology, and even
artificial intelligence.[41] Blending the scholarly terms and parents'
insights, I've come to see rich talk as having three main elements.
Think of it as the "alphabet" of rich talk, with the acronym ABC.

Rich talk is:

A: Adaptive. You adapt your talk—your words *and* tone—based
on what you hear and see from your child. This adaptation has two
pieces: you shift *in the moment* and reflect *after* conversations, which
lets you tailor your approach longer-term. You notice what your
child needs now, as opposed to yesterday, or last year, or what his
sister needs. You encourage him to do the same for you. With adaptive talk, you're primed to meet a child's precise needs: not what she
"ought to" need, given her age, stage, or grade, but what she *actually*
does need now. That's the key to hitting that Zone of Proximal Development, providing the just-right level of challenge and stretch.
Through your model, kids learn how it feels to connect deeply,
which sets a foundation for making those deeper connections with
others. They hear how you're making sense of what they say, which
teaches them while boosting their perspective-taking skills.[42]

Being adaptive also lets you decide what support and guidance
to give at any one time and how to give it. Maybe your three-year-
old is far more verbal than most at his age and would be excited to
hear you read a complicated book. Or maybe your eleven-year-old
still has trouble reading facial expressions and would benefit from
talking over how people with different expressions might feel. In
both cases, recognizing your child's individuality lets you respond
in a way that best matches his or her wants and needs.

These needs might not make sense at first glance, or might be
easy to brush off. Say your generally calm five-year-old gets hyster-

ical over a paper cut, as once happened to a friend of mine. Apparently, the child had never hurt herself and had never seen blood. It wasn't so much the pain, but the surprise of seeing red on her finger, that startled her.

"It's only a paper cut," you might say. Sure. But that doesn't mean she wasn't upset—or that she didn't need a bit of comforting, along with the knowledge that it wasn't the end of the world. That's the power of adaptation. It lets you pay close and careful attention, at every age and stage, to how your child is developing, then change tack in response.[43] It also lets you be flexible. You don't get hung up on "shoulds," but instead focus on what the moment requires. The same goes for what you do as you speak: you might bend in and ruffle your child's hair,[44] or stand back, sensing that your child wants to be left alone. The important thing isn't *what* you do specifically, but how you pay attention: the ways you notice your child's cues and respond.

B: Back-and-forth. Using this principle, you're both participating, engaged, and taking turns—or all of you are, if talking in a group. That doesn't mean fighting to get a word in. Sometimes it's the smallest signals that offer the most opportunities. You might show you're listening through comments like "Hmm" or "Oh, really," showing that what a child says holds your interest and you want her to go on. You might point out something you notice on a daily walk and wait for her to comment. Or you might give your opinion, then ask for hers. The psychologists Roberta Michnick Golinkoff and Kathy Hirsh-Pasek, authors of *Becoming Brilliant*, call these back-and-forths "conversational duets." This talk, at its best, feels like dancing.[45] It's open-ended. You don't decide on the endpoint beforehand. You leave room for your child's talk to change your perspective—and for your talk to change hers.

Many times, these back-and-forths are what's called *contingent*. Your response depends on your child's, and hers depends on yours. When two things are contingent, they're yoked together. For instance, say you want to buy a new car but don't have the money. Your ability to buy the car is *contingent* on whether you're able to sell the old one for a good price. In conversation, a contingent response shows you're emotionally and mentally there. You're attentive and responsive, even if you don't give your child what she wants. Say your child says, "We don't have any sugary cereal." You might say, "We ran out," or "I'll go to the store tomorrow," or "I don't want to buy Lucky Charms," or any number of responses, depending on how you feel. It's not about whether you buy the cereal or don't. Instead, the key is to acknowledge what your child said and answer it, in whatever way makes sense for you.[46]

This back-and-forth gives you both the chance to get your conversational needs met. Without it, you may end up missing what your child means or leave her feeling lost. Say your child asks a question and you give a long explanation, then say, "Okay, hope you got it." While your answer is perfectly fine, she doesn't get the chance to clarify her question or say she's confused. Instead, if you talk a little, then check in, or ask what she thinks first, you let the conversation teach *you* about what your child needs, as much as it teaches her. You're both actively listening and open to new perspectives. The learning goes both ways.

C: Child-driven. What exactly should you talk about? Most often, the answer is right in front of you. The child-driven principle means you start with what's salient for your child. That might mean an idea or question he brings up, but equally, something you notice him excited by, worried about, or struggling with—or even some new skill you've noticed him developing. Often, you don't need to search for what your child cares about. He might be begging you to talk about his new Lego construction, his video game set, or his dance moves. At other times, it takes attention to notice. Downtime can help. Say he comes home each week from soccer practice grumpy, even though he scores a lot of goals. Maybe he's jealous of his teammate who scored even more goals, or he's exhausted or has stopped enjoying the game. Staring with the *child-driven* principle, you take the time to reflect aloud about what might be going on. Or you ask how he feels, rather than assuming he must feel good. Starting with his perspective primes you to reach him at his level and work with his energy. From the outset, he's more interested and more likely to connect. He's building his own self-awareness, even as you get the chance to understand him better.

From early on, being child-driven is about responding in a timely, appropriate way. Even if he's not talking yet, you can base your conversation on what he seems interested in, attracted to, or scared of. Your baby looks at something, and you follow his gaze and respond by pointing or describing what he sees. He coos, and you comment that he sounds happy. He shrieks and you see what he needs, while noting how upset he seems. You're mind-minded, meaning you base your response on noticing how he acts and seems to feel.[47]

....

How you respond in these early months matters for your child's later well-being, social functioning, and language skills.[48] In one study, six-month-old infants of mothers who showed more mind-mindedness had greater levels of well-being and social functioning, fewer behavior problems, and better language skills at four and a half years old.

....

Even an infant has feelings about wanting to be soothed and kept clean and dry. As her senses heighten, she's increasingly drawn to exploring her world. The better she can see and hear, the more she wants to explore. As you observe her, you put words to her joys and frustrations as you imagine them. You reflect on her feelings and thoughts, then voice your ideas out loud. This ability is known as *mentalizing*, and it's a powerful component of conversations, especially before kids can talk.

Mentalizing means recognizing that even a young child can think and feel. Cries and coos aren't random. Your child's mind is separate from yours, and experiences that feel off-putting to you might feel enjoyable to her, and vice versa.[49] When you give voice to her unspoken feelings—when you "get it right," or come close— she feels heard and understood. She's comforted, sensing you want to help her get her needs met.[50] Later on, since she knows you'll be attentive, she's more likely to be open to talking—and more honest and vulnerable.

The "ABCs" of rich talk matter because they let you and your child work as a team. You're not at cross-purposes, even if you disagree. Instead, you're open to hearing what your child says and feels, and you're encouraging her openness. You gently challenge a child's beliefs and assumptions in a way that lets her question them without feeling judged. That lets her grow more independent in her thinking and her relationships. She learns not only *to* learn, as in take in facts, but *how* to learn, in a way that honors her own style and needs. She picks up on *what* you're feeling and explores *why*. When you're upset, she learns how to respond in a way that helps, or to ask questions that help her understand. And she grows to understand the nuances of others even as she learns more about herself.

Doing the ABCs Leads to Talk Success

With the "ABCs" of rich talk, you're on the road to satisfying conversations. Your interaction feels good in the moment. You might have clarified a misunderstanding, worked out a frustration on your part or your child's, resolved an argument, had some insight, or even simply enjoyed each other's company and made each other laugh. There may be bumps in the road, but overall, your talk feels pleasant, not effortful or forced. What's more, the conversation has moved you both forward: toward a greater understanding, a new feeling of empathy, or a deeper awareness of what each of you wants and needs. You feel more bonded. You want to do it again, and your child likely does, too. You feel more aligned, like two strings in harmony. See the diagram below for a summary.

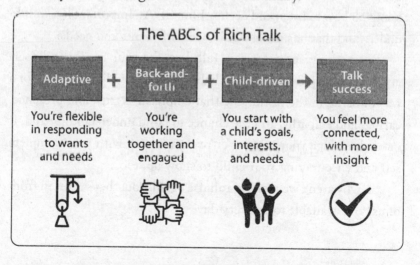

The ABCs of Rich Talk

Adaptive + **Back-and-forth** + **Child-driven** → **Talk success**

Adaptive	Back-and-forth	Child-driven	Talk success
You're flexible in responding to wants and needs	You're working together and engaged	You start with a child's goals, interests, and needs	You feel more connected, with more insight

It's not about more talk, and still more. It's equally about the pauses and silences, making room for talk *and* time to process and reflect. In the safe space of your family, kids learn to make mistakes and repair them: all skills they can later apply. As they grow, they're primed to see you as a partner, mentor, and guide: someone they can confide in, reflect with, and tell jokes to. With that foundation, they're *less* likely to be needy over time. They're better able to resolve conflicts, empathize, and think through problems themselves.

That doesn't mean making everything about your child—and it certainly doesn't mean neglecting your conversations with other adults. Having many people to talk with enriches all your lives. It keeps you sane as a parent while giving your child many models. Not everyone thinks or talks the same way, he learns; and that's a good thing. "Everyone speaks the same language differently," as Megan-Brette Hamilton, a speech-language pathologist and professor at Auburn University, told me.[51] It's through hearing multiple ways of talking that a child learns to appreciate these differences. When he's not at the center of every conversation, he also develops skills in knowing how to listen and occupy himself. An important lesson is to understand that he's not the only one with wants and needs.

But making space for rich talk benefits your family and society.[52] In developing it as a daily habit, you're providing a model for a way of being in the world: one that emphasizes trust and presence, caring, and empathy, and the chance to build understanding and, if needed, change your mind. You're showing up with your complete self and encouraging your child to show up, too.

So why aren't we making full use of this tool that's right in front of us, and available to us every day?

Why We're Missing the Rich Talk Opportunity

The principles of rich talk rest on something fundamentally basic: talking with your kids in ways that engage you both. Having fruitful conversations might seem an incredibly simple, even obvious path toward helping kids learn and develop to their potential. And, in a way, it is. So, if we want kids to do well, and we're trying to help them, what makes it tough to take this opportunity?

There are three main reasons:

1. *The achievement-oriented focus of traditional schooling,* which trickles down to our home lives.

2. *Intensive parenting ideals* that suggest we need to be "on" all the time.

3. *The ways our kids and we use technology,* especially while we're together.

Let's consider each of these in turn.

First, our society too often pushes achievement and progress, in ways that at times rise above children's overall well-being.[53] High-stakes testing, measuring skills and progress in math and reading, has come to frame talk about learning in profound and sometimes insidious ways. What's tested is what many teachers prioritize and what kids learn to care about.[54] Conversation becomes more about strategizing to find the right answer than about thinking creatively or critically. When kids constantly focus on questions that can be answered with bubble-filling, deeper discussion naturally takes a backseat. Talk focuses on one right way, not many possibilities. We don't value the brainstorm, or the unusual idea—even though brainstorming well is key to developing creativity.[55,56]

True, conversations don't have the same metrics of success as those all-important grades and test scores. It's far easier to do an activity—ideally a structured one—to feel you're moving your child along. Take swimming class. After five lessons, the coach says, "She's doing well with backstroke, but needs to master her kick." Saturday finished, mission accomplished. You walk away, happy your child has made visible progress. Talk isn't like that. It leaves no obvious trace and has no checklist or recipe. Because of that, it's like the proverbial nose in the middle of your face. Unless you're self-conscious—or vain—you probably almost never think about it. You just want it to do its job.

The vast majority of noses work fine without any help from us. But talk isn't the same. Our default "talk modes" do get the job done, in terms of getting us from here to there, making sure kids eat dinner or do their homework. But quality conversation, at its best, can do far more to open their worlds.

This isn't an argument for watching every word that comes out of your mouth or your child's, or for meticulously planning what you say. Quite the opposite. That intensive focus, as parents, on being "all on, all the time," can make those richer conversations *harder* to have. Parenting, in this mode, has become a "relentless" pursuit, as the title of a 2018 *New York Times* article stated.[57] We want kids to reach their full potential, now and in the future. But we too often end up often talking *at* them, in a one-way stream. We direct and manage, becoming chauffeurs and tutors, playmates and coaches, doing our best to meet our kids' needs while not neglecting our own.

It's natural to want to be involved. But when we're involved too often or too intrusively, it's easy to leave behind kids' actual, in-the-moment interests and goals. We don't pay as much attention to how they're talking and what lies behind their words. Instead, we tend to look ahead to the next goal, activity, or metric of success— whether a test or a soccer practice, or simply a smooth playdate. We forget to notice what *is* happening and focus on what *should* be.

When we see ourselves as lecturers and managers, rather than conversational partners, our talk often isn't *adaptive*. We tend to pass over what a child is trying to tell us. We arrive in a rush, often with our own agendas: a point we want to make or a message we want to get across. We don't notice when we're at cross-purposes. We forget to slow down.

You can see this in the most everyday situations. Imagine you've just returned from work and you greet your toddler, who's playing with a toy train, running it up a track and into the wall. "How was your day?" you ask. He responds, "Look, the train's out of battery." And then you ask, "Were both your teachers in today? Was Jason still sick?" and he answers, "I need the little batteries." That's a natural-enough conversation. But you're focused on your own agenda. You want to hear about the details of his day—maybe you're secretly wondering whether you've picked the right school for him—but he's deeply focused on his present reality.

In the moment, you might not notice anything wrong. But if you keep on, you'll both probably feel frustrated. He'll start whining or tugging on you. You may get irritated, wishing for quiet. He's lost the spark of his interest, and you've missed the chance to engage with him. And so, in these small, everyday ways, the cycle of disconnection starts. But that cycle isn't inevitable.

....

Many of us want to parent intensively, even if we can't afford to. I spoke to Patrick Ishizuka, a postdoctoral fellow at Cornell, who found in 2019 that three-quarters of parents across income brackets favored the intensive parenting style.[58,59] *This ideal has become widespread, he argues. With it comes pressure to make that ideal a reality.*

....

The "do-it-all" mentality—and the fear of being judged if we don't—cuts down on the quality of our talk. We tend to judge and guilt-trip ourselves. Our attention grows scattered. We pile on stress, losing out on the true benefit of conversation. If we try to "perfect" our sides of the conversation, we're missing the point. These conversations should leave us *less* stressed, not more.

Our default talk, in contrast, often feels labor-intensive. In our scheduling of multiple activities, nagging about homework, or even our directing of little kids, we often focus on *logistical* and *transactional* talk, or talk focused on "getting things done." We emphasize teaching lessons or making a point. The slower pace needed for a more meaningful back-and-forth gets lost. It's not just the *adaptive* part of rich talk that goes missing. It's the *back-and-forth*, too. Either you're not engaged, or your child isn't. You miss the chance to let conversation flow, or give feedback that lets your child's ideas expand. Say your child is playing a word game out loud. He says, "L is for . . . llama. J is for . . ." You might join in with "jellybean" or "juice," then wait as he adds "jam" or "jumping gorilla." In contrast, you might say, "Oh, I don't know . . . let's get your shoes."

There's nothing wrong with the second response. When you're in a hurry, it's the one that makes the most sense. But at least sometimes, it's important to make room for the first.

Equally important, when we focus on success, we may leave behind the *child-driven* aspect. We tend to emphasize what a child seems naturally good at, from the youngest ages, or where he shines. We don't give as much encouragement for activities he's only just begun, or those he loves but is only mediocre at, or even for new aspects of his personality. Say he's only started playing soccer, while his friends have played for years. While he finds it fun, he's not very good. If we overemphasize being at the top—or getting there—he may feel too discouraged to keep trying. Or say he feels shy but has been working to meet new friends. If we focus on how social his older sister is, as compared with him, he may stop trying or say, "I give up on making friends," which can lead to him retreating more. A critical part of childhood has been lost: the need to be seen as a full person, at every age and stage, and let traits and skills evolve.

Even during play, we often miss chances to start with what a child cares about. You can see this with a young child playing with Lego blocks, dreaming up a castle and moat. "What's that?" we ask, pointing to one block. "Is it blue or orange?" He forgets his questions about how high to make the castle or whether his toys will float or sink. His thinking gets cut off at the pass.

The same goes for older kids in different ways. Say your child is talking excitedly about video games. When you're overfocused on academics, it's easy to ignore what he's saying or turn your attention to whether he's done his homework. While you *do* want homework to get done, you don't take time to notice why he cares about gaming, or how those interests might transfer. Maybe he likes the risk taking aspect, which could lead into starting outdoor adventures. Or maybe it's about connecting with his friends, which could lead to him making more real-life meetups. Finding those links, and helping your child find them, is key to enriching his world.

Then there's the issue of the phones and computers themselves, and other electronic devices. Are they helping our conversations along, or constraining them? It's easy enough to jump on the bandwagon and say kids are always on their phones and rarely lift their heads up to talk in person. But the real picture is probably more complex. True, when kids are on devices for most of their waking hours, there's not much time for embodied talk. In 2019, teenagers spent more than seven hours a day on their phones, and kids from ages eight to twelve just under five hours.[60,61] This tech use can change how kids think and can shift their perspectives. For example, studies have found higher rates of depression when teens engage in "upward social comparisons," or using social media to compare themselves with friends who seem happier or better off than them.[62]

What's more, using tech devices changes our interactions in the moment—whether it's kids playing games on their tablets or us checking email. Habitually turning to your phone can shut dialogue down. It's less about what you say or don't and more about your attention. Keeping your eyes on your phone signals that you're not fully open to conversation. What probably started as a small escape or a need to check the news can morph into a consistent habit. In response, your child may start whining or clamoring for attention. Or—if they're old enough—they may turn to their own device and disappear down a wormhole of videos and memes.

Especially at first, kids might comment on your lack of attention. Five-year-old Sophie, before showing me a dance she'd invented, demanded, "Phones off, please!" Other kids may get irritable or whiny. After a while, though, it gets to feel normal to talk while

....

As one study found, when parents of toddlers gazed at their phones, the toddlers explored their environments less and had less-successful reunions with their parents once the parents put their phones away. The biggest effects were found for parents who said they habitually turned to their phones.[63] Over time, when kids sense they won't get an engaged response, they tend to stop trying. The quality of your interactions goes down— and with it, your child's openness to talk.

....

scrolling—so no one says anything about it. But this halfhearted talk can't go into much depth. We can't notice our kids' subtle cues or encourage them to notice ours. So much goes unheard and unsaid.

I often talk about our current society being a language desert. We have a lot of communication—if you look at the constant barrage of news, texting, and tweets—but far less that is profound, that connects us deeply or feels meaningful. In this language desert, it's even more important that we pay conscious attention to the quality of the conversations we have with kids. You can prioritize these conversations as ends in themselves, but also as acts of resistance against a trend to use more words, send more texts and tweets, but to miss out on deeper communication. Even if we're busy, there are ways of using small pockets of time to start up habits kids can take on. The opportunities for rich talk are great, if we pay attention. And we should: the positive dynamics of our families depend on it, as do our children's happiness, learning, and well being.[64]

CHAPTER 2

Conversations for Learning: Sparking Your Child's Lifelong Curiosity

Our care of the child should be governed, not by the desire to make him learn things, but by the endeavor always to keep burning within him that light which is called intelligence.

—MARIA MONTESSORI[1]

One afternoon soon after Sophie's fourth birthday, Philippe and I sat at a meeting with her preschool teachers in Brookline, Massachusetts. I shuffled in my child-size chair. An hour earlier, I'd been meeting with parents at the school where I worked. Now I was on the parent side.

"She has trouble making mistakes," the first teacher, a grayhaired, gentle woman, told me. "That's typical of many kids. She's independent, and a perfectionist."

"And she blames her mistakes on other people," the second teacher said. "It's hurting her friendships. We're talking a lot about responsibility. At home, I'd reinforce that."

"I'll see what we can do." I gulped, having noticed those ten-dencies as well.

Throughout a busy workday, I let that conversation fade. But that evening, as I walked home, it started pouring, and I arrived home drenched and uncomfortable.

"You're wet." Sophie wrinkled her nose. "Didn't you bring an umbrella?"

"I didn't check the forecast," I admitted.

"You should have."

Peeling my socks off, I wanted to snap. Then I had an idea.

"That was my mistake for today," I said. "What was yours?"

"My what?"

"Your mistake." I met her gaze. "What wrong or silly thing did you do today?"

"I don't make mistakes." Huffing, she walked away. But then came dinnertime.

"Your mistake," she demanded, with a twinkle. "Tell us."

"I forgot to lock my bike up," Philippe said. "I left it outside."

"So, it got *stolen*?"

"No, I got lucky." He sighed. "But next time, I'll bring the lock. And what about you?"

"I don't bike in the rain." She flashed a smile. "And I *didn't* have a mistake."

I changed the subject. But at dinner the following night, she asked, "Your mistakes!"

Philippe described sending an email too soon, then picking up the phone to clarify.

"You didn't *check your work*?" She jumped up.

"I was in a rush. But tomorrow, I'll give myself more time."

"My turn," she said, and explained how she'd run into a boy

at the playground by accident. He'd started crying, but she hadn't apologized.

"You didn't explain what happened?" I asked.

"It wasn't my *fault*."

"You didn't have to say *sorry I pushed you*. But what do you think he thought?"

"Probably that I meant to do it." She scowled. "I'll explain next time."

That conversation was a small revelation. It allowed her to own up to a mistake, but not let that mistake consume her. Mistakes are common to all of us, she started to realize, and reflection can let us strategize for the next time. This realization arose *from* her, through our back-and-forth dialogue, not from any lecture I gave. After thinking through and wrestling with the ideas, she expressed them in her own words. Such thinking-through— and talking-through—lets kids learn more deeply than they otherwise would. Putting ideas in their own words makes those ideas more solid and allows them to take ownership of what they've learned. Think about constructing a toy car from scratch, rather than learning, in the abstract, how a car works.

Dialogue Shifts over Time

Over the next few weeks, Sophie brought up mistakes: some days in a silly mood, some days more seriously. We did, too. As the weeks passed, we started seeing her attitude shift. She was taking more responsibility, the teachers said, and making more friends.

Reflecting on those conversations, I was reminded of what the psychologist Carol Dweck refers to as a "growth mindset," or the belief that intelligence isn't fixed.[2] With a growth mindset, kids believe that effort will help them improve. It's not that talent doesn't exist, or that kids don't have natural abilities in certain areas. Of course they do.[3] But hard work, along with mentoring from us and their teachers and friends, can help. In her work on mindset, Dweck talks about the use of the word "yet," as in, "I haven't learned how to do multiplication—yet." Skills can be developed, and mistakes are only a sign that you have room to grow.[4]

The "growth mindset" idea has become so popular that it's now a kind of catchphrase. And it is important. As Dweck found, kids can develop a fixed mindset even as young as three and a half years old.[5] They start believing that mistakes show who you are as a person. As I heard three-year-old Paul say, "Well, I'm just bad at Legos." Watching Sophie build a more complicated structure, he found himself lacking. But these ideas can be changed with dialogue, for kids of all ages. As David Yeager, a professor at the University of Texas, has found, teenagers with fixed mindsets can, with conversation, change to growth mindsets, boosting their motivation and even their grades.[6] In his study of more than 18,000 ninth-graders, he found that students taking growth-mindset workshops later sought out more challenges. In this way, talk led to action, as kids stretched themselves and stayed open to making mistakes.

How should we help kids with this openness? Dweck's recent work offers important insights. As she found, even if we have a growth mindset, our *reactions* to our children's failures or mistakes might suggest we think their abilities are fixed.[7] If we rush in to soothe a child quickly and anxiously, with a comment like, "Well, it's okay if you're not good at that," the child can get the message that she can't change. Instead, Dweck suggests, emphasize strategies that worked, or how kids managed to solve a problem. When a child makes a mistake, show you're embracing that mistake as information. Ask what that mistake teaches you.

As I saw with Sophie, "mistake" conversations are critical for learning. They set the stage for kids to feel all right being wrong. Through looking at errors compassionately, we create room for kids to pinpoint *why* they've made those errors, which helps them strategize for next time. We also help them build empathy. When Sophie talked about having pushed a child by accident, she gained insight into how that child must have felt. In this way, kids gain both empathy and comfort with not being perfect. When we share our mistakes, they grow to recognize how they—and we—are always learning. This foundation of self-compassion lets them stay curious and engaged. Just as important, these conversations help them identify highlights in their journeys, letting them see where they've gone *right*.

Still, "mistake" conversations are only one of countless examples of talk that boosts learning. It's less what you talk about, and more about *how* you talk. In fact, all sorts of everyday topics let kids see where they are in their learning journeys and understand more about themselves and the world. Quality conversation helps them notice their own false beliefs and take steps to change them. These conversations also give *us* insight into how kids are thinking, which lets us bring them to the next level. When supported to follow their interests, kids pursue budding passions and, ideally, learn to make those passions a part of their everyday lives.

To be fair, long-term changes in beliefs aren't simple or immediate. But they *do* happen in small moments, in dialogue that shifts over time. To get there, helping kids embrace mistakes is only the start. This chapter reveals two main ways conversation can boost learning. First, it can spark lifelong curiosity, encouraging kids to explore ideas and take intellectual risks. Second, it supports them to learn *how* to learn. Thinking about your thoughts, a skill known as meta-cognition, is key to learning strategically. Rather than trying to do *more*—accumulate more facts, study for longer—kids see how to learn better.[8] That boosts their school success and, more important, lets them become lifelong learners, hungry for knowledge and optimistic about their abilities.

The End Goal of Learning

What's the end goal of learning? It's not getting straight As, or even getting into a top college—even though we often think of schooling with that mission in mind. It's not even securing a well-paying job. It has far more to do with giving kids the tools they need to pursue what interests them. In fact, learning goes far beyond grades. Learning to learn well is key to children's mental and emotional health. As they grow, this learning lets them find work and hobbies they love: lose themselves in books, imagine new worlds, invent, create, and engineer. "It's essential for our well-being that we connect with our true passions," as Ken Robinson, author of *The Element*, argues.[9] When kids find and connect with their passions, they're also more motivated. Over time, they learn to persist with challenges until they succeed.

But what if we define success only as good performance? That ignores important skills such as critical thinking and creativity. Worse, it leaves many kids without the mental flexibility or confidence needed to explore new ideas or persist long enough with tough problems to solve them. Instead, when we take a broader view of success, we help kids focus on what they care about. That leaves them more motivated to keep exploring. They face challenges more easily. When kids engage in authentic activities—when they see the *point*—learning often comes along for the ride.

How Daily Talk Helps Kids Learn

A few weeks after my "mistake" conversation with Sophie, I visited the "train park," a Boston playground overlooking a crossing of local and express trains. One father stood with his young son, peering through the fence.

"Guess which color train will come next," the boy said.

"Green, maybe."

"I think orange." The two of them waited. Soon, a green-colored train flew past.

"How did you *know*?" The son jumped up and down. "You guessed?"

"Not exactly." The father turned to him. "I realized there's a pattern."

"What's that?"

"It's when one thing comes after another. And repeats. Like there." He pointed to the boy's striped shorts. "See, green, blue, green, blue. Like that."

"Or like in the sky." The boy craned his head back. "Cloud, blue sky, cloud."

"Exactly." The father smiled. "And they do that with trains, so each direction gets a turn."

"They want to be fair," the boy said.

As they turned to watch more, I listened to a family nearby: a mother with a girl of about the same age. Hearing a loud honk, the girl jumped back.

"Is that the purple train?" she asked, eyes bright with excitement. "That's the fastest one. I hear it. The faster trains sound different, I think."

"Let's work on your alphabet," her mother responded. "What's after D?"

"I don't know *why* they sound different, though."

"E, F, G." Her mother sounded annoyed. "And then?"

Soon the conversation dissolved. Ten minutes later, the mother said they had to go home.

Those two conversations might have sounded similar, but they couldn't have been more different. In the first, the father piggybacked on his son's interest to offer him a window into the world. Sparked by his son's question, he introduced the idea of patterns: an interesting concept, and the foundation for early math.[10] He connected that idea to his son's shorts, which his son could easily see— important, given his son's age and stage. And he offered the chance for his son to contribute, in a natural back-and-forth, in a way that made the learning meaningful.

While the second conversation wasn't "bad" or "wrong," it didn't do any of those things. Neither the mother nor the daughter was listening to each other. Their interests left them at cross-purposes. The girl *wanted* to learn—just not, at the moment, what her mother wanted to teach. It would have been a far more interesting conversation if the mother had stopped and listened to the girl, and noticed that her question was actually pretty deep. Why do faster things sound different than slower ones? That's far more engaging than the ABCs—and lends itself to lots more questions and thinking. Why do things sound higher- or lower-pitched when they come closer or go farther away, like ambulance sirens? What does that tell us about sound and about our ears?

We might not have answers to all these questions—or even one. But that's exactly the point. Not having answers means we can go on the journey with kids: explore, ask more questions, maybe even learn something ourselves.[11] Taking on these questions gives kids a much richer understanding of what learning is all about. Yes, the ABCs are important, but learning goes far beyond memorizing facts. It has more to do with attitude: asking the hard questions *because* they're hard, taking the time to pursue them, and not stopping with the first answer we hear.

Capitalize on Passions and Goals

We don't always see chances to make learning authentic, especially if we get hung up on having kids learn in a certain way. When we overfocus on details of assignments or tasks, we can lose sight of the end goal or what kids care about. Especially with the pressures of school, it's easy to leave behind kids' interests and forge ahead with assignments and homework. Yes, the homework needs to be done—but even then, there's often room for a more creative approach.

This idea especially hit home for me once Sophie got old enough to have homework. In second grade, her teachers started asking students to read for twenty minutes a night. At the time, reading didn't come easily for her. One night, she lay in bed, flipping through *Rainbow Magic* and *Henry and Mudge* and complaining bitterly.

"I want to help put Paul to bed," she said. "Why won't you let me?"

Typically, I'd have kept trying to convince her to do her reading. Instead, I had some ideas in mind and wanted to try them out. We could work *with* a child's energy, I'd started to think. In seeing what drives her, at any moment, we can harness that drive to make learning smoother and spark motivation for the long haul.

"Paul likes to have someone read to him." I held out a stack of books. "If you want to put him to bed, I'd start there."

"You think?" She brightened.

"Haven't you seen him asking?" Luckily, it was true.

Taking the books, she walked over to Paul, then sat and opened *Curious George and the Puppies*. He cuddled up. Thirty minutes and four books later, I had to convince her to stop.

We can waste so much time insisting that learning happen in a certain way. If I'd nagged her to read, she probably wouldn't have enjoyed what she read. She'd have ended up frustrated, and not in the mood to start again the next day. Instead, through focusing on her goal of taking care of her brother, we got to the same place far more enjoyably. Reading became a means of connecting, not a dry assignment, and she saw the immediate benefit, in calming Paul down and letting the two of them connect. It all had to do with how the conversation turned.

Going back to the ABCs of rich talk, my conversation was A: *adaptive*. It paid attention to what she wanted in the moment—to her drive—and shifted based on her interest. It involved a B: *back-and-forth*, offering her an idea, then checking in to see what she thought. And it was C: *child-driven*, keeping her perspective in mind as well as my own.

Letting a child choose how or what to learn or practice—in a guided way—tends to let her want to do more. Motivation snowballs. Better skills lead to more interesting questions, leading to more practice, and on and on. Even becoming a better reader often makes kids want to read more, since reading feels easier and more fun.[12] When kids aren't stumbling to read individual words, they have more mental space to focus on *what* they're reading.[13,14] With this principle in mind, you can help kids decide what they care about and which questions to pursue. Of course, there are limits and boundaries. Of course, the homework has to get done. Still, creating space for kids to make their *own* learning decisions is a critical way to support them long term.

Rich Talk for Learning in Action

But what does this support look like? To learn more, I sought out one school I'd heard much about, the Atlanta Speech School, which puts a deep focus on everyday dialogue.[15,16] The school was famous for its ability to help kids with learning challenges make great progress and return to public schools. The school's philosophy is inspired by the work of Dr. Maryanne Wolf, a world-renowned literacy scholar and UCLA professor. Several months back, I spoke to Wolf about her recent work on the challenges of helping kids read deeply in a digital world.[17] She pointed me to the Speech School's powerful work supporting kids who had trouble reading. What's more, she told me the school focused not on drills or lectures, but rather on everyday talk based on what kids were passionate about.

Intrigued, I called the Speech School's CEO, Comer Yates. With a catching enthusiasm, Yates invited me to visit, and I gladly agreed. Soon, I headed to Atlanta, where I visited several classrooms and a school-wide "book tasting," a book-preview party complete with related snacks: licorice wands inspired by *Harry Potter* and *Diary of a Wimpy Kid*–themed cupcakes.

Later, I sat with a group of teachers to discuss their experiences. One spoke of her students learning of Thomas Edison's innumerable failures. Along the way, Edison wrote of finding himself in a valley, when he felt he'd fail. But, he claimed, if he kept going, he'd find success.[18] The teachers talked about these valleys as "dips," drawing from Seth Godin's 2009 book *The Dip*.[19] "I'm really in the dip now," that teacher recalled a student saying with a laugh, as he worked on a math problem. Using that phrase let struggle feel tolerable. Such self-talk, over time, lets kids tackle hard problems without getting overwhelmed.

At the Speech School, as I came to see, failure and persistence weren't abstract philosophies. Instead, these kids had understood Edison's lesson and internalized it, making it part of their way of thinking. When they might have given up before, this self-talk let them hang on. They embraced failure as inevitable—part of the process of moving toward mastery—and worked to stay curious about what that failure meant. As many studies have shown, positive self-talk, such as "Let me give it another try," helps kids manage their feelings and behaviors in ways that let them learn more effectively.[20] When they're confused, they talk themselves through problems, instead of saying, "Forget it," or immediately asking for advice. One study even found that kids who repeated positive statements about their hard work did better on math tests than those who did not—and the effect was stronger for kids who thought they weren't good at math.[21] That's powerful evidence that we should help kids notice and enhance their self-talk—and that we can.

That's the most valuable takeaway: these learning conversations can thread through your daily lives, in ways that let kids take ownership of their learning while letting them feel good about themselves. It's all about what kids learn to say, and what they internalize. It's not about the words we put in their mouths.

How the Three Es Set Rich Talk in Motion

So how can these learning talks happen in our lives? Inspired by my research into the interactions between adults and kids, I started using what I call the *Three Es* in my clinical work. The Three Es have a strong research base in developing language, thinking, and social skills across the age span. They serve as the foundation of rich talk, letting each of you participate and giving your conversations flow. Think of them as strategies you can keep in your back pocket, bringing them out when the moment demands it. They are as follows:

The Three Es for Rich Talk:

Expand on a child's thinking

Explore aspects beyond the here and now

Evaluate the process and product of thinking with a reflective, compassionate eye

What Are the Three Es?

Let's look at each in turn.

1. *Expand.* You take a child's comment and stretch it. You add phrases or words, or clarify. Simple expansions set the stage for more complex ones. One study found that, the more

mothers made such expansions, the greater a child's language development between ages two and three. If the child said, "Big truck," and the mother said, "That is a big truck," she stretched the child's comment, promptly, keeping to the topic, in line with the child's interest. That study focused only on mothers, as much of the research on parent-child interactions has. But luckily, researchers have begun to study fathers as well. Other studies have shown the power of fathers speaking to their kids, especially in terms of vocabulary use. For example, one study of fathers from rural communities found that the level of vocabulary they used with their six-month-old infants while reading related to the children's language development at one year and three years old.[22]

Imagine a child says, "Truck fall down." The mother responds, "Yes, it fell because you pushed it into the wall. It crashed." Her comment shows she's attending to the same thing as her child. That's known as *joint attention*, and it forms the basis for learning and social development for years to come. She gives her child feedback related to his interest, which makes it more meaningful. She models more correct and complex language, including vocabulary words that may be new to him, which teaches and stretches him beyond what he could do on his own.[23]

As a starting point, use questions that help kids open up. Take an *expanding* question: "Tell me more." Especially for younger kids, we tend to make "labeling" questions or comments: "Nice airplane" or "What a pretty flower" or "What color is that?" But when you say, "Tell me more," you're showing you're present and eager for the next idea.

Labels do help with early learning.[24] But in overfocusing on them, we miss the deeper thinking young kids are capable of, and the full range of their imaginations. Instead, try simply: "Wow, neat. What's that about?" or "What's the story here?" If your child explains a bit, then pauses, ask, "And after that?" That's far more conducive to conversation than the guessing game: "Is that a tree?" Try not assuming you know what a child will say. Instead, sit, look, and listen. Allow your child to do the explaining. Let his ideas surprise you. You must realize that what you thought of as a tree was actually a two-toed monster, or what looked like a house was really an outer-space satellite, or a nest for imaginary birds with purple wings.

2. *Explore.* Here, you go beyond a child's immediate surroundings to discuss the past and future; imagine distant landscapes and unfamiliar people; and consider solutions inventively. Continuing the truck example, you could say, "Where do you want the truck to go?"

"Outer space," he says.

"And after that?" you ask, after he zooms it up. Or maybe the truck keeps ramming into the table. You might ask, "What could you do to make it not crash?" or "What other road might it take?" These kinds of questions help him think abstractly and creatively, consider new ideas, and explore scenarios he might not have experienced. Just as books let him expand the borders of his world, so too do these opportunities to imagine, to hypothesize, to predict.

When you explore, you tend to use *decontextualized language*, or talk about abstract ideas, or things not right in front of you. "House" is concrete, but "architecture" is decontextualized. This decontextualized language builds kids' vocabularies, storytelling abilities, and the language they'll need to succeed in school.[25] From the research on this language, we know that the best way for them to build it is for us to model it.[26] You can start by telling stories. You might talk about the ideas in books or simply talk in ways that go beyond the here and now. One way to do this is by focusing on open-ended questions, or questions without "yes" or "no" answers. An open-ended question can be as simple as "What happened?" or "Where do you think he's going?"[27,28] Or you can ask about motivations or feelings; for instance, "How did the boy feel when his friend went away?" or "Why do you think he didn't cry?" Closed-ended questions, in contrast, could be "Was he happy when he moved to a different school?" or "Do you think he'll go back to his old home?" The close-ended versions have their place, especially if your child feels confused or says he doesn't know. But the open-ended questions are where his imagination can shine.

But, especially with young kids, start concrete. Base questions on what you and your child can see. Get increasingly complex, then check in with your child: what he's learned, whether he's interested or bored, engaged or confused. When you read, explore the ideas in books, instead of focusing only on words. Even young kids can think more abstractly if you *scaffold*, or support their thinking. Say you have a picture book of a child petting a bunny. It starts raining, and the bunny runs off. "Oh, no, the bunny's lost!" the child cries. Then the bunny appears, along with a rainbow. The most basic of all basic books, right? But your talk doesn't have to be.

Consider questions like "Why did the bunny run away?" "Where do animals go when they need shelter?" "How do humans do much the same thing?" "What types of shelter keep us safest?" "What other needs do humans and bunnies share?"

Or look outside for rainbows. "Rainbows come after storms," you say. "Our houses give us shelter, like trees do for bunnies. What do you like about your house?"

With only a brief conversation, you've gone from reading a tedious picture book to discussing fundamental human needs. And you've done it at your child's level, in an engaging way, without artificially using "hard" vocabulary. That's the beauty of talk. It lets us shift from the concrete to the abstract, while bringing kids along. Even if a question or topic feels a bit over your child's head, keep supporting your child and see if she can get there. Don't force or push, but try it out in small doses, and check in with yourself about how it went, and how you both feel.

This process engages kids while building their self-awareness and pride about how much they already know. You gain closeness and insight into how they're thinking, which helps you target questions better the next time. Often, you'll be surprised by how deeply they can think, or by connections they're making. You also get the chance to clarify misunderstandings. A month ago, I heard a five-year-old ask, "Why doesn't a meteor shower make you wet?" He'd recently watched an astronomy show. Hearing his question let me clarify that a meteor shower wasn't like a shower in the bathroom. But we then discussed how a meteor shower and a cleansing shower were alike—they both involved a collection of things, whether water droplets or meteors.

The same goes for conversations *not* based on books, and

those with older kids. Try the question: **What if . . . ?** For example: What if humans were as small as ants? We'd have to build smaller houses and cars. There might be less pollution. Explore these sorts of domino effects.

3. *Evaluate.* Encourage kids to think about their thoughts, ideas, strategies, and plans with a critical eye. With the truck example, you might ask, "Why did the truck's wheel break when you crashed it?" or "Hmm . . . why can't we fix that broken truck?" It's not about being "right." It has far more to do with answering questions such as: "Where are the gaps in my thinking?" "What am I missing?" "What else do I need to know?"

Emphasize that everyone, adults and kids, has gaps in his or her thinking, and we're all on a learning journey. To learn well, kids need self-compassion. Without it, they can end up deeply self-critical. "Maybe add?" one first-grader asked me, pondering a word problem. "No, that's stupid," she said, before I could tell her she was right. Like so many kids I've seen, she'd learned the habit of second-guessing herself at a very young age, in ways that undermined her confidence and that could eventually sabotage her intellectual growth.

Evaluation doesn't mean being critical in a negative way. Really, it's a positive, letting kids consider thoughts and feelings more objectively. Think of *evaluation* questions as pause buttons, creating chances to reflect. After that reflection, kids can come back with far deeper questions and ideas. That's the foundation for harnessing learning and making it more profound. It's also key in teaching kids how to trust themselves—which boosts their independence over time.

How the Three Es Look in Practice

Soon, I started putting those Three Es into practice. When I met Caroline, a sixth-grade student with trouble brainstorming ideas and expressing herself, I sensed she'd benefit from this approach. After having assessed her reading comprehension and writing, I found that she was reading and writing two years below her grade level. In her writing, she had particular trouble getting started. She second-guessed herself so much, questioning whether her ideas were good or whether she had anything to write about, that she often ended up paralyzed. But once she got into a flow, she was able to finish without much trouble.

Over the course of the year, her feelings about her challenges had started to snowball. As soon as she hit a roadblock, she started criticizing herself. "I'll never be able to write," she often told me. "I guess I'm just not a writer. My ideas are terrible."

In that way, her challenges with writing had led her to label herself as someone who wasn't capable and wouldn't ever be. In working with her, I wanted to help her change that perception, even as I helped her build her writing skills.

One afternoon, we sat as she struggled to write a persuasive essay. A great animal-lover, she started by saying there should be a "pet day" when kids brought pets to school. "Dogs are the *best*," she said, clearly excited, but soon complained, putting her head down, "I have *no idea* what to write." To scaffold her thinking, I started with *expansion* questions.

"Why do you think there should be a pet day?" I asked.

"I just do."

"Anything else?"

"I'm not sure." She met my gaze. "It sounds fun."

"How do you think kids would feel, with pets at school?"

"Good."

"Well, how did you think of the idea?" I sensed she had more to say. "It's pretty creative."

She brightened. "I saw a show where kids brought pets to each other's houses. The kids were arguing, but then they started getting along."

"Why do you think?" I asked, wanting to *explore*.

"Pets bring out good feelings. They're even used as therapy."

"Great. Let's think of other reasons."

Together, we worked to outline her ideas, and afterward, *evaluated* if she'd captured them all. She stumbled over her words but persisted. I was surprised at how such a simple prompt—along with an attitude of open curiosity—helped her talk more. Over time, she began expressing herself more fully. She grew more comfortable putting thoughts on paper and felt more confident. One day, I was surprised to hear her say, "This is actually *fun*." And soon after, she told me, "You know what? I read what I had written to my teacher, and she loved it. She even read it to the class afterward." The process had allowed her to view her work differently, and equally important, to see herself more positively.

Through changing the way she thought and talked about herself, Caroline changed what she was able to *do*. In a virtuous cycle, doing more let her feel better about herself. As she progressed, we were able to have more construction conversations. She became more open to learning. Her improved self-perception was founded on an improvement of her actual skills.

Kids Don't Need an Oracle

That experience with Caroline was followed by many others and confirmed what research had shown about talking through ideas. This skill, known as *verbalizing*, is a key way of boosting learning. To enhance children's reading and writing skills, Nanci Bell, author of the reading program *Visualizing and Verbalizing*, teaches them to make "movies" in their minds, then speak those "movies" aloud.[29] This helps them to visualize what they're reading or want to say, then to express those ideas more completely. As several studies have shown, verbalizing helps kids make sense of what they learn and remember it better. Even more important, kids who verbalize their ideas tend to have more positive attitudes and cope better with roadblocks.[30,31,32,33] Often, they don't need a lot of prompting, but simply encouragement and a few check-ins along the way.

For kids of all ages, use an attitude of curious waiting. Ask a question, or propose an idea, then step back and wait. Show him you sense he has more to say, and you're all ears. Notice what your child wonders about, then investigate alongside him. One parent friend, Jae Cody, now a high school German teacher in Minnesota, described such an experience: "As part of my teaching job, I was chaperoning a group of high school students and had my first-grader along. He had run into some raspberry bushes on a hike the day before, and, as we walked along a path surrounded by bushes, he asked me why the plants had to be so mean and scratchy."

Then Jae asked how animals protect themselves, and he said they run or use claws. She responded that plants can't run or attack, so they use thorns.

"That's pretty smart," her son said.

Jae could have just said, "I don't know," or answered, "To protect themselves." Instead she opened up a wider conversation. Not
only her son's question, but her response—with another question
and prompting that asked him to expand beyond the here and
now—created the high-quality talk. In a simple, everyday way, she
expanded on her son's initial question, which helped him make a
deeper connection to the world.

What's more, high-quality talk often engages people of all ages.
Isn't it more interesting to consider how creatures protect themselves, or how weapons and thorns are related, versus only answering what a thorn is? The same goes for kids.

We often assume that young kids can't think deeply, but that's
a misconception. True, if kids hear only simple sentences and yes-
and-no questions, they'll probably respond in simple ways. But
even young kids can—and often want to—take on complex ideas
and questions, having fun as they explore. It's all about giving an
opening and showing you believe in them.[34]

Conversation Shows Kids We Think They're Capable

At its best, our talk lets kids know they can take on intellectual
challenges. Simply showing interest and curiosity is a powerful
way in. Start with expressing implicit approval: "Mm-hmm" or
"Yes?" These openings suggest you're a conversational partner,
wondering what will come next. You're offering time to think
while encouraging storytelling. That lets ideas take on their biggest form.

A while back, I saw this recently in my house. One evening,
climbing up to the windowsill, three-year-old Paul asked, "Where's

the raccoon?" As we'd recently learned, there was a raccoon living in a tree outside.

"You can't see him," Philippe said, "but he's probably awake."

"It's my bedtime," Paul insisted. "The raccoon's, too."

"He plays when you're asleep," I said, "and sleeps when you're awake."

"He gets tired?" Paul looked quizzical.

"Yes—but at a different time than you do. When do you think?"

"When it's light." He went to the window. "Wake up, raccoon! Time for your morning."

With that simple conversation, he'd understood that for certain animals, the day could be flipped. Our schedules aren't universal. We could have used "hard" words, such as "nocturnal," but we didn't need to. Instead, he was able to grasp the concept in his way. There would be time to introduce "hard" words later, at a time when it felt natural.

The same goes for concrete observations. When you start with what a child notices or points out, you validate his interest and prime him to explore those ideas. Say he asks, "Why do ants march in a line?" Your discussion might lead to talking about differences between insect and mammal behavior or to questions like: Why do insects follow a leader? What about people?

Small wonderings can be gateways to big ideas. When kids expand on what they know, they think of more questions, leading them to want to know more. That's the foundation of raising a lifelong learner, someone who *knows* there are interesting things to learn and who wants to learn them. You can help by asking *your* hard questions; ones you don't have the answers to. Those harder questions engage you more, which enriches your interactions. Think about "What's the capital of Germany?" versus "How did the first country get started?" or "What are the names of constellations?"

versus "Why do we see most stars only at night?" In the first cases, there are answers you know or could find easily. But in the second, the answers aren't simple. You need to really think.

To be clear, I'm not arguing against learning the capitals, or saying that "hard" questions are better than "easier" ones. As in all things, a balance is key. But I am saying we often overemphasize questions with obvious answers, leaving the more complex or less obvious ones aside. To shift that trend, focus on exploring alongside your child. Voice your ideas and doubts. Emphasize questions coming *from* her. Initiate, then step back. See what she has to say. Kids often are delighted to realize there are things grown-ups don't know or haven't figured out yet.

That being said, you won't always have the energy to go beyond the quick response to engage in a full conversation. On other occasions, when you're talking to another adult and your child asks a question, you might not have the time. In that case, it can be helpful for a child to learn when *not* to talk! Still, when the time is right, these conversations are critical. Every time you have them, you're building habits kids can later adopt.

For Everyday Learning:
Explore Reasons and Causes

At their root, these habits let kids make sense of the world. They have an innate drive to learn, starting young. When young kids ask the same question a million times (as research shows, at least ninety-three questions per day), they might sound annoying, but they're often trying to scratch the "question itch."[35] When they don't get a satisfying explanation, they're twice as likely to ask the same question again.[36] These questions often jump around from topic to topic, seemingly randomly. As seven-year-old Sophie asked, "I have three questions. Who invented the word 'stop'? Why are there stars? And what happens to your brain when you sleep?"

··

What Does the Research Say?

In one study, four- and five-year-olds remembered information better when it was given in response to their questions than when it was presented without their personal prompts.[37] In another, when fathers asked "Wh" questions of their two-year-olds ("who, what, where, when, and why), the kids used more complex sentences and harder words. When fathers asked more of these questions, the kids' reasoning skills were stronger a year later.[38]

··

We often think we have to know the answers. While such questions are almost never about us, we make them about us, worrying when we don't know how to answer correctly, or feeling frustrated if those questions feel unanswerable. It can be much simpler, and more engaging, just to say we aren't sure—but here's what I think, and what do you think? Afterward, add on why you think that way. When kids hear you voice your thought processes, they learn a model for how to think things through. They also gain comfort with not knowing everything.

From young ages, kids benefit from *causal explanations and questions*. Think of "How things work" and "Why things happen." These questions—whether your child is two years old or thirteen— help explore and make sense of the world.

Ask *why* and *how* questions and answer your child's questions thoughtfully. Take that question about your brain when you're asleep. You might say, "I guess it shuts off." But what about when you dream? Does it start working differently? Tell what you know; for example, maybe you've heard that dreams help you process your day. Or say you have no idea. Try googling "your brain on sleep," or ask your child what it feels like to fall asleep. Does he remember his dreams? Talk through what you think, even if you're not sure. "I don't think it *shuts off*," you might say, "but maybe slows down? Let's look it up."

Taking on questions honestly—and *starting* conversations with them—helps you bond with your child, letting him feel you're less controlling and more responsive.[39] Start with everyday interactions. Rather than pivot *away* from the question, try a deeper dive. Say your four-year-old notices clouds gathering. You ask, "What do the clouds mean?" and he says, "Rain or snow." Take his thinking further. Say it's ten degrees Fahrenheit. Does he think it will rain or snow? Why? Has he ever seen a snowstorm when it was warm outside? Surf the wave of your child's curiosity. When possible, stay curious yourself. Your energy and curiosity feed his. That's as true for older kids as preschoolers. Let's take two examples. First, with a younger child:

Making Small Shifts: The Deeper Dive

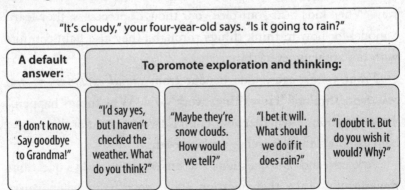

"It's cloudy," your four-year-old says. "Is it going to rain?"				
A default answer:	**To promote exploration and thinking:**			
"I don't know. Say goodbye to Grandma!"	"I'd say yes, but I haven't checked the weather. What do you think?"	"Maybe they're snow clouds. How would we tell?"	"I bet it will. What should we do if it does rain?"	"I doubt it. But do you wish it would? Why?"

Second, with an older child:

Making Small Shifts: The Deeper Dive #2

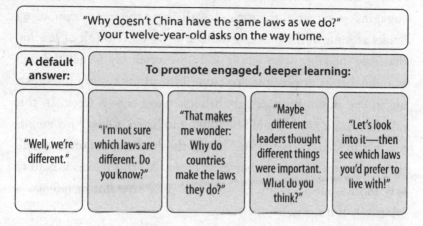

"Why doesn't China have the same laws as we do?"
your twelve-year-old asks on the way home.

A default answer:	To promote engaged, deeper learning:			
"Well, we're different."	"I'm not sure which laws are different. Do you know?"	"That makes me wonder: Why do countries make the laws they do?"	"Maybe different leaders thought different things were important. What do you think?"	"Let's look into it—then see which laws you'd prefer to live with!"

In both these examples, the parent wasn't all-knowing. She didn't have the perfect answer. Instead, she saw the question as a chance to explore. Conversation became an invitation to stretch a child in new ways: to teach that everyone has questions, and that not knowing can be an opportunity, not a shame.

You can take on similar ideas and questions with older and younger kids. The only differences are how abstract you get and your vocabulary. Take a "big idea" such as gravity. Even a three- or four-year-old can engage at a basic level. Say, "Why do things always fall *down* and never *up*?" An older child can consider: "What if we had less gravity? Would everything float, or move up toward the sky?" Or she can discuss more nuanced questions; say, why some objects take longer than others to reach the ground. Check in regularly about how your child is making sense of the conversation. Unless you ask, you may think he's missed the mark or hit it—but you can't know for sure.

Help Kids Love Reading: Using the Three Es

Asking these kinds of questions can also make reading feel fun and engaging—no matter the topic. It's all about the interaction, using books as jumpstarts to deeper talk. But we don't think of reading that way. Starting with young kids, we often try to get through as many books as possible. You should read for twenty minutes a night, you might hear, or get through two books a week. In this mindset, young kids should be quiet and listen. Older kids are often told to focus on how many books they've read, not on how well they understood or what they care about. All this makes it hard to stay motivated. So many kids find reading stressful or tedious—especially if it doesn't come easily.

"Please don't interrupt," I've heard parents say when reading to their kids. But interrupting during reading is actually a good thing. It shows a child is engaged and following along. In fact, as many studies have found, how much kids *participate* matters most for their learning. It's not only how much you read.[40] *Dialogic reading*, a proven way to boost understanding, means having a conversation about a book.[41] You start by paying attention to what your child is drawn to. You comment on her comment (*evaluate*) and encourage her to say more (*expand*). You rephrase what she says, add to it, and start again. In fact, kids who interrupt and ask questions during reading learn more and end up more motivated and curious. To get there, shift questions based on their evolving skills. Emphasize questions that relate to their worlds and encourage imaginative thinking.

Say, in a *Curious George* book, the monkey George goes up in a hot-air balloon and can't get down. "What would you do next?" you might ask, or "Why couldn't he get down?" Or *evaluate*: say, "Were you surprised when George got saved?" or "What part was the funniest?"

Making Small Shifts: Talk for Reading

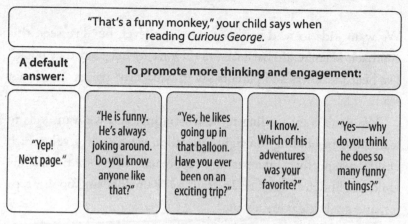

"That's a funny monkey," your child says when reading *Curious George*.				
A default answer:	**To promote more thinking and engagement:**			
"Yep! Next page."	"He is funny. He's always joking around. Do you know anyone like that?"	"Yes, he likes going up in that balloon. Have you ever been on an exciting trip?"	"I know. Which of his adventures was your favorite?"	"Yes—why do you think he does so many funny things?"

Already, you've opened a richer conversation than if you read straight through. Yes, you didn't get through as many books—maybe not even one. But you *did* use reading as a gateway into talking about ideas. That engages your child far more.

For older kids, ask what books they like to read or are reading for school. Take a theme they enjoy and search out related books and magazines. Especially for a child who doesn't like reading, magazines about his hobbies can be a great way to start. Have nightly read-alouds, or check out a second copy and read along. Ask: What surprised you? What did you like and dislike? What do you think will happen next? What topics should we explore later on?

> ***Talk Tip:*** Engage with the same book together. Read aloud to your child, have her read to you, or listen to audiobooks. Ask her which parts she enjoyed. Especially with funny books, let her be the storyteller. If she can't read yet, encourage her to retell the story using the pictures.[42]

Bend the Rules of Reading Toward Learning

We want kids to read books at the right level, but I've seen this approach become almost militant. "Don't *let* her read that book," I've heard teachers and parents say in whispered voices. "She's not ready."

We don't want reading to be frustrating, and we want kids to learn. But in holding too tightly to rules, we forget to value each child's perspective, interests, and approach. What motivates one child might defeat another. Instead, focus on choosing books, topics, and goals kids care about.

"Check if it's too hard," I told seven-year-old Sophie one morning at the library after she'd picked a book. We went through the "five-finger rule." Popular in many schools, the rule goes like this: five words you can't read per page means it's about right. More means it's too difficult. And if there are *no* words you can't read, it's too easy. You won't learn much. In fact, practice with "easy" books is often fun and builds confidence. Reading the same book over and over—tedious as it may be for us—is one of the best ways to support children's abilities to read fluently.[43] And five "too hard" words per page can frustrate many kids, causing them to give up before they get far. No matter: many teachers still use that rule as if it's set in stone.

"There are five in just the first *paragraph*." Sophie sighed dramatically.

"Let's find another one."

"I want this one." She insisted—and I felt ridiculous. So I said yes.

Every night, she took the book out. I helped with the hard words.

"That's not at your *level*," I heard myself say.

"I don't *care*."

For weeks, she kept reading, never more than two pages a night. "Can't we find a better book for you?" I asked, more than once.

"No," she insisted, and I gave up.

But something funny started to happen. As we worked through the pages, she started reading less choppily. She commented, "That was so silly, wasn't it?" She started to need me less. And she felt proud. "It's a hundred pages!" she exclaimed. "This is a really hard book."

I saw the effects of her progress in reading *through* that book. Was it the best choice? Maybe not. But that was the goal she'd set. Reading a "too-hard" book suited her personality and her wish to prove she could. Our talk let us check in on whether she was getting too frustrated or overwhelmed. If so, we could take a step back.

That's not to say throw out the rules and let kids read whatever they want. But it *is* to say that we should see reading rules—and rules about learning—as guidelines, meant to be bent depending on each child. In schools, that's not always possible, although small, flexible groupings of children go a long way. But we can definitely think about this individualized approach at home.

The Second Way In: Learning How to Learn

Soon after that discussion, Sophie started noticing more about how hard or easy books seemed. Opening one, she commented: "This one will be a bit hard, but I can do it," and another, "This one is *way* too tough." Her comments let us enter into a conversation with her about her reading, helping make her judgments more precise while still challenging herself. For example, I might say, "That one does have some hard words, but I think you can handle it," versus "That one's meant for high schoolers, so let's put it aside." And that journey, like those of many kids I've taught, highlighted how conversations can help kids learn *how* to learn. Talk helps them think about their thinking. That skill, known as metacognition, lets them see what they know and don't; where they need help and how they might get it. In the past three decades, the study of metacognition has blossomed, as researchers have recognized its importance in raising resilient, successful learners.[44]

Not only is "thinking about thinking" useful—it's even more effective when kids learn to do it proactively. When kids think ahead about how to approach a task or project, they learn to strategize, then monitor as they go. For example, a child who needs to do a science experiment but doesn't have the ingredients might plan to go to the store before five. The store, he knows, is closed on Sunday nights. When he gets there, he sees that the store has all the ingredients except for one. When he returns home, he reads the assignment. He's supposed to make a volcano and predict whether it will explode. He gets started and makes a prediction, writing that he thinks his volcano will explode.

But then he stops and says to himself, "Well, I'm missing one ingredient, right? Maybe I shouldn't jump to conclusions. I might *want* it to explode, but maybe that one ingredient is key." He recognizes that his excitement might have led him astray. He then researches which ingredients are required for the explosion and finds the missing one on the list. He changes his prediction to be more accurate. He tests it out—the volcano doesn't explode—and then decides to try again when he's bought the missing ingredient. Not only has he learned more, but he feels less disappointed when his experiment doesn't work. He has a better understanding of the reason—and he secs how to make changes to find success the next time.

When a child thinks metacognitively, he keeps an eye on his learning and his feelings. If he's confused or unmotivated, he stops and makes a change. In this way, seeing the whole landscape makes it easier to decide on the next steps and know where to put their energy. That's especially important for older kids, as they grow more independent and need to drive their learning more.[45]

. . . .

A 2017 Stanford study tested two groups of college students taking statistics. Before each test, one group was randomly assigned to strategize how they would study. By the end of the class, that group was more reflective, used study aids more effectively, and got better grades.[46] Patricia Chen, a study author, explained that many students thought they were better-prepared than they were. Those who didn't reflect kept doing poorly. Those who did were able to see where they were going wrong and recognize they needed to study more.[47]

. . . .

Metacognition Means Us, Too

Soon I began seeing how these nudges boosted kids in many areas of learning, and even in our relationships with them. Metacognitive thinking, I began to see, could benefit both parents and kids. Once, I was meeting with Brianna, the mother of a ten-year-old boy, Jeremy, to discuss Jeremy's progress in reading. Jeremy was dyslexic and had trouble both with decoding, or reading the words on the page, and reading comprehension, or understanding what he was reading. While he was improving on both fronts, I sensed he was exhausted. He told me of late nights after basketball practice, trying to catch up on homework. He often put his head down in our sessions. His teachers had said much the same and worried he wasn't getting enough sleep.

"We work for *hours*," Brianna moaned, when I asked her about how homework was going. "I want to be involved, and I don't want to leave him with wrong answers."

"Does he finish?" I asked.

"Oh, he finishes," she said. "I make sure of that."

"But how do your sessions make you feel?"

"It feels like overkill." She gave a sharp laugh. "And I know he hates it. By the end, he's exhausted, and I'm furious."

"What about being honest?" I suggested. "Say you don't understand his math. Ask your actual questions. See if he can teach you and catch his mistakes."

"What if he can't, and the teacher's upset?" she asked. "Or if the teacher grades him down?"

A fair point. But I knew few teachers who'd be upset if a child really tried. And even being graded down—while never easy—has an upside. I've talked to many teachers who see kids struggling in class but turning in perfect homework. That makes it tough to pinpoint a child's misconceptions. When many kids miss the same concept, most teachers notice and shift their teaching. As I discussed with Brianna, it's helpful to monitor our own thinking around learning as well. Did *she* feel anxious or panicked at the thought that he might not finish? Did she see his incomplete homework as a reflection on her? Answering those questions lets her find the most effective next step. Maybe it would be best to step away and let him manage—or maybe he does truly need more help in order not to feel frustrated or give up completely.

In this way, noticing your own impulses and reactions to a child's learning lets you find the best compromise between helping and overdoing it. Also, talk with your child's teachers about his challenges, or encourage him to. Emphasize strategies that helped, especially those he can do on his own. Such conversations help close the loop between his home and school lives. They also make it far easier for his teachers to know what's happening and how they can support him best.

Notice Your Own Attitude

As I've found in talking to parents of school-age kids, finding the right balance in these learning conversations can be tricky, especially these days. In the United States, since the introduction of Common Core standards in 2010, we've entered a new learning era.[48] These standards, designed to create a uniform set of goals for all students, were adopted by more than forty states—but later dropped by more than twenty of them.[49] Still, the methods have profoundly changed the ways teaching and learning happen. Many of the ways teachers teach don't map onto how *we* learned as kids.[50] Take math. Rather than applying formulas—say, "flip the fraction to divide"—kids are asked to try many approaches, even invent strategies themselves.

This new math, meant to help kids develop deeper understanding, often *does* resemble how we use math in everyday life. Say you give a twenty-dollar bill to buy something that costs a dollar and ten cents. To figure the change, do you take out a calculator or scribble numbers on a paper? Probably not. You'll likely estimate—"Around nineteen dollars"—or count up—"Ninety cents, then eighteen dollars more." The "new math" is designed to teach this kind of thinking. How well it works is still up for debate—but it's left many parents confused.

"Shouldn't I be able to do third-grade math?" parents have asked me, half-joking, but with obvious anxiety.[51] Feeling anxious, as parents, teachers, or caregivers, makes it hard to help kids learn. As one 2015 study found, children of "math-anxious" parents learned less math over a school year. When their parents often helped with homework, the kids tended to become math-anxious themselves.[52,53] That's not to say don't help, but keep your attitude in mind, especially if you start feeling frustrated and stuck. Do you suggest math is scary or too hard? Shifting those messages is important, especially for girls, who go from being as strong in math as boys in the early grades to weaker by the end of high school. Take a relaxed approach. Focus on tinkering and talking through ideas aloud. Encourage strategizing like "I might try this way, or that."[54]

Ask kids to explain right *and* wrong answers, at least sometimes. That solidifies their ideas and shows if they're thinking incorrectly. Taking a nonjudgmental tone, ask: "Interesting, how did you get that?" or "I'd like to hear how you're thinking." Or: "How sure are you of your knowledge, from one to ten?" Have an older child weigh in. Or ask your child to teach a younger sibling. Explaining his knowledge cements his ideas while letting him feel proud of his skills.

More broadly, try these habits to make learning conversations a priority:

Conversational Habit #1:
The "Why" Talk—Answering Causal Questions

For "how" and "why" questions, try the following:

Own up to not knowing. You don't need to master any subject. Telling your child "I'm not sure" sets you up to explore together.

Check in with what kids know. Say your child asks, "Why did dinosaurs die?" You might say, "Because of a meteorite," and launch into a discussion about extinction. But start by checking his understanding. Does he say, "A rock killed them" or "Cars ran over them?" His answer changes your response. The first child's theory needs only a little tweaking, while the second needs an overhaul.

Support ideas in the right direction. For example, "Mongolia isn't the biggest country, but it *is* bigger than France."

Take a child's question seriously and answer with real information. Say your child asks, "Why are plants green?" or "How do rockets work?" Try that same check-in. "Why are you asking?" or "What made you wonder that?" buys you time while letting you understand his thought process. Maybe he'll think of other questions or realize his real question was different. As he talks it out, his thinking becomes more nuanced and precise.

If there's no obvious answer, find out together. Ask friends, family, or neighbors, or look in books or online. Collaborate in answering, then generating new questions. Reflect on where you found answers and why. Note surprises: maybe you hadn't realized your neighbor knew about botany, or that old maps showed where different plant species grew.

- ***Leapfrog questions.*** "Chlorophyll," your child says, in answer to why plants are green. "Why is *that* green?" you might ask.

Keep going, following his interests, until you've exhausted the line of questioning or he feels "done."

- **Help hypotheses bloom.** Try a game I developed with students called *Yes, No, Maybe So*. Take a hard question and develop a few possible answers: what you think is most likely ("Yes"), least likely ("No"), and in between ("Maybe so"). Have one person give their answers, and let the other guess which is which. Then switch. When you have time, investigate which answer is right.

- **Encourage linked questions and lines of questioning.** "Why do we see color?" "Is there a purple plant?" "Are there colors that *don't* exist in nature?" "What makes a color artificial?" Let questions evolve. Write them down and track how they change, as you answer some questions and as new ones bubble up. Highlight how asking more challenging questions is a sign of progress, not failure.

- **Expand your idea of research.** Don't underestimate the value of local experiences. A trip to a nearby river can teach about how salmon are spawning.[55] A visit to a video game arcade can offer insight into virtual-reality driving. Rock climbing can let a child learn about momentum and balance while testing a new sport—and, most important, having fun.

- **Offer up more than one theory.** "Stars come out because they're there." "Trains run because a person made them." It's easy to give a simple answer and leave it at that. But even young kids benefit from realizing that the real story is more complex.

    "Not everyone agrees about that," you might say, in answer to why dinosaurs died. "Some people think an asteroid caused them to become extinct. Others say it was because the weather changed. I'm not sure. Let's look it up." Ask your child what she thinks. If you keep your attitude curious, she learns that lacking knowledge can be an opportunity, not a threat.[56] This perspective benefits her in the moment and in later years. Think of an adult working on a vaccine. To succeed, she needs to start with what she *doesn't* know, and use that to drive her research. Progress means asking more precise questions, not finding one answer and closing the book.

Recognize when you're out of time or not in the mood. Don't beat yourself up about not being ever-present. That's an impossible goal, not to mention a false ideal. Kids need downtime, alone time, and time with other relatives, siblings, and friends. Try "bookmarking," saying you *do* want to answer, just not now. Make a game of it: for example, "Can you remember that for when I pick you up?" or "Can you invent five questions by dinner?" That gives you thinking time and piques your child's interest throughout the day. Or try a playful approach: "The question-answerer is not available. Please come back in one hour. Until then, ask your brother." Try a question-asking contest with friends, family, or siblings: Who can ask the hardest or silliest question? Have your child brainstorm answers, the craziest to the likeliest, and rate which ones he likes the most.

If your child has constant questions, write them on scrap paper, or have him do it, if he's old enough. Put them in a jar, then take out a few when you have time. Don't worry if they're impossible to answer fully. Break them into parts. Instead of "Why do we see color?" try starting with "How does the eye work?"

Conversational Habit #2:
Big-Picture Talk

Daily routines and rituals are a great way to start this step-by-step approach. Say your two-year-old has a habit of looking out the window after dinner. One evening, he watches firefighters rescue a cat from a tree and asks if the cat is safe. The next evening, he checks for the cat again.

In response, test out a nightly game like "What will we see outside?" Help him put ideas in "buckets," like "Will it be an animal or a person? A normal or exciting thing?"

Or say he notices it's getting darker earlier, or complains it's too early for bed, since it's still light outside. Use that as a springboard: Discuss how days get shorter in winter. Notice how late sunsets come. Or, if you're out for a walk, step on each other's shadow, noticing whose is bigger. Reflect on when we see shadows and don't. When you pick him up from school, ask: "How bright is today versus yesterday? Do you think we're closer to spring?" Connect ideas to bodily sensations: "In winter, I start getting goose bumps. What other signs of winter do you notice?"

Dry facts don't do much to draw us together. They're not particularly interesting. It's only when we weave those facts into bigger questions, and start connecting them to our lives, that we see how powerful and fun conversations for learning can be.

Conversational Habit #3:
Take the Aerial View

To raise self-awareness: Have fun thinking about thinking (meta-cognition). Use games, playtime, and downtime to help.[57] Say you're playing basketball. Which strategies work best to make a basket: shooting underhand, or standing three feet farther back? Test out ideas, then see if you're right. Talk through the results, playfully rating your efforts: "better," "best," or "not so great."

In harder times, metacognitive talk can help your child manage and learn to regulate herself.[58] Say she feels anxious. Help brainstorm soothing strategies—taking a bath, say, or deep breathing—then try them out and reflect on how they made her feel. Focus on all the senses: a warm blanket, the smell of baked bread. Emphasize that comfort looks different for each of us.

Test out "self-checks." Self-checks build your child's awareness about her learning while giving *you* a window into her strengths and needs. Try these strategies:

- *Encourage reflection on thinking and habits.* Say your middle schooler doesn't know if she's studied enough for a quiz. Reflect on how much she studied last time, and how well she did. Ask her to pinpoint which strategies helped most. Encourage her to develop practice quiz questions, then test herself. Use earlier tests as models. Or say she can't get started with a research project. What's the problem: not knowing enough, or not having chosen a topic? Pinpointing the issue lets her take an effective next step.[59]

- *Help a child see areas of strength and challenge.* Try questions like: *What's coming easily and less easily? Where am I getting stuck? What can I do to help myself?* As Jae Cody, the parent friend you met earlier, told me, her older son was struggling in second grade and she wasn't sure why. One day, he burst out, "There's too much writing and it takes too long and I hate it." While she'd suspected writing was hard for him, hearing this let her know he was aware of his difficulties. She could then empathize with him and brainstorm about how to support him best. Otherwise, she might never have known, or might have assumed he was just unmotivated.

- *Help kids recognize and overcome challenges.* To promote independent learning, I often use the metaphor of driving. I talk about three elements:
  - "Roadblocks" make it tough to get a task done or problem finished.
  - "Speed bumps" slow you down.
  - "Yield signs" are places you can pause and reflect.

- *If your child faces a tough assignment or problem, try questions like these:*
  - Roadblocks: Ask, "What needs to change before this can go better?" Maybe he feels hungry or needs a movement break.
  - Speed bumps: Ask, "What could you smooth out?" Maybe sitting in a new place would make focusing easier.
  - Yield signs: Ask, "What works for you? What strategies have you already tried?" Maybe he's confused about the directions and could call a friend.

Afterward, look to the future. How could he change his strategies for next time?

To understand how each other learns: Make "meta" talk a family affair. Once or twice weekly, discuss your "jolt." The "jolt" is an event, moment, or idea that lets you understand something new. Maybe it was a news story you read or a family member you talked to. Take turns describing your jolt and how it changed you: "I used to think things were like ____, but the jolt made me realize ____. Now I think/feel differently." What new questions do you have? Did the other person's jolt surprise you? Why or why not?

Even with the best of intentions, our conversations around learning may shut kids down. We focus narrowly, trying to pour in knowledge and facts; a sort of "fire-hose" approach. But kids don't need that blast of words or information. They're already full of their own curiosities and questions that only need a little support to grow. Making sense of the world and developing their curiosity are far more important goals than "test success." Boosting their thirst for knowledge will help them learn deeply, and *want* to learn more over time. What's more, it doesn't have to be one or the other. You can help kids question deeply and follow their budding passions, even as they learn skills to succeed in school. It's definitely not about having all the right answers. Instead, it's all about feeling relaxed enough to explore.

CHAPTER 3

Conversations for Empathy: Fostering Your Child's Understanding of Others

Empathy is about finding echoes of another person in yourself.
—MOHSIN HAMID, NOVELIST[1]

In our apartment, the air filled with the sounds of kids squealing and the sweet smell of blue frosting and cake. It was a Saturday morning in early November, the weekend after Sophie's seventh birthday, and I was supervising a slime-making party: Sophie's choice. She and most of her friends were obsessed with slime. With eight girls busily mixing sequins and glitter into "unicorn slime," the excitement was palpable. After cleaning up pizza and setting out cake, I headed over to the girls and listened in.

"Can we take the slime home?" Frances, one of the girls, asked as they sat on the floor.

"Sure," Sophie said. "We have way more than I'll use."

"Great, thanks."

Sophie asked how they should divide the slime up, and Frances suggested they each keep what they'd been working on until then. The girls agreed, and I headed to the kitchen for plastic bags. But as I walked away, I saw one girl, Elizabeth, hold up a tiny ball of slime and say, "Look. Mine is basically nothing." It was a small thing, but I could sense her disappointment.

The girls looked at her, then at one another: they did have much more than she did. For a moment, there was silence. Then Frances leaned over and put a bit of her own slime on the table.

"Let's each give her a bit of ours," she suggested. "Then nobody loses a lot, and she'll have as much as we do."

Without hesitation, the other girls agreed and piled up glittery gray slime, which Elizabeth took with a broad smile.

"Thanks, guys," she said. "That's just what I needed."

Soon they left the party, carrying their slime-filled Ziploc bags. They gave one another warm hugs before saying goodbye.

That scene, minor as it was, stuck in my mind. At first, I wasn't sure why. The girls hadn't seemed to think much about it. For them, it hadn't been a big deal. But then I realized it was precisely their ease in fixing the problem that made the moment memorable. They didn't struggle or have a long debate. Instead, they'd showed empathy, thinking and feeling into Elizabeth's mind and heart, then responding based on what they noticed.

So how had they managed the situation so easily? They were good friends from school, for one. That shared base had surely made it easier. But more than that, they'd learned to feel empathy and act on their feelings, in a way that helped their friend. That's not to say they'd *always* be empathetic—but that, at that moment, they'd been able to let their empathy shine.

Conversations can spark children's curiosity and let them learn how to learn. But learning isn't all we want kids to do. We want them to take one another's perspectives, connect meaningfully, and take action that helps. How? If a child can recite "emotion" words from the dictionary, he might win a spelling bee. But if he does nothing when his friend falls down, or when someone bullies his brother, all his knowledge doesn't count for much. He needs empathy to understand others' perspectives, share feelings, and take action that helps.

But that birthday party conversation, and countless others I've heard since, made me think. It aligned with observations I've made through the course of years of research and work, as well as my experiences parenting two kids. Over the course of those years, I've been heartened to see so many kids showing empathy to friends, family, and strangers in surprising ways. Raising kids to have empathy is possible—and we don't need to hover over them to get there. Kids *can* strengthen their empathy muscles, understanding and feeling into others' perspectives in ever more nuanced ways. To help, we need to start by getting clear on what empathy is.

Empathy Is More Than "Nice to Have"

If you find the concept of empathy vague or confusing, you're not alone. So many people throw the term around, as something we want kids to have, but without ever defining what it means. Others lump it together with similar qualities, such as kindness or caring. Or you might have heard the saying, "Put yourself in the other person's shoes." That's not a bad start. But what do those "shoes" look like, and what do you do once you've put them on?

We tend to think of empathy as good to have; a quality related to being nice or giving to charity. Or we see it as pleasant and sweet—the emotional equivalent of watching *Mister Rogers' Neighborhood*. But empathy is much more exciting and powerful. Think of it as being open to the world. Rather than having high walls, you're porous. It's not only about negative emotions. You can also empathize with a person's happiness. And doing so is the key to feeling connected, understood, and loved as a full human being. Empathy lets kids be social and avoid cruelty, while bringing them out of their individual bubbles. When they feel empathy, they're primed to connect and bond in far deeper and more meaningful ways.

In fact, kids have a natural capacity for empathy that needs nurturing. It's like a gas tank that needs to be filled. With a honed sense of empathy, a child recognizes what a person *really* feels and expresses herself in ways that let *her* full self be recognized. She gets to know who others authentically are, while at the same time, they get to know her. And the ability to feel and show empathy builds throughout childhood and beyond. Even as adults, most of us are still working toward mastering empathy. Think of road rage, or simply of getting annoyed at someone taking too long in the checkout line. We often let our anger, annoyance, or frustration get the better of us, not stopping to think of why the other person might be behaving as he or she is. Our natural capacity for empathy gets cut off.

But where does our empathy come from? For decades, scientists thought it had to do with mirror neurons, or brain synapses that fire both when you do an action and when you *watch* another person doing it. It's a "monkey see, monkey do" idea that literally started by studying monkeys. But we now think empathy involves far more than an isolated brain network. It's an interwoven set of skills that may *start* with mirror neurons, but draws on a whole lot more.[2]

Empathy, as the psychologists Daniel Goleman and Paul Ekman define it, has three parts: taking another's perspective, a skill known as *cognitive empathy*; feeling what another person is feeling, known as emotional or *affective empathy*; and being moved to help, a skill known as *compassionate empathy*.[3,4]

The girls at the birthday party had drawn on all three. They'd taken Elizabeth's perspective, using *cognitive empathy* to realize she didn't have as much slime as they did. They'd felt what she was feeling, using *affective empathy* to share her disappointment.[5] And they'd acted to help her in a way that didn't inconvenience any of them, using *compassionate empathy*. What's more, they'd applied those skills independently, in a way that left everyone feeling connected and happier. To grow up to be caring, a child needs all three parts. Having only one or two doesn't mean she'll act in a caring way. As research has shown, kids who shine at perspective-taking can actually be *crueler* to classmates, since they understand which actions will hurt the most.[6,7]

Also, understanding empathy in the abstract isn't enough. Kids also need skills in applying their knowledge about feelings. They need to feel moved to care. At times, this comes naturally, but not always. Our conversations with them are critical in helping them recognize their empathetic strengths and develop in weaker areas, while helping them understand their moral agency.[8] Essentially, in our dialogue with our kids, we're helping them fill in their empathy gaps. By coaching them to understand and express emotions, rather than dismissing them, we're supporting their empathy skills from the earliest years.[9]

Luckily, from infancy, we're all innately primed to understand others and want to connect. We find joy in vicariously sharing in positive and negative emotions. Think of watching a horror movie and sharing the hero's suspense. But simply *having* the capacity for empathy doesn't mean that kids will develop it. We need to help foster empathy—and we can.[10]

Empathy in Everyday Life

In everyday life, it's easy to see kids having trouble empathizing. When Sophie was around four years old, I took her to the birthday party of another four-year-old, Layla. Two weeks earlier, Layla's mother had sent out an invitation, saying, "Please, no gifts—we're serious."

There are good reasons for "no gift" policies: the kids already have enough toys, or we should emphasize the people, not the presents. Not every party needs to have gifts. Still, when we got to the party, I saw the birthday girl standing in the driveway, sobbing, saying, "Where are my *presents*?"

Soon the other kids came over, asking, "What's wrong?"

Her mother walked over and explained they'd give money to charity instead. But Layla wouldn't stop sobbing. After several minutes, her mother ushered her into the house, saying, "We'll find some presents for you—or, right after the party, we'll buy some."

Layla's mother had wanted to teach her empathy. The idea of giving to charity was well-intended. But Layla was too young to understand the concept of charity without specific examples, or without seeing the recipients of her gifts. Contrast the idea of sending a check with, say, bringing cans of food to a food pantry. There, the discussion of charity could start from a concrete place.

We want to teach our kids empathy, but it's easy to aim too high or too low for their developmental stages. We want our kids to care for others, but the conversations we have may assume too little or too much. This chapter will help you refine your conversations to target your kids exactly where they are on their empathy journeys. That's the key to helping them develop the skills to understand empathy—and, just as important, to apply their knowledge when they're on their own. We won't always be standing right beside them, so this independence is essential.[11,12]

So what's stopping us from these more targeted conversations? For one, we don't always notice simple ways of building empathy that show up in daily life. These ways don't have to be fancy or complicated. Gift-giving, for example, pushes on each of those three parts of empathy, making it the perfect opportunity to stretch. You need perspective-taking to think about what another person wants and how he'll make sense of your gift. A book about exercise or a purple shirt might be fine presents—but if your friend is sensitive about his weight or hates purple, those "gifts" can feel cruel. Through empathizing, you think of a gift that would feel meaningful and act based on what you realize. Receiving a "just-right" gift is fun in the moment and lets you feel the giver "gets" you. Long-term, it shores up your bond.

But empathy isn't only about actions or presents. It starts with taking off your blinders and getting to know others for who they really are.

Soon after Layla's party, I read a book to Sophie from the popular *Daniel Tiger* series.[13] That children's book series features the tiger Daniel and his friends. In this book, we meet Daniel's new friend Chrissie, who needs crutches to walk. Daniel, trying to be friendly, keeps asking Chrissie if she needs help. They won't play the running game he likes, he tells her, since she can't run fast. He assumes he's being caring and nice. But Chrissie tells him she *does* want to play the game, just in a different way. What's more, she doesn't need help—and if she does, she'll make sure to ask.

Just as Daniel did, kids often make assumptions about what others feel or think. They may even have the best of intentions. Still, they can forget that each person has a unique perspective and wants to be known for who she or he is. In that way, empathy isn't about caring *in general*. It's about specifically leaping into another person's world, understanding her real thoughts and feelings, and seeing that she's far more complex than any one group or category. The seeds of this ability can be planted early—but there's often a long road toward its full development.

How Does Empathy Develop?

Empathy doesn't pop out of kids when they turn six, or thirteen. Rather, glimmers appear early on. From infancy onward, many babies wail when they hear another baby crying, a "viral cry" that's practically contagious.[14] Already, they're sharing another's pain. Perspective-taking also shows up early, but not all at once. For example, children from one to two years old start showing signs of distress for others, particularly caregivers and infants in pain. Interestingly, that's around the time they become better able to imagine and use symbols, and when they start distinguishing others from themselves.[15,16] By sixteen months, kids often start soothing others in basic ways, such as offering hugs and saying they'll "make it all better."[17,18]

As they get older, kids improve in their understanding of feelings; a key underpinning of empathy. Already, many preschoolers are capable of sharing a character's emotion.[19] In general, they tend to **recognize** emotions—seeing that another person is happy—before they can **describe** them. Broad strokes come before nuance. Young kids have a limited emotional palette; say, mad, glad, and sad. Their abilities to understand and talk about "mixed emotions"—say, a combination of happy and nervous—develop later.[20] Many three-year-olds can connect feelings and wants; for example, predicting that a young child will feel excited to get a balloon.[21] From ages four to five, many kids start being able to take another person's perspective. They recognize that someone can believe something that's not actually true.[22] "She thinks we're going to the beach," your child might say of her friend, for whom you're hosting a surprise party. Your child sees that the friend doesn't know what everyone attending the party does.

From around seven to eight, kids have an easier time recognizing feelings but tend to draw conclusions based on what *they* feel. Say, if *they* would feel sad to miss a field trip, they assume their friend would too.[23] In later years, they get better at imagining how a character in a book might feel, based on what he or she does and says.[24] With that foundation, kids have a much easier time understanding literature. For example, why does a character hide backstage at a talent show? It might be because he's shy or doesn't want to perform. Or maybe it's because he hasn't practiced enough. When kids talk through these theories, they're building their understanding of how others think and feel.

As kids grow, they also learn to ask reciprocal questions, in which asking and answering goes both ways. If I ask, "How was your weekend?" you might tell me, then ask, "And what about yours?" I look for this ability, especially when assessing kids in middle school and beyond, as it shows kids realize not everyone is like them. The same goes for understanding that the world doesn't center around them. This skill develops over time, often bumpily. "What are you saying about me?" I heard a seven-year-old ask her parents, who were talking about finances. These kids need help to realize how much *doesn't* have to do with them.

Still, all the knowledge of child development won't let you fully understand *your* individual child. In my experience, the development of empathy is more complicated. It depends in part on a child's temperament, and also on the others around him. For instance, I've seen many middle school kids struggling to take another's perspective, and much younger kids who shine. We can't know a child's level of empathy only through knowing his age or stage, I began to realize. There has to be a lot more going on.

Each Child Has an Empathy Profile

One January morning a few years back, I was working at an elementary school when I went out to find the playground covered with snow. In this school, I was working with children one-on-one and in small groups on their reading comprehension and writing skills. Often, I dropped by their classrooms to pick them up, then brought them back afterward—a common model in many schools, known as "pull-out." As a result, I had the chance to see how the kids interacted with their classmates and how they managed the transitions back into class. On this day, I was bringing a group of third-graders out to recess. One nine-year-old boy, Darius, ran out in front of me, pulling his friend Robby toward the playground. Robby had a downcast look.

"Isn't it *awesome*? Playing in the snow?" Darius asked, then turned to his friend. "Come *on*."

"Yeah, I guess," Robby said, clearly unenthused.

"What first—the swings or the monkey bars?" Darius asked, running ahead, as he yanked his friend's arm.

"I don't think your friend wants to go," I told Darius.

"Of course he does."

Soon Darius had run out onto the playground. Finding a blank patch of snowy ground, he balled up a fistful of snow and said, "Hey, let's have a snowball fight."

"No, thanks," Robby responded, looking glum, and headed to the corner.

Ever more excited, Darius balled up snowballs and started playfully pelting Robby and a few other kids. While the other kids laughed and fought back, Robby only sat still. A minute later, I noticed tears streaming down his face. When I went over, he hid his head in his jacket. Nothing was wrong, he said. But then I sat beside him and let him cry. Gently, I asked if he wanted to talk. After a minute, he poked his head out and said he was moving in a month and would have to change schools. His parents had just told him that morning.

Listening to him, I was reminded all over again of the importance of noticing feelings as a pathway to empathy. Clearly, Darius hadn't noticed how Robby was feeling—or, if he had, those signals hadn't changed his mind. While he might have wanted to make Robby feel better by distracting him, he hadn't picked up the subtler signs of how his friend felt, and hadn't used those signals to change how he responded. In fact, he struggled with similar issues in his reading. He could read the words all right but had trouble making inferences, or "reading between the lines."

That reading between the lines is a key part of empathizing. It's rare that someone meets you and simply says, "I'm excited," or "I'm sad." Instead, those feelings come across in body language, tone, and facial expressions, as well as *how* a person is speaking. To empathize well, kids need to become attuned to these cues. They need to master their own and others' emotions—but that doesn't mean becoming more rigid. Quite the opposite: it's in growing *more* open and flexible about emotions that kids learn to accept a fuller range. They recognize feelings and know how they look and sound. They see emotions as welcome guests. Marc Brackett, director of the Yale Center for Emotional Intelligence and author of *Permission to Feel*, talked to me about the need to raise "emotion scientists," not emotion judges.[25] You examine an emotion thoughtfully, noticing what's behind it. You recognize and embrace it, then explore how you might best express it. You sit with your emotions, which lets you process them. You don't force them away.

Brackett is the founder of a curriculum, known as RULER, that focuses on teaching exactly these sorts of skills—to kids, but also to their parents and teachers.[26] The curriculum focuses on five major areas: kids are taught to *Recognize* (R) their emotions, to *Understand* (U) them, then to *Label* (L) them, or give them a name. Afterward, kids are taught to *Express* (E) their emotions to others, then to *Regulate* (R) or manage them using different strategies. For example, a child who senses himself getting frustrated with a project learns to recognize and understand his frustration, tell others about his feelings, and perhaps stop and take some deep breaths.

While I've used and taught Brackett's approach with kids and their teachers, I've found it has stumbling blocks. For one, it asks kids to name and express their feelings. Yet, for younger kids especially, it can be tough to match feelings with words. Naming feelings publicly can also leave kids vulnerable, as I've seen especially with older kids. If everyone else feels hyper and excited, do you want to be the only kid admitting to feeling down in the dumps? Instead, if you see empathy as a *conversation*, you can draw a child's emotions out while keeping her feeling safe. That's especially important when emotions are negative or leave her open to embarrassment.

That conversation matters because empathy doesn't look and sound the same with each child. Instead, each child has a different empathy profile. Some have trouble knowing *how* to help, while others struggle to take a friend's perspective or pick up signals of how others feel.

Even with affective empathy, the "feeling" side, not all kids are the same.[27] Some kids are naturally drawn to feeling another's feelings, picking up the slightest change in facial expression and asking, "Are you okay?" Others overempathize, or struggle to separate what they feel from what others do. I've met highly sensitive kids who feel very deeply or cry when they see their friends in tears. And still other kids struggle to read facial expressions or take others' perspectives; a particular trouble for kids on the autism spectrum.

As a result, many people falsely assume that kids with autism aren't interested in friendship or can't empathize. More often, they're eager to relate but don't see *how*. They feel empathy but struggle to express it. In fact, a high percentage of people with autism have alexithymia, or trouble understanding and naming feelings. People with alexithymia "could be sad, angry, anxious or maybe just overheated," says the researcher Rebecca Brewer, but they're not sure which.[28] Ten percent of the population has it—but up to 50 percent of people with autism do. That makes it hard to express their feelings or connect—and hard for us to connect with them.

In nurturing empathy in kids, there's no one size fits all. Instead, it's most important to see your child's strengths and challenges as they evolve over time in a unique pattern. It's also important to recognize where these challenges come from; in fact, they may be more common than ever.

Why Kids Struggle with Empathy These Days

Especially today, our society's overfocus on achievement and success makes it harder for kids to think deeply about others. It's a sort of "everyone out for himself" mentality. Kids can get wrapped up in their own emotional bubbles, with little space to recognize how others feel—or even what they're feeling themselves. When they're hyperfocused on being right, they don't have much mental space to notice feelings. They're too worried about being judged to extend a supportive hand.

This holds true for kids of all ages, even young adults. In 2010, college students declined on most measures of empathy when compared with students ten years prior. Levels of "empathic concern," or worry for those who are suffering, went down the most, along with perspective-taking skills. That's not to blame kids. They're only responding to their environments, which all too often *don't* prioritize understanding and caring for others, or even seeing each other face-to-face.

In one Stanford study of girls ages eight to twelve, the one factor most strongly linked to positive social feelings was the amount of time spent communicating face-to-face. Those who spent less time on devices and more on face-to-face communication tended to act more social and feel more "normal." They also had more success socially, had fewer friends whom the parents considered a bad influence, and even got more sleep. While the study didn't prove face-to-face communication caused this success, the strong links are worth noticing. In contrast, the girls' amount of video watching, online communication, and especially media multitasking—for example, texting while watching YouTube videos—were all linked to negative social outcomes.[29] Another project sent teenagers to camp for five days without screens.[30] The teens came back better able to read nonverbal cues. Practicing that verbal and nonverbal dance—the mix of what's said and *how* it's said—seemed to have helped improve their noticing skills. They were able to show up for one another and be more fully present. That's the foundation of richer relationships.

True, digital connections can shore up empathy. Whether we're expressing condolences over a death or excitement over a baby photo, nearly all of us, and our kids, do some form of empathizing online. But how deep is this empathy? Most often, in the sea of "likes" and "*so cute!*" comments, the complexity of feelings gets lost. The same goes for kids, especially in terms of social media. When they carefully groom social media profiles and respond to others' perfect-looking ones, they're often moving *away* from the thoughtful understanding and the nuance that empathy requires.

But if that fuller empathy is truly so important, why aren't we focusing on it? That question is one that's haunted me for years. As I've spoken with more parents and researchers, I've come to see that many of us have a few key misconceptions that limit us, in terms of our conversations for empathy. First, we think of empathy as a fixed quality, not something that can shift or be actively enhanced. Second, we focus on building empathy through lectures, not dialogue. And third, we emphasize talk about *what* kids are doing over *how* they're doing it, or how they feel.

How Misconceptions Limit Us

"He's such a good kid, so caring," I've heard many parents say. Or "good luck getting *him* to care about his brother—or anyone. He's totally selfish." Influenced by a culture that often puts kids into boxes, we tend to label kids from early on. Those labels, while we often don't think much about them, can create problems. For one, they're almost always too simplistic, in failing to capture the full child. Worse, they can create a vicious cycle. Such labels, especially the negative ones, can cause kids to act into the roles we assign. A child who hears he's "uncaring" may act even more uncaring, which makes us think we were right all along.

These cycles speak to the first misconception: we often think about empathy as a fixed quality, something kids have or don't. But every child's empathy skills are in development. And each child has empathetic high and lows, depending on who he's with, his current mood, and even whether he's hungry or tired. Even a child who calls his brother stupid might later tell you not to step on ants.

Second, we often treat empathy like a vitamin. We assume we can give it to kids with lectures and good deeds. As one fifth-grade student told me of a bullied classmate, "Why should I care? He's not my friend." This student wasn't the bully, but he *was* a bystander. He needed to imagine how the bullied child felt. He also needed the ethical sense that he *should* step in.[31]

Worse, that "vitamin" idea makes it hard to help kids develop empathy effectively. Our standard talk, while well-intended, doesn't always help. Often, when we discuss feelings, it's with the goal of teaching a lesson or making a point. We're distracted, reacting to problems as they come up, usually just hoping to fix behavior or help a child feel happier. "Just say you're sorry," you might tell your child whose friend is crying, or "It's not a big deal, okay?" when a child says he's jealous of his friend. These comments might help in the short term—and clearly you can't stop to discuss every argument. But such talk doesn't do much to help kids take others' perspectives or figure out what they or their friends need most. It also doesn't raise their self-awareness; the biggest key to nurturing their empathy long-term.

So how *can* we raise their self-awareness? Let's take a simple example. Say your three-year-old son, Nick, hits his friend John with a toy.

"How do you think John felt about that?" you ask. You want Nick to understand that hitting hurts, and you want him to respond with "sad" or "bad." This helps him connect his action to John's sobbing, and ideally, avoid hitting John the next time.

Or, with an older child, you might reflect his comment back to him. Say, "How would *you* feel if you tried on a dress and your friend said, 'Well, I guess it looks okay?'" The words weren't hurtful, but the tone said it all. Pointing out the *effects* of a child's words or actions can help them notice the hurt they've caused. Still, these examples are far from the whole answer. A fuller sense of empathy requires an ongoing back-and forth, as we help kids learn how they and others feel.

What else keeps us from exploring that fuller sense? In part, it's lessons we've absorbed from our culture. When we're focused on getting kids ahead or having them fit in—that is, when we emphasize short-term performance—we tend to talk about relationships as transactions. We might ask who could write a recommendation, or get a child into private school, but neglect to consider caring for its own sake. If we do talk about caring, we may emphasize show over substance. "I told him he needs to join the Boy Scouts, or do *something*," one parent of a ten-year-old told me. "He needs to show he cares. That's what colleges want." But good deeds without reflection don't change children's thinking. They become simply more activities. What we need ideally is dialogue to make those experiences meaningful. That's the way for kids to learn from those experiences and, over time, to want to do good deeds on their own.

Also, when we focus on performance, we tend to want things to go smoothly. We may not make time for harder or more complex emotions to rise up. Often, we stop at the first emotion we hear, with questions and comments like "Oh, you feel happy?" or "Yes, that's sad." It can feel hard for a child to get a word in edgewise. In fact, kids often need quiet time to process their feelings, recognize those of others, or consider how to apologize. Feeling rushed can lead to them talking impulsively or acting out—and that can make it even harder for us to feel empathy toward them. We forget to notice where they shine, empathetically speaking, and where their challenges lie. In fact, compassion and empathy can be taught—but that teaching requires a back-and-forth over time.

My Road to Understanding Empathy

My understanding of building empathy in kids grew from observing teachers at a Boston preschool. Some seemed to have nearly infinite patience, especially an older teacher who took the time to sit beside each child at least once a day. But sometimes even that teacher's patience broke; for instance, when a child asked for the fifth time whether she could go home *now*.

"I said *no*," she snapped, turning away.

But a few minutes later, she returned, leaned in close, and said warmly, "Oh, I'm sorry. We all have only so much water in our buckets. And mine was running dry. And my mouth was tired from answering so many times."

The child smiled and hugged her, then said, "Go and fill your bucket. Then you'll be good."

This interaction, I later realized, arose from a curriculum, known as "Fill your bucket," the school had in place, emphasizing how each person carries around an invisible "bucket" representing their mental and emotional health.[32] When you show caring and kindness to others, you fill their "buckets," and when you're mean, you "dip" into their buckets. That was a great idea, I thought. But I was equally intrigued by what the teacher had specifically said. She apologized, showed self-compassion, *and* hinted that the constant questions were getting irritating. In that way, she showed empathy while giving the child feedback. She supported the child to link her *own* feelings to reasons, even while learning social skills.

Even in moments our kids are frustrating us, there's often a chance to discuss empathy. It might have to be after the fact. As any parent of a toddler knows, the middle of a tantrum is no time to reflect deeply. The same goes for the outbursts of older kids. The key is to find the right moment, after tempers have cooled. Suit your talk to the situation, hear what your kids have to say, and encourage them to participate. And—the most important of all, but most challenging—don't forget to direct empathy toward yourself. If the talk doesn't go perfectly, or even well, there will be other opportunities.

The Key of Self-Compassion

Celia, the mom of Eric, a five-year-old with autism, came into my office a few years back, frustrated at Eric's third meltdown of the day. She'd dropped him off at school, still flailing. "I feel like such a bad parent," she said. "But he has to try." I empathized with Celia. I also saw how harried and distracted she felt, as she hurried off to start her own day.

When your child has such challenges, it's especially important to extend empathy to *yourself*. Talking to yourself in a positive, loving way can stop the spiral of "shame, guilt, and self-blame," as the researcher Kristin Neff puts it.[33] When kids can't communicate easily, meeting their needs can feel like a mind game. Developing a mantra, such as "This is just hard," has helped many parents I know.

But the same goes for parents of kids without special needs. We often think about empathy *as opposed* to self-compassion. Either you direct attention and care to your child, *or* you offer it to yourself. "He's having a hard time," you might say of a teething toddler, when you're up at night for the third time in a row. But then you snap at your older child when he whines—and feel guilty afterward. You offer empathy freely for your child, but leave little for yourself. So many of us judge ourselves so harshly. Instead, I often advise parents to speak self-compassion out loud. Explain if you're distracted or worried. Use a neutral tone. Remember that kids notice the ways we talk to and about ourselves. Notice phrases like "I should have" or "It's all my fault." How could you frame those ideas in a more compassionate light? Perhaps you could talk about what you'd like to try the next time.

I know from my own experience that this is far from simple. Still, for our own well-being and that of our kids, it's worth a try. I've seen so many examples of well-meaning parents who miss this critical self-compassion piece, especially in times of frustration or upset. At that same elementary school where I spoke with Celia, I met Nicole, the mother of Robin, a nine-year-old boy. One afternoon, Nicole sat down with me at a meeting and, teary, told me Robin was having trouble being "nice."

"His friend said he was going camping." Nicole looked uncomfortable. "The friend was so excited, but Robin said, 'I'm sorry. Camping is *terrible*.' And it only went downhill from there."

"And what did you do?" I asked.

"Oh, I sent him to his room." She frowned. "But he said I was mean and asked what was wrong with telling the truth. I was so annoyed, we ended the playdate. Afterward, I felt bad—but I didn't apologize, since I didn't want him to feel like he'd won."

Her story isn't uncommon. Often, when kids show a lack of empathy, we don't dig down into why. The situation is awkward enough already. Why explore it? In fact, Robin's response showed a lack of social skills, but also difficulty with perspective-taking; specifically, *theory of mind*, or recognizing that person might feel or think differently than you do. Understanding the other person's perspective gives you far more insight into how to respond.

A classic theory-of-mind test, developed by Simon Baron-Cohen and Uta Frith, is called the "false-belief" test. It asks kids to imagine a child, Sally, who puts a ball in a basket and goes for a walk. While she's gone, her friend Anne moves the ball to a box. When Sally comes back, where will she look?[34] If kids say the box, they're not taking Sally's perspective. True, that's where the ball is—but Sally doesn't know that.

We often think of empathy in this way, as something to build up in our kids. But really, as I came to see with Robin, empathy has two parts: our kids and ourselves. In fact, honing our abilities to show empathy is the key to raising empathetic kids.

This idea hit home for me one afternoon, when Sophie was about two years old and we flew south on a vacation to the beach. On our first day, a girl around six years old sat beside us, as her mother smeared sunscreen on her back. For a few minutes, the girls played contentedly. Then, without warning, Sophie threw sand in her new friend's face.

....

Developing Theory of Mind: Tips for Young Kids

Theory of mind tends to emerge in kids around the ages of four or five years old, but as I saw with Robin, many kids struggle with perspective-taking long afterward. Encouraging this skill lets kids become more social, as they learn that not everyone thinks or feels as they do.[35,36]

Starting with young kids, notice and respond to their comments in real time.[37] Say your child notices a shadow that looks like a dinosaur. "See?" he asks, pointing. Try giving your own perspective and comparing it to his. Do you see a dinosaur, or a cloud? Also, explore his perspective further, going beyond the here and now. Ask: What else does he see? Or, What's the most interesting thing he can imagine seeing? Your excitement serves as the foundation for empathy—since you're sharing positive feelings about the same idea.

....

"I can't see," the girl wailed, rubbing her eyes.

"Open your eyes." The girl's mother grabbed her tight. "Just a crack." She sounded fearful, desperate. I felt ashamed.

"I *can't*," the girl said.

Sophie stared with the look of someone waking from a dream.

"She's hurt," I said. "The sand hurt her."

I asked Sophie to apologize, but she only watched me.

"It's all right," the girl's mother said, but winced.

"I'm so sorry," I said. "Is she all right?"

Tight-lipped, the girl's mother nodded.

"We should go," I said, my frustration rising. Later, once it was just the two of us, I asked Sophie to explain.

"I didn't know that sand hurt." She pouted. "I'm sorry."

Suddenly it came to me. Sophie had spent her past winters in Boston throwing snow. "See if you can hit my hat," I remembered saying, as she'd tossed snowballs with obvious glee.

"I see." I softened. "Now you know we don't throw sand, all right?"

"Okay, Mama." She curled up next to me.

That afternoon, I recognized the importance of *our* lenses as parents. Too often, we assume our kids lack empathy, when there's really something else to blame: a lack of knowledge or social skills, or confusion about how to apologize. In the moment, that can be tough to recognize. But when you react out of frustration, your child reacts to your reaction, in a vicious cycle. Instead, take a moment to reflect: Is there something your child might not know, or a need or want that hasn't been discussed? Could she simply be hungry or tired? Recognize how much you might *not* know, even if you spend every day with her. And what about you? We often give so much to our kids, we forget about ourselves. But if our basic needs aren't being met, that makes it doubly hard to feel or show empathy.

· ·

When Your Child Seems to Lack Empathy

Ask: What's behind your child's hurtful actions or comments? Maybe he doesn't understand the situation, or maybe he's embarrassed and wants to save face. I remember watching the father of a sixth-grader, Brian, swoop in during an argument, telling Brian, "You hurt your friend's feelings." Brian turned red-faced, then shouted, "I don't care.*" Clearly, he felt embarrassed at being called out. If his father had let the interaction unfold, then reflected on the situation later, Brian would probably have reacted better and learned more.*

· ·

Empathy Means Accepting Mystery

To learn more how our talk can build empathy in kids, I visited the well-known psychologist Jean Berko Gleason. For years, I'd heard about Gleason's work. A longtime professor at Boston University, Gleason was renowned for her decades of research into how children develop language.[38] I was most intrigued by her work on apologies.[39] As she found, young kids mostly hear apologies through times their parents apologize *to* them; for example, "Sorry I got mad." And that's not a bad thing. We often see apologizing as a sign of weakness. But really, it's a strength. It shows kids you're willing to admit your failings, and that you can repair things when you've messed up. It also gives them a language model they can use. When they see they've hurt a friend's feelings, for example, they can draw on what they've heard you say to apologize well. All that's critical in helping them fix misunderstandings. But, beyond apologizing, how else can we build kids' empathy?[40]

After contacting Gleason, I was pleasantly surprised when she suggested I visit her at her house in Cambridge, Massachusetts. Soon afterward, I knocked at her door. She welcomed me in with plates of Girl Scout cookies. We headed to her sunny kitchen as I took out my tape recorder, watching in awe as she—over eighty years old—bustled to make coffee, gesturing with seemingly boundless energy.

While her research fascinated me, it was one of her personal stories that stuck in my mind. For years, she told me, she'd asked her children to give her a store mannequin as a birthday present. She'd come up with the idea on a whim, but then she couldn't forget it. As the years passed, though, her kids bought her every other kind of present. Only after several years, and her repeated half-joking requests, did they finally (grudgingly) buy one.

"We named him Ralf," she told me, "and we dressed him up at holidays. Every time we moved, we brought Ralf along."

Decades later, Ralf "lives" with one of her daughters and makes appearances at holidays.

"Can you believe it," Gleason asked me, with a laugh, "that after all this time, we still have that ridiculous mannequin?"

I *could* believe it. That gift had become not only a funny present and a part of their family lore, but a symbol. Through it, her family showed they accepted her uniqueness, and would accept the uniqueness of everyone else. That's the key foundation of empathy. As I thought back to Layla's birthday party, I was reminded of an important point: things aren't only things. They're signs of how we feel about one another, or the aspects of one another we accept. That acceptance goes far beyond gifts. It means learning to notice and care for the full person in front of you, even if his or her wants and needs, thoughts and feelings, may surprise or annoy you. That's where quality conversations come in. No matter how close you are, you can't know for sure how a child thinks or feels without asking. Empathy starts with accepting and welcoming that mystery.

Quality Conversation Braids Heart and Mind

Quality conversation fills a child's empathy tank, offering daily opportunities to reflect on their own thinking and feeling, and to explore the thoughts and feelings of others. What's more, when you have quality conversations, you help kids make their *own* feelings and thoughts clearer, using language in more precise ways.

You model self-compassion and compassion for a child, as you wonder what's behind his or her apparent lack of empathy. You show how you welcome all emotions, not only sunny ones. And you notice *your* challenges in extending empathy, then do what you can to support yourself.

When you engage children with these "empathy conversations," the benefits are surprising, and often hugely helpful to their long-term relationships. I remember when three-year-old Paul had suddenly become scared of going to the bathroom alone. Surprised, I asked what he was worried about.

"It's the robot." He gave me a stressed-out look. "He's in the dark. He'll find me."

"It's from a cartoon," Sophie explained.

"That robot wasn't real," I told him.

But he didn't seem convinced. After a bit more discussion, Sophie raced off, returning with a flashlight.

"This magic flashlight makes the robot dizzy," she said. "Try it."

Soon, Paul went to the bathroom himself, flashlight at his side. A few days later, he'd forgotten the flashlight and went to the bathroom alone. The robot, he told me, had disappeared.

Empathizing let Sophie help Paul break through his fears. More than advice, he needed someone to join *with* him in his imaginative world. Empathy lets kids figure out *how* to care for others, which starts by getting to know who others authentically are. In my insistence that Paul would be fine, and my focus on *my* reality, I was only putting up walls. We'd had similar talks with Sophie at that age, I soon realized, which had most likely been the foundation for her to help Paul later on. For kids to show empathy, we need to show it to them first. The models we offer will serve them for years to come.

....

Kids Need to See Empathy to Build It

To develop empathy, you can have "conversations" even before
your child can speak. When you promptly notice and respond to a
child's cues, you acknowledge he's a thinking, feeling being. You
make appropriate comments, depending on how he seems to feel.
If he looks at a toy, you might say, "Oh, you like it?" or "That looks
interesting." If he starts sobbing, you look around. "Oh," you say,
when you notice spilled cereal on the floor, "are you sad because of the
cereal?"[41] You're being "mind-minded," or imagining what he feels
or thinks. That shores up his trust, since he sees you recognize what
he meant—or got close.[42] Being comforted primes him to comfort
others. Your empathy is the springboard for his.

....

Find Time to Name Emotions

In later years, young kids need to know *what* they're feeling to
help themselves feel better. In my house, inspired by the work of
the company Generation Mindful, we started using a simple chart
with the two questions: "How are you feeling?" and "What do you
need?"[43] On one poster, there are faces depicting each feeling, and
strategies listed for "What do you need?" The strategies are simple:
count to ten, hold a soft toy, or do a puzzle, for example. At first,
I was skeptical. But soon I found that three-year-old Paul, even
mid-tantrum, responded to the words "Run to your chart." Sobbing, he'd run over and stare at the pictures. At first, the distraction
calmed him. As we talked through each picture, he got better at
pinpointing his emotions. Sometimes he surprised me. "I'm lonely,"
he said, when I thought he was sad. "I need a hug." Such tools can

make your conversations far richer, as kids identify more precisely what they feel and need.

Using the Three Es to Raise Emotion Masters

While those charts are a start, kids need far more as they get older, and as perspective-taking becomes much more complex and nuanced. I remember a thirteen-year-old boy, Alex, I evaluated at a private school and was working with twice a week. Diagnosed with a language-learning disorder, Alex had trouble retrieving words and expressing himself. He often spoke using simpler words and shorter sentences, even though he had a good vocabulary. In part, this left holes in his conversations, and left others challenged to understand what he meant. For example, I once heard him say, "I went over there, you know? To that place? To get that thing?" While many kids speak like this once in a while, Alex's tendencies were far more extreme.

In our sessions, I was working with Alex on expressing himself both in speaking and writing. We worked to find synonyms, if he couldn't think of the exact word he wanted. I taught him to describe something about an object or a person: what a thing looked like or how it smelled, for example, or what a person did for a job. He might even use gestures, or talk about what a thing was like or not like. For example, for a helicopter, "It's like an airplane, but smaller, and it lifts straight up." That could help others guess what he meant.

One day, Alex told me, he'd asked Naomi, a girl in his class, to go out with him. Naomi had politely rejected him. He told his friend Jackson about the rejection, and ended by saying, "Whatever.

She's a snob." Jackson, who'd been scrolling on his phone, looked up and said, "Huh? I thought she was nice." Alex walked away feeling hurt and told me he never wanted to talk to Jackson again.

When I talked to Alex afterward, I used the Three E's, in this case applied to empathy:

1. *Expand*. Help kids use more specific emotional language.

2. *Explore*. Dive into fresh ways of discussing the past (especially negative or confusing experiences) and reading into others' minds.

3. *Evaluate*. Test out compassionate actions or responses, then ask: "How did that go?"

With Alex, I first *expanded* on his feelings. In fact, he agreed with Jackson that Naomi was nice. Jackson, to his credit, had stood up for Naomi. While Alex had felt the comment was heartless, I sensed that he was upset that Jackson hadn't validated his sense of entitlement. But it wasn't so much Jackson's comment that upset him, he said. Rather, it was that Jackson hadn't seemed to notice how hurt he felt. We then *explored* how Jackson had acted in the past. How had he been as a friend? Jackson, as Alex explained, had been caring during hard times, such as when Alex's mom had been diagnosed with cancer. But, in the discussion about the girl, he'd missed the subtleties. Recalling the high points of their friendship let Alex recognize that Jackson wasn't fundamentally bad or uncaring. Quite the opposite: their friendship was valuable, and the rift deserved repair. In fact, Jackson's comment about Naomi being nice had been another sign of his caring nature. In response, we role-played ways Alex could share his feelings of upset about his rejection in a socially acceptable way. While he didn't want to let those feelings go, he also didn't want to overstate them. He decided to bring the incident up once after basketball practice, explain how he felt, then move on. At our next session, we *evaluated* together how the process had gone: what had worked well and what he could try tweaking in the future. Alex told me he was mostly satisfied. He'd apologized for being rude about Naomi and had explained how he was feeling upset about being rejected. Jackson had apologized for not paying attention to Alex's hurt. However, as Alex told me, Jackson had seemed confused when Alex had first brought up the issue and had asked what Alex was referring to. As a result, Alex decided that, the next time, he'd bring up problems closer to the time of the conversation.

In that way, empathy-building conversations work best when anchored to real experiences. They also need tailoring to each child. Robin and Jackson needed two different conversations. While Robin had trouble with perspective-taking, Jackson wasn't fully listening.[44] He needed a gentle reminder to really be with his friend—and put down his phone.

That's all well and good if a child can easily tell you what his problem is or pinpoint where he needs help. But what about times when you sense he needs support, but he doesn't want to talk about it? Or when your child seems upset but can't or won't clarify? For these times, reflective listening can help. This listening, inspired by a movement known as "mindful parenting," goes beyond simply hearing what a child says. Instead, you "check out" what a child really thinks and feels by directing your attention to everything about him: words and body language.[45] You bring all your awareness to the present moment. You then reflect what you hear back to him and see if you're right. This lets your child feel respected, heard, and understood—and that process sets him up to do the same for others later on.

Reflective Listening: Use the Four Ps

Reflective listening, as I've come to practice it, has four parts. Think of four Ps: **Puzzle, Piece Apart, Pare Down**, and **Process**. Broken down, they look like this:

1. *Puzzle*. First, *be a detective*. Notice cues about what your child is thinking and feeling, using silence and body language. Is your child sitting close or far off? With which kind of expression? Where have you seen that expression before?

2. *Piece Apart*. *Sift through* those cues to figure out which is the most important, or which seems to take priority.

3. *Pare Down*. What ideas do you have about his feelings? What do you think might have happened? *Decide on* one or two major takeaways.

4. *Process*. Finally, *express* that takeaway and listen to see if you're right.

Try what the researchers Neil Katz and Kevin McNulty call "door-openers," or open-ended invitations to talk.[46] State what your child's behavior suggests. For example, "You look upset" or "It looks like you're excited." Then invite him to talk, with words or simply by waiting. Offer open-ended comments like "Oh, is that right?" or "Oh, I see." Finally, once he does talk, reflect back what you hear, checking in to see if you're right.

Let's look at this process, using the example of a parent friend of mine, whom I'll call "Jasmine," the mom of three kids. She writes of her son "Luke," now a teenager:[47]

"Ever since I can remember, my son has had trouble processing anger. When he was younger, he would seemingly get very upset about small things. On his tenth birthday, for example, his friends (being rambunctious boys) did not sing happy birthday properly (instead, they ran around yelling it), and he got really upset and rushed to his room, unable to articulate what was wrong."

As the years passed, Luke seemed to have an easier time. But then one afternoon, he got into trouble with his dad and left in the middle of an argument. Soon, he headed to his room. As Jasmine later told me:

"I heard a lot of stomping, yelling, hitting things, etc. I went upstairs, aggravated, and as I got to his door, I fully intended to open his door to play the authority figure—telling him to stop all the foolishness, stop acting like a baby, or he was going to really be in trouble. I stopped, took a couple of deep breaths to calm down, then opened it and simply looked at him. He said, 'Before you say anything, I'm not doing this because of dad.'"

When Jasmine asked what was wrong, Luke explained that his friend had sent him some hurtful texts, including one that said he didn't want to be friends anymore. In response, Jasmine didn't say much, but only sat quietly, trying to "acknowledge his pain and be there with him." After a while, she told him she'd had a similar experience at his age and understood how he felt. She encouraged him not to keep reading the texts, and if he did, give himself time to respond. Maybe she could take his phone for a bit, she suggested, so he could step away and calm down.

Later, she reflected that she was "very thankful I didn't go into his bedroom that day with 'guns blazing,' because I might have missed out on that conversation, and missed the opportunity to talk him through how to deal with friends who hurt you."

Jasmine started by centering herself, then *puzzled out* what was happening, leaving space for her son to explain. She *pieced apart* possible triggers and *pared down* her response, focusing on the texts. She then *processed* out loud with him, making sure he knew she was on his side. Her response let him save face while not escalating the situation. She also raised his self-awareness, encouraging him to wait before texting back.

Think of how differently this would have turned out if she'd demanded to keep his phone. That's not to say take away phones unthinkingly, but rather to let our conversations offer insight into children's maturity levels and stages of development. Through back-and-forth dialogue, we get to know what they're ready for—and make changes if we sense we've been too strict or permissive.

. . . .

Principles for Empathy

- *Notice and attune to what kids want and need. Listening to their signals, you mirror their emotions. "Are you hungry or tired?" you ask an infant. "Let's see if you need a bottle." With school-age children, note their body language, in a neutral tone. "You have lots of energy today," for example, or "You're quieter than usual." When you speak without judgment, you let your child see you're open to all emotions.*[48]
- *Check in with your child and yourself. Sit quietly, noticing both of your energy levels. How exhausted or refreshed is he or she? What about you? Notice your child's tone of voice, level of excitement, and pauses. Ask yourself: What "talk needs" does he have at this moment? How much does he want engagement versus downtime? And what about you? Many great conversations have started with sitting together quietly, knitting, cleaning dishes, or fishing. Don't underestimate the power of quiet and downtime to help more vulnerable feelings, thoughts, or questions arise.*

- *Find creative ways of seeing into others' hearts and minds.*
  Use characters in books or movies as examples. Fiction gives
  us a window into other minds, and often uses feeling words
  such as "flustered" or "irritated," which we can reflect on and
  discuss. Wonder aloud how each character felt and why. Use
  exploratory questions: Would you have acted that way? Which
  reactions surprised you? With whom did you identify?

Accept Sunny and Stormy Emotions

When you engage in reflective listening, it's especially important not to tamp down or ignore negative feelings. We want kids to feel happy, but focusing only on positive feelings can send the message that other feelings are "less than." In response, kids may hide their fear or worry, or even shame those emotions in family or friends. When feelings go underground, they often fester, leading to guilt and even anxiety. To support all your child's feelings, try *emotional reminiscing*.[49] Focus on small moments from the past, especially stressful or negative ones. Talk over what happened, emphasizing your child's resilience, and strategize for the next time.

Say your young child says, "That doctor's visit was terrible." Try the Three Es. *Expand* on that memory. *Explore* his emotions. *Evaluate* his reaction, reframing it from a position of strength.

"Yes, he gave you a shot, and your face got red," you might say. "You cried, but you were so brave." Leave space for your child to participate. Ask: What else happened? How did you feel? What helped you get through the hard parts?

Talking about worrisome or stressful experiences, with a good listener, improves children's mental health. As Susan David, au-

Making Small Shifts: Emotion Talk

"I feel sad," your child says while packing up from a beach trip.					
The quick answer:	**To promote deeper connection and thinking:**				
"Oh, you'll be okay."	"What are you sad about? Did you have a favorite part?"	"I'm sad to leave too—but also glad to be seeing school friends."	"I understand. Are there special things you want us to do again?"	"What does that feel like in your body?"	"Yes, I see. Anything else? Sometimes, I feel especially sad when I'm tired."

thor of *Emotional Agility*, and I discussed, it's about reminding kids that they can experience their feelings fully and *still* act.[50] In one study, when mothers and nine-to-twelve-year-old children explained more and used more "feeling words," such as "jealous" or "disappointed," in discussing a stressful event, the kids showed less depression and anxiety and acted out less.[51] Another study with preschoolers found that, when mothers elaborated more on emotionally difficult events, talking about their feelings and reactions, children tended to show stronger abilities to regulate their feelings.[52] Such reflection primes kids to understand who they are as emotional beings. How do they react to challenge or fear?[53] Bringing up your experiences shows them they're not alone in their feelings. It's not a shame to talk about being sad, upset, or scared. And it's not a shame to feel those things.

All this might sound simple, but in practice, it can be really tough—especially when you're rushed, tired, or stressed. In talking with dozens of parents, psychologists, and researchers, I've identified four main "empathy challenges" and four solutions.

Language Challenges and Solutions for Empathy

Challenge #1: The language of judgment. You should feel this way.

Say your son says, "It's stupid to feel upset about that." That's clearly judgmental. But judgment can come in more subtle ways, too. Take an *embedded question*, or one with an answer already included. For example, think about the comment "We all had such a great time at the party, didn't we?" While that sounds pretty neutral, it suggests we all feel the same way, which makes it harder for anyone to admit they wish they could have stayed home.

Solution: The language of openness. It's all right to feel what you feel.

To welcome all emotions, start by noticing your family "emotion culture." Which feelings get discussed or shared, and which ignored or ridiculed? In each family, this culture is different, depending in part on your families of origin. Maybe anger was forbidden in your house, or maybe expressions of excitement or joy. Notice how your spouse, partner, or other relatives differ in terms of which feelings they're comfortable expressing or seeing expressed.

Challenge #2: The language of projection. You do feel this way.

Too often, we confuse our emotions with the ones our kids have, or we tell kids how we assume they feel. For example, "That movie wasn't sad" or "You aren't mad." Your opinion gets presented as fact. But your child *may* be mad or sad, even if it's not logical. Ask yourself: How does the world appear from his perspective? How do his body language and tone give clues to his true emotions?

Solution: The language of separateness. We might not feel the same way.

Support kids to expand on their emotions. Explore what happens when you stay with topics they bring up. Sitting with emotions doesn't mean wallowing in them. Instead, talking through feelings, whatever they may be, helps kids make sense of them. The sociologist Charles Derber at Boston College describes two types of responses: *shift* versus *support.* A *shift* response means you turn the conversation toward yourself. A *support* response keeps to the topic your child introduced.[54] Imagine your daughter says, "I feel nervous about going on the diving board." A *support* response might be "Why?" or "What are you worried about?" A *shift* response might be "Diving is fun. One time, when I was diving . . ." While you wanted to help, her nervousness never gets discussed—and she may end up feeling *more* stressed the next time.

Most conversations naturally balance shift and support. But focus on *support* responses when you sense your child has more to say, or when she seems especially vulnerable.

Challenge #3: The language of shame. You should feel bad about how you feel.

Comments like "It's dumb to cry about that" or "Only babies are scared of that" are obvious ways of shaming a child. But "It's not a big deal" or "Okay, enough already" are also signals that tell kids, "That's not how I want you to feel."

Solution: The language of process. It's all right if another person's feeling (or yours) doesn't make sense at first or doesn't feel "good to feel."

Emotions can take time and talk to understand. So often, feelings can blindside kids: a sibling crying at a playdate, for example, or a friend getting offended at a joke. Their own feelings can also surprise or confuse them. It happens more often than you'd think. "I'm mad," a child might say when he's jealous; or "I'm sad," when disappointed. Dialogue lets them pinpoint their emotions more precisely. That lets you understand what sort of support they need.

Frame feelings as neutral and changeable, like the weather. Fo-

cus on moving through a range of emotions in constructive ways.
Emphasize that no emotion is "bad." Constant happiness isn't the
goal; it isn't realistic or even healthy for kids. If a child says he
wants to feel differently—say, he says he feels "cloudy" and wants
to feel "sunnier"—ask: "How can we shift those clouds?" Let him
see his responses are under his control. Also, emphasize that we
can feel more than one thing. If a child names a single emotion
but looks unsure, ask, "Is that all?" Or suggest, "That *does* sound
exciting. Anything else?" Give kids time to think and talk it over,
or offer a model. "I'm excited but nervous to give a presentation,"
you might say.

*Challenge #4: The language of isolation. You're alone in feeling
how you feel.*

Comments like "It's so bizarre that you feel that" or "I don't
know anyone who feels like *that*" can leave kids feeling their emotions make them weird and shouldn't be shared.

*Solution: The language of togetherness. We can work through these
emotions together—and your uniqueness doesn't have to keep us apart.*

A collaborative, encouraging tone helps a child feel he's not
alone. It also helps when conversations feel stopped or stuck. That
can happen with this kind of emotion talk, especially if a child is
new to it. When he repeatedly says, "I don't know," but still wants
to talk, for example, or when you've reached a standstill, focus on
these principles:

....

Troubleshooting: Tips for Stuck Conversations

If your child seems stuck with her side of the conversation:
- *Give choices: "Is it more like this, or like that?"*
- *Ask a simpler question, focused on her experiences: Instead*

of "How might you feel if that happened?" (asking her to imagine) try "How did you feel about what happened yesterday?" (asking her to discuss something that has already occurred).

- **Offer an example from your own life:** "I felt disappointed when we didn't go on our winter vacation this year. What do you feel disappointed about?"

- **Suggest an emotion you sense your child is feeling, then check in:** "It looks like you're upset. Is that right? Or is it upset mixed with something else?"

- **Notice how emotions feel in the body:** "When I feel disappointed, I get a sinking feeling in my stomach. Sometimes my face feels flushed. How does disappointment feel to you?"

- **Return to an earlier topic or comment:** "I remember this morning, you were talking about your friend moving away. Can you tell me more about that?"

- **Gently explore your child's point of view:** "You said you didn't want to go on the camping trip. Can you tell me more about why?"

- **Step away and give some breathing room:** "I feel like we're both getting worked up. Why don't we take a break and talk about this later?"

- **Encourage your child to describe what she needs:** "What would help you feel better? Do you think you should [take some alone time, do some deep breathing, get a hug, talk it out]?"

- **Emphasize that you're trying your best:** "I want to understand and help, and I'm trying to figure out how. What do you think we could do differently?"

More generally, try out these conversational habits:

Conversational Habit #1:
The Empathetic Risk

Teach kids to take *empathetic risks* in their thinking and actions. These are ways of relating to and helping others that might not feel simple or obvious, or that your child might not have thought of at first. Think of it as stretching a child's "empathy muscles." For example, maybe he could go up to the classmate who seems lonely or ask a friend on the sidelines if he wants to join in a game. Help kids decide which actions suit the circumstances and their personalities. Also, notice when you feel uncomfortable about their ideas and why. Do you not think it's a good plan, or is it simply out of your comfort zone?

Conversational Habit #2:
Using the "If"

To help kids see other perspectives, try *conditional conversations.* Use "if" and "as-if" talk to help kids creatively imagine their ways into different lives. Start with what they notice in their own environments. Or use books as jumping-off points. What strengths might they need if they were farmers in Brazil, or businesspeople in Mexico? What obstacles might they face? Encourage them to play around, talking *as if* they were Olympic contenders, superheroes, or scientists facing a failed experiment. Especially at first, it can feel hard or even stressful for a child to imagine himself as lonely, or poor, or hurt, if he's none of those things. But exploring a range of feelings in a safe way primes him to understand and accept those feelings later, when he *does* feel them , or when he meets someone who does.

At the same time, encourage your child to share in others' joy. Model an attitude of celebration. Say she whines about her friend winning a competition. Let her know it's fine to feel jealous, but explore how *she'd* feel if she won. Ask: How would you like your friend to respond to you, if you'd been the winner? How could you show you're impressed or proud?

Stay Open to Mystery

Empathy is such a misunderstood concept, it's no wonder our conversations lead us astray. We may think emotions should turn out perfectly, like a cake in the oven —and then, when they don't, we turn away and shut the door. But raising empathetic kids means raising "emotion masters," in Marc Brackett's words—kids who know what emotions look and sound like and who welcome a full range. That starts with us; with the openings our conversations offer and with the self-compassion we show. When more authentic thoughts and feelings rise to the surface, we get to explore the mystery of the child before us. To be sure, that isn't always easy, but, when it goes well, it can be surprising, enlightening, and even fun. As Po Bronson, author of *NurtureShock*, notes, "It's when children are at their most mysterious when we, their caretakers, can learn something new."[55]

CHAPTER 4

Conversations for Confidence and Independence: Encouraging Your Child to Embrace Challenges

I am not afraid of storms, for I am learning how to sail my ship.[1]
—LOUISA MAY ALCOTT

W hat can we *do?*" seven-year-old Sophie whined with two playmates at a Fourth of July barbecue on our shared roof deck. "This is taking *forever.*"

"Here." I held out stray pieces of sidewalk chalk.

"But we don't have a chalkboard." She stared at me quizzically.

The wooden floor slats looked washable. We had an hour till dinnertime, and I couldn't have the kids close to the grill. "Color on the floor, okay?"

"You're letting us make a mess?" she and her friends shrieked.

"Just clean it up afterward," I said.

"Okay." Soon they'd scampered off, busily drawing hearts and hopscotch squares. Even Paul grabbed fistfuls of chalk. Our neighbors wouldn't be thrilled, I thought, as I watched the drawings develop. Soon, the entire floor was covered with them. Two hours later, I took out the hose.

"*We're* cleaning." Sophie raced up, her friends trailing. "You said we should do the whole floor, right?"

"That's right." I'd forgotten. "But it's getting late. I'll do it."

"No!" they practically shouted. "It's our job."

Defeated, I handed them the hose. A ploy, I assumed, to stay out late and see the fireworks and fighter jets. But they'd asked to help—and I wasn't one to micromanage chores. So I let them scrub and scrape, add chalk and clean, until sunset, when Sophie's friends had to leave.

"Take a picture," one friend said, smiling broadly. "Look, the whole floor's clean!"

Kids Want and Need to Help

At all ages, kids want and need to help—even if the impulse has been trained out of them. They're like the proverbial houseguests asking, "Can I help with dinner?" or "Do you need someone to make the beds?" Often, our default reaction is to say, "Oh, no, there's no need." And so the guests wander around, well cared-for but feeling useless, wishing you'd just say, "Yes, would you mind putting away the dishes?"

For kids, helping is a natural instinct that promotes empathy while binding them into a community. This is especially obvious in the early years. But even the most sullen teenager is likely to perk up if you ask him to help you choose music for a party, pick stocks, or fix the car. It all depends on his interests and personality, as well as his developmental stage. Contributing in valuable ways builds their confidence and gives them dignity, in a world where they've become "economically worthless but emotionally priceless," in the sociologist Viviana Zelizer's words.[2] When we do it all ourselves—with the best of intentions—our kids miss out and eventually develop an "allergy" to chores. What's more, our own talk suffers, as we highlight their neediness, rather than their capacities and progress toward goals. We do more directing and managing, less encouraging of their initiatives. Worse, when tasks pile up, especially those we know kids could do, we tend to feel resentful. The less kids do, the harder it is for us to see them as independent or imagine how far they can stretch.

As we saw in the last chapter, we want kids to care for others in nuanced ways, taking their perspectives and imagining into others' hearts and minds. We also want them to feel confident and strong, ready to attempt increasingly complex challenges. As they grow up, we'd like them to take the reins of their own lives: to set goals they care about and make steady progress toward them. We'd like them to feel proud of themselves.

Letting them help, even in seemingly minor ways, is an important start. From the youngest ages—before they're old enough to whine about chores—start with what they naturally gravitate to. There's a big difference between a child challenging herself to "clean the whole floor" and us handing her a mop, then saying, "Clean there." In the first case, she must consider what's most efficient, what she has time for, even how she might convince friends to help. In the second, she has little to think about. In brainstorming solutions and following through on tasks, kids build confidence and independence in a grounded way. They don't need fancy competitions or Olympic-level tournaments. In fact, maturity, self-awareness, and other foundations of confidence are built in the smallest ways: with activities kids can master, which they choose, and on which they can reflect.

We often think about confidence as bravado, getting out there and conquering mountains. But in fact, it's deeply connected to empathy. When kids understand the feelings and thoughts of those around them, and when they can help others get their wants and needs met, they're primed to feel good about themselves. They also get positive feedback from others, who see and respond to their better sides. That virtuous cycle builds their confidence, even as they build their skills.

This chapter will explore those twin qualities, confidence and independence, and show how they develop through dialogue, starting with the actions they take and the signals we give. Building confidence doesn't mean running around with pom-poms. Rather, it means using talk that acts like a mirror, helping kids see themselves more precisely and feel in control. Over time, as they do more, they get into the habit of overcoming obstacles. They might not be fearless, but they'll bring their full selves to the challenges they face. They'll learn to help in more useful ways. That's key to the kind of confidence that lasts.

This chapter will explore two main conversational habits that make this lasting confidence a reality. First, help kids **get clear** about their situations—their skill levels and the challenges they face—in a way that notices and responds to their growing edge. Think about letting them see just *beyond* their current abilities. Second, test out **what works** to overcome challenges. Try out strategies and support them to reflect on how well those strategies worked. Help them celebrate the road they've taken and the path they still have to go. These habits let challenge feel like a normal—and maybe even exciting—thing. That all starts with *us* feeling comfortable with challenge and getting clear about what confidence means.

What Is Confidence Anyway?

What comes to mind when you hear the word "confidence"? For many of us, it conjures up ideas of Dale Carnegie or other public-speaking gurus. Or you might think about a skateboarding or rock-climbing star finishing an amazing trick. Those *are* examples of confidence, but really, confidence encompasses far more—and doesn't always look flashy or incredible.

Instead, think about confidence as an "I can" reaction. It has to do with the belief that you *can* achieve your goals, even if you haven't gotten there.[3] You feel a general sense of strength in your capabilities. You believe you can work toward big things and regroup after failure. It's different from what's known as *self-efficacy*, or your belief in your skills in any one area. You can have a high degree of self-efficacy in math, but not in sports, for example. The same isn't true for confidence. It's a more general sense that applies to all areas in your life.

What's more, confidence matters for kids' well-being and achievement. In several studies, how competent they *thought* they were linked more strongly to their achievement than how competent they *actually* were.[4,5,6] Why? It has to do with the decision point *after* failure. Will a child try again? If she might not succeed, will she still give it a shot? More practice builds stronger skills—so the more a child keeps trying, the further she's likely to go. In the long run, you help them develop *grit*, psychologist Angela Duckworth's term for passion and perseverance toward long-term goals.[7,8] As she and another psychologist, Carol Dweck, found, having a growth mindset tends to make kids grittier.[9] Faced with challenges, they think, "I can get past that."[10,11]

Independence has to do with the ability to strike out on your own and take appropriate risks. It's not about "going it alone," but about knowing when to ask for help. It's about a child feeling he has what he needs to reach his goals or knows where to look.[12] Independence and confidence are tightly linked. When you have that "I can" sense, you're less likely to need prodding or hand-holding. You may well ask for help to get over a hump or face fears, but you're likely to give the hard thing a shot, even if you're scared. That confident attitude especially matters in childhood, since all skills are still developing. Kids can *learn* from that sense of being in process. In fact, they have to. Otherwise, they risk feeling paralyzed.

Childhood Can Build Confidence— or Self-Doubt

Whether it's learning to throw a pitch, do a cartwheel, or solve a math equation, childhood can be a confidence training ground. When kids see themselves throwing farther or climbing higher, they're primed to notice their progress and celebrate their skill development. Finding areas of weakness, they can take concrete action to improve. And yet the sense of being constantly in progress can leave many kids feeling anxious or insecure. Especially if they hear a lot of success-oriented talk, they can feel as if they're never "finished," or their best is never enough. I've heard many kids I've worked with express such feelings. And over time, I've come to see how much our talk plays a role.

Even the ways we frame everyday activities can make a difference in how confident kids feel. In 2019, Ryan F. Lei, a psychologist at Haverford College, and colleagues published a study showing that, from the ages of six to eleven, children lose confidence in their capacity to "be scientists," but not to "do science." As the authors noted, it seems that many children believed they could "do science" as an everyday activity, but that they weren't likely to become scientists. That difference matters in terms of the language we use. When we focus less on who children might become, and more on what they can do in their daily lives, they're likely to engage more. Over time, as they gain stronger skills, they're likely to feel more secure and confident in themselves. This is especially true for subjects, such as science, that can feel tough or intimidating for some kids.[13]

Our talk matters equally in terms of how we reflect on and handle children's failures or challenges. Josiah was a second-grader I worked with at one private school who was great in sports but struggled with reading. Because of his challenges and his quiet personality, he was often confused in class, but didn't say anything or ask for help. He avoided reading aloud, since he feared classmates would make fun of him.

Before working with Josiah, I met with his father, who said, "I tell him he'll do awesome, but he says he doesn't agree." It turned out that he'd been cheering his son on for months, while Josiah's skills hadn't improved. As Josiah fell further behind his friends in reading, and as he saw the simple books his teachers gave him, his belief in his skills wavered more. When I assessed Josiah's reading, I found he had many signs of dyslexia, including trouble reading longer and unfamiliar words, and multiple spelling errors.[14] His teachers and I decided on a different, more intensive approach to improve his reading skills, and I began working with him several times weekly.

Along the way, I had many conversations with Josiah about how he talked about himself. When we first met, he told me gloomily that he was a terrible reader. "Everyone else is crushing reading," he told me, "and I'm not." We talked about how he didn't have to "crush" reading or anything else. Instead, he could try sounding out words when he didn't know them and, if he couldn't, ask his teacher or me for help. To build his confidence, we decided on a tracking chart that he could use to see his reading progressing. We also decided on a mantra, or a saying that he could repeat before reading. He chose "I'll give it a try. If it gets too hard, I can stop." That let him move from thinking about success as "all or nothing," and instead start seeing his progress in increments.

This idea of incremental progress reminded me of a talk I had with Dr. Rory Devine, a psychologist at the University of Birmingham in England.[15] Devine studies how parents can support kids' executive function, or the ability to shift, multitask, and plan: a key foundation of confidence. Fluid conversations, he's found, can be especially effective. In these conversations, you stay flexible: offering help or assistance, but then quickly stepping back.

"Ramp up your help when a child is struggling, then back off when they no longer need you," he suggests. "Be flexible and don't intervene too quickly." Think of conversations for confidence as going in, like the tide, when kids are stuck, then retreating once they've gotten over a hump. Use a warm and understanding tone, helping kids see that struggles aren't things to fear.

For example, imagine your four-year-old is trying to make a peanut butter and jelly sandwich. He carries all the ingredients to the table but then pauses, saying he doesn't know what to do. You can help by coaching him more at the start—for example, talking him through opening the jars and putting the bread on a plate—but then stop as soon as he's gotten the idea. Try giving the minimum amount of help he needs, then stepping back. Start conversations with the mindset of "you know what to do." Even if a child isn't sure, help him along with questions like "How have you seen me do it?" or "Hmm, what do you think should go next?" This helps your child feel he's driving the action. By shaping your side of the conversation, you help him feel strong and in control.

To Build Persistence: Let Kids Feel in Control

As we see in that small example, to avoid fearing struggle, kids benefit from feeling in control. Having an internal "locus of control" means that kids believe they can create change. Progress is—at least partially—in their hands. They don't need to depend on someone else, or on luck. When they fail at crossing the monkey bars, they can step back, strategize, and try again. Decades of studies have found that children with a stronger internal locus of control persist longer and experience more personal success.[16,17,18] They believe that the power to change lies within them. They don't feel helpless. Kids who explain bad situations as being their fault and good events as luck tend to be more depressed and achieve less than kids who do the opposite.[19] They also tend to be more depressed in later years. Over time, their self-talk affects what they believe about themselves, which in turn affects how they act and how people treat them. With positive self-talk, kids tend to expect others to treat them well. Others often respond by treating them better. That's something we all want for our kids.

The good news: through quality conversation, you can help kids enlarge that locus of control, showing them that more lies in their power than they think. This talk *empowers* them to choose their goals, decide on steps to progress, and evaluate new strategies when theirs aren't working well. Such talk is especially important for kids who've started feeling helpless, saying for example, "Well, there's nothing I can do." Instead, their questions can take a more optimistic stance; say, "What next step can I take?" Putting more in their control allows them to do more and reflect on failure in more constructive ways.

Say your teenager did worse in a wrestling match than he expected to. Why? Maybe he was competing against stronger wrestlers or was placed in a new age class. He can't do much about that. But how well had he been eating and sleeping? How effectively had he been training? And how had he talked to himself in the moment, when he'd started losing? Noticing and reflecting on these factors—especially his self-talk—serves as the first step in making changes. With an attitude of curiosity and compassion, you can support him in identifying places to improve and in exploring how. As much as you can, use active language, focused on the future. Ask him what he thinks he can do differently. Over time, as he starts looking to himself for solutions, his confidence in his decision-making builds.

Conversations for Confidence

I didn't always see the link between confidence and control—and how much our talk affects both. One day several years back, I sat at a local playground with my daughter. She wanted a break, so we sat and started watching a group of kids who were clambering up a climbing structure. Breathing in the brisk winter air, I noticed there were really two groups, both around four to six years old, but behaving very differently. The first was higher up, climbing across a suspended ladder, with holes for dropping down. The second was much lower, near to the ground. Those kids looked terrified, even though the drop was less than a foot.

Intrigued by the difference between the groups, I listened closer. In the first group, as the kids climbed higher, I noticed something surprising: the parents or caregivers were relatively quiet. There wasn't much interruption: no clapping or cheering, and no, "Go, go, go!" Instead, the adults stood off as the kids made their ways across. "That's right," one said approvingly. "You took three more steps than before—how many more do you think you can do?"

Another said, simply, "Yes, you got it. And if you fall, you know what to do."

In that group, the kids were talking to one another, but not in a comparing "I'm-higher-than-you" way. Instead, they were jokingly reminding one another how far they'd gotten earlier. "You said you could get halfway, right?" one asked the other. "Now you're way farther."

"Well, watch this," the second child responded, taking another step.

As they climbed together, and as a few nearly toppled, it looked like an intricate, fumbling ballet. "You're not there yet," an adult said to one child as she dropped, mid-climb. "But just wait—I bet you'll get there later today, or maybe tomorrow."

"Maybe." The child nodded, then headed back to the start.

The same wasn't true of the second group. There, the adults were *noisy*, with high fives and cheers that echoed in the tree-lined space. Standing closer to their kids than the first adults were, they talked constantly, pausing only when the kids stopped to look down. "Don't *look*," one woman said, as a younger boy *did* look, then took one hand off the bars. A second later, he'd tumbled off and was sobbing, curled up, on the ground. As the playground surface was soft, I didn't imagine he'd gotten very hurt, but the woman held him tight, then spoke sharply. "Come on, stop crying. Listen, just stop. You're not a baby. I *told* you not to look down, right?"

"I know," the child said, mid-sob. "I shouldn't have. It was my fault."

After I left, those conversations hung in my mind. From afar, the two groups looked similar—but had there been something about *talk* that had helped the first group go on, in ways that stretched their current abilities? While the adults hadn't spoken much, they'd given feedback about how far the kids had already come. They'd used the word "yet," as in "you're not there yet," suggesting optimism and hope. As we saw in Chapter 2, that's a word Stanford psychology professor Carol Dweck has emphasized using, since it implies a child *will* get there eventually.[20] In her 2014 TED talk, she discusses the "power of believing you can improve."[21] Those adults had put the power to improve in each child's hands, implying that each was in control of how far she went. The message seemed to be: Keep going and you'll succeed. Do what you feel comfortable with, but also take risks. Stretch yourself. Check in, but don't worry if you fall.

And what about the second group? The child who'd fallen seemed fearful and had blamed himself for looking down. That self-criticism, I imagined, had only made him feel worse—and wasn't likely to help him when he tried again.

After that day at the park, I started thinking more about how the most minor interactions could shore up or cut down a child's confidence or faith in himself, both in the moment and over time. It wasn't any big proclamations or lectures that mattered, or even any activities designed as "confidence-building," such as zip-lining or rock climbing. The smallest moments, and the most everyday challenges, were opportunities—if we could recognize them.

Soon, after seeing this scenario play out with many other kids, I started asking: What does confidence in kids really look like? How can we build it, not only through actions, but through back-and-forth talk, in a way that put kids at the helm? It isn't only what we *say* or don't, as Dweck suggests, that builds confidence. It's equally important how actively we listen to kids: how well we hear their hidden fears and insecurities, and how open we are to discussing them.[22,23]

As discussed in Chapter 2, having a growth mindset is critical for kids to achieve well and feel motivated.[24] Recall that, with this mindset, kids realize that their efforts can make a difference in their skills, and that their intelligence and skills can be changed. That's in contrast to a *fixed* mindset, in which you think that "smart" is something you are or aren't, and no amount of effort will help. To promote a growth mindset, I'd read of Dweck's and her colleagues' advice, in terms of phrases you should emphasize. Praise a child's effort, not her as a person. Say your child did well on a math test. Try "You must have studied hard" instead of "I guess you're naturally good at math." Help her see that her effort changed the outcome. It wasn't just that she was smart. Putting a focus on effort also builds her confidence, as she sees she can master challenges by working hard. Studies have found that kids with a growth mindset tend to persist longer than kids with a fixed one. They're less likely to give up early and say, "Well, I guess I'm not good at that."

Also, be specific in your praise. Instead of, "You got a ninety-five; I guess you understand," try "You got the fraction questions right." That shift lets a child see exactly where she's succeeded, raising her self-awareness and showing her where she has room to grow. Finally, emphasize strategies that worked: "You knew to flip the fraction to divide it." That helps her see *specifically* which aspects of her effort led to her success. The next time, she's more likely to use that strategy or a similar one.[25]

That's all well and good. And yet, that focus on what *we* should say seemed to leave out something important. What about the back-and-forth of dialogue? What about helping kids with the ways they talk to themselves and others? What about confidence that builds not only with what *we* say, and the praise we give or don't give, but also with what *kids* say and do?

The Two-Way Dance of Confidence

Soon I had the chance to explore those questions further. I was finishing a clinical internship at a bilingual hospital clinic when I met Ruth, a three-year-old girl with a severe speech delay and cortical blindness, or vision loss caused by brain damage.[26] At birth, Ruth's brain had been deprived of blood flow. She also had physical disabilities, leaving her able to crawl but not walk.

Before Ruth, I'd never met a child with cortical blindness. How, I wondered, would she interact? I imagined her sitting motionless, wanting to engage but unable to. Before our first session, I pulled out toys from the top closet, searching for something she might like. I was surprised when the door opened early and a woman wheeled a stroller in, saying brightly, "We're here!"

After they came in, her daughter immediately unbuckled herself and got down on the floor, then crawled around to each corner. Gravitating toward a plastic box her mother held, full of stuffed toys, she grasped one after the other, smiling as she said, "I like that one. No, *that* one!" As Ruth continued exploring, the woman introduced herself as Jill, Ruth's mother and a pediatric nurse.

"So where next?" Jill asked, as Ruth crawled under the table. "You remember, if you get stuck, just roll yourself out." Then Jill turned to me.

"Can you believe it?" she asked, gazing at Ruth approvingly, as Ruth returned to the toy box and inspected the balls and sticky tape. "Almost every day, she's able to do something new, or *say* something new. She's so busy, so curious. I can't keep up with her."

We watched as Ruth continued playing, and as I started my assessment with her. The forty-five minutes flew by. Jill watched her explore, and occasionally commented on her choice of objects— "Oh, you like that one?"—but mostly stayed silent.

Afterward, I was intrigued enough by Jill's energy and care that I asked her directly how it felt to raise a child with this condition. In Ruth's first year of life, she told me, she'd taken the opposite approach. The diagnosis had nearly broken her. At first, she'd feared her daughter would be quite limited in her life options, even ostracized. But time and experience had let her take another tack. She'd decided to compare Ruth with Ruth; to see her development as having a unique arc. She'd focus less on what Ruth could or couldn't achieve, and more on the joy, fun, and interest she brought into everyone's lives. Instead of emphasizing Ruth's deficits, Jill's focus turned to helping Ruth contribute to her family and community.

"And I learned to do the same with David," she told me, referring to her eight-year-old, who didn't have any disability. "He's benefited from that approach, even more than she has."

As she explained, David had always been tentative and risk-avoidant. She'd often responded by encouraging him—really, "over-encouraging," she said with a laugh. When he did even the smallest thing well, she'd say, "Great job!" or "I knew you could!"

To her frustration, he'd often responded in the *opposite* way she'd hoped. Rather than being encouraged to do more, he argued back, saying, "No, it's *not* a great job." If he'd been reading, he shut the book. Afterward, he sulked, saying, "I knew I wouldn't be good at that." Her conversation, while well-intended, was shutting him down. But when she adopted the same approach she'd used with Ruth, things started to change. Instead of giving constant praise, she reserved it for times she was genuinely surprised. Starting with questions about what David wanted to achieve, they discussed how he could get there. Based on those goals, she checked in on his progress, asking his ideas about next steps.

Soon our session was over. As Jill buckled Ruth in her stroller, she told me she was glad to see her two children thriving and— even at their young ages—showing initiative and taking ownership. Hearing her talk, I thought of the psychologists Edward Deci and Richard Ryan's influential work on intrinsic motivation. When driven by intrinsic motivation, kids work toward goals because they want to, rather than because of a carrot someone dangles at them (known as external motivation).[27]

We encounter both kinds of motivation all the time. Say you have a goal of running three miles. Maybe it's because your doctor warned you that you needed to get in better shape or risk health problems (*external motivation*). Or maybe you find running fun (*intrinsic moti-*

vation). Intrinsic motivation is the key to sticking with things, practicing more, and finding meaning and pleasure in what you do.

Reflect on Skills and Challenges: Help Kids "Want to Want"

To have intrinsic motivation, as Deci and Ryan argue, kids need three elements in place: *autonomy*, or the ability to make their own choices; *competence*, or the sense that they can master skills and develop weaker areas; and *relatedness*, or a warm bond with others.[28] With Jill, these three elements came into action in a braided way. Jill gave Ruth *autonomy*, or a sense of choice. Instead of directing, she asked Ruth where she wanted to go next. She gave lighthearted advice about risks (getting stuck under the table), but offered a sense of *competence* by telling Ruth she'd know what to do. And she showed *relatedness* by sitting with Ruth warmly, offering a sense of comfort and excitement as Ruth explored.

Such conversations, I came to realize, had all the elements of *rich talk*. Jill's talk was A: *adaptive*, shifting as Ruth's interests did. It involved B: a *back-and-forth* between them, not only a one way talk stream. And it was C: *child-directed*, focused on jumping off from where Ruth showed interest or where she seemed most engaged.

With these ideas in mind, I soon delved into the research on praising kids. What I found surprised me. We tend to answer the question "How should I raise confident kids?" with the answer "Praise them." Or maybe "Praise them well." But that's only part of the solution. In fact, heaping on praise tends to make kids feel *less* confident, especially if they have low self-esteem. In what Ohio State University researchers call the "Praise Paradox," inflated praise, or exaggerated comments such as "That's so incredibly beautiful," tends to lower self-worth when kids struggle or fail.[29] The same goes for "person-focused praise," or praise focused on who a child *is*, rather than what they've *done*. That is, "You're so brilliant," versus "I was glad you managed to swim so far." Person-focused praise seems to make "children attribute failure to the self,"[30] says Eddie Brummelman of Utrecht University, a study author. Yes, when a child succeeds, he may feel he's smart. But what about when things go south? Does that make him "dumb"?

From the youngest ages, kids sniff out false praise. They notice our body language and the exaggerated tone of voice. Overpraising is a natural habit, and one I've noticed in myself. "That is just *awesome*," I said when Sophie was struggling to ride a bike and rode for two seconds before tumbling down. But this overzealous praise is often counterproductive. In Brummelman's study tended, adults gave inflated praise to kids with lower self-esteem: but that praise actually *decreased* the kids' tendencies to seek out challenges.[31]

Most kids want to hear the truth about their skills, delivered in a compassionate way. They want to talk through the good and the bad. Overpraising sends the message that they can't handle the hard parts: that failure is a scary thing, rather than a natural fact they can face up to. Hearing overdone praise too often, they can start trying to avoid failure, shying away from useful challenges. What's more, when we push their failures under the rug, we don't let them *see* failure long enough to reflect on it. This prevents them from learning from their failures, or even recognizing the lessons it can bring.

In fact, failure is a rich store of information, if kids can see it objectively enough. Mastering the art of learning from failure—whether in academics, social life, or elsewhere—develops more skills than any lecture can. As Jessica Lahey notes in *The Gift of Failure*, the "toolbox, the accumulated store of skills students earn through their failures, adaptations, and growth, is more important than any mathematical formula or grammatical rule."[32] Still, as I know from experience, helping kids with this art isn't easy. Many tears and frustrations line the path. What's more, kids must be open to learning. It's not because we *want* them to learn from failure that they will.

So how can our conversations help? Ideally, they support kids to see their progress clearly, identify roadblocks, and use failure as a catalyst to thrive. Start by emphasizing *process*. Explore the grays of experience, not the black-and-white of failure versus success. Think less about "bad" or "good" and more about "how," "where," and "why." How did it feel to take on that challenge? What was enjoyable or boring? Where did you get stuck? What strategies did you use? And how could you set a new, more challenging goal? Encourage specific, objective language about their accomplishments. Emphasize the joy of trying things out and—when possible—laughing over ambitious but failed attempts. As I heard one girl say at the playground, attempting a handstand, "Wow, I fell—but that *was* a crazy cartwheel!" Or see the following example:

Making Small Shifts: Praise for Growth

"Look at what I built," your child says while holding up a model rocket and the directions he used.					
The quick answer:	**To promote growth and exploration:**				
"Great! Good job."	"Which part was your favorite to build?"	"Wow! How much did you use the directions? Do you think they helped?"	"Those wings look complicated. How did you put them together?"	"It looks like it might really fly. Do you want to take it outside to test?"	"How did it feel to build it? Were there places you got stuck?"

The Signals We Give

Focusing on process helps kids not get too tied to their failures and successes. To boost their willingness to take on challenges, it's equally important to notice our talk about the ways *we've* succeeded or failed. Sometimes, we're not even aware of how we limit ourselves or disparage our abilities. I think back to the time after Paul's birth, in the middle of a blizzard, when I had to stay in the hospital for a few days for medical complications. As the extra stay was unexpected, we hired a new temporary babysitter, Janine. In previous winters, Sophie had asked me to take her ice-skating, but I'd never been very good at it and said she should go with her dad. I'd go with her sometime later, I told her, trying not to sound evasive. Somehow, the time never came. Later, she'd told me she thought ice-skating was scary—and I sensed I'd contributed to that idea.

But one late afternoon, Sophie burst into my hospital room, followed by Janine, and said with a smile, "We went ice-skating for hours—and it was *easy!* I even got to use a blue whale."

As it turned out, the ice rink had plastic whales the kids could hold on to as they practiced. Sophie had used one for a while, then had followed Janine around, who herself was a confident ice-skater and who'd made the activity seem fun.

Why had Sophie's fear apparently disappeared? When I thought back, I realized we'd had several conversations where I'd laughingly suggested that I'd never be able to ice-skate. I'd grown up in the south, I said, where it rarely snowed. While I'd happily swim far out in the ocean, I'd never be good with snow or ice. In those talks, I'd conveyed a message about who I *was* as a person. I'd given her the idea that my skills could never change. And that's how many conversations end up being framed. Our own subtle messages about what *we're* able to do and how much we can grow, or can't, can trickle down unconsciously to kids.

Confidence Needs Room to Grow

With this idea in mind, I started asking: How could our everyday conversation show *we* felt comfortable giving new things a try? How could reflecting on our skills and assumptions about our capabilities help kids do the same? To learn more, I contacted Lenore Skenazy, founder of the Free Range Parenting movement and author of a bestselling book by that name. I was intrigued by that movement, but even more by her latest initiative, the Let Grow Project, which she designed precisely to encourage confidence and independence through everyday talk.[33]

Over the phone, Skenazy spoke at a rapid-fire pace, with clear enthusiasm.[34] Conversations about confidence, she argued, start with us. Her own work on the Let Grow Project began when she noticed a few extreme cases of kids doing far less than they were capable of, many of them from well-off families. Twelve-year-old kids weren't allowed to use sharp knives. Teenagers weren't allowed to go to the corner store. The Let Grow Project was her answer; she hoped it would start conversations that loosened the reins and let kids see themselves as capable of more.

At its heart, the project sounded so simple, I wondered if there was a catch. Kids are asked to choose an activity or task they think their parents would forbid. They check in with their parents, get permission, do the activity, then reflect on how it went. The activity could be anything: walking to a neighbor's house alone, ordering a pizza, auditioning for a dance show. They could also do things for other people. As Gary Karlson, then a teacher at the Riverhead Central School District in Wading River, New York, told me, one third-grade student in his class took the opportunity to teach his mother some English words.[35,36] The key was that kids chose their activities and reflected afterward. "The best part," Skenazy said, "was how the project changed the conversation between parents and kids." When talk started with a focus on kids' capabilities, it became far more positive. Given permission, kids pushed beyond their comfort zones and often succeeded. That built their confidence, and equally important, shifted the dynamic. Challenges became a good thing. Talk turned to what kids could accomplish, and how.

It's easy to get in tugs-of-war with kids, as they ask for more independence, and we focus on the risks. We may start conversations about new challenges by listing dangers or laying out the rules. But confidence can't develop in a vacuum. Kids need to challenge themselves. By identifying just-right challenges, we make it easier for them to encounter obstacles, stretch their boundaries, and reflect on their capabilities. If a challenge seems out of reach or too risky, discuss similar ones they could try. Maybe a child can't ride the train alone but could go with a friend.

When your attitude suggests that you welcome his initiatives, even if his specific plan won't work, you show you want him to challenge himself. You present yourself as a mentor, eager to help. The activity matters, but more important is how you frame it. How do you respond when your child wants to try something new? Do your tone and body language suggest openness when he mentions a new task that's challenging, but slightly beyond his grasp?

The Three Es for Confidence: Choose and Reflect on Goals

To build confidence, support kids in choosing and reflecting on goals, by using the Three Es:

1. *Expand* on the reasons a child chooses a challenge. Clarify: What is his motivation? How does it meet a need or let him grow beyond his current skills?

2. *Explore* what success means to him. What metric does he want to use? Maybe a child wants to get better at running. Does he want to run to his friend's house, or run in a race? Or does he want to get fast enough to keep up with friends? As much as possible, help him get specific and objective, so he has a metric he can meet. Brainstorm possibilities to meet that goal, staying open to all ideas. Discuss likely obstacles and strategize proactively. What if he gets out of breath, say, or starts running but realizes he's gone out too fast? Focus on both *feelings* and *facts*: How would he feel to meet his goal? How can he avoid panic if he gets stuck? Personalize success: How would he like to celebrate? And notice the difference between *when* and *if*—one seems like a matter of time, while the other might not happen at all.

3. *Evaluate.* What if a child makes a goal, then decides he wants to change it? That's fine. In fact, it can be a sign of self-awareness, if a child realizes his goals don't suit him anymore, and he doesn't want to waste time continuing to pursue them. Help your child sit with a goal for a while. But emphasize that changing goals doesn't mean failing. Maybe the goal needs to be different, if his interests have changed: say, he wants to bike

or do karate instead of run. Or maybe he was overambitious in his first goal and needs to tone it down: say, try to run *one* mile, not three. Rethink these goals alongside him and make a plan. Also, help him see if he's changing goals just because something is new or hard, or if he seems to have a new goal all the time. In that case, it might be worth sticking with the goal for a while.

After he's started making progress toward that new goal, help him reflect. Compare his expectations with reality. What surprised him positively? What presented an unexpected obstacle? What does that tell him for next time? Say, in the running example, he started out too quickly and got fatigued. Next time, he can learn to start slow and pace himself. Emphasize that finding "just-right" goals is a process for all of us. Just by having the conversation means he's on his way.

See Beyond the Mess

What about when your child wants to do something messy or counterproductive? Especially with young kids, that can be hugely frustrating—not to mention exhausting to clean. Still, behind the mess often lies the drive to explore. Recognizing that can help you frame his attempts less negatively; the first step in collaborating with him. Take the Terrible Twos (or the "Terrible Toes," as Paul used to call it; his favorite response when someone asked his age). Danish parents call this the Boundary Age.[37] Through their antics, toddlers are testing: How many plates can I stack before they fall? How much ketchup can I squeeze out? Often, they're just curious. But we interpret their curiosity as defiance. Add to that the unstoppable tantrums, and you've got a recipe for stress.

But try recognizing their limit-pushing as natural, if maddening. Ask yourself: What interest lies behind this behavior? What idea is a child trying to work out? You'll probably still be annoyed, but you'll less likely take it personally. Usually, it *isn't* personal. The wall and a piece of paper are both drawing surfaces, he thinks. Or he's motivated by the intrigue of not knowing that delicious question "What would happen if . . . ?"

Take that classic example of a young child pulling all the toilet paper from the roll. Irritating, for sure. But he's at the age where he's interested in questions like: How much paper is there? How hard do you have to pull to get to the end? What *is* at the end? That's not to say you should let him do it. But you *can* have a different conversation than the typical one, which goes something like, "Hey, stop that," and ends there. It's natural to get annoyed or even lash out. But he'll likely find your reaction exciting and even interpret it as a game (the "make mommy mad" game, as a friend of mine sarcastically called it). Soon you'll find yourself in a back-and-forth battle of wills—with a lot of wasted toilet paper.

Instead, you can set limits, telling him no while still building his confidence and perspective-taking skills. Take a deep breath and approach the situation lightly. "Whoa, that makes a mess," you might say. "How long do you think it'll take to put it back?" Casually *expand* on his thinking; say, "It looks like cotton candy. What do *you* think it looks like?" Bring up the effects of his actions on others. Ask: "Would *you* want to use dirty toilet paper?" or say, "Pulling it all out wastes it for everyone else."

Then ask yourself: What impulse is driving him? Maybe it's the yanking action he likes, or the question of what's at the end. *Explore*: direct him to a similar, less messy activity; for example, pulling scarves out of a drawer. Make a game of cleaning up afterward, and *evaluate* whether his impulse was satisfied, or whether you could try something new the next time.

These discussions support his independence while showing him that there are rules, other people matter, and not everything is up for grabs. You're working in partnership, and in not reacting too strongly, showing him a model of how to regulate himself. Reflecting on his impulses, you guide him toward decisions that work better for everyone. You're also showing that messes aren't permanent—but he *does* need to take initiative and clean up.

The Three Es for Failure

Learning to shift their decisions with feedback isn't only key for young kids. Older kids also need that skill, especially when they fail or only partially succeed. Really, failure is in the eye of the beholder. How much it brings kids down depends, in part, on their biology, but equally, on the conversations they have. Resilience, or the ability to overcome hardship, is most likely to develop when kids have at least one secure, loving relationship with an adult.[38] Think of your role as a personalized support system. At your best, you notice what response they'd benefit from at any one time. You sense whether they need a nudge or encouragement to try more, or comfort, or a chance to reflect. They might have big feelings that need to be aired. When they're supported to do so, they often feel better—and build key skills like planning and strategizing for the next time.

One friend's ten-year-old son, Jake, talked to me of training for a statewide cross-country race with his friend Nico. For the whole season, the two friends had run at the same pace, and they'd talked about crossing the finish line together. But on race day, Jake got a cramp and slowed down, then watched as Nico sped by and won. Not only did Jake feel disappointed and lose confidence in himself, he also felt that Nico had betrayed him in not slowing down.

In that way, confidence and friendship challenges became intertwined, in a way that left Jake feeling distant from Nico and from his team. After the meet, in fact, Jake told his mother that he didn't want to run anymore and didn't want to be friends with Nico. He needed talk that helped him see that failure isn't forever and doesn't define you. He also needed to rebuild his confidence.

Soon, Jake's mother used the Three Es to help him get over his disappointment in a way that didn't alienate him further. First, sensing that the loss was a sore spot, she let it go for a while, giving him time to process. When he was calmer, she reflected alongside him:

1. **Expanding** on his thinking, she asked: "What made you most disappointed? What was hardest about that?"

2. **Exploring**, she asked: "What do you think Nico was feeling in the moment? Do you think he wanted to hurt your feelings—or was he caught up in the excitement of the moment?" Jake realized that his teammate probably hadn't known about his cramp and hadn't meant to be cruel. While he still felt hurt, he didn't have to cut off ties with Nico. He also explored why he'd panicked in the moment. He realized he'd never had such a bad cramp and hadn't known what to do. Next time, he'd slow down and do some deep breathing exercises. He'd also focus on pacing himself.

Using a gentle approach, take the perspective of *both-and*: learning from failure can be painful *and* helpful. Especially in

the near term, failures can loom large in a child's mind. Kids
can all too easily identify themselves with failure, shifting
from "it failed" to "I'm a failure" without even realizing it.
Your conversation can help by holding these failures lightly,
reframing them as chances for learning—while *still* validating
their upset. There's no reason to brush over feelings of
disappointment or anger. Exploring these feelings calmly lets
you show they're not shameful. You're open to hearing the
hard parts, and you're on your child's side.

3. *Evaluate*: Encourage your child to try again, with his plan
   in mind. Afterward, reflect. Use questions like: "How well
   did that strategy work?" "What outcomes did you expect
   and not expect?" That lets him keep up the cycle of reflection
   and action and shows that success might not be immediate.
   Resilience isn't a onetime event. Rather, it builds over time.

Harness Self-Talk: Support Kids to Coach Themselves

What we say matters, but confidence ultimately has to do with the
ways kids talk to themselves. What experiences do they label failures? When they fail, how much do they beat themselves up? How
easy is it for them to forgive themselves and try again? It's great if
kids hold themselves to high standards, but not when those standards are so high or rigid that they get overwhelmed.

Negative self-talk, on the other hand, doesn't only make them
feel bad in the moment. The way kids talk to themselves often becomes their reality. As research starting in the 1960s has found,

when kids have too many experiences of things being out of their control, they can develop *learned helplessness*. They feel that nothing they do makes a dent in their lack of success, so why try?[39]

Kids who've experienced trauma or are biologically predisposed to depression are more likely to experience learned helplessness. But any child can develop it, or a shade of it, even if it's not so extreme. "That's too hard for me," I've heard kids say, glancing at math problems they haven't even read, or "I'll never cross *that*," looking at a tall set of monkey bars.[40]

Instead, when they harness their self-talk, they're far more likely to keep trying and eventually succeed. I've relied on the power of this self-talk often in my clinical work, especially to build self-awareness.

One middle school girl I worked with, Vivian, had trouble understanding language and expressing herself. She had been diagnosed with auditory processing disorder, meaning that her hearing was fine, but she had trouble processing the sounds she heard. She had particular difficulty when more than two people were talking at once. To her, it all sounded like a blur.[41] She'd been a "worrier" for years, her mother told me, but her troubles with language had left her even more prone to self-doubt. While her coaches praised her soccer performance, she thought she was a poor athlete.

When working with her, I first asked her to *expand*. Why did she think she wasn't good at sports? She said she fumbled on the field and often felt paralyzed by indecision. "I always ask if I'm right," she said, frowning. "My coaches tell me to just try, but I can't. Sometimes, after just one mistake, I decide I'm done for the day."

We then moved to *explore*, and I questioned her "I can't." Why couldn't she make in-the-moment decisions easily? Did she not know enough, or did she think she'd fail? Or was it more that she feared her decision would be wrong?

Sometimes, she explained, her "I can't" reaction had to do with self-doubt. It wasn't that she'd heard negative feedback from her coach. In fact, she'd been the negative "coach" to herself. Her self-talk was tearing her down. She was saying to herself, "I'm just bad. I won't score a goal." As studies have found, negative self-talk plays a role in maintaining anxiety and depression, while positive self-talk is linked to improvements in self-esteem.[42,43,44]

With that research in mind, I worked to help Vivien counter her negative statements with positive or neutral ones. I asked her for her ideas, and I gave mine, writing them on the whiteboard on a big brainstorming "web." Then I asked her to talk through the list, cut out some, and settle on the one she thought would help most. It's often not helpful to go to the opposite extreme and be hyper-positive. Instead, it's better to seek out a realistic but hopeful middle ground. After our discussion, she decided on, "I have work to do, but I'll get there." This comment allowed her to recognize her current challenges but not become overwhelmed by them. Taking that perspective helped her move forward comfortably, in a way that didn't leave her feeling paralyzed.

At other times, her trouble had to do with not understanding the coach's directions. Confused, she let the game go on without her. That spiraled into her doing even more poorly and to more self-doubt. For those times, we role-played asking the coach for clarification. She did much better, she explained, when she could see strategies in action. We practiced questions like "Can I see what it looks like?" or "Could you show me?" We also developed a mantra she could use when she felt paralyzed: "Decide, do, reflect." It looks like this:

Decide, Do, Reflect: Getting Unstuck

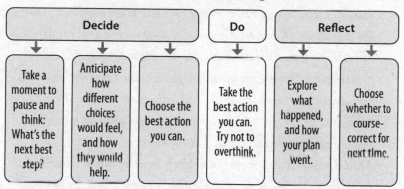

At practice, she paused briefly and thought through options, with catchphrases like "go for it" or "stand back," then chose one and followed through. After practice, she *reflected*, using her judgment and the coach's commentary to decide how well that had worked. Right or wrong, that approach gave her information. That's what she needed, far more than perfection, to feel in control.[45]

After a few weeks, Vivien told me, she'd started acting more decisively and feeling more confident. Of course, all her challenges hadn't disappeared, but she'd started finding workarounds. Most important, she'd developed independence and self-reliance, foundations for her long-term confidence.

. . . .

Principles for Confidence Conversations

To raise kids who can embrace challenge, focus on the following:
* *Help kids chart their progress and celebrate their many aspects holistically. Maybe your child isn't a great trombone player—yet. Maybe she never will be. That doesn't mean she can't enjoy playing or make progress. What's more, poor performance doesn't have to define her. Even if she truly*

*is the "worst" trombone player in class, she has other great
qualities. Encourage her to bring up those other qualities when
she gets down on herself. Emphasize that no one is great at
everything—and we don't need to be. Help her clarify her
priorities and where she wants to put in time. Say she doesn't
care about the trombone at all and only plays because it's a
requirement. In that case, maybe she should practice music
enough to get a decent grade, but no more.*

- **Model progress and forward motion in your life.** *Reflect on
how you're trying to meet challenges, even if you're struggling.
Use a lighthearted tone, considering many areas in your life.
Maybe you're working on your driving or accounting skills.
Where have you improved, and where do you have room to
grow? How close have you come to your goals?*

- **Notice your child's growing edge and gradually let her do
more over time.**[46] *If your child is hesitant, ask her: What's
the next natural goal? Say she's finished a recipe with a few
short steps. What about trying one that's more complicated, or
experimenting with some new ingredients? Show her it's "all
right to be wrong," and that you're proud of her open attitude.*

More broadly, to develop grounded confidence and independence,
try these conversational habits:

Conversational Habit #1: Get Clear

To raise self-awareness and help kids feel in control: *Get clear.* What
is the feedback or situation? Can your child articulate it?

Take the example of three-year-old Paul. "Where are we going?" he asked, on our way to pick up Sophie from a playdate. I told

him, but ten seconds later, he asked again. And again. After the sixth time, I said, "To pick up *Sophie*, okay?" After he kept asking, I turned the question around. "Tell me, where?" I asked him. And he responded, "To pick up Sophie. But *where*?" I added, "To her friend Alex's house." We then had a conversation about who Alex was, and how excited Sophie had been for the playdate. And finally he let that question go. In fact, I realized my first answer hadn't answered his real question, about which friend Sophie was visiting.

Putting the idea in his own words solidified it in his mind. Through taking control of the conversation, he clarified his question, which we could then take on. That broke the spiral of repetitive questioning, while giving me insight into why he'd felt out of control. For older kids, the strategy looks different, but the goal is the same. Try this three-step process, which I call **Clarify, Talk it Out, and Plan**:

1. *Clarify*. Answer: "What is the world telling me?"
   • Support her to rephrase feedback as objectively as possible. See what happens when you strip away some of the more extreme language and related emotions. Did the coach say she would "never" be a good soccer player, or only that she should work on her kicks?

2. *Talk it out*. Teach her to analyze feedback, in the context of her experiences.
   • After she gets feedback, discuss:
     – How does she *feel* about the feedback? Motivated, discouraged, or in between? Say her coach tells her, "Well, you still have a ways to go." For a child who really cares about her performance, that can be hard to hear. Hearing her reaction lets you notice if you need to talk her down.

    – How can she best *use* what she hears? Not all feedback
is equally helpful or actionable. Compare the coach's
comment about having a ways to go to a comment like
"Step back before you kick." The second comment teaches
her far more about what to practice. Distinguishing
helpful from unhelpful feedback is harder than it looks. It
asks kids to think critically and not accept all comments at
face value. Ask: Which feedback gives you insight about
what to do next? Which can you minimize or ignore?
- Teach her to self-coach, using strategies like these:
    – Break failures into steps she can examine: Why did she
fall off the rock wall? Did she not reach far enough, or did
her foot slip? Or was she more tired than usual?
    – Promote self-encouragement: Teach a child to check for
growth and celebrate the progress she sees. Use visual
evidence; say, review old workbooks to see her spelling
improving, or check landmarks to notice how much
farther she's run this time as compared to the last.

3. *Plan*. Use feedback to drive her next steps.
   • Start with what's already working well. Ask her to reflect on
strategies that helped, then talk over tweaks for next time.
    – Say she wants to take on a bigger Lego project than
usual, which you sense will frustrate her. Discuss how she
made the last project work. Did it help her when you read
the directions to her, when she looked at the brochure's
pictures, or both? Which strategies could she apply to this
new project? Are there new strategies she could try? As
much as possible, focus on letting her drive the project.
Reflect together on her ideas.

Conversational Habit #2:
What Works? To Boost Independence:

Let your child see what's working well and plan for success. Strategize about taking small "bites" out of bigger projects. For example, "That's a more complicated project than usual. How many parts do you think we should try?" Use one day's benchmark as a guide for the next. "Three pages was easy yesterday; how many could you do today?" If he tends to think small, encourage his ambition. It won't be the end of the world if he doesn't finish it all.

Help paint a child's confidence "self-portrait." Maybe he's eager to point out his flaws but doesn't notice the positives. Or maybe he ignores the context. For example, he says he's a bad photographer, since he takes blurry pictures, but he only started using the camera today. Or maybe he can't distinguish between feeling frustrated and overwhelmed. In these cases, talk can clarify how he sees himself and how he feels. It can also let him rethink those blanket judgments. To do so, model thinking about your thinking. For example, if you're feeling annoyed with a craft project, "I'm starting not to like what I'm working on. I'll stop for tonight. Tomorrow, I'll see it fresh." Offer insight from your life, focusing on noticing *shoulds*. Normalize problems you're having; for example, "I get frustrated when I think I *should* know how to fix the computer, but then I realize half my colleagues have the same problem." Instead of "shoulds," emphasize an attitude of self-compassion.

Give the role of praise and critique over to your child. Try coming at problems from a realistic but hopeful angle, instead of using a critical "judgement." What part of the picture did your child like the best? What does he want to improve?

Try not to overdo support. It can feel hard to step back when there's an obvious answer, or one piece of the puzzle left. But how much are you taking on tasks your child could do? Think of yourself as an interpreter and guide, helping your child develop his or her own measuring stick.

Offer a model of being open to struggle. "I climbed the baby rock wall," I heard my friend Deborah saying at our rock-climbing gym. She gave a thumbs-up to her teenage son, who'd climbed far higher. "Good job, mom," he said with a laugh. A joking interaction, but a powerful point. That morning, she'd described her fear of heights. She wasn't a "climber," she explained. But later, she wondered, "What message am I sending? That you're either a 'climber' or you aren't?"

To counteract that idea, she tightened her harness and climbed. What's more, she talked to her son about her attempt. "Even at his age," she told me later, "he's watching how I react. He's noticing how I manage fear." Climbing didn't make that fear go away, but her talk modeled how to work within it. If your child sees you struggling but coping, he's likely to do the same, or try.

We all have a blend of fixed and growth mindsets. Watch for the ways these mindsets show up in all your lives. I've found Dweck's suggestion to notice your own fixed mindset triggers a useful one.[47] For some of us, it's about technology. Perhaps, when your computer hangs up, your first reaction is "I'm just bad at computers." Ask yourself: When do you feel defeated or like you'll "never" get something right? Check your self-talk. If it's often negative, emphasize that we're all works in progress. We all deserve compassion for our attempts, and we should celebrate that we're trying things out of our comfort zones.[48]

To let your child stretch: check your assumptions. We know our kids so well, but at times, we still might not see all they're capable of. Or we want to keep them comfortable, so we don't stretch them as much as we could. Try this self-check:

Self-check: Testing your assumptions

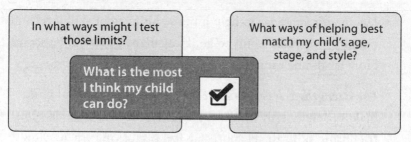

In what ways might I test those limits?

What ways of helping best match my child's age, stage, and style?

What is the most I think my child can do?

- Afterward:
  - **Hone in on interests and skills.** Even with young kids, discuss which tasks or chores they could take on, tailored to them. Think of budgeting skills for a high schooler who enjoys math, or dishwashing for a ten-year-old who likes cleanliness. Highlight the results of their work and who benefits; say, "The whole family will enjoy clean dishes." Those "rewards" offer a grounded sense of pride.[49]
  - **Focus on the end goal of any task, the more concrete the younger the child.** Say a young child has a shirt she wants washed. What about sorting clothes or checking if the dryer is done? For a child who wants more allowance, what about trying to reduce the electric bill? Offer choices based on what appeals to her and what seems an appropriate stretch.

Conversational Habit #3:
Visualizing the Journey

Focus on *objective* and *comparative* conversations.

Objective conversations help your child see his skills clearly and optimistically, and not beat himself up for flaws. Try this process:

- *Use specific language* to help him see his current skill level and visualize where he wants to go. How many goals did he score? How far did he run? How much farther does he *want* to go?

- *Use strengths as levers to shore up weaknesses.* Say your child makes friends easily but struggles in sports. He could use his friendship skills to get sports advice; say, asking friends how they learned to throw overhand.

- *Use semantic webs*, or word maps, to reframe failure as learning. Semantic webs are the associations we make with a word.[50] For instance, many kids equate "failure" with "stupid" or "bad." Notice if your child makes negative leaps, such as "It's embarrassing to fail" or "I'm such a loser." Encourage him to shift to more positive talk: "I don't have to feel embarrassed if I'm trying," or "It's not being a loser to keep practicing," or "It might feel bad now, but if I keep working, I'll feel better."

Comparative conversations help your child see where he's been and where he wants to go, using himself as a measuring stick. Try the following:

- *Compare past and present skills.* Point out signs of growth and encourage him to do so. Use visual evidence when possible. For example, "Let's read the stories you wrote last year. How are they different from now? What specific skills have you learned since then?"

- *Question negative labels.* Emphasize actions that brought him closer to or farther from his goal. Help him notice thoughts, like "I *knew* it wouldn't work," that stop him from persisting. Give these thoughts a name, such as "confidence blasters." Strive to make them conscious, then challenge them. In working with kids, I've drawn from what psychologists call *cognitive distortions,*[51,52] with a focus on these:

➡ **Black-and-white thinking: "I'm either good at it or terrible."**
Move to "Seeing the grays": "I might be not great at
        swimming, but I'm not too bad either. Also,
        I'm a really good soccer player."

➡ **Fortune-telling: "I know it will turn out horribly."**
Move to "Being open to possibility": "I'm not sure how
        it will go; it may be fine."

➡ **Labeling yourself or your child: "I'm such a bad basketball player."**
Move to "Naming the action": "I didn't get that one shot
        right. But I did get close. Maybe I'll get it the
        next time"

Kids don't become confident by talking themselves in circles. Instead, it's the *cycle* of action and reflection out of which confidence springs. When they learn to take on harder challenges, then reflect, they raise their self-awareness and their knowledge of what worked. That helps them try tough things, dream big, and show up with courage. Believing in themselves doesn't mean thinking they'll always succeed. It means knowing they might not succeed, but they'll be all right. They can give the challenge a try anyway. The surprising part? That doesn't only build their confidence. Just as important, it changes how *we* see them. When they raise the bar, we raise our expectations. We speak from a place of appreciation. We even celebrate failure, hard as that seems, because it shows they were stretching themselves; the only way to find success eventually. We meet their struggles with compassion and show them we love them no matter what. That encourages them to try more.

CHAPTER 5

Conversations for Building Relationships: Cultivating Your Child's Social Skills

Friendship is born at that moment when one person says to another, "What! You too? I thought I was the only one."

—C. S. LEWIS[1]

I'll always remember Linda, the nanny we hired to care for Sophie while I was finishing my dissertation. As a nervous new mother, I felt torn up about the idea of leaving Sophie. Still, the research study I was working on was taking place *that* year—and I didn't know when I'd have another chance. So, when Sophie was a few months old, my husband and I started looking for a day-care or nanny share.

Linda was the first nanny we met, a Swedish woman my age with long blond hair and a crinkling smile. As soon as she walked in and sat beside Sophie, I sensed she was the one. There was a warmth and efficiency to her, and a sense of gentle playfulness, as she picked Sophie up, and as Sophie—typically afraid of strangers—gazed back, quiet and calm. As we sipped coffee, Linda told us her story. She'd nannied for years, and had recently moved with her Spanish husband to Boston. Her baby, Malou, had been born within weeks of Sophie at the same hospital.

"Funny you don't look familiar," I said, thinking we must have crossed paths at some prenatal appointments.

Soon Linda brought up a question: Could she bring Malou along? Of course, I said, thinking it would be a great setup. Soon, though, I started worrying. Maybe she'd spend more time caring for Malou, or go too far in the other direction, and care for my daughter at the expense of her own. Maybe the girls wouldn't get along. Maybe Sophie would be jealous of Malou having her mother around, or I would feel guilty heading off every morning, not staying at home, as a part of me wanted to. Still, Linda seemed so competent, and the solution so simple, that we agreed.

Little did I know that, in the months to come, Linda and Malou would grow to feel like family, and the girls like sisters. Sophie was round, bouncy, and blond, while Malou was brunette, with a narrower face. In fact, as we all noticed, Malou looked more like my child, and Sophie like Linda's. And in the end, my worries were unfounded. Linda took care of both kids astoundingly well. I still have the pictures where the two girls are lying back, six inches apart, on an owl-patterned mat; where they're taking their first sips from cups; where they're bundled up to play in a January snowstorm ("no bad weather, just bad clothes," as Linda always said); and where Malou—an early walker—pushed a plastic cart while Sophie, mid-crawl, looked on. I still remember Linda meeting me one day and saying, with her typical offbeat humor, that she'd taken the girls to the local

Indian buffet—free for kids—where they'd tried their first puree, a spicy *matar paneer.*

"They loved it," she said, and I smiled, having planned to start Sophie on bland oatmeal.

And I still have the memories of meeting them outside one summer on the Boston Common, where they splayed on a picnic mat, as Sophie tried on oversize sunglasses and Malou giggled and grabbed for them. In the sunlight, watching their antics, I felt truly blessed to have found them—not only Linda, but Malou as well, who became Sophie's first companion and her first experience with a friend. Yes, the two kids squabbled, but that seemed part of the puzzle. No relationship could be without its flaws. In fact, as I'd learned from the research, it was *within* the context of those safe relationships where kids learned to care for each other and to play fair. The earliest of friendships sets the stage for all later skills.

My time with Malou and Linda reminded me of the work of John Bowlby, founder of the influential idea known as attachment theory. In his words, early relationships mark kids "from the cradle to the grave."[2] From birth, infants' close attention to faces and voices lets their "social brains" mature.[3] No matter which way you turn it, early experiences matter, in building social talk and social skills. What's more, the quality of *our* relationships as adults trickles down to our kids.

With that in mind, I'll always remember how our nanny arrangement ended, when the girls were a year and a half old. One morning before I left, Linda leaned in and said, "I have something to tell you."

"Yes?" Startled, I set down my bag.

"I'm pregnant." She gave a broad smile. "With twins. And we're moving to Spain."

I hugged and congratulated her, then said, "I guess those are three good reasons to quit."

Of course I was glad for her—but still, I felt myself shaking on the way out.

Linda's presence, in the end, had been a gift for our family. It made leaving for work not easy, but tolerable. It also reminded me of the importance of adult friendships for our own well-being, which in turn affects our kids. Especially in the early years of parenting, it's lucky to have someone who "gets" it, and who *also* wishes she could go to the bathroom alone.

At the same time, this experience highlighted the importance of *children's* friendships and relationships, starting far younger than we think. As I knew, even six-month-old babies get excited when they see a similar-age child, and often make noises to attract the other child's attention.[4] By the time they're a year old, they often show preferences for some playmates over others, long before they can have full-fledged friendships. And even two-to-three-year-olds can show kindness to others, based on their developing perspective-taking skills.[5] I remember hearing a three-year-old tell his friend who was crying after a bad fall, "Don't worry. Your dad will make it all right."

I knew all this research, and still, it surprised me to see friendship developing, on a day-to-day basis, as Sophie and Malou asked for the same books, imitated each other's play, and followed each other down the stairs. But most of all, seeing their developing bond made me wonder: What was friendship exactly? What made it so important—essential, even? How did its dynamics work? And how could we nurture not only children's friendships, but more broadly, the social skills needed for close, connected relationships?

Friendship Is a Fundamental Need

Social relationships are key to children's health, well-being, and happiness. We can't overstate their importance. When kids struggle to make or keep friends, it's natural to worry. And even when they don't have serious friendship challenges, the simple ones are often more than enough to keep us up at night. At the same time, the joy of childhood friendship can't be overstated either. I've rarely seen kids as happy as when they meet friends at the playground, squeal in recognition, then race on their scooters for hours. That goes for kids in every culture, on every continent. Even if their play looks different, the smile when one friend meets another makes *us* happy and is its own kind of gift.

We want kids to be confident and independent. We also want them to have strong relationships, including good friends. Not only are friendships hugely meaningful on a daily basis, they also convey benefits into adulthood, in terms of psychological and even physical health. One study found that boys who spent more time with friends as children tended to have lower blood pressure and be less overweight as adults than those who didn't.[6] Friends promote well-being, starting even in preschool.[7,8,9,10] And we know their importance intuitively. At school meetings, we don't typically ask to see every assignment. Instead, we want to know how kids are getting along with others, whether they're bullied, popular, or in between—and how we can support them to build and maintain strong bonds.

And that's what nearly all kids care about, too. "If kids wrote parenting books," as the play expert Peter Gray told me, "those books would look different than what we have now. There would be so much more about 'What do other kids think of me?' and 'How do I make and keep friends?' Those are the questions kids want to have answered."[11]

In their focus on friendships, kids are onto something. Friendship is a fundamental biological need. In friends, kids find protection, comfort, and connection, even calm for their nervous systems. They also practice their social skills.[12,13] This capacity for friendship is ancient. Some scientists even think having friendships made early humans smarter. We grew larger brains not only to hunt better, but—equally important—to socialize. In a virtuous spiral, that socializing built our brains. And it's not only humans who have friends. Many other big-brained species also do. Horses, zebras, hyenas, monkeys, and dolphins can form friendships—at least of a sort—that last for years.[14]

But what is friendship exactly? The idea goes back centuries. In classical Greece, Aristotle wrote of *philia*, or an affectionate regard that binds people together.[15] It involves a special care for the friend, as he or she truly is. Friends have generally positive feelings for each other and want to spend time together. They do each other favors because they want to. In healthy friendships, each person wants the other to be happy and fulfilled. At its heart, friendships are based on acting cooperatively over time. They depend on your memories and plans: say, recalling a fun party you went to or deciding where you'll go on vacation together. Those memories and plans bind you. If you had no memory and no ability to think about the future, it would be nearly impossible to make and keep friends.[16]

That's because, in most definitions, friends *care* about each other. They have close or *intimate* relationships. And they *do things* together, choosing activities based in part on what each other wants.[17] Those three pieces count for children's health, well-being, and happiness. With strong friendships, they become more available for learning, more open to new ideas, and more motivated.[18] Those who have more friends report being happier on average. They do better in school, are better-liked by teachers, and even have an easier time as adults getting jobs. They're healthier and less anxious than those who say they're lonely, and they experience more fun and joy.[19,20] In contrast, kids suffer when they lack friends or feel they do.[21] A lack of friendships, at the extreme, can be almost as hurtful, physically and emotionally, as actual poverty.[22,23]

Why is this? Long back, friendships were about physical survival. Early humans helped their friends stay alive. These days, the survival is more psychological—but not only, as having more friends has been linked to better health.[24,25] Kids need friends to feel good in their own skin and manage the inevitable storms and stresses of growing up.[26,27,28] One study surveyed more than four hundred kids, ages eleven to nineteen, from poorer backgrounds and found that having a best friend let them more easily overcome obstacles. Most important was how the friends offered emotional support and reframed problems in a positive light.[29]

Equally important, friendships let kids explore their personalities. Through socializing, they figure out who they are and who they'd like to be. In the highs of the best friendships, kids can let down their guards. Their conversations let them feel truly heard and seen. As one ten-year-old told me of her best friend, "It's like we're speaking the same language that no one else knows." One of the easiest ways you can recognize good friends is listening to their casual conversations. Close friends often pick up where they left off, with dialogue that may make little sense to outsiders. They develop inside jokes and shortcuts, so they don't have to start from scratch. "Did you get the orange one with sparkles?" I heard one seven-year-old girl ask, telling her friend about her purchases of tiny collectible Shopkins. "The special edition ones are the best, but I need more allowance. Sad-face emoji. If you have an extra, can I have it?" Afterward, I saw her turn to her mother and ask, "Mommy, can I have your phone to look up the special edition ones?" Clearly, she'd had practice with "texting" language, including emojis, even at her young age.

Back in 1971, Basil Bernstein talked about a "restricted code," or talk that assumes a shared background and experience. Those who use this code feel included. They use this sort of insider talk to show care and to feel cared for.[30]

Boys and girls may show this care in different ways, but the differences are smaller than you might assume. Starting in the late 1980s, the psychologist Eleanor Maccoby argued for what she called the Two Cultures Theory. Boys and girls, from her perspective, grow up in two different friendship cultures.[31] By middle school, boys tend to have bigger friendship groups and focus more on physical play and shared activities, while girls tend to have more one-on-one friendships and focus more on confiding in each other. In more recent years, scientists have found that boys' and girls' friendships are more similar than different. It may be that many girls talk more to share secrets and resolve conflicts, while boys tend to do so through shared activities. But really, all friendships are complex and can't be put into a single box based on sex.[32]

To build these friendships, kids need skills learned from their earliest relationships. Our comfort teaches them how to care. Whether it's by changing a diaper quickly or soothing a tantrum, we show we're there for them and want them to feel better.[33] When they cry or smile, they learn, someone responds. Other people can meet their needs, in interactions that can bring pleasure and joy. Those early lessons set the foundation for a dynamic of caring and being cared for.

Friendship Develops in Phases

Past those early years, friendships tend to develop in phases. While every friendship is unique, there's also some predictability in terms of the social skills kids master. From around three to six years old, as the Harvard psychologist Robert Selman argues, kids have "momentary playmates," in which they want play to go their way and may shun others with different ideas. Starting around age five (there's some variance), kids often think about friends as other kids who get along and do nice things for them. But they often have a "What can you do for me?" perspective, as I saw with the seven-year-olds earlier. Whether it's a cool toy or a chance to swim in a nice pool, many kids prioritize friends for the advantages they bring.[34]

It's only around age seven that kids start having a two-way collaboration, in a stage Selman calls playing "by the rules." They may have rigid ideas of fairness and can drop a friendship if they feel slighted. They may also start noticing and fearing criticism from their friends. As an eight-year-old girl told me about choosing a Halloween costume, "I just want one my friends won't laugh at." Starting around age eight, kids (girls especially) tend to confide more and turn to each other for problem-solving. They may be "joined at the hip," as I've seen with so many kids whispering in pairs at the back of a classroom.[35,36] More mature friendships, around twelve years old and up, ideally focus more on mutual trust and support, and less on possessiveness and material goods.

Far from a Friendship Ideal

Still, as I soon discovered, helping kids develop friendships to that mature stage isn't easy. So many kids are far from a friendship ideal. At work and on the playground, I've met kids of all ages who feel lonely and isolated, without the skills to maintain deeper friendships or repair rifts.

These difficulties, I soon discovered, mirror national trends. As the psychologist and author Jean Twenge found in a survey of more than eight million kids, the percentage of high school seniors reporting loneliness rose from 26 in 2012 to 39 in 2017. The rates of those saying they often felt left out increased from 30 to 38 percent.[37] Twenge cites social media and phone use. Those in the later generation, Twenge argues, are less likely to get together with friends in person. They're more likely to be scrolling on their phones—alone. Many teens I've met say they rarely see their friends in real life but have memorized every aspect of their friends' virtual lives, from vacation plans to the prom dresses their friends plan to buy.

But really, technology is only a piece of the puzzle. Friendship is complex, as is loneliness. Both have less to do with the number of friends a child has, and more with how she feels about her social life. To John and Stephanie Cacioppo of the University of Chicago, foremost researchers on loneliness, social media is a scapegoat that doesn't explain everything. Most likely, the problem goes deeper. In a national Pew study, teens cited too many obligations as their main reason for not seeing friends. Next on the list? Their *friends* are too busy.[38] When they're overscheduled, kids have little of the downtime they need to make and keep strong friends.

In my research, I've found three major challenges keeping kids from these stronger friendships. First, academic stress and the structures of most schools, which push socializing aside or don't make it a priority. Second, intensive parenting beliefs that leave us feeling we have to either butt in or stay out. And third, digital disruptions, which can stop in-person friendships in their tracks.

The Challenges of Kids
Making—and Keeping—Friends

First, academic stress and traditional school structures keep kids from having much time and encouragement to build or maintain strong friendships. Kids who spend hours studying hardly have the time or mental space for socializing. That's especially a problem when schools don't allow for much social talk among kids. With a focus on individual achievement, schools don't often focus on collaborative learning or the social-skill-building that comes along.[39] I remember working at one high school, where I saw a fourteen-year-old, Mark, sitting alone during a group project session. In Mark's classroom, I was serving as a co-teacher. The school had adopted the co-teaching model as a way to make the classroom more "language-rich." My role was to teach alongside the classroom teacher, infusing vocabulary and complex sentences into the lessons. I'd preview and review the ideas the students would encounter in their books. I'd show them how to decode complicated words they were about to read. Instead of taking individual kids out of the classroom, I'd support the whole class, with a focus on the kids who had the most trouble with reading and writing. Seeing kids in their classrooms, rather than one-on-one, was new to me. This model gave me insight into how kids interacted, and especially into the social dynamics that helped or hurt their learning.

"I don't want to cheat," Mark told me, when I explained he was *meant* to talk to classmates. Apparently, he hadn't done any group work that year. Already he was a quiet child, with a tendency to isolate himself. But his school experiences had made these tendencies worse. His experience of school was that of striving ahead alone. Talk was reserved mostly for answering the teacher's questions or asking for help. Recess and lunch, often cut short, were the only times for the social talk that could boost his friendships—and even then, kids were supposed to talk quietly.

Contrast those dynamics with a scene I witnessed in a Boston-area Montessori school. In that school, I worked mostly with kids one-on-one and in small groups. I also advised their teachers about the methods that would help their students learn best. In order to do so effectively, I spent a good deal of time observing students, in class and out. One morning, as I went to pick up a child for a reading assessment, I found a group of elementary school kids clustered in the hallway. Bent over maps and puzzles, they chatted with each other, then fell silent, not even seeming to notice when whole classes of kids traipsed by. I stopped to listen. Older and younger kids were working together, blending advice with playful teasing. Their social talk washed in and out like the tides.

"I think Zimbabwe goes *there*," one girl told a younger boy as they sat over a world map with colorful country-shaped puzzle pieces. "What do you think?"

"Probably." The boy put the piece in, then smiled. "Hey, your mom said you'll come over this weekend, right?"

"Yeah." The girl picked up a second piece. "Here's China. Try that one."

"You know, my baby just started crawling yesterday. It's cool."

"*Your* baby?"

"Okay, my mom's baby." The boy sprawled over the map. "But he's my baby, too."

So many kids, I saw, engaged in this comfortable back-and-forth: chatting and studying, thinking and socializing, in ways that crossed age and grade boundaries. Even as they had fun and developed their relationships, they learned. Their interaction reminded me of research showing kids achieve more when their teachers focus on social skills. As one study found, when teachers taught empathy, cooperation, and assertiveness, children's academic scores in math and reading increased. That was especially true for kids who began as low achievers.[40] It's a virtuous cycle that too much of schooling doesn't emphasize. So often, we as parents tend to emphasize what our schools do. As a result, we stop thinking of friendship as a deep-seated want and need, and often push it to the margins of kids' days.

Second, our culture's encouragement of intensive parenting doesn't help. We tend to think that either we hover over kids and fix every conflict, or we leave them alone. We don't want to butt in. That's a natural tendency, but if we keep away entirely, we leave kids without the support to reflect more deeply, or to think critically about social dynamics.

Then there's the opposite extreme. Out of fear of being judged—especially by other parents—we may over-manage conflicts, trying to prevent arguments. We see our kids' conflicts as reflections on us. I'm as guilty of this as anyone. One day, two-year-old Paul was playing in a sandbox when a girl his age took the shovel he was using and refused to return it. The everyday stuff of toddler conflict, I thought, and waited, hoping they'd resolve it. But soon the girl's mother bent in, took the shovel, then handed it to Paul.

"She's so sorry," the mother told me. "She didn't mean it."

"It's okay, we're fine," I replied, as—argument averted—the kids played on.

Only afterward did I realize how absurd that interaction was, on both our parts: the mother for apologizing for her child's behavior, and me for accepting the apology. Why hadn't we let them work it out?

In part, the answer is cultural. As the journalist Pamela Druckerman argues in her 2012 book *Bringing Up Bébé*, French parents don't tend to act as "intensively" as Americans.[41] I've seen as much on Parisian playgrounds: most parents stay on the sidelines, chatting or drinking coffee, and I've had to stop myself from traipsing into the sand. But even more than physically getting involved, we tend to overmanage talk, and not only in the early years. In trying to keep kids happy—an impossible goal—we can prevent them from hearing negative messages. We stop their conflict before it gets started. "That's mean to leave her out," we might say to a child keeping her sister from a playdate, before we even know if the sister is upset. Or, if she's hoarding tokens in an arcade game, "Stop it. You can't keep them all."

Sometimes, kids need these directions and reminders. Things can go haywire otherwise. Certainly I've had enough "stop hitting" discussions to last a lifetime. But more often, kids need to hear feedback from those who are directly affected. Comments from peers often help the most. Say your child hoards tokens, and his friend complains, "No fair!" Whether your child hands the tokens back or argues about fairness, there's been learning, and without any effort on your part.

In fact, conflicts and arguments—if harnessed productively—both *draw on* language skills and *build* them. You can see this naturally with groups of kids. A month ago, I heard a friend's child, four-year-old Reese, ask to borrow his friend Shae's truck. When Shae said yes, Reese grabbed it and started playing, shouting, "My truck." Shae lunged, insisting, "That's not yours—it's mine."

"You said I could borrow it," Reese complained.

"Okay," Shae said, "but just remember whose truck it is."

In fact, Shae didn't mind Reese playing with his truck, but *did* mind Reese thinking he owned it (probably because Shae feared Reese not giving it back). Their back and-forth helped to clarify the situation, even as it stretched their language skills.

At other times, negative feedback helps kids figure out how to assert themselves. Say a classmate tells your child he looks "weird." How does your child respond? Does he change his behavior? Maybe he understands the comment but wants to maintain his quirks. Reflecting on feedback helps kids decide if they want to conform. That's the foundation of being emotionally intelligent, able to adapt to their circumstances in ways that suit them personally. But when we either "butt out" or over-manage, we miss out on opportunities to help this reflection along.

A third challenge in social skill-building is digital disruption. There's a paradox: to socialize well requires reflection, offline downtime, and solitude. As Cal Newport states in *Digital Minimalism*, reflection lets kids resolve social dilemmas, identify their values, and decide how best to show up for others. That's ever harder today, when many kids grow up "solitude-deprived"—always on the go, involved in structured activities, or on a screen.[42] They're constantly faced with input from other minds. Their opinions can meld into the peer pressure sea. With little time or support for introspection, they often struggle to figure out what *they* think, versus what others do.

Constant input from scrolling and tweeting can feel like a fun diversion, but it's distracting more often than not.

At worst, it leaves kids on edge, hyperaware of how they're being perceived. Popularity becomes public—visible to anyone who visits a child's page—and quantified, as a number of friends or likes.[43] Even for kids to have their own "pages," especially if publicly accessible, constitutes a failure of safeguarding. Kids often aren't aware of potential predators, and most certainly aren't able to protect themselves. Those dangers aside, there's also the trouble of kids getting into a pattern of chasing approval from family, friends, and strangers. I've heard many teens complaining, after posting, "I thought I'd get more thumbs-ups." Focusing on the number of thumbs-up ratings or likes may, in the long run, leave them hyper-aware of others' reactions and ignoring their authentic thoughts.

At the same time, going online can help kids find community, especially if few friends share their interests in real life. One teenage girl I know, living in rural Texas, found friends online who were also interested in fashion. For months, they emailed each other sketches and designs. Later, they even applied to college together. That's only one example of how technology can build friendships—if we help kids harness it. To support them, try out the following:

....

Principles for Social Talk in a High-Tech World

- *Don't confuse "conversation time" with "screen time." Focus on contingent interactions, where kids can ask questions and get responses, and where they can see or talk to each other. Explore what it means for conversations to have more and less depth; say, the difference between high-fiving someone and writing a longer comment.*

- *Build empathy through talking about responses friends might prefer. Say a friend posts that his grandmother passed away suddenly. Would it be better to write on his feed, where everyone sees it, or message him privately? What would your child prefer? The point isn't to make artificial limits on screen time. It's all about using the technology to jump-start conversation and reflection. If kids are passively scrolling, encourage more active and social ways of using technology: say, what about writing to a friend of his, instead of checking his friend's profile repeatedly?*

- *Use social media as a starting point for discussion about kids' habits—and yours. Ask: Which online uses help your child feel connected and engaged? Explore using technology to strengthen friendships. Discuss how to engage, and how much. As I discussed with Jane McGonigal, game designer and author of the book* SuperBetter, *explore how technology is helping or could help your child. For instance, are gaming habits connecting him to classmates or isolating him? If he's gaming solo, could he play with others? How much online time does he—and you— need to maintain friendships? When is he chatting or texting, versus scrolling mindlessly? Examine his tech use together. Emphasize taking a tailored approach; he might need a different schedule than his brother, or a different time allotment this year as opposed to next. This framing keeps technology from being a battleground. You're there to help him make good use of technology. Rather than nagging, your conversations can start from a more constructive place, which will serve him better when he needs to make his own choices later.*

The Way Conversation Helps Friendships

But what about real-life interactions? In the interest of not over-parenting, should we do nothing when there's an issue and hope kids figure it out? Not exactly. Rather, we can serve as mentors and guides. We can help kids become socially flexible, able to adapt to many situations. Through reflecting on their experiences and emotions, they can develop better gut feelings about relationships: which to maintain, *how* best to maintain them, and how to stretch themselves socially. Think back to perspective-taking skills from Chapter 3. Kids who hear more "mental state" talk, or talk about what other people feel, want, and need, have stronger perspective-taking skills than those who hear less.[44] Those skills serve as the basis for strong friendships. Kids who have trouble understanding social situations tend to be less well connected than those who don't.[45]

Discussions about friendship obviously matter for kids who struggle to make friends. Oftentimes, as I've seen, challenges with language play a role. Kids with lower language skills are more likely to act out and be rejected as early as preschool.[46] When kids have language challenges, they may not have the mental space to notice social cues.[47] Being rejected hurts and can leave them stressed and anxious. Rejection even links to lower grades and higher drop-out rates.[48,49,50] "Nobody here knows me," one middle schooler said, after I asked how she was adapting to a new school. "It's like I don't belong with anyone." Isolation can feel as tough as academic failure.

But "friendship talk" is equally important for kids who find it easy to make friends. Kids can learn to use their social strengths "for good," to bring groups together and support outsiders, rather than exclude classmates or build cliques. Dialogue about how they and others act as friends lets kids learn to be flexible, adapting easily to different social situations. At times, they might want to conform to the group, while at others, they might want to highlight their quirks and individuality. Equally important, this dialogue raises their awareness of how they present themselves and relate to others. Having stronger friendships builds their confidence and makes it easier for them to reach out to those they don't know as well.[51] That's the key to closer connections and better social skills.

Social Talk Doesn't Have to Be Tough

Why don't we tend to think of helping kids make these moves? For one, we're busy, and our kids often are too. If a social problem doesn't come up, we don't always ask. We think kids will tell us if they're having trouble making friends. But kids are learning these skills in real time. They often don't know what they don't know; say, that their knock-knock jokes sound juvenile to their friends, or that their excited renditions of characters from *Diary of a Wimpy Kid* don't mean much to kids who haven't read the books. They might not know how to talk about friendship troubles. It can be hard to articulate when they're lonely or out of sync. As a result, they can end up isolated, even embarrassed. They can also start feeling bad about themselves. Many kids I've worked with describe friendship challenges as a personal failing.[52]

"It's my fault," one fifteen-year-old girl, Maria, told me in tears, after realizing she hadn't been invited to a party. "I sounded too eager when they mentioned the party. They all hate me." I was working with Maria twice weekly to help improve her reading comprehension. While she didn't have trouble reading the words on the page, she had quite a hard time understanding what she read. She struggled to make inferences, or draw conclusions when information or emotions weren't stated outright. Consider a simple example. You read in a story that a child's pet fish dies. The child goes out and stares at the sky for a long time. Then she comes in and says she doesn't want dinner. In that story, it's fair to assume that the child is sad about her fish dying, even though she never specifically said that she was.

Making those leaps was hard for Maria. She could recall the facts of a story but had trouble "reading between the lines," as Robby, back in Chapter 3, also did. As I soon realized, this trouble extended to social situations as well. She had many friends, but as she'd reached high school, her friends' conversations had grown more nuanced. There was more sarcasm and joking, and more left unspoken. As a result, Maria had been having a far harder time making sense of her interactions with her friends. She'd also grown more anxious and prone to worry. She'd begun to "catastrophize," a term psychologists use for jumping to the worst possible conclusion.[53] When her friends didn't invite her to the party, she immediately assumed that they all hated her, and that she was to blame.

In cases like Maria's, it's easy to groan and change the subject when she brings up her fears, or say, "Don't be silly. I'm sure your friends don't hate you." But avoiding conversation leaves behind the chance for her to feel validated. It can also worsen her anxiety, since her worry still isn't resolved. Many kids struggle with similar issues as Maria, especially in the preteen and teenage years, when much less is stated outright. Misunderstandings and miscommunications can cause drama and stress, especially when emotions (and hormones) run high.

Still, hovering over your kids or probing them about their social lives is only likely to backfire. Instead, try acting as a partner in reflection. While it's often far from simple, it *is* possible, especially if you build in enough silence and downtime. As your kids get more comfortable talking with you about personal topics, they're likely to express their feelings more easily. With a good dose of humor, humility, and self-compassion, you can grow closer in these years and—in the best of times—become a listener, mentor, and guide.

How Talk for Relationships Helps: The Three Es for Relationship-Building

When speaking with Maria, I used the Three Es, tweaked in this way:

1. *Expand*. Ask gently: "What's going on?" Clarify her version of the situation, as specifically as possible. Encourage her to recount what her friends actually said, rather than jumping to interpretations. Take breaks if you need to stay calm.

2. *Explore*. Why might your friend have said or done that? Give others the benefit of the doubt. With Maria, we discussed other potential reasons for the slight. I encouraged her to question that "everyone hates me" idea. She reflected on her many meetups over the past weeks. Maybe the friends didn't mean to be hurtful, she recognized. She'd talk to them.

3. *Evaluate*. After your child takes action, evaluate! What has she learned? As Maria later learned, her friend's mother had limited the guests to ten. The friend had picked guests within walking distance, so their parents wouldn't need to drive. While Maria still felt hurt, she saw her fear wasn't justified. Discussion helped her manage her self-talk. Without it, she might have avoided her friends—a vicious cycle that could lead to her feeling more rejected, and to her friends leaving her out more. Instead, she repaired the dynamic and, in the process, learned more about her friends' situations.

But what if the friends *had* meant to leave her out? That's no fun to hear, but even then, talking it out can help. With your support, she can think through whether the exclusion was part of a larger pattern, and if so, how she should respond. Does she need to confront her friends about it? Has the friendship become too one-sided? We often think of banning kids from seeing friends who aren't good for them. But in the case of toxic friendships not based on mutual support, kids need to come to their own conclusions.[54] If we do try to "ban" friendships, kids can end up feeling even *more* drawn to those friends, as forbidden fruit.

Talking with Maria reminded me how much kids of all ages can use help with perspective-taking skills.[55,56] While it may be easier simply to reprimand them or tell them, "You hurt your friend's feelings," that won't lead to much growth or change on their parts. Instead, imagine how much more they can learn when they reflect. Over time, they're more likely to notice when they label themselves negatively or start feeling bad about themselves. That lets them make conscious changes, shifting gears in the moment to feel more empowered, self-aware, and open to change.

Help Kids See Their Many Social Aspects

Kids don't always see themselves evolving. Over time, they may get into social ruts. If they behave in a certain way, their friends respond to that behavior, labeling them the "clown," the "shy kid," or the "pushover." Given those labels, kids often double down and act even more that way.

When I first started moving around for my clinical placements, I wasn't fully aware of how these ruts developed. Crisscrossing the neighborhoods outside of Boston—going from a middle school in Charlestown, to a clinic in Chelsea, to an elementary school in Winthrop—I met so many kids in a short period. These communities, vastly different in terms of the residents' backgrounds, revealed to me just how much diversity existed even within a thirty-minute drive.

At the middle school in Charlestown, an urban school right near a community college, most kids walked or took the subway home. Many spoke Spanish as a first language, and I wished I knew more than basic Spanish. At the Chelsea clinic, serving young children and their families, many of the community members were also native Spanish-speakers, and most of the clinicians were bilingual or trilingual. Many families had parents who worked multiple jobs to make ends meet, and some kids spoke of needing to share computers with siblings. And at the school in Winthrop, nestled close to the ocean, the population was almost entirely Caucasian and more affluent. Many families I met there had multiple computers and easy internet access. It was common for kids to go sailing or swimming on weekends.

Seeing kids from all these communities confirmed my understanding of how much their environments can shape their perspectives and routines. Firsthand, I saw the effects of systemic racism, inequality, and poverty on children's development. I also began to see how these larger inequalities impacted individual students, such as the students in poorer districts having far less access to school counselors. In one school, a student would be counseled about his problems, while in another, he'd be sent to detention with no chance to talk. These experiences were an education in themselves. Still, I often didn't see those kids for long enough to understand their own unique arcs or see how they evolved over time.

It wasn't until I'd worked at one high school for six months that I had a chance to see this evolution. For instance, Jeremiah, an eighth-grader, I knew as quiet and studious. With close-cropped brown hair and an easy smile, he had a few close friends and was a solid math student, even though reading was hard for him. In our sessions, in which we focused on reading comprehension and writing, he was reserved, but always polite. He consistently worked hard and tried his best, even as he told me that he felt embarrassed, even ashamed, to read out loud. But one day, I heard he'd been sent to the principal's office and would miss our session. Wanting to know more, I went to see him.

"He's such a behavior problem," a teacher said as I waited outside.

Inside, Jeremiah sat with his head slumped, staring at his shoes. Soon he told me what had happened: his classmate Brendan had a noticeable stutter. A few weeks back, Jeremiah had jokingly imitated him, and the class had laughed.

"They thought it was funny," he said, looking sheepish.

"And so what?" I asked.

"So I did it again."

Every morning, Jeremiah asked Brendan to say words he stuttered on, then made fun of him. Jeremiah's friends laughed and gave him attention. He kept it up even after his teacher told him to stop. This wasn't because Jeremiah and Brendan were enemies. In fact, as Jeremiah told me, "I *like* Brendan. He's a cool guy." Rather, peer pressure and Jeremiah's insecurity had pushed him to continue. Teasing had let him feel higher on the totem pole.

"I guess I'm just not a nice person," he said glumly.

I sensed he'd let his behaviors drive his self-talk, in a negative spiral that needed to shift.

. . . .

Principles for Social Talk

• *Be aspirational. Help kids* expand *on their best selves, focusing on social values. Highlight how they're already good friends and could do better. In the above example, I asked Jeremiah to clarify: How did he want friends to see him? Which qualities was he proudest of? Perking up, he told me he wanted to be seen as someone others looked up to and enjoyed being with. His older brother was his role model.*

"He's so cool," he said, "but he's still nice, and even lets me tag along to parties."

We used that comment as a starting point to describe qualities he wanted to cultivate. He brainstormed "fun-loving," "generous," "cool," and "nice." We pared it down to two qualities: "fun-loving" and "generous." Then we made a plan. Before acting, he'd think whether his actions would show those qualities. If not, he could try to act differently. If he messed up, he'd apologize or find a way to repair things. Think about these qualities as a North Star that kids can return to and can easily keep in mind.

Discussions about these ideal qualities are critical, especially in the teenage years, when kids can be thoughtful but impulsive. When we skip this step, we lose the chance to talk through why they'd want to act differently. Any change in behavior isn't likely to feel authentic, or to stick. But through reflection, kids can develop a vision of how they want to be. You can strategize together: the best recipe for making that vision a reality.

• *Discuss aspirations versus reality.* Explore *the discrepancies between how he thinks others view him and how he wants them to view him. As Jeremiah told me, he was unhappy that his classmates had started seeing him as a troublemaker and a clown. Taking a constructive mindset, I asked: How could he change? I asked him to describe his daily routine as specifically as possible. He described sitting beside Brendan and asking him to say "S" words (his "stutter" words), then smirking.*

"As soon as I sit down, it just happens," he said.

These ruts get started and maintained like many routines, often unconsciously. Noticing how a routine unfolds is the key foundation to making a change.

- *Help a child make changes, then evaluate how the changes went. At first, Jeremiah assumed he was stuck. But he could break the cycle, I suggested, and we explored how. Maybe he could start with something simple; say, choosing a different seat, or talking to someone else first. Then, instead of imitating Brendan, he'd simply say hello.*

  Afterward, he'd evaluate how he felt and how everyone responded, then consider his next steps. Focus on developing empathy and making repairs, with questions like "What might your friend need to feel better?" Jeremiah decided he wanted to apologize to Brendan but not in front of their mutual friends. Instead, he'd catch Brendan after school, chat, then apologize. Our conversation raised his self-awareness and helped him live up to his values while staying socially comfortable.

To support this self-awareness, encourage talk that explores your child's multiple social sides. Think about *how* and *why* he behaves as he does, and *where* and *with whom*. For instance, he might easily make friends during structured activities like tennis camp. But maybe he shuts down at parties or in activities where he doesn't know anyone.

When your child gives himself a negative label, say, "bad" or "mean," encourage him to remember times he's been a good friend or socialized easily. Link actions to descriptions. For example, "That was generous to share your toys without asking," or "That was gracious when you asked your friend about his mother feeling better." Making those links builds your child's ability to tie actions to behaviors, which supports him to do the same later on. That also lets him see he's complex, like all of us. Making negative choices doesn't mean he's fundamentally bad.

Help Kids Make Sense of Social Dilemmas

Seeing this complexity also means noticing times your child or others don't play by the social "rules." Think about social tendencies like a rubber band. Some pull can give a child a fresh perspective or let him adapt to new situations. Too much pull, or in the wrong direction, can cause the band to break. Of course, kids are resilient, but you get the idea. Encourage pulls that question your child's assumptions about himself. Maybe a "quiet" child can be the first to suggest an idea to his friends. Afterward, *evaluate* his feelings. How did his friends react?

Focus on what your child does well naturally. Susan David, author of *Emotional Agility*, told me of working with a boy who worried about making new friends at camp.[57] The boy loved strategy games and enjoyed planning every move, so she capitalized on that. Starting with kids he rode the bus with, and those whose personalities seemed similar to his, he planned out which kids he'd talk to first. That gave him control while suiting his natural style.

Other kids might need a more playful approach: say, deciding to join an in-progress game, or planning to meet one person at the playground. Emphasize trying out the pull in a relaxed way, having fun. He can always go back to the older way. If he says he's anxious, validate how he feels; for example, "It can feel stressful to be the new kid at the party." As the Yale psychologist Eli Lebowitz discussed with me, anxiety works differently for kids than for adults.[58] For kids, anxiety is social. They come to us for soothing, and we often respond by "fixing" things; say, skipping the party. We want to keep kids from feeling discomfort, but that doesn't help them build skills. Instead, as Lebowitz suggests, tell a child he can cope with some distress. Enlist friends, siblings, and teachers to give a similar message, supporting your child's attempts to stretch himself.

Expand on his expectations. Ask what he anticipates happening. Discuss who might be at the party and what he might say. Practice introductions. Explore strategies he's tried before. Try comments like "I bet other kids are also feeling nervous." That can help normalize your child's feelings and raise his self-awareness about how he feels.

The Social Pragmatics Dance

These social situations can be tough to navigate, especially if they're new—say, first party, first dance, or first interview. But really, any situation can come with social challenges, as friends' expectations change, or as your child develops and acts differently. Say, maybe he becomes more confident and starts telling jokes—only some of which go over well. You can help by reflecting on pragmatics, or the social use of language. "Pragmatics" means the words we use and *how* we use them: timing, tone of voice, and what's implied but not stated outright.[59] It has to do with understanding context—say, talking to a teacher rather than a friend—and managing conversations, such as deciding whether to stay on topic.

But if pragmatics is a dance, the floor matters. "I'll get you" can be terrifying if shouted by a stranger, or fun if you're playing a game. The *absence* of talk also requires pragmatic skills. Imagine, at a teacher conference, you ask, "How's Michael doing in math?" The teacher says, "His reading is coming along." The lack of a straight answer says a lot.

Kids develop skills in this dance as they grow, but the steps can be jolting. These skills, important as they are, are often late to develop. It's not as easy as it sounds to learn, for example, when and how to interrupt, how to take turns, and how to add to a conversation in a way that supports the flow rather than shutting it down.[60] Young kids, who haven't had as much practice as conversationalists, are prone to "breaking the rules," in ways that can be funny, irritating, upsetting, or all of the above. I recently heard two girls around seven years old in a toy store looking at dolls.

"This one's twenty dollars," one said. "My mom would never go for that."

"What, your mom's poor?" the second girl asked.

"I didn't say *that*."

Clearly, the second girl had made a big assumption based on the first girl's comment. Kids don't always mean to make such assumptions. They can speak impulsively, without realizing how their comments will be interpreted, or without the needed perspective-taking skills. I know many kids who have trouble noticing cues to change the subject or let someone talk. During a reading group one day, I sat with middle schoolers having a book discussion.

"How do you think the story will end?" I asked Brian, the quietest of the group.

"I know," his friend Xavier said.

"What does *Brian* think?" I asked pointedly.

Xavier barreled on, not noticing Brian's reddening face. Finally, after two more times, I asked Xavier to stop and pay attention to what Brian's facial expression and body language were telling him. While Brian might not have said what he was thinking, his upset was clear on his face. We took the time to notice these implicit signals and bring them into the conversation. Xavier said that Brian looked upset, and Brian said he was. I asked Brian to explain why he was upset.

"You never give me a chance to talk," Brian said to Xavier.

"Well, you never asked for one," Xavier said.

Their interaction opened the door for us to talk openly about the interactions of our group. We then discussed how we wanted turn-taking to happen, how much time each person should have to talk, and what we should do if we felt someone wasn't getting his or her fair share of airtime. The important thing wasn't making rigid rules. Instead, it was simply clarifying what we all wanted and needed in order to make the group function well. In this case, Xavier didn't need a lecture on turn-taking. He needed a clearer signal that he was preventing his friend from talking and was frustrating him.

Help Kids Master Social Pragmatics

More broadly, to support kids in this pragmatic "dance," try the following:

- **_Talk about expectations: What's the rule?_** Maybe your child doesn't know the expectations for a situation. This can happen especially when she goes somewhere for the first time. I remember going to my first classical music concert and clapping after the first song, only to hear laughter. That "song," I realized, was only the instruments being tuned. Before heading somewhere new, check in about what your child already knows. Make unspoken rules obvious; for example, if you see kids playing soccer, you wouldn't jump in to play immediately. Instead, you might ask if you can play, or wait on the sidelines to see if one of the teams could use an extra player.

- **_Talk about going against expectations: What's the cost?_** Maybe your child knows the expectations but chooses *not* to follow them. That may be awkward, but it's not always a negative. At times, it requires us to step back and let go. It's not because *we* want our child to behave in a certain way that he has to, or will. But it's important for him to recognize the cost. Maybe, if he doesn't follow the coach's directions, he'll get left on the sidelines. Focus on your child's long-term wants. Ask: How will the person probably respond? How do you feel about that? How do you want him to feel about you?

- **_Ask kids how they'd like to behave: What's your choice?_** Take a neutral stance. Help your child strategize, weigh possibilities, and make a choice. Maybe he wants to go with the flow, or maybe he doesn't mind the consequences. Discuss aligning his choice with his values, recognizing that those choices may change over time.

Role-Play with Humor

Role-playing, or imagining you and your child in the roles of other people and talking through a situation, can be a great chance to clarify social norms. This might mean imagining you and your child as a teacher and a student, or as a soccer coach and a player, or even as two classmates or friends. This role-playing allows you to take on hard, difficult, or nuanced topics in a relaxed and even playful way. It doesn't have to be boring or tedious. In fact, it can be far more engaging than having a lecture about the ways one should behave in any one situation.

I've often done this sort of role-playing with students, as have many of my colleagues. As inspiration, I've looked to the work of Michelle Garcia Winner, a speech-language pathologist and founder of the Center for Social Thinking. Her approach, initially focused on children with autism, emphasizes the need for "whole-body listening," or "listening with the eyes and brain."[61] In this way, you notice social cues actively and help kids pay attention to them. Garcia Winner focuses equally on helping kids make inferences when they hear sarcasm or jokes and on supporting them to understand others' perspectives. That work helps kids see the big picture about what they hear or read.

I've found her principles helpful in working with kids of all ages, and not only those with disorders. Often, kids don't know what they don't know, socially speaking. They may have blind spots, especially if they're entering new situations or new groups. For example, I've seen many kids struggle to keep up friendships when moving from elementary to middle school. They're no longer with a single group of friends, since they often change classes multiple times, and their conversations often involve more sarcasm or jokes. Conversations at these transitional times are key to helping them manage friendships and process big or conflicting emotions. The same goes for helping kids work through upcoming challenges, or times when they'll be trying something out for the first time. Role-playing can be a wonderful way to take on those challenges proactively, especially if you sense kids are worried or struggling.

My colleagues and I have focused especially on these role-plays with students who have trouble with language pragmatics and those who struggle to apply language skills in real time. That is, many kids might be able to tell you what you *should* do in any one situation, or what would be most effective—but when they actually get into that situation, they freeze. Role-playing can help you and your child pinpoint where they might run into trouble. You can then brainstorm strategies to make the interactions smoother. At the same time, this role-playing can help anxious kids prepare for potentially stressful or overwhelming situations. Instead of feeling they're facing the unknown, they can come to feel that a successful interaction is within their reach. The resulting conversation might not be easy, but the kids have gained a great sense of control. They feel better about themselves, and those around them tend to respond more positively.

You don't have to approach these role-plays as lectures or rules about "what should be done." In fact, you can take the opposite approach, at least at times. In a playful way, try going to the extreme of what should *not* be done. Depending on your child's personality, this can help them clarify and practice social norms in a pressure-free way.

I remember seeing this kind of role-playing in action with a colleague of mine, before I began doing it myself. One afternoon, I walked into my shared office to find my colleague sitting beside

"Lenore," a fifteen-year-old student, who was leaning back in her chair, smacking gum.

"I don't work on Fridays," Lenore said, looking bored. "And I want my phone with me at all times."

"We'll see about that." My colleague frowned. "We don't typically allow—"

"And I don't want to sign in," Lenore interrupted. "This isn't middle school, okay?"

Soon my colleague stopped the "interview," laughed at Lenore's acting, and started discussing how the *real* interview should go. In fact, Lenore had been role-playing the "worst" interviewee to prepare for upcoming internship interviews. My colleague had asked her to brainstorm "non-examples," or the opposite of what she should do, then play them out. They used each non-example as a springboard. Instead of talking about work she *wouldn't* do, Lenore would emphasize her strong work ethic. Rather than slouching, she'd sit up straight.

Letting kids see the effects of such "non-examples," in the feedback they receive and the impressions they give, can be far more effective than nagging them to "be nice." This unorthodox approach can help prepare kids for social challenges, especially when they feel nervous. Playing out ridiculous "non-examples" shows them they know far more about how to act than they think.

To Resolve Conflicts: Reflect After the Fact

Expanding on what kids already know supports them on many levels. Take conflict. Often, kids implicitly understand each other's wants and needs but have trouble putting that knowledge into practice, especially mid-argument. Reflection can't happen when kids are emotionally "hot." But wait until they've calmed down, and you have a chance to help resolve conflict, build empathy, and prepare them for the next time.

Certainly, conflicts don't feel good to have. Yet they often do offer opportunities. Last Valentine's Day, I brought home an enormous red velvet cupcake from an office party, planning to split it between the kids (not sure what I was thinking). But soon Paul whined, "Don't *cut* it! I need the *whole* thing!" After arguing, Sophie shouted, "Fine! He can have it all," and stormed off. After kicking myself for not having brought two cupcakes, I used a strategy from my clinical work, which I call Reflect, Brainstorm, Compromise:

- *Reflect* back each person's wants,

- *Brainstorm* solutions, and

- **Talk through** a possible *compromise*.

First, Reflect back. Encourage your child to articulate each person's wants and needs specifically. Use the Three Es. *Expand*: Who wants what? *Explore*: What's *behind* each person's desire? Go beyond his first response. Is he afraid his friend won't play fair, or he won't have enough? For siblings, emphasize stages of development. Ask: What does he or she understand? Try a compromise. Then *evaluate*: How well did it go? How satisfied was each person? What other strategies might be equally or more effective in the future?

With Sophie, I first validated her goodwill in letting Paul have the cupcake. Still, that didn't teach him the lesson he needed—and it wasn't fair to her. When I asked how she'd felt in the moment, she explained she was tired of hearing Paul cry and wanted to fix the problem.

"And I don't get to talk to you when he cries," she added.

I listened, then *reflected* her want back, assuring her that we all wanted dinnertime to be quieter. If it couldn't be, we'd find time to talk before bed. We *explored* Paul's want together. He usually did all right sharing. It was the *cutting* he didn't like. As we'd seen in past dinners, he liked having "the whole thing," even if it was tiny. If it had to be cut, *he* wanted to cut it, which I supposed let him feel more in control. With that in mind, we *brainstormed* solutions.

"We could just give him everything, right?" she asked.

I said he'd be happy in the moment, but what about over time? And what about her?

"He'd get spoiled," she said. "And I'd feel mad."

I then asked how *she'd* want to feel if she were him.

"That I got my fair share. Even if I was little."

"How could we help him feel that—but *also* learn?"

"Let him cut it in half," she said. "But let *me* choose my piece."

I agreed. While that wasn't a perfect solution, it was a start. It validated Sophie's "big sister" role while making sure her needs were met. It encouraged her to see Paul's behavior through the lens of his current stage. Even though he was learning, he couldn't act however he liked. Our compromise let him keep learning while not stepping on anyone's toes.

When Conflict Becomes Bullying

What about when conflicts aren't so simple? Ellen, a friend of mine and mom to eleven-year-old Mike, called me and said another kid, Quinn, was bullying Mike—pushing him against the lockers, stepping on his homework, even making him hand over money. This had been going on for weeks and was getting worse. Ellen asked his teachers to intervene. The teachers suggested that Quinn and Mike meet and talk, under their supervision.

"Do you think that'll work?" Ellen asked. She wasn't optimistic. Every time Mike had defended himself, Quinn only bullied him more, waiting until the teachers weren't looking.

In fact, conflict isn't the same as bullying. Bullying is repeated, aggressive conflict that involves a *power imbalance*, say, a popular against a less popular child. Sadly, it's surprisingly common. As of 2017, one in five school-age kids in the United States reported being bullied.[62] Cyberbullying, or using online technology as the means to bully (for example, posting embarrassing images or impersonating someone else in order to cause harm), has become even more problematic in recent years, and can be harder to catch.[63] One synthesis of studies found that 20 to 40 percent of children and teens reported cyberbullying, with girls at higher risk.[64] Another review found that the most common reason for cyberbullying was relationship issues, with girls most often on the receiving end.[65] This bullying can be devastating for kids and their parents. I've seen parents crying at school meetings, hurting because their children hurt. They often feel out of control, not knowing what to say or how to intervene.[66] The worst pain is of course for the children themselves. In addition to in-the-moment suffering, there are well-established links between being bullied and many short- and long-term mental health challenges, including moderate to severe depression, suicidality, and substance use.[67] Research has even found that consequences of bullying can affect some children until mid-life.[68]

To be fair, not all bullied children will develop mental health problems or experience long-term consequences. Still, with all this in mind, bullying should never be ignored.

So what about having kids "talk it out"? In fact, that's often counterproductive. The bullied child feels worse, and the bullying child becomes crueler. Instead, kids who are being bullied need to be protected. The bully needs to be stopped. It's when bullying becomes chronic that the effects are more likely to stay with a victim for years.[69] Ideally, preventing bullying takes a whole-school approach. Kids learn to speak out against bullies and become "upstanders," defending friends rather than standing by and saying nothing. Adults create a culture of respect. But all that takes time. In the meantime, what can you do?

With a bullied child, start by asking for details: *where*, *when*, and *how* the bullying happens. Support him to tell his teachers. Discuss his ideas about the best strategies to stop it. Follow up with his teachers to ensure they're taking action. Ask how they're handling it and how well that's working. Regularly *evaluate*, checking on how he feels. In addition, try the following:

1. *Expand on his self-talk.* If he's started feeling bad about himself, emphasize self-compassion, with the message that he did nothing to deserve this treatment. Focus on maintaining his sense of self-worth. Remind him that you're on his side and will help him through it. He won't have to defend himself alone.

2. *Explore* what the child who's bullying might be feeling. Typically, kids bully when lacking attention elsewhere. It's a learned behavior. While it shows a lack of empathy, it doesn't mean they're fundamentally "bad."[70,71] Hating a bully can feel natural. Still, encourage your child to realize bullies aren't typically happy and secure in themselves. The bully himself likely isn't doing well. Of course, you can't expect a child to empathize when he's hurting. But over time, empathizing lets

him see himself as more than a victim, which offers him a sense of control.

3. *Evaluate* deeper issues at play. As Denis Sukhodolsky, a professor at the Yale Child Study Center, argues, differences in development and learning need attention, for both bullies and bullied kids.[72] A bullying child needs to understand bullying is wrong. He may need support managing anger and noticing nonverbal cues. Issues such as ADHD may be contributing. Yes, he's hurting others, but he may need help as well.

Even a child without any bullying problems can benefit from discussions about standing up for friends. When a bullying child sees others opposing him, he often stops. Through being an "upstander," your child learns what it means to be an ethical and moral person. That courage will serve him, now and later. He'll be a better friend and reap the rewards of knowing he's done the right thing.[73] More broadly, try these conversational habits:

Conversational Habit #1: Storytelling Conversations

To help kids take other perspectives flexibly: Focus on *storytelling conversations*. These stories don't need much: only one or more characters, a place, and a problem. You describe a problem or conflict from beginning to middle to end, exploring how a person tried to meet her goals, how she felt, and how she did or didn't change. Reason through strategies, letting your child see that not everyone thinks or solves problems the same way. Start with your own life and everyday situations.

For example, say that morning you couldn't get your car to start. "At first, I turned the ignition on, and nothing happened," you might say. "I was so frustrated. Finally, I checked the oil and saw it was too low. I was able to fix it then, and I ended up feeling better. I was able to do more than I thought."

- *Give me people, a place, and a problem.* I often encourage kids to play storytelling games, especially if they don't want to talk about themselves. These games help kids consider characters, feelings, and motivations in a fun, nonthreatening way.
  - *Try out:* "Give me three characters, a setting, and a problem." Or, for younger kids: "Tell me three animals or people, a place, and a problem." Especially with younger kids, show them an example, then give them a chance to try.
  - For example: "The characters are a policeman, a garbageman, and a teacher. The place is school. The problem is the lights aren't working." Maybe the policeman checks the switch, the teacher searches for bulbs, and the garbageman opens the trash. The policeman feels upset to be missing work. The teacher is frustrated because she can't teach. The garbageman is glad for a break. Finally, the lights go back on. Turns out, a storm had cut the electricity. While the garbageman is annoyed, the others are relieved.

To challenge negative social talk: Use action-focused language: Notice when your child uses a negative label about herself or someone else ("I'm such a bad friend"; "She's mean"). Emphasize growth and the possibility of change. Remind her of how she acted oppositely at other times. If she's arguing with her sister, remind her, "You helped her with her homework yesterday." Focus on specific actions. "I didn't say hello to the new girl" and "She stole my friend's toy" are more objective descriptions than "I'm shy" or "She's rude." These leave room to explore how and why the person acted as she did, without playing a blame game. You might find there's a good reason for the other person's behavior. At the very least, your child will gain practice in taking an empathetic perspective.

Try out *redemptive moves,* or discussing the positive effects of working through challenges. Without minimizing hardship, explore the learning or growth that results from tough experiences. Maybe being cut from the basketball team led a child to practice drills with friends, or failing a test led her to connect with more studious classmates. Encourage her to try those moves with friends. When she hears that classmates were sad to miss a trip, help her validate their sadness while also looking for any positives Ask: "What good came out of that?" or "What ways could you make it better for your friends?"

Conversational Habit #2:
Play the Believing Game

Imagine the story behind a person behaving oddly or badly. Give the benefit of the doubt. Maybe the child sobbing at the library is sad because someone checked out her favorite book. Maybe the scowling teenager in the grocery store wishes he were out playing soccer. Emphasize playing what Peter Elbow refers to as the "believing game," or being open to and welcoming of many ideas.[74] Tell compassionate stories about others' wants and needs.

Discuss "bad behavior" as signs that kids need to grow. Turn "she's terrible at sharing" into "she hasn't learned to take her turn," or "she's such a bad climber" into "she's working on getting past the second rung." Emphasize that all kids are developing, and all of us (adults included) will make mistakes.

Model how we're all works in progress, socially, and that's all right. Teach a three-part strategy when kids see someone upset, or when they've hurt someone: "Sorry. Are you okay? How can I help?" That shows empathy and a desire to help—in a way that suits each person specifically.

Use books and movies to explore characters and conflicts. Focus on *spoken* versus *unspoken* motives, the difference between "what he says he wants" and "what he really wants." Maybe a friend says he wants to win a science competition, but really, he wants to beat his rival. Imagining both options helps kids understand their friends more deeply and respond to their authentic wants and needs.

Focus on humanizing language. Move away from "those people" or "that group" and toward more specific, objective language. Instead of "the mean girls," encourage talk about "Jeanne and Jasmine, who were tattling on my other friend." Help a child get beyond sweeping judgments about whole groups and focus on what's really happening. Often, there's far more nuance than what kids see at first.

There's a reason why, at the end of life, many people mention a top regret as not staying in touch with their friends.[75] In our everyday busyness, it's easy to set aside friendship, or simply forget to keep up with those we care about. As adults, we start losing friends, as one study found, at age twenty-five; a decline that continues until retirement. But focusing on friendships and other relationships can help kids—and us—slow down and reprioritize. Through quality conversations, we can help kids take others' perspectives in a way that lets them connect and relate more easily. Even conflict can deepen friendships, if we use dialogue to work through it and clarify what each person needs. Through reframing friendship challenges and dilemmas as chances to reflect, we can help kids shift their perspectives. They become more open to repairing rifts and building new ties. Over time, as these strategies come more easily, kids are more likely to find the fun that long-term friendships allow in the moment, and the health and well-being that they bring. Keep in mind that these talks take time. Friends don't develop over the course of one conversation, or one day. In the words of the Greek philosopher Aristotle, "Wishing to be friends is quick work, but friendship is a slow-ripening fruit."[76,77,78]

CHAPTER 6

Conversations for —and Through—Play: Promoting Your Child's Joy and Creativity

The most fruitful and natural play of the mind is in conversation. I find it sweeter than any other action in life.
—MICHEL DE MONTAIGNE[1]

The first time I heard the comment, I didn't think much of it: "My teacher doesn't want me to waste time playing. She wants me to do my work."

It was Friday afternoon at an elementary school, the day before winter break. The air filled with the sounds of kids practicing songs for a musical down the hall, and the smell of gingerbread from a cooking party a parent had set up outside. My work was part of a model known as Response to Intervention, in which we give increasing support to students, depending on how well they are or aren't progressing in their academic work.[2,3] Students can move from having no support—being in the general education classroom—to taking part in extra small group lessons, and then to additional lessons given one-on one. Ideally, this model works like a conversation, adjusting to students' needs as we go.

In this school, I was responsible for collaborating with teachers to assess children's language and learning needs. Based on what I found, I advised the teachers to work with some children in small groups, and I worked directly with the highest-need students.

I enjoyed this work in part because it let me toggle into and out of the classroom. Over weeks and months, I got to know students individually and see how they behaved in class. As I saw them interact with other students and their teachers, I began to pick apart which situations brought out their best sides and which dampened them. On this particular Friday, Josie, a fifth-grade student, and I were working on an essay she'd been assigned. As she had trouble getting started, I'd asked her to brainstorm ideas on a whiteboard. We'd play around with them, I said, not wanting to pressure her. She'd struggled with anxiety for years. Recently, she'd had been shutting down in class, saying she didn't know what to say whenever her teachers called on her.

But Josie had no time for playing, she told me. She wanted to get the work done.

"But the play will *lead* to the work," I said.

"I said it's a waste of time." Josie gave a preteen sigh. "Can't you just tell me what to write?"

I couldn't do that, but we could try another way, I said. She agreed, but without conviction, and we set to work outlining her ideas. When we ended, she seemed relieved. As the day wore on, I convinced myself it was bad timing—no one likes working before break—and that she'd return with more motivation after the holidays. I told myself it was her anxiety keeping her from feeling playful. When she felt more relaxed, she'd have an easier time.

But as the months went on, I realized that Josie's comment about "wasted time" wasn't an isolated one. Indeed, I started hearing echoes of that attitude everywhere. Often, it had to do with how kids approached learning. "I made up this song to learn the times tables," one third-grader told me, "but my mom says just look at the sheet." Another child showed me her vocabulary list, then said, "I have to memorize them. There's no point using them in sentences. That's playing around."

"Play" and "learning," I began to see, were on two opposing sides—at least that's how kids and teachers often talked. As I started observing younger kids, I saw this opposition even more clearly. I often went into a classroom with the purpose of understanding how a child with a potential learning challenge performed in class. However, I couldn't help noticing all the other kids as well. What I saw was often sobering. So often, even in classrooms with young kids, I saw play happening only on the sidelines. I saw kindergartners bouncing in front-facing chairs, worn out by the tedium of sitting still, or answering questions that didn't much engage them. "What day is it?" the teacher asked, pointing at a calendar. "Thursday or Friday?"

"It's a firefly," one of the kids whispered, running to the window.

"No, a *dragonfly*," a second child responded, peering at it with cupped hands.

"It's Friday, Friday," the other kids chanted, following the teacher's song.

"Come on back, okay?" the teacher asked the kids at the window.

Most of them groaned, but one—the most rule-following—told the others, "Stop *messing around*."

Play, I sensed, was a distant thing, a shining beacon they waited till recess to find. Even those recesses were twenty-minute affairs; hardly enough time to put on jackets and make it outside before the bell rang and they returned, glum-faced and still bustling with energy. They had no time to discover dragonflies or anything else—or even talk much to their friends. That shortened playtime reflected the national average. It wasn't even as extreme as some schools, such as those in Gadsden City, Alabama, which cut kindergarten nap time in favor of more "instructional time."[4] That's a sad irony, at a time when even the American Academy of Pediatrics has released a statement, as of 2013, arguing that the downtime of recess helps kids learn and is a "crucial and necessary component of a child's development."[5]

In fact, downtime—and even nap or rest time—can benefit children of all grades. Research has linked more sleep to better well-being and even higher intelligence. As one study of nearly three thousand Chinese children from ages ten through twelve found, children who napped three times a week were found on average to be happier, have more self-control and grit, and have fewer behavior problems than those who didn't nap. They also did better in school. While such studies show only links and not causes, it's worth considering whether a child who seems unmotivated may be simply overtired.[6]

Not letting kids play, on the other hand, can lead to other problems. When we take away playtime, few kids can sit and pay attention. They simply have too much energy. That's especially true if their schools take a traditional approach to learning, where kids sit at desks and listen to a teacher. We often think more is more— more instruction, more time sitting—forgetting that play is *the* foundational way of learning, and of learning to be in the world, for kids long past the early years. I've seen so many young kids stymied in their play that I'm reminded of the recent maxim "Preschool is the new kindergarten, and kindergarten is the new first grade." As Erika Christakis argues in her 2016 book *The Importance of Being Little*, play has little role in this push for academics, even as studies show that the most profound learning arises from discovery and from the trial and error associated with play.[7,8]

In the months after seeing those kindergartners, I started wondering: How *were* kids playing? I started observing more closely. Often, I found, play was separated by sex, especially for younger kids. The girls had their Barbies, squishy toys, scented stickers, and locking diaries. The boys had their fireman hats and dinosaur costumes, salvaged from Halloweens past, and swords and Transformers ("the pink ones are for girls," one four-year-old told me, when I offered him one). I was startled to see how early on traditional gender stereotypes were being perpetuated. When I took Sophie to the toy store, I was even more surprised at how rigidly these stereotypes were on display, with "boy" and "girl" aisles, packed with robots and battleships on one side, and princesses and toy ponies on the other. As sociologist Elizabeth Sweet has noted, toy companies began this intensive gender segregation and marketing in the 1980s, and since 2000 have intensified the push, making assumptions by leaps and bounds about what kids might want.[9]

To be fair, the older kids I saw had traveling sports teams, fantasy football, screens and consoles, online solitaire, and rock-climbing trips. But for so many kids and parents I spoke with, play—and playful attitudes—was sidelined, as we focused far more on achievement and getting ahead.

Yes, we want kids to succeed, be empathetic and confident, and have friends. We'd also like to raise creative kids who know how to laugh, who don't take themselves too seriously, and who can connect joyfully. We want them to play well with others and by themselves. And we'd like playing with our kids to be fun for *us*, at least occasionally. To get there, we need to think through what play really is, and realize the powerful role it can have in all our lives.

Play Is an Attitude

What comes to mind when you hear the word "play"? For most of us, the answer has to do with games: sports or board games, video games or tag. There's an activity with rules, which you can choose to follow or not. You might play Monopoly the "real" way or the "cheater's" version (which you can actually buy), selectively bending the rules. Or you might think of kids playing in the sandbox or climbing a tree: *unstructured play*, without predetermined rules.[10] As a concept, play can feel fuzzy, or idyllic, bringing up visions of clambering through open fields or shooting marbles, 1950s style, in someone's backyard. The idea feels connected to a happy childhood, as if childhood and play are completely intertwined.

In truth, play can look totally different depending on age and stage. Consider a child playing field hockey, a teenager playing chess, a ten-year-old inspecting a science project, a toddler building a tower, or an infant examining his toes. In an ideal world, play lets a child be in control. Driven by curiosity, he explores. According to Stuart Brown, founder of the National Institute for Play, play is anything "done for its own sake" that leads to greater mastery. It needs to be challenging, but not *so* much as to frustrate you. In Brown's ideal, play should be *pleasurable*, or fun; *intrinsically motivated*, so you don't need a reward; and *process-oriented*, so you're not worried about the outcome.[11] It's less about winning or losing and more about the road. I've been surprised to see Paul building a complex Lego structure, only to say, "I'm done," or "Let's destroy it," and knock it down. He's like many young kids, lost in the time-lessness of the moment, building sandcastles over and over, each time letting the sea snatch them away.

That kind of construction play *is* vital to a child's development. The same goes for guided play, or play in which we share in children's play, offering new words and concepts as we go. Your child directs his play and has fun with it; you're there to provide gentle guidance.[12] For example, your preschooler shakes a box with beads inside and says, "It's loud." You agree, then encourage him to shake it harder and see how the sound changes. Or maybe you support him to make a pattern of louder and quieter sounds, or you ask what shape he thinks the beads might be, then open the box to see if he's right. This type of play has been found to boost language learning and early learning about shapes as well as children's abilities to multitask and plan.[13]

But if we think of play as an *activity*, we're only seeing a fraction of its potential. Instead, consider play as an *attitude*. It's about being open to tinkering and testing, to brainstorming and trying again, without anxiously worrying about being right.[14,15] This playful attitude lies at the root of creativity and brings out the best in kids. It's actually less about what you're doing, and more about how you or they *approach* an activity or task.

Say you're out for a bike ride. You might be playfully enjoying yourself, or doing it only for exercise. When kids are playful, they can have fun without needing a lot of stuff. A garbage pail can become a toy truck, or a cardboard box can be cut up and turned into a video arcade.[16,17,18]

As a family, a playful attitude can bond you, letting you relax and resolve conflicts more easily. It can help kids approach even tough challenges positively. When kids think playfully, they're less likely to moan, as I've heard students do, "I just can't *do* it." They'll test a new way.

Playful thinking and learning are driven by children's interests and questions, and connect meaningfully to their lives.[19] When they enjoy activities and find them relevant, they're more engaged and reflective. They notice if they need a new approach and shift gears. They try harder and persist longer, because they're genuinely interested. Consistently working through failures leaves them more resilient. As they succeed with experiments or get questions answered, they grow more independent and confident.[20] A playful attitude can make the difference between kids following through on projects versus dropping them because they're overwhelmed.

What's disturbing is how quickly this attitude disappears, replaced by the anxious need to succeed or get things right. Play starts getting murky pretty fast. What about a child crying because he *has* to play soccer? Or fearing, if he doesn't win, his team won't advance to the finals? He's likely not having fun. He's motivated by pressure, not love of the sport, and he's quite worried about the outcome. He might be "playing," but it's far from that play ideal.

Why Play Matters

For kids, that ideal play matters. In fact, play is essential to the development of their brains and one of the most powerful ways to learn about themselves and the world.[21] When kids engage in free play—play with rules they invent or adopt themselves—and negotiate complex social interactions, their brains build new circuits in the prefrontal cortex, the part of the brain that supports planning and impulse control.

More broadly, play offers nutrition for both body and mind. It's not only fun, it also lets kids process big emotions, connect authentically, repair arguments, and soothe hurt feelings. Talking through emotions helps them marry "thinking" and "feeling," as they imagine *why* characters feel as they do.[22] When Paul says, "The dog was sad to be sick," he connects a feeling with a situation. When he adds, "I get sad when I'm sick, too," he identifies and verbalizes his own feelings. Over time, such talk helps kids recognize and label emotions: the first steps in understanding their feelings and learning to manage them in healthy ways.[23]

Play is equally key for social bonding. In play, kids build alliances, make and strengthen friendships, and build capacities to tolerate the unknown. How do they react when a friend wants to play house, not rocket ship, or when the bridge they've spent hours building collapses? In play, they can apologize in silly or exaggerated ways, showing they're sorry without losing face.

Finally, play promotes deep and expansive thinking like nothing else. In pursuing questions through tinkering, kids lay the foundation for the creative thinking they'll need to solve complex problems in later years.[24] Even a young child can develop deep questions through pouring water into buckets or twisting strings. I love to study the play of young kids especially. I imagine their questions forming in real time, bubbling up as they tinker and test. One summer day, I sat with a group of three-year-old girls at a playground, where they were running around a sprinkler, using buckets to collect water, and putting stems into the stream flowing down the steps. After dropping the stems in, they raced to the steps, then watched intently as the stems sailed down and settled in a muddy pool. They gathered the stems up, smearing them in their hands, before setting the mess of stems and mud into the sprinkler again.

"More flowers," one girl called, gathering some, as another shouted, "More mud."

In such moments, I have seen how easily young kids engage in flow. Flow is the experience of being so focused on an activity that you're immersed and lose track of time.[25] There's no multitasking, only the immersion in that single-minded question or pursuit. In a world where we, and our kids, are so often distracted, simply making the time for flow is a worthwhile goal.

But play's potential goes far beyond that. There's a reason why many Nobel-winning scientists have had "aha" moments when staring at water beads in a stream, or watching light flicker on the window, or taking long walks through the woods. These moments allow for the quiet out of which deeper thought comes, and for the kind of attentive attitude that helps a child explore the "whys" of the world. Pursuing questions through play fires up curiosity and scientific thinking: How many pokes does a leaf need to fly off a branch? What direction do dandelion seeds scatter when you blow—and why? Why can't you *see* seeds as they fall to the ground?

It's not only about pursuing questions in nature. Think about even the simplest of video games. Say, what happens if I push this character to the right? Will he fall? And does that dragon only breathe fire, or does he spit gold coins if you catch him? These questions are more premade than those you find in nature—but that doesn't make them any less fun to explore.

Over time, as a child's questions develop into deeper ones, she starts noticing what most intrigues her, which lets her pursue her interests more effectively. As seven-year-old Sophie told me, "I really like science stuff. How the body works. How stars get made. You know—mysteries!" As questions and interests evolve, kids start finding their passions, without the anxious need to tie themselves down. Maybe an interest in stars will lead to studying astronomy, or a love for knitting will blossom into an interest in fashion. It's not that young kids need to think about their future careers. In fact, it's the opposite; immersion in the moment is key. And, over time, it's about letting interests deepen and evolve, and letting curiosity flourish.

That curiosity is clearly on display during imaginative play, where kids invent scenarios and characters. One morning recently, Paul brought an empty Lego ice cream store structure to his face and asked, in a serious voice, "What would you like? Chocolate chip or vanilla? Or hot dog- or pickle-flavored?" When I asked if he had coffee flavored, he laughed and suggested cactus-flavored instead. This kind of back-and-forth is key to building language and social skills. It supports mental flexibility, as kids change roles and invent ideas on the fly. It also links to longer-term creativity.[26,27] In one study, it was discovered that obviously creative people, such as Nobel Prize winners, spent more time playing make believe games as children than a control group had.[28]

The Play-Creativity Link

But creativity seems to be decreasing in kids, especially the youngest. In 2010, in a series of studies, Kyung Hee Kim at the College of William and Mary analyzed the results of more than 300,000 creativity tests over the past thirty years. Since 1990, she found, kids have become less able, on average, to generate unique and unusual ideas. They're also less funny—as far as a study can evaluate—and less able to elaborate on their ideas.[29] Why? It's easy to say "kids these days" aren't as innovative as those in the past. Maybe they were born that way. But that doesn't make a lot of sense. Really, kids are born with an innate creative drive. It's more that, according to the University of Oregon psychologist Ron Beghetto, their creative drive can be either nurtured or suppressed.[30,31]

Since I started working with kids more than a decade ago, I've noticed an increasing trend for them to freeze in the face of creative assignments. This is certainly true for older kids, but even for kids who were a long way off from AP classes or college prep.

"Is that fiction or nonfiction?" a fifth-grade girl once asked when I introduced a poetry unit with a prompt on where you'd like to travel. "I don't think we've covered that yet." When I explained that she was supposed to use her imagination, she said she didn't like to imagine places she hadn't been.

"It just feels awkward." She smiled uncomfortably. "I don't know the facts. And I don't like starting from a blank page."

Her comment echoed the experiences of many kids I've worked with, who do fine when given a multiple-choice test or asked to fill in the blanks, but who struggle to brainstorm or start from scratch. There's an anxious need floating through so many kids to get things right immediately. That need only gets worse when we don't make the time for encouraging creative play, and the open-ended, generative talk that often comes along. Think about asking questions rather than answering them, and of brainstorming freely rather than feeling paralyzed or shut down. Strengthening their asking and brainstorming muscles through play is key to nurturing creativity in kids.

materials. The more you pile up, the harder it is to see the chance for playful thinking hidden underneath.

I saw this principle in action a few weeks back. After dinner, Sophie and Paul went into a dark room with a flashlight they'd found in a toolbox. It was the end of a long Sunday, after they'd exhausted their toys and argued enough that they were bored of arguing. Soon, Paul stretched out his arms, making the shadows of his fingertips touch the ceiling.

"It's a chicken dance," he said, and they both laughed. After transforming their shadows into "giants," they took out a stuffed toy beach house and threw the giants a beach party. After playing for a while, they sat in silence. I thought of bringing out more toys or books, but, seeing how engaged they were, I asked how they could make their shadows smaller.

"Like this?" Sophie stepped away. "No, that's bigger. Let me try again."

"Or can you make it touch the window?" I added. "Or disappear?"

"Can we make our shadows hit?" Sophie asked. They crashed, then collapsed, giggling.

"What changed the size of your shadows?" I asked Sophie.

"We were farther from the light," she said, then: "No, from the *wall*." Paul flicked the flashlight on, then asked why his shadow didn't "work" anymore.

"It's because there's no darkness," Sophie replied, bringing him to a darker room.

If it hadn't been for their boredom, this play would never have happened. The same for if I'd followed my initial urge to bring out more toys. It was through finding a new way to play with an old thing, and expanding on their initial ideas, that let them get truly immersed.

Intensive Parenting Pushes Play Off

That scene also reminded me of the importance of stepping back as parents and simply noticing. Especially with younger kids, we often assume we need to be constant playmates, always "on." We sit in the sandboxes or beside the Lego bins. When we talk, it's often with streams of commentary: "Is that a doggie?" "Is that the blue one?"

Yes, talking like that builds vocabulary. But, if we make it a habit, it doesn't allow for the interior thought and self-talk kids need to verbalize plans or let simple questions simmer into deeper ones. It's also exhausting. Play becomes yet another parenting duty, not an outlook and practice to encourage in kids. That duty is echoed by many parents I know, who feel the need to get and *stay* involved—and make sure everyone's having fun.[37,38] So what if we're resentful or worn out? Isn't that inevitable?

Worse, when we're always "on," kids and parents alike can end up frustrated. Especially young kids are drawn to doing the same tasks over and over. Repetition boosts learning and feels inherently satisfying. But, as a result, their play *can* seem endless and tedious. Constantly watching means we're bound to get bored. The same goes for turning play into teachable moments: labeling objects, teaching colors, asking, "How many go there?" It's not that we shouldn't ask questions. But when those questions crowd out the chance to explore, the point of play gets lost.[39]

Play is supposed to be pleasurable. But when we see it as a burden, we tend to act inauthentically. We're bored but try to project excitement. Kids notice pretend emotions. They want our real selves to show up and enter into a conversation about their play. They want to be observed and noticed (a toddler's nonstop "watch me!"), and to have ideas commented on. They want our talk to *see* them, stretch and challenge them, and at least occasionally, view them with delight. This challenge starts with *their* big ideas; say, "How could I get this dinosaur to fly?" That's a far more interesting and complex question than "What color is it?"

The same goes for the play of older kids. We don't always see kids' flow experiences for what they are, or talk in ways that value them. Video games are one clear example. Many parents I speak with see them as a waste of time or a drain on kids' mental health. Really, the research isn't clear.[40,41] There are potential downsides, such as gaming being linked to kids being more aggressive.[42] But even that link is far from certain. One study of the long-term effects of violent video game playing found no evidence of lowered empathy, or even brain responses that might underlie such changes.[43]

In fact, gaming may help kids multitask and even boost cognitive skills. Many games encourage kids to take on new roles, imagining themselves as a knight or a soldier, or building imaginary worlds. Still other games, such as Fortnite, ask kids to collaborate to collect resources, save survivors, and defend equipment. While the rules are predetermined, there's no doubt that the role-playing and strategizing does exercise their "play muscles" and encourage them to think of many possibilities. Some early research suggests that certain "pro-social" video games, designed with collaboration and joint problem-solving in mind, may actually increase perspective-taking skills.[44]

The Play Battleground

What's more concerning than the games themselves is how fear-based our talk becomes. In 2017, a national Pew study found that

65 percent of adults in the US believed that video games contributed to gun violence.[45] Such fears constrain our conversations, causing kids to feel they can't talk about gaming or have to hide it. When that happens, we lose out on the chance to help them process what they're seeing. Too often, our talk becomes a battleground.

This battleground isn't limited to gaming. It also tends to come up around questions of organized sports. On the one hand, sports are obviously healthy. They offer a physical outlet and the chance to learn teamwork. They're also simply fun. But in recent years, there's been a push for kids to specialize in a single sport year-round, at ever-younger ages. I've met many parents worried that their kids haven't "picked" a sport at age ten or eleven. They'll be more successful, goes the idea, if they focus on what they're best at.

But early specialization wears many kids out. As a study of more than 12,000 kids showed in 2018, it increased the risk of injury for both boys and girls. Emotionally, kids feel the burden of too-high expectations and often quit or burn out. In one study, early-specializing kids were the first to quit their sports and were *less* physically active as adults.[46] Starting early isn't even necessary for success in college sports. On average, one study found, college athletes didn't specialize until age fifteen.[47]

What's more, having kids specialize early changes our talk. Often, we emphasize doubling down on what kids are already good at, or focus on skills that seem to come naturally to them. Many kids focus more on pleasing their coaches and us than on developing skills. If they fail even once, their self-talk can turn negative. Their self-worth gets tied up with their last loss or win. These kids especially need a reframing of play.

So what does this reframing look like? It starts with focusing on that playful attitude.

Play—and Playful Thinking—Both Count

It was 7:30 in the morning, in a classroom on the campus of Michigan's Grand Valley State University, and I—never a morning person—was wide awake. I was taking part in a nationwide competition known as the Science Olympiad, where high school kids gathered for countless events: identifying tree species, testing machines to shoot tennis balls into cans, and navigating landscapes using only a compass. My event, known as "Write It, Do It," involved putting one child in a room with a complicated structure, and another child in a second room with that same structure taken apart and all the pieces piled in a box. The goal was for the first child—the "writer"—to offer precise directions so the second child—the "doer"—could correctly build the structure in a specified time frame. Afterward, the judges awarded points for each correct element and deducted points for mistakes. The winner was the one with the highest score.

The morning of my event, I sat in a row alongside a dozen kids my age, each with a stack of lined paper, a pencil, and an odd contraption constructed of Lego and Styrofoam. I stared at the contraption: six inches tall, a foot wide, round as a sun, with irregular rays. Dozens of popsicle sticks dotted it randomly, along with stickers, star-shaped beads, even potato chips. *What a mess.* All around me, kids were scribbling busily. A shiver ran up my spine. An hour to go, and I hadn't started. My partner, the "doer," was sitting in a room down the hall. She'd be furious if she got a blank piece of paper.

Sensing my mind freezing up, I breathed deep and shut my eyes. For a second, I stopped worrying about my partner or about winning, and started to think. How could I paint the most accurate picture—and fast? *Look for a pattern.* I bent in.

Reeking of craft glue, the thing didn't look remarkable. But then I saw it: the popsicle sticks had been arranged in the shape of a smiley face, with two potato chips for eyes. *A smiley face. That's the key.* The rush of finding a pattern, which I knew from weeks of practicing, filled me. Hurrying back to my desk, I put pen to paper and started to write.

Looking back, I found this event meaningful, not only because of the cheese hats and metal pins I collected at the precompetition meet-and-greets. Rather, it served as inspiration for what writing could do. All I had was a pencil, paper, and a strange object. Out of that, I had to create the most precise description. Drawing was forbidden. I had to rely on words.

At the same time, this event reminded me how play—and playful thinking—is all about our attitude. It was a competition, with a "winner" and "loser" outcome. This very contrived situation didn't seem to lend itself to play. Indeed, as I heard kids filing out afterward, I realized many had experienced the time very differently than I had.

"I failed," one moaned, searching for his parents. "I took too long with the first part, and I never got to the potato chips."

"Who cares?" another asked, looking sour. "This is stupid. My mom made me come."

Behind them, two younger kids jumped around, trading high-fives.

"That's first place for sure!" one told the other. "We'll get the pizza party after all."

For the first-place kids at least, play wasn't *pleasurable*, or fun. They focused on an external reward—the pizza party—not their own motivation. They emphasized the outcome—getting first place—not the process. Using Brown's definition, this "play" wasn't

play at all. And while I'd found myself in their position on countless occasions, this time was different. In the midst of that competition, I'd managed to take a playful approach. Brainstorming
options, I wondered, "Should I try this way? Or that?" I let myself
forget the question of winning and losing, and simply explored.
And I found myself having far more fun than usual.

Playful Conversations
Supercharge the Imagination

Fostering this playful attitude doesn't have to be difficult. In fact,
it starts with the simplest conversations about nature and the world
around you: in real life, and in stories and books.[18] Seeing a cloud,
you imagine a ship or a dinosaur. Seeing a pile of bricks, you start
constructing a rocket. You don't need to fly to Michigan—or anywhere. But so often, we forget to take the time for these small
imaginings. Instead, we often mistake play for a problem, as kids
seem distracted, or worse.

Several years back, I spoke to a kindergarten teacher about one
student, five-year-old Brett. Both she and Brett's parents were concerned that he wasn't learning at the same pace as his peers. He
also often ignored his friends, not responding when they called his
name. And during class Brett was constantly off-task: wandering
around and even occasionally walking into walls.

"Do you think he needs glasses?" I asked. His parents had already
had his vision and hearing checked, the teacher explained—and attention deficit disorder had been ruled out. Frustrated and stumped,
she told me his mother described similar problems at home.

When I met him one-on-one, I asked him what he thought was

happening. Brandishing a pretend sword, he jumped from his seat. "I pretend I'm in the Gobi Desert," he told me. "I shut my eyes and feel the wind whipping, and imagine riding on a camel."

"Really." I hadn't expected *that*. "Where did you hear about the Gobi Desert?"

"A documentary." He grinned. "I've watched it six times. I can repeat every word."

"I bet." How easily we leap to conclusions. He didn't have attention problems; he was simply immersed in his imaginative world. He needed talk that valued his play but also let him know when he'd be better served by turning his mind to other things.

Principles for Pretend Play: Use the Three Es

To support Brett, I first asked him to *expand* on his scenario, bringing in all his senses. What did the desert feel and sound like? How did it smell? Were there others with him? Had he ever been to a desert in real life? How did he feel when he thought about it?

Soon after, I helped him *explore*, validating his strong imagination. I asked him to flesh out his scenario, making it even richer. He imagined himself as a character in the Gobi Desert, among a group of travelers. We discussed three kinds of conflicts: conflict with other people, with nature, and with yourself. What kind of conflicts might he face? Excitedly, Brett told me that his fellow travelers argued about water, then met robbers they had to fight. They felt terrified but had to stay strong—and eventually, they made it to their destination.

At the same time, we *evaluated* when his imagination was working for, rather than against, him. I asked: When did his imagining distract him, stop him from socializing, or even get him injured? We decided, when he found himself "in the desert," he'd look around for signs he needed to rein it in. Was a teacher calling him, or a friend asking to play? Together, we developed two mantras: either "tone it down" or "turn it up." "Tone it down" meant shut off the scenario, at least for the moment, while "turn it up" meant free rein to delve into his made-up world. Such talk raises a child's self-awareness while giving you a window into his imaginative life. In the daily rush, many kids don't share what they're really thinking. Having this window lets you bond more deeply as you get to know him better. At times, you may find yourself truly surprised.

This surprise can also come through exploring and expanding on kids' in-the-moment play, rolling with ideas as they unfold. I saw this process in action a few weeks back. After dinner, Paul took my yoga mat and said, holding it up, "It's Zobo the robot" (in reference to a *Lego Friends* episode—don't judge). He stared through it, declaring, "Zobo is a camera." For a while, he and Sophie played peek-a-boo with it. Finally she got tired, and he started whining.

"What else could Zobo turn into?" I asked.

"A spear!"

Soon, he and Sophie started up a tug-of-war game he playfully named Monkey Attacking Spider. I hardly had to say more, and they were off.

This open-ended play doesn't need much: only empty time and space, and the sense that many ideas can be right. When you have time, pause and sit. Wonder out loud what will happen next. Open-ended questions such as "Then what?" or "Okay, and what else?" let a child lead. Use *exploratory* questions: How could a napkin become a helicopter or an ice cream truck? Try out his ideas, then *evaluate*: "What was most fun?" "What do you want to play again?"

Think of going lower-key, not ratcheting up; of making plans and testing multiple ideas. Move away from talk about who's failing or who's first.[49] Encourage everyone to participate. Offer the freedom to think differently, use failure as information, and try again. If the helicopter doesn't fly, maybe it could be a submarine. If the science experiment didn't work, ask what *did* happen, and explore that instead. A playful attitude lets kids wonder instead of racing for right answers, and see failure not as an embarrassment, but as an opening.

A Playful Attitude Is Contagious

The need to see play as wonder came to me in glimmers, through watching kids on playgrounds and in schools, and heightened once I became a parent. Over one long Northeast winter, I felt the tedium of endless searching for places to run around: bouncy houses, indoor play spaces with worn-looking kitchens, and easy-enough hiking trails. Finding space to play, in the way we traditionally think of play, was tough.

One dreary February afternoon when Sophie was five, I decided to take her to Boston's Museum of Science. Apparently, half the families in Boston had the same idea. A line snaked to the dinosaur exhibit. We decided to wait outside till the crowd thinned. I listened as two kids nearby, around four and six, started yanking on their dad's arm.

"Can't I have my video game?" the younger kid asked. "Or your phone?"

"Let's play hopscotch," the older kid said, jumping into a puddle. "Puddle hopscotch."

"No phone." The father frowned. "And no hopscotch. You're already drenched."

"This is so *boring*." The younger kid yanked harder. "Let's go."

"Be quiet, okay?" the dad said, wincing as the older one sprayed him with water.

Soon I turned to a second family: a father with three young boys in rainboots, their jackets soaked. As the boys jumped and splashed, their father watched them with a small smile.

"I wonder what that puddle could be," he said, "if you pour water in. Say, an ocean?"

"Don't be ridiculous." The oldest boy laughed. "But I bet it could be a lake."

"With frogs?" the middle one asked, jumping around.

"Maybe." The father gave a wry smile. "Or—*sea monsters!*"

"Ooh," the youngest boy said, as the middle one chanted: "Sea monsters, sea monsters, one two three. Won't you come and play with me?"

"*I* play." The youngest boy lunged for a puddle.

"Sure." The father smeared mud around with his shoe. "Maybe we could make a mud monster?"

"A dinosaur," the oldest boy said, adding to the mud. "A T. rex."

"A *dolphin*," the middle boy argued.

The father made the mud puddle bigger, then said, "There's room for a T. rex and a dolphin. And maybe a landscape they could fit in."

"A desert," the oldest child said, as the middle child offered, "An aquarium."

"Okay." The father laughed. "A desert-aquarium. A layer of sand, a layer of water . . ."

"And it's getting hotter!" the middle child said, as he gestured, throwing in pretend fire.

Soon the line thinned, and we headed into the museum, but not before Sophie proclaimed, stomping in the puddles, "Hold on. I want to make a dolphin, too."

Her excitement reminded me of a simple fact: a playful attitude is contagious. When you support one child's creativity, you'll likely inspire those around him or her as well.

As we explored the museum, I thought back to those families. We'd only spent ten minutes waiting, but in that time, one of the families had only gotten more annoyed, while the other had transformed the mud into a desert-aquarium, complete with fire. That second family's interactions were more pleasant and fun, but even more, the kids were thinking playfully, and the father's conversation helped. Their talk reminded me of two questions suggested by the researcher Rikke Toft Nørgård: "What might be?" and "How might we?"[50] These questions invite your child to explore possibilities, draw on his curiosity, and think in an open-ended way.

The second father had followed the thread of his children's interests, in the moment. He listened and combined their ideas creatively (the "desert-aquarium"). Singing the "sea monsters" chant and rhyming let them all play with language. Such language play, including rhyming and punning, might sound silly, but it's great for bonding and even boosts learning. It gives practice in phonological awareness, or the ability to recognize and manipulate the sound structures of language, a key foundation in learning to read.[51]

At the same time, the father showed his openness to different ideas. He encouraged many ways to play, and no one right answer. Through his question about the ocean, he took his children's thinking beyond the here and now. And, by going along with their suggestions, he offered them an attitude of collaboration and respect.

Notice Your Own Play Attitude

To be fair, there are many reasons we don't, or can't, have conversations like the second family's. We might be tired, frustrated, drained, or stressed. There might be other things on our minds. When our kids ask to play, our reactions have as much to do with us as with them. I laughed, a few weeks back, when noticing how differently I responded to the exact same situation at dinner. One evening, both kids were playfully blowing bubbles in their drinks, and Sophie asked, "Do milk bubbles look different from water bubbles?"

"Good question." I encouraged her and Paul to test it out.

Only a few nights later, I came home late, then rushed to get dinner ready. When I finally sat down and they started their bubble-blowing contest, I snapped, "No bubbles at dinner, okay?"

"But you *said*." Sophie blew a bubble for emphasis.

Of course she was right—but our own attitudes toward play can ebb and flow. Simply noticing your own attitude—and *why* you have it—can help get everyone's needs met. When you're not in the mood, try explaining, in a neutral tone, why now isn't the best time. That's another reason to focus on self-care. It lets you come back with more mental space. Give yourself compassion when you simply don't have the extra energy or patience you need to joke around.

Playful Conversations Break Up Arguments

What about more drawn-out conflicts or arguments? A playful conversation can also help. I like the way Lawrence Cohen, author of *Playful Parenting*, frames it.[52] Rather than push when your child pulls, try dropping the rope. Meet his upset with expansiveness.

Say your preschooler refuses to eat his toast, because you didn't let *him* butter it (a recent argument at my house). It's tempting to say, "Just *eat* it, okay?" Instead, validate the *idea* behind his desire, then creatively expand it. Say, "Try buttering the other side," or "Pretend you're a pirate, and spear the toast." Or laughingly tell him you did it "wrong," since you missed the corners, and could he help?

Having a collaborative attitude gives you options beyond "no" or "later." It also puts your child in the driver's seat. He saves face and doesn't feel he's lost the argument. The same goes for repairing upsets. Say your child comes to dinner crying over a broken toy. You put pasta sauce on the broken spot, asking, jokingly, "Hmm . . . will that fix it?" A pretend fix can nudge him out of his rut while giving him a chance to add ideas.

Playfulness can also make apologizing easier on both sides. Say you snap at your child. You apologize, but he's still upset. With a younger child, pretend to be a bear who left hibernation. Now he's grumpy. Ask, "What animal do you feel like when *you're* grumpy?" This talk offers a new topic and a fresh chance to reconnect.

More broadly, try these principles to make play work in all your lives:

To Help a Child Play Well: Use Talk as a "Barometer"

Talk can be a play barometer. Just as a barometer measures air pressure, a "talk barometer" lets you reflect on how much pressure your child feels and what might need a shift.[53]

- *Encourage kids to reflect on their play lives.*
  - *Focus on feelings.* Maybe a child's least successful activity is his favorite, or he hates when he doesn't do well. Notice

how much "I have to" versus "I want you" he uses. How much is he focused on getting praise, versus simply enjoying an activity?

– *Let new activities offer a fresh mirror.* Say your child wants to start up a new, time-consuming activity. Reflect on his schedule and priorities. Ask: What appeals to him about the activity? Which skills does he want to gain? If he does start, *evaluate* regularly how he feels. Is he finding challenge or excitement? Does he have supportive friends? And what does he complain about: total exhaustion or frustration, or simply some fatigue? See this example:

Making Small Shifts: The Play Barometer

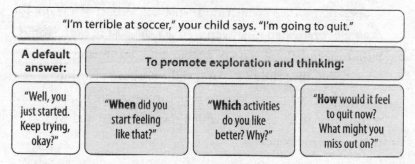

"I'm terrible at soccer," your child says. "I'm going to quit."

A default answer:	To promote exploration and thinking:		
"Well, you just started. Keep trying, okay?"	"**When** did you start feeling like that?"	"**Which** activities do you like better? Why?"	"**How** would it feel to quit now? What might you miss out on?"

If he's frustrated at not succeeding initially, remind him we all have a learning curve. Support him to keep up with the activity long enough to have some aspects come easily.

• *Rethink sports specialization, especially if it isn't on your child's terms.* If your child feels very intensely about a sport, watch for signs of burnout or fatigue. Does he need a break or a change in pace? Take stock over time, especially if his involvement increases (say, he joins a new traveling team).

Leave time and space for other conversations. If your child

talks about his sport or activity nonstop, guide him gently to other topics.

Notice your *own* feelings about his sport and how you'd feel if he cut down. Did you play his sport in high school or college? If so, what feelings does your child's participation bring up for you? Ask yourself if your excitement about his sport is more about him, or about you wanting him to shine as you did.

- *Help your child cooperate as he competes.* We often think about kids either cooperating or competing in their play: they're building a Lego tower together, *or* they're competing against each other in a Lego tournament. But it doesn't have to be either/or. Many kids feel more motivated when focusing on cooperation *within* competition—playing as part of a team, for example, against another team. To get the best of both worlds, talk through helpful ways of encouraging teammates; say, praising another child's kicking skills or sportsmanship.

In games, encourage kids to take turns making up and testing new rules. *Evaluate* which they like best, and what they'd like to try next.

Making Small Shifts: Talk for Inclusive Play

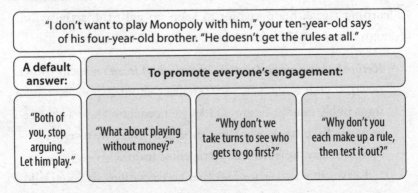

"I don't want to play Monopoly with him," your ten-year-old says of his four-year-old brother. "He doesn't get the rules at all."

A default answer:	To promote everyone's engagement:		
"Both of you, stop arguing. Let him play."	"What about playing without money?"	"Why don't we take turns to see who gets to go first?"	"Why don't you each make up a rule, then test it out?"

Conversations for Gaming: Keep an Open Mind

With some types of play, these reflective conversations can be especially challenging. Take video games. Most parents I meet wonder if they should ban them. Arguments often center around what's on the screen. While understandable, such a focus doesn't get at what truly matters: the meaning kids make from those games. Maybe your child is terrified of a scary-looking bear in his game, but doesn't mind the fighter jets. Maybe he's overfocused on the blood and gore, or maybe he's only thinking about accumulating points. Those differences matter in terms of how the games affect him— and in the kind of support that would benefit him most.

Instead, as I discussed with the video game researcher Jane McGonigal, author of *SuperBetter*, notice how kids engage with technology.[54] Focus on the sense they're making of them. Rather than banning a game based on its title, ask what intrigues your child about it. Is it the graphics, the levels, or how it lets him engage with friends? When you don't start by saying gaming is "bad," he's less likely to get defensive. You'll better understand why the game matters to him and what kind of talk he needs. Maybe it's a discussion about violence, or maybe simply a talk about what's real and not real—or whether he'd actually see a zombie in real life.

If a video game seems scary or violent, ask: How do you feel before and after playing? *Expand* on a child's comments. Point out signs of stress or anxiety. That raises his self-awareness. One day, he may sense *himself* getting agitated and stop playing.

To be fair, some teens are playing video games excessively, even addictively, and need gaming boundaries and rules. But even then, start collaboratively. Calmly state the evidence. Ask him: What have you missed out on, due to gaming? Plot out homework and gaming times he can sign off on. See it as an ongoing discussion. If you feel stuck or sense there are bigger issues, it's worth checking in with a child psychologist or therapist.

For All Ages: Conversational Habits for Play

What if your child isn't old enough for gaming? While play looks vastly different from one child to the next, there are key habits that can support kids of all ages. These emphasize exploring words, ideas, and feelings from many angles, encouraging everyone to participate.

Conversational Habit #1:
Pattern-Seeking: Play with Language

To explore play with language, try these principles:

- *Encourage kids to join you in language play.*
  - Start by noticing. Kids are already playing with language if you listen closely. Even toddlers in their cribs rehearse their day, sing nursery rhymes, or tell stories, unprompted by anyone. Use that as a springboard for your talk. Ask to hear more.
  - Test out the silly and extreme. Say, for a young child: "Row, row, row your boat, gently down the *lake*; if you see a crocodile, don't forget to *shake*." This lets a child learns to rhyme while having a fun social experience. For older kids, play around with common sayings. For example, "*Brown* is the new *black*; *hip-hop* is the new *rock and roll*; *banana* is the new *papaya*."

– Give your kids—and yourself—the license to defy logic, brainstorming elements and patterns that don't make obvious sense. Talk through your reasoning afterward, and encourage them to do the same. "People call something the new black because it's fashionable. What's 'the new black' of video games? Of nail polish?"

- *Link language play to real-life experiences.*
  – Go outside, listen to a new piece of music, or try a new food. Use concrete, sensory language to talk about subtle differences. **Concrete** language focuses on what you can experience: people, places, art forms, things. **Sensory** language emphasizes how you make sense of experiences; for instance: What does a *crunch* sound like, versus a *clack*? When does music sound *mournful* versus *exuberant*?
  – Emphasize all five senses. Try out visual descriptions (*maroon* versus *violet*) and tactile ones (*slimy* versus *sticky*). Ask: Which textures, sights, and sounds is your child drawn to? Which annoy or irritate him? And what about you?

This process heightens children's attention to the outside world while helping their language become more precise. Having grounded sensory experiences also calms their minds.

Conversational Habit #2:
Play *Through* Language: Talk that Transforms

For talk that sparks wonder and curiosity, try out these strategies:

- *Explore multiple ways of seeing the same issue, object, or idea.*
  Explore how objects can transform. Say your child is playing with a rubber band. Try asking, "Can you knot it so there's

no flat part left?" or "What might happen if you knot it, then shoot it?" Or ask him to turn it into a bird or a flag. Encourage him to add his ideas or give you some challenges.

Consider many possibilities for the same object: How many ways can you use a stick? How could a bucket become a rocket ship? How many designs can you invent for a solar-powered roof? How would a ball bounce on the moon? Or imagine how a situation would look in the future or past. How might you build a house with no electricity? Model asking a few questions, then encourage kids to pursue their own.

To Raise Scientific Thinkers: Play the Believing Game

At its best, science is a playful thinking process, sparked by wonder. You ask "why" and "how" questions when facing a new experience, or revisiting old ones.[55] You test out opinions, hypotheses, and ideas. Try the following:

- Reflect on your gut reaction to any one idea. Does it "seem right"?

- Question how new thoughts or ideas fit with what a child already knows.

- Take on hard questions with a playful attitude.

As Stanford researchers suggest, "Try believing one idea and see what you can figure out about it. Then try believing another."[56] Ask: Which idea wins out? What are problems with thinking either way? Say your child asks whether his plaster-of-paris boat will sink.

Talk through each option together; for example, "Let's say it would float."

1. *Expand* on that idea. Why would it float? How much weight would make it sink? Then suggest: "Let's say it *wouldn't* float. Why not?" If he says, "It's too heavy," *expand* on that; say, "What about that material makes it heavy?"

2. *Explore* that idea and related ones: for instance, "Would cutting a hole in it help it float?"

3. Afterward, *evaluate* which idea was correct, and which ones you believed more.

Conversational Habit #3: Reframe Play as Wonder

When you wonder, you come with your full attention. You use a fresh lens, exploring the mystery of common things. Try out these strategies:

- *Promote expansive ways of thinking.* Test scales on the piano. Try out new materials for a treehouse. Go cross-country skiing, or head to the playground, noticing the sounds shoes make on mud and on ice. Compare how you and your child describe sounds. Maybe you thought the ice cream truck's song sounded *tinny*, and she thought *delicious*. Notice how responses evolve. How does your child hear songs differently after learning to read music? What happens to sound when it snows? How does the windshield look when covered with pollen?

- *Value intuition. Explore a new solution because it feels right, then discuss why.* Maybe the stove won't turn on. Ask: Is the burner broken? What does he think you should do next? Why? Try his solution, then yours. This encourages his helping impulse while valuing his imaginative thought.

• *Notice what doesn't work. Comment on doubts and frustrations as well as positives.* Why doesn't the screwdriver open the compartment? Is it too big, or does it have the wrong tip? Test, reflect, and try again.

• *Highlight and reflect on everyday mysteries.* Why are some rocks lighter and heavier? Why does the microwave beep if you don't take out the food? Start with everyday questions, then gradually get more complex. Do microwave sensors work based on weight? Could you design a device that "knows" there's nothing inside the microwave?

Conversational Habit #4:
Promote Child-Driven Play

You both need physical and mental space—and it's impossible to be interested in all a child does. Here are some suggestions to move away from "always-on" play:

• *Try silence and watchful waiting.* Invite a child to drive his play, then bring you in on his terms.[57] If you're tired or "talked out," sit beside him, offering your eyes and ears, and an open attitude. Encourage him to play alone and come when he needs you. Your watchful waiting—and the sense that you're available—is more than enough.

• *Give quiet encouragement.* Kids tend to play more and benefit more from play when they sense you approve. In one study, parents' attitude about play predicted their children's levels of imagination.[58] Offer time, space, and props inspired by scenes they suggest. If a child always plays fireman, let him paint a cardboard box for the firehouse.

- ***Use the Three Es.***
  - Try *expansive* questions such as: "What were you thinking when you built that bridge?" or "What made you choose those colors?"
  - Use *exploratory* questions to extend play to the limits. For instance, "If you had every color in the world, which would you choose?" Imagine a bigger or smaller stage: "What if each block was as big as this room?"
  - Use *evaluative* questions after play to help kids judge their progress and name their likes and dislikes. For example, "What about your building do you like best?"

- ***Find alternatives.*** It's better to be occasionally but fully engaged, than always only partially listening. If you don't feel like playing, try these strategies:
  - Ask your child to finish his project or activity, then show what he's done.
  - Encourage him to teach a game to a sibling or friend, then play together.
  - Build the first part of a structure, then challenge him to finish it.

In the end, these conversations don't have recipes. You're noticing and responding to your child's individual spirit with an individuality of your own.

Rethinking play isn't a feel-good initiative or a fix to all the changes needed in society.[59] But it can challenge the prevailing thinking in our culture and empower kids to stay open to their inner creative drives. As Maria Montessori famously noted, "Play is the child's work."[60] She meant that play and work can be braided, letting kids blossom as they stretch. Playing well is a way of learning deeply. Playing together, in ways that suit our tendencies, is a powerful way of showing love.

At its best, our talk can act as an invitation. Through providing inspiration, stretch, and creative openings, we have the chance to let our children's biggest ideas blossom, and their dreams shine.

CHAPTER 7

Conversations for Openness: Raising a Global Citizen

Those who cannot change their minds cannot change anything.
—GEORGE BERNARD SHAW[1]

I don't like kids with accents."

"I'm sorry?" I asked. It was my first year working as a speech-language pathologist. I was sitting with William, an eighth-grader, in my office. William had come to me with struggles in expressive language, or communicating his thoughts and ideas out loud or in writing. He had particular trouble, as many kids with this profile do, with grammar and syntax, or the structure of sentences. That is, he had a strong vocabulary, but he often spoke and wrote using only simple sentences. In elementary school, when many kids were using mostly simple sentences, his problems hadn't been as evident. But as an eighth-grader, he was now required to write much more complicated essays. At times, he was asked to convince the reader of a point, using persuasive writing to build an argument. William found these assignments especially stressful and frustrating. As a result, we often brainstormed using media, such as radio shows, podcasts, or videos, designed to pique his interest. We worked on specific ways of honing his arguments, such as using "however" and "although" to connect his ideas. He typically seemed to enjoy our sessions. For my part, I'd had fun finding videos and shows that engaged him and related to the topic at hand.

This morning, we'd just watched a video where a boy from Mexico City was talking about how much busier the city had become since he was little. William was meant to write an essay about urbanization, but that didn't seem foremost on his mind.

"His accent." William imitated the boy's speech. "It is *not so good*, ma *life* here."

"That's not how he talked," I replied, "and it's natural that he has an accent. English isn't his first language." Already, William had complained about the video, saying he wasn't interested in how other people lived.

"So?" He met my gaze. "He ought to practice. He's such a loser."

"A loser?" I paused to let the word sink in. "He sounds like he's doing well to me."

"*He's* the one that made the video. It's *his* job to try to sound decent, okay?"

As calmly as I could, I discussed why it was wrong to say such things, and to have such a negative attitude about people who were different from him. Shuffling his feet, he mumbled an apology, and we moved on. In the moment, I recognized his attitude as all too common. It had come in part from his environment, then hardened from interactions that didn't question his stereotypes. As the psychologist Marguerite Wright argues, intolerance is learned.[2]

But soon it came time for parent-teacher conferences. I sat with William's teacher waiting for his parents to arrive. As his teacher told me, William's family had immigrated from Poland when William was two. While William had learned English fluently and spoke without an accent, his parents had had a harder time. In recent months, William had stopped having friends over, since the "friends" had made fun of how his parents spoke.

All of a sudden, I understood his reaction to the video. He'd been treated badly and, as soon as he could, had passed that same treatment along. When kids feel insecure and hurt, they often lash out at others even more vulnerable than they are. Or else they turn that insecurity inward, becoming anxious or depressed.[3,4,5] That's not to say William's comment was justified. Quite the opposite: it was wrong. Still, learning about his situation had allowed me to understand why he might have spoken as he had.

But what about how I'd responded? I'd focused only on lecturing him. That likely hadn't changed how he thought. I hadn't asked him to question his ideas. He'd probably tuned me out.

So what could I have done differently? I wondered. And, more broadly, how can we help kids move from having ingrained assumptions to becoming open and curious? How could we get beyond teaching them to "say the right thing," or to *tolerate* those who aren't like them, to help them want to understand others and engage in positive ways?

As we saw in the last chapter, we want kids to stay playful, but not only with their immediate friends and family. Ideally, we'd also hope they understand and appreciate others who are unlike them. We'd like them to stay curious about differences and have empathy for those with backgrounds and profiles unlike theirs. Especially in a complex, interconnected society, teaching kids to be open and interested in difference is one of the most powerful ways to help them thrive. This openness lets them collaborate, cross national and cultural borders in building friendships, and adapt to the vast changes in work, school, and society they'll surely experience. Even creativity arises from the productive clash of ideas, not from having more of the same.

Yes, such openness is a quality employers will ask for. But far more profoundly, it's a quality that will help kids learn, build empathy and creativity, and experience their diverse societies as a positive, not a problem. Engaging well with difference is a powerful gift, if we can help kids get there—but how? To start, let's get clear about what difference means.

What Difference Really Means

Difference has to do with more than how kids look or act, or the languages they speak. Yes, race, ethnicity, and/or language is part of it. But really, difference and diversity mean more. It's also about kids who come from more or less well-off families, who are different in age or sex, or who live in different types of family structures. Maybe a child has two moms or lives with his single mother. Or maybe he lives in a multigenerational household with his grandmother, parents, and aunt. Difference may also have to do with ability; say, kids who shine in sports but struggle with reading, versus kids with the opposite profile or kids who have physical, mental, or emotional disabilities.

Not all differences are visible. Some may be easy to pass by. Difference also includes those who *think* or learn differently, or have strong differences in personality, which researchers call "deep-level diversity."[6] Neurodiversity, or differences in the ways each person's brain works, is also critical for kids to understand.[7] Maybe a friend has autism, or maybe she's unusually sensitive to sound. When a child recognizes these differences and meets them with compassion, she's primed to have a better relationship with that friend. What's more, she learns more about who that friend is—and more about herself. How does she react to those who are different? Which differences leave her excited, versus frustrated or uncomfortable? And how do those attitudes change over time? Reflecting on attitudes is the first step in changing them.

On the surface, it might sound like a lot to lump all these differences together. Certainly they're not all the *same*. Some bring advantages. Others come with stigmas or biases that leave kids vulnerable. In the United States, students of color attending majority Caucasian schools are a clear example. There's a long history of overt racism and implicit bias that persists in both obvious and subtle ways. One 2017 study of about 10,000 high school sophomores and their teachers found that teachers held lower expectations for students of color than they did for Caucasian students. In turn, these lower expectations linked to how much the *students* believed they'd succeed.[8] These biases trickle down to how kids talk to one another, and to their beliefs about themselves.

These types of biases need to be addressed specifically. Our conversations are critical. We need back-and-forth dialogue, evolving over time, to raise kids who embrace difference. These conversations focus on developing a few key skills: **knowledge**, or insight about the world; **morality**, or an ethical sense of what's right; **social skills** to relate to others with diverse backgrounds; and **experience** putting into practice what they learn.[9]

It's not enough for kids to be "tolerant." Sure, that's better than being cruel. But emphasizing tolerance is doing the bare minimum. Even the word has a negative tone.

Think about a person sitting too close to you on a bus. "I don't like it, but I'll tolerate it," you might say. It's definitely not the highlight of your day. Sonia Nieto, a leading scholar in multiculturalism, talks about tolerance as "low-level" support for differences.[10] It's not really changing children's worldviews. I've seen this myself, walking the halls of so many classrooms, with bulletin boards posted with the message "We're all okay." Inevitably, there will be pictures of kids of many different races, often from clip art or stock photographs.

That's certainly better than *intolerance* or hate. And yet, among all the kids I've worked with, I don't know one who wants to be only "okay." They want to feel truly cared for and known; to feel loved, in all their uniqueness. They want to be celebrated—and not in a sort of earnest, birthday-party celebration way, but with a genuine interest in who they really are.

As I saw one morning, observing a fifth-grade classroom, one child asked another, "What does it *feel like* to have autism?" The second child had just given a presentation on her recent autism diagnosis, and had opened up the floor for questions. With a broad smile, she talked about how her mind had a sort of "tunnel vision," where she got very focused, then tuned everyone else out. "I *am* interested in people," she said. "It's just that everything else—for a minute—feels more interesting." The first child nodded and said, "I get it. That happens to me sometimes."

In their interaction, I sensed that the child with autism had felt understood, not simply as a category or a diagnosis, but for the particular workings of her mind. She felt celebrated and lifted up. That same celebration can hold true for differences of all kinds. Whether it's sex, race, ethnicity, language, or thinking—whether differences are obvious or invisible—kids can learn to take a celebratory perspective. That's a profound way of bringing them together and bonding them even while they learn.

Instead of tolerance, Nieto argues for "affirmation, solidarity, and critique."[11] In this mindset, kids embrace differences as positives and see them as a means to learn. They *affirm* one another's differences, or bring them to the light, rather than keeping them hidden. They show *solidarity* with those who are unlike them, using empathy to realize we're all in this together. And they *critique* the unfairness of their societies. They don't simply accept the way things are.

To get there, kids need to talk actively about differences. They need to have hard conversations, challenging one another to look beyond their gut reactions to wonder *why* they're having the reactions that they do. We can help by showing them that we're on the journey with them. Opening up and examining our own assumptions shows kids it's okay to be vulnerable. More than in any other area, our attitudes about difference trickle down. It's not only about what we say, but how we say it; our body language, tone of voice, and warmth. It's also about the friends *we* make and don't make and the ways we approach potential friends.

Upending prejudices starts with understanding what kids know and don't about others; recognizing assumptions, then checking them. When you talk openly about differences, you help kids separate facts from assumptions. When their understanding isn't based on fear, they're more inquisitive and curious. These conversations can start early. You meet kids where they are, with their questions in mind. This lets you target your talk. It's not about dictionary definitions. It's as simple as defining someone based on a characteristic or group: "You're the blond one," or "You're the Mexican one." Defining bias gives you a springboard for discussion. Does your child know what a "stereotype" is? An "assumption"? What does he think when he hears those terms?

Moving beyond these stereotypes lets kids learn to love the surprise of novelty, and to direct empathy and compassion toward those who might feel vulnerable. They move from hearing an unfamiliar language and thinking, "Oh, that sounds weird," to saying, "Wow, that's different. I wonder what those words mean." They learn to feel delighted to realize a person's mind works differently from theirs. As one ten-year-old told me, on hearing his cousin was color-blind, "I wanted to know what he could see and couldn't. I kept holding up stuff to see what he'd say."

That's not to say we should be hyperaware of the ways we interact. Instead, through focusing on our discussion with kids and our beliefs, we can raise kids' self-awareness and move us all along in the direction of embracing differences—naturally.

The "Kids Don't See Difference" Fallacy

"But young kids don't notice differences," I've often heard. That's a false assumption.

In fact, kids are highly attuned to differences in language, race, gender, social class, and even learning, thinking, and social skills. Take gender as one example. As research has found, kids often start using the words "boy" and "girl" around eighteen months to two years old. By preschool, they often show preference for playmates of their own gender.[12] And by age three, many use basic gender stereotypes—such as boys being rough—which grow more sophisticated by four and a half.[13,14,15] The same goes for differences in race. As one study found, kids can categorize people by race and gender, at a basic level, by only *six months* of age.[16] Yes, they're not speaking, but they look longer at faces of familiar races than unfamiliar ones. Researchers think they may be aware of racial differences even earlier. And even kids as young as three to five years old not only categorize based on race, but also show bias for their own race group. In part, this is due to their developmental stage. Preschoolers can often only work with one category at a time; say, "red things" or "circles."[17] It's much harder for them to see the nuances. But that means, without any direct teaching, they're already drawing conclusions based on what they see. Not talking about these categories only hardens them in children's minds.

And this awareness only gets more nuanced as they develop. For instance, many two- and three-year-olds notice differences with cultural influences, such as boys in the United States being given trucks to play with. From age three to four, their thinking gets more nuanced, and they may ask why our words for people's skin tones don't match their actual skin—say, "Why is a white person not really 'white'?" Some kids, as many I've met, are curious about which parts of their bodies, and your body, are open to change; say, "Are you going to keep growing?" or "Will I change color when I grow up?" And by age five, many kids start asking questions with scientific explanations; for instance, why she has green eyes, while your eyes are brown.[18]

And beyond age five, their thinking and questions only get more nuanced, as they start seeing these differences play out in their schools, families, and communities. Discussions of racism and xenophobia, or the fear of strangers, can become much more powerful and complex. But there's no reason to wait till middle or high school to have these discussions. From early on, kids know that others are different from them, and they want to know why.

The Familiarity Principle

Yet we often assume we shouldn't talk about differences; that kids can't handle it or aren't interested. These talks can feel uncomfortable. Some of us fear our kids will say the wrong thing, or that we will. So instead of bringing these topics up, we shut them down.

We want to protect kids, but end up keeping them in a bubble, and *more* likely to make false assumptions. We don't capitalize on their curiosity. We're also not responding to a natural fact of their development: a preference for the familiar, and a tendency to avoid the unknown.

In fact, even young kids have a default "familiarity" preference. For example, five-month-old babies prefer native speakers and accents over foreign-sounding ones.[19] This preference probably served an evolutionary function. A caretaker who sounds like your mother is likely from your family circle, and less likely a stranger who could harm you. The same goes for race. Babies look longer—a sign of interest—at faces whose racial group matches theirs. They tend to interact with and imitate adults who look like them.[20]

But that doesn't mean babies are racist. Instead, they simply feel comfortable with what they know. In contrast, the biases kids later develop are far less personal. They apply to all members of a group: for instance, "all Spanish-speakers," "all kids from China," or "everyone in wheelchairs."[21] It's those biases that quality conversation is most suited to upend.

Prejudice and discrimination have to do with positive attitudes directed only toward the in-group, and negative attitudes or behavior toward all others. It's based not on each person, but on group membership.[22] While prejudice has to do with beliefs and ideas, discrimination refers to *actions* taken based on those beliefs.

Any group can be the subject of prejudice; for example, "jocks" or "blonds."[23] Still, some prejudices are clearly more rooted in history and centuries-old injustices, such as those based on race.

In a famous 1950s study, the psychologist Gordon Allport argued that prejudice develops slowly, as the brain learns to make and rely on categories.[24] Putting things into boxes lets us function in the world. Kids learn that an animal with four legs and a furry tail is a "dog," or a thing with bark and leaves a "tree." They need this ability to help make sense of what they see. If they had to decide, from scratch, what to call every object, they'd be paralyzed. But the problem comes when they make these groupings for people, then *stereotype* or make broad judgments about whole groups.

These stereotypes are all different for each of us. The same goes for what kids see as "different." Say your child is the only Polish boy in his class, or the only African American girl, or the only child whose parents speak Spanish. How different a child seems depends on many factors: How diverse is the rest of the class? Do they know kids from other countries? What about the teacher's attitude—and that of their parents? These assumptions change over time, as kids have conversations with friends that either lift these differences up or squash them down.

Not all differences are treated the same. Our society teaches us some are "good," some "bad," and some in between. To take a simple example, wearing glasses is typically seen as neutral, unless a kid is the only one in his grade or class. Then he might be called "four-eyes" and teased. The same goes for having braces. But kids in wheelchairs often face far more bias and stigma, as do kids who have hearing aids. This isn't fair, of course, and often results in kids getting left out or teased. These messages need to be considered critically. If we just go with the flow, we're setting them up to have lots of wrong assumptions. They may treat others unfairly without even realizing *why* they're doing it.

With explicit prejudice, kids say they don't like members of a group. With implicit bias, they don't even realize their stereotypes. Most kids have both.[25] Many studies have found that kids of all ages tend to prefer those in the same language group, gender, and race. They look to group members to learn information, prefer to reward group members, and tend to think members of their group will be more loyal. Our conversation can take on both these implicit and explicit biases.[26,27,28]

Bias Versus Curiosity

Still, pointing out differences doesn't mean kids are biased.[29] They may be trying to learn about the world. At times, they don't have the pragmatics, or social skills, to do so effectively. "Who am I *raising*?" one friend asked me as we walked around our block. Her four-year-old son had pointed to a man in a wheelchair. "Is he from the circus?" the child had asked—loudly enough that the man clearly heard.

We often take these instances—embarrassing as they can be—as evidence of our children having an issue with *morality*. Certainly, the question wasn't polite—at least, not if it had come from an adult. But kids aren't mini-adults. At all ages, they're trying to understand their world's borders, drawing assumptions based on what they see. It's *we* who make the connection between their curiosity and being "rude" or "mean."

Ironically, the more we try to squash questions or comments, the more weight we give them. Shying away sends the message that there's something fearsome or terrible about the question. In fact, the child was simply wondering—albeit in a socially awkward way. Responding with a real answer, calmly, does far more to quench his curiosity. For example, you could discuss how some people's legs don't work well. You can ask him why he thinks that is, and discuss his reasoning. And you can give him social feedback, suggesting he ask questions quietly. If it feels right, encourage him to go up to the man and talk. While everyone is different, many people will welcome a child's interest, especially if it comes out of genuine curiosity.[30]

But we can do more than take each bias or assumption one by one. Instead, we can focus on difference in general. How do we and our kids react to someone unlike them? What conversations do we open or shut down? Which questions delight us, upset us, or stress us out? Answering that means knowing our own difference "stories," including where our biases and assumptions began.

Making Sense of Difference: My Own Road

As a child growing up in the Deep South in the 1980s, my understanding of difference was a gradual awakening. In many ways, I didn't "know what I didn't know." Looking back at photos of my swim team and Girl Scout troop, I didn't consider how we were almost all white, middle-class, native speakers of English. It wasn't until I reached middle school that I was exposed to kids from a diverse range of racial, ethnic, cultural, and income backgrounds.

At that time, my public magnet school drew kids from across the county with a positively antiquated "quota" policy. As I recall it, around 30 percent of students would be "white," 30 percent

"Asian," and 30 percent "Black," with the last 10 percent "Other." I didn't consider the problems of that policy, or the controversies of busing kids away from their neighborhood schools. To me, the whole thing seemed natural. On the positive side, the policy *did* mean that my friends came from across the county and were racially and ethnically diverse. But my teachers mostly taught us to be "color-blind," pretending we didn't see any differences, especially in race. It wasn't just my school: this philosophy was common nationwide.[31]

On the surface, pretending to be color-blind may be well-intentioned. Kids wouldn't be racist, so goes the idea, if you simply say you don't *see* any differences. But if you don't see differences, you can't have conversations about them. You can't reap all the richness they can bring. And, in any case, no one can *actually* not notice race. That's just a fiction, and not a very useful one. In fact, it can even be dangerous, keeping those who hold it from noticing and talking about inequality, discrimination, and biases as they play out in everyday life.[32,33]

Embarrassingly, it wasn't until college, when I reconnected with my high school friends, that I saw all I'd missed about their lives. One friend was celebrating Diwali, the Hindu festival of lights. Others told me of celebrating the Chinese New Year and of spending vacations in their hometowns in Jamaica and Vietnam. Other friends were engaged in political and social-justice movements related to their backgrounds: educating immigrants from Mexico about their voting rights, or helping kids from poorer families apply to college.

In these friends, I recognized a passion and engagement that I hadn't noticed in our high school years. Certainly these passions had probably developed further during college. But what surprised me was how little I'd known about their backgrounds, and how I hadn't even thought to ask. In fact, I would have seen asking as rude, an imposition. So instead of connecting with my friends at a deeper level, I knew them only from cross-country practice and study hall. Pretending we were all the same—that old American dream of assimilation—had actually kept us apart. It also kept me from realizing that race, ethnicity, and culture aren't equivalent.[34,35]

In fact, there are as many cultural differences within a race as similarities. For example, a Caucasian person from the rural South and one from Hawaii are likely to have different ways of speaking and different views, and perhaps different religious beliefs. The same goes for people of every racial group.[36] The risk of not getting to know others deeply is that kids will develop fears about those "others." Or they may overgeneralize, thinking that all people from one group are the same. For instance, in one elementary school class I observed, a Russian student arrived midyear, and the kids interviewed him. "Now I know how Russian people are!" one exclaimed afterward. Great enthusiasm, but a lot of room to grow.

We all come with our own histories. Our talk can help uncover these histories—and, more important, explore how each person makes sense of them. We can move them beyond lumping everyone into a box, or even a series of boxes, based our assumptions about who they are. Even recognizing someone's background doesn't help kids relate, if they don't get to know the specific person. When kids say, "That's the Mexican girl" or "the kid in the wheelchair," they're no closer to understanding than they were before. That's especially true for differences that are stigmatized. Subtle messages about stigma trickle down.

Soon after working with William, I met Adriano, a fifth-grader whose family came from Brazil and who was bilingual in English and Portuguese. I knew Adriano as a fun-loving boy, very close to his brother and to his extended family abroad. He often spoke to me about his family's traditions and holidays, and one day even brought in slices of *bolo de leite condensado*, or traditional Brazilian condensed milk cake, to share. Over the weeks I worked with him on writing and vocabulary, he spoke with interest of the differences among English, Spanish, and Portuguese—and he seemed excited about learning all three.

But one day, he came into my office frowning and tossed his books in a huff onto the desk. I asked what was wrong, and at first, he didn't want to say. He seemed distracted, though, and so I asked again, gently, emphasizing that he didn't have to talk. Soon he told me, "My brother had friends over last night. All of them only speak English. And it was so weird. He told them we only speak English, too. I wanted to say something, but I didn't."

After the friends had left, Adriano had talked to his brother about what had happened. As it turns out, his brother had wanted to fit in with his friends, all native English speakers. He'd also, I sensed, internalized shame about his language background. That's all too common in a world where kids hear that some ways of speaking are better than others, or some groups are superior to others.

The impulse to join a privileged group is natural, as I discussed with Adriano, but that doesn't make that impulse right. When kids feel they have to hide aspects of their identities, that's a symptom of a bigger problem. Assumptions and biases they've learned from their environment have likely trickled down. Conversations can't undo all those messages, but they *can* help kids question them critically and regain pride in their backgrounds. Discussing stereotypes openly takes the air out of them, letting your child see that there's nothing natural about stereotyping. Instead, stereotypes are created by humans, like buildings or factories—and they can be undone.

If you find your child is stereotyping or being stereotyped, try the Three Es:

The Three Es to Bust Stereotypes

- *Expand on what he or she says.*
  - Ask: Where did you get that idea? What evidence or specific facts do you have?
  When your child hears a negative stereotype, ask: Where do you think that stereotype comes from? What is its history? Does everyone feel that way about it?

- *Explore possible reasons things are as they are.:*
  - Ask: Why might that person be acting or talking as he or she is?
  - Investigate counterexamples from people they know, or images in the media. If you hear a broad generalization, ask: Who *doesn't* act or speak that way? Why not?

- *Evaluate: Talk to the person you're stereotyping, or read about the issue.*
  - Ask: What did you realize after talking to that person (or reading that book)? What surprised you? See the following example:

Making Small Shifts: Bust Stereotypes

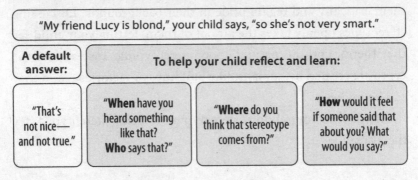

"My friend Lucy is blond," your child says, "so she's not very smart."

A default answer:	To help your child reflect and learn:		
"That's not nice— and not true."	"**When** have you heard something like that? **Who** says that?"	"**Where** do you think that stereotype comes from?"	"**How** would it feel if someone said that about you? What would you say?"

It's not only targeted kids who should have these discussions. It's equally important for kids who *aren't* targeted to notice injustice, as a starting point to making things right. Help your child notice the times he's used stereotypes, either in positive or negative ways. Ask: What does the stereotype miss? Why is it wrong to lump everyone together? How could we talk instead?

Talk About the Terms of Bias

Speaking with parents from a range of backgrounds, I've heard many reasons they feel uncomfortable discussing these kinds of terms with kids. Encouraging kids to stay silent about difference—especially hot-button differences like ethnicity and race—feels to some parents like teaching them to be polite. These discussions do ask us to be vulnerable and question our own assumptions, which isn't always easy. And then there's the question of pointing out differences. We still have that old idea of being "color-blind" circulating. As one mother asked me, "Doesn't talking about differences only make kids more aware of them?" In her opinion, the best way forward was to stay silent, shut down any questions, and hope for the best.

Soon I had the opportunity to talk to Andrew Grant-Thomas and Melissa Giraud, a husband-and-wife team and the founders of the nonprofit organization Embrace Race.[37] In 2016, they started their nonprofit precisely because of questions like these. As parents, one Black and the other multiracial, they felt alone on their journey in discussing the complexities of race with their kids. They wanted to create a community and gather resources to help parents of all backgrounds discuss race openly, in nuanced ways, and not shy away from hard topics.[38]

As we discussed, assumptions can harden into long-term biases.[39] Sometimes, those assumptions come from a lack of exposure; say, a child has never met someone from Germany, and so takes all his knowledge about Germans from cartoons he's watched. Other times, it comes from comments kids hear in their environments, sometimes repeatedly. When I talked more to Adriano, I found out that he and his brother had many assumptions about what it meant to be American, which deeply affected their relationships. "It's not cool to speak more than one language," Adriano told me. "My friends say it even makes you dumb."

These assumptions, all too common, fly in the face of what we know about bilingualism, as an "experience that shapes our brain for a lifetime," as Gigi Luk, a former colleague at the Harvard Graduate School of Education and now at McGill University in Montreal, Canada, argues.[40] Speaking two or more languages seems to prime kids to be more empathetic, even as young as age three.[41] When kids need to think about which language their conversational partner speaks, they need to take that partner's perspective and notice social cues. There may even be benefits in terms of executive functioning and attention. With two or more languages, kids need to pay attention to language switches and stop their initial impulse to speak one language, if they see that another one is needed.[42] But more important are the real-life opportunities bilingualism creates to enlarge a child's social circle. Being able to talk to people in Senegal or Spain, Mexico or India, in their native tongues is a gift—and one that we should encourage in our kids.

True, a few conversations can't undo years of judgment from society. But they can help kids question their judgmental stances and explore where their biases have come from. Adriano's understanding of what being American meant left him lumping all Americans into one category. It also meant drawing a negative conclusion about himself.[43] Later on, when he meets another bilingual person, he's poised to think, "Oh, he might not be smart." He may look for signs that confirm his biases. That's the tricky part about assumptions. Left unchecked, they can balloon.

But there's a positive side. Quality conversation lets kids get up close with difference: to learn *from*, rather than *about*, others, in compassionate, reflective, and nuanced ways.[44] Through dialogue, they can see differences between people as something to celebrate. They develop compassion for a broad spectrum of backgrounds, including race and ethnicity. They raise their awareness about others' abilities and needs, and their self-awareness about their own. Our conversations are a key way to help this compassion along, to keep kids engaged and curious. The key is to reach beyond tolerance and acceptance. We should challenge ourselves to raise global citizens.

The Power of Raising Global Citizens

A global citizen, as the nonprofit Oxfam defines it, is aware of the wider world, sees himself as a world citizen, feels outrage at injustice, and values diversity. He or she also acts: taking responsibility, participating actively in his community, and working to make his world more equal and sustainable.[45,46] Global citizens see beyond the borders of house and school. They're open to adopting new perspectives while not losing sight of their own. They allow their beliefs to shift in the face of new facts, and they educate others about difference without alienating them. As a result, they're poised to become true leaders, flexible thinkers, and engaged citizens.

Clearly, this openness isn't simple to develop. And it's naïve to think that kids can stay open all the time, especially in a world that tends to encourage the opposite. But developing it, even in glimmers, can vastly enhance their relationships. Openness snowballs. The more kids learn about others, the more interested they get— and the more open the *other* person often becomes.

The Stakes of Intolerance

What if kids *don't* become global citizens? The stakes have never been higher. When messages of intolerance, racism, and hate fill airwaves, online forums, and screens, kids can start seeing such messages as commonplace. Intolerance doesn't stay in its corner, but leads to bullying, discrimination, and even disconnection in families.[47,48] As one twelve-year-old told me, he thought it was "stupid" to speak Arabic, his family's native language. As a result, he couldn't talk with his cousins overseas. His assumptions literally led to him not being able to communicate—and to a family rift between the speakers of the two languages.

Certainly, conversations about difference can be tough to have. But if we ignore this "difference talk," or put it off, we let biases and misunderstandings fester. That limits the quality of children's relationships. In the rush of the everyday, we push aside talk that might involve hurt feelings or discomfort. We move forward quickly, without the pauses or thinking time that this talk requires. And we don't always take the time to see how attitudes about difference are all connected. How kids feel about someone who *looks* or *sounds* different than they do and about someone who *thinks* or *learns* differently tend to go hand in hand.

Instead, we need to start seeing difference to be a bigger idea. It's an umbrella that covers many elements, from language and race to religion, ability, personality, even learning style. And seeing that umbrella—and talking about it—is key to raising kids who engage with difference positively. As with most complex topics, we need to start local and concrete. Big, abstract ideas and principles don't connect easily to kids' lives. Instead, the most profound way to help kids embrace difference comes from talk that starts small. This talk is personalized, meeting kids at a level they can understand.[49]

Conversations About Difference Open Kids Up

After Sophie started elementary school, I saw firsthand how these kinds of conversations could work. In her art class, kids were asked to mix colors to find their precise skin tone, then paint a portrait with it and write what it reminded them of. When I visited, I saw an array of colors from light tan to black, along with scribbled words: "candle wax," "honey," "coffee," and "charcoal." When I talked to the kids, I was surprised and pleased to hear how openly and proudly kids talked about "their" color, and how easily they compared them: "Her skin's more olive," one child explained, "and mine's like caramel."

Exercises like those can teach powerful lessons. Difference isn't "out there." Everyone is not average in some way, as the Harvard professor Todd Rose writes in his 2016 book *The End of Average*.[50] Each child is also, in one way or another, in a minority, as compared with friends, classmates, or community members. Maybe he has relatives who speak a second language, or maybe *he* does. Maybe he belongs to a different religious group than most of his classmates, or has a physical or learning difference. Even though not all differences are equivalent, the *fact* of being different is common to us all. To help kids understand, try these principles:

....

Talking About Difference: Key Principles

- *Start with optimism. Ask: Is my child stereotyping, or does he have a genuine misunderstanding?*
  - *Look out for phrases that accompany stereotypes: "all," "those people," "always," "nobody," and "never" (for example, "All Chinese people are good at math," or "Nobody from Mexico speaks English"). Older kids may use may subtler signals, such as "Obviously" or "Of course" (for example, "Of course she's not good at soccer; she's a girl").*
  - *When you hear such comments, help your child revise. Encourage him to become more specific, give context, and focus on positive qualities. For example, "My friend Matt is good at math, and he's from China." Use the metaphor of painting: your child is using too broad a brush when really he needs to see all the variation and range of color in each category.*
  These questions lend themselves to real-life experiences. Say your child says, "All poor people eat fast food." Take a moment not to snap. Simply pause and try speaking in a neutral tone.

- *Start with concrete observations, then move to reasons.*
  What did he notice that prompted the fast food comment?
  Talk about why you eat the food you do, and why some
  families might not be able to afford that. Ask: What does
  "poor" mean? Do you know anyone poor? Are we poor?
  Why or why not?

- *Use real experiences. Explore how processed food often costs*
  less than fresh. Compare your neighborhood or town to nearby
  ones. How does yours stack up, in terms of services? For
  example, how far do you drive to the grocery store?

- *Look critically at images in the media. Do they promote or*
  reinforce negative stereotypes? Ask: What message does that ad
  send? When a child names a stereotype, he can hold it at arm's
  length, not buy into it unthinkingly.

Kids Learn About Difference from Us

All conversations about difference start with us: our own assumptions and biases. To help kids embrace difference, we need to look in the mirror. How do we react when a child points out that someone is unlike them? How calm or upset do we seem?

As Professor Beverly Daniel Tatum, author of the classic 1997 book *Why Are All the Black Kids Sitting Together in the Cafeteria?*, argues, "Many people seize up and don't know how to respond, conveying to the child that there is something *wrong* with difference."[51] We're embarrassed or uncomfortable, or we feel a child's comment reflects on how we've raised him. So we quiet the comment or shut the discussion down. Tatum speaks of a white child asking, "Mommy, why is that person so dark?" and the mother responding, "Shh."[52,53]

When kids receive this sort of feedback, they miss out on developing their understanding. Instead, Tatum suggests explaining that skin comes in different colors, just as hair and eyes do. Responding objectively shows we're open to exploring the nuances, and that we won't push off their questions or shame them for asking. The same goes for noticing our own assumptions. If we don't, we can get caught up in biases, often from our own childhoods. That's especially true for differences with stigma attached.

I remember one afternoon, when the father of ten-year-old Brandon came into the school's conference room for a team meeting. We were planning to discuss Brandon's progress in reading and other academic areas. But Brandon's father arrived early and looked worried. Before the meeting started, I asked whether he wanted to talk.

"My son's so upset," he told me, near tears. Recently Brandon had been diagnosed with dyslexia and had become antisocial, not wanting to leave the house.

"He says his brain is broken." His father wiped his eyes.

"Have you talked to him about dyslexia?" I asked, wincing.

"He'll get cured, I told him—but he doesn't believe me."

"What do you mean?" I asked, meeting his gaze.

"Isn't that what you're here for? To help find a cure?"

This talk, I realized, aligned with national patterns. As one national 2017 survey found, a full 33 percent of US teachers said that a learning or attention issue is often just "laziness," while 43 percent of parents said they wouldn't want others to know if their child had a learning disability.[54] I've seen much the same, with parents whispering that a child "might be dyslexic." It feels scary or shameful. Imagine the heartache a child experiences if he gets these messages.

Brandon and his father, I realized, would benefit from more education. Dyslexia is a neurological difference, not a disease. As such, it can't be "cured." While it has many components, it's defined at the broadest level as difficulty learning to decode (read aloud) and spell.[55] Later on, even if children with dyslexia learn to read individual words well, they often struggle with reading fluency, or reading texts smoothly and appropriately fast, with the right intonations.

Dyslexia is quite common, affecting between 5 to 10 percent of the population, but isn't related to intelligence. In fact, as much as 15 to 20 percent of the population has some symptoms of it, including slow or inaccurate reading, a tendency to mix up words, and challenges with spelling and/or writing.[56] Highly creative adults, including Richard Branson and Walt Disney, have or have had dyslexia, as have historical figures such as Leonardo da Vinci. Indeed, new research has hinted at links between dyslexia and creativity, although the findings are mixed, and education seems to play an important role.[57,58] Kids who have dyslexia might not learn *worse*, but *differently*.

At the same time, as decades of studies show, you *can* teach a child with dyslexia to read.[59] It might never be his favorite subject, but many do just fine. Decades of research have shown that dyslexia can be remediated through the use of structured reading programs. We now know very well which types of reading instruction help kids with dyslexia make progress and thrive.

Beyond this education, Brandon needed to see himself as a complete individual: a great friend, a solid soccer player, and a curious thinker, as well as someone with a learning challenge. Dyslexia didn't have to define him. Exploring many aspects of their identities lets kids realize they're more than any set of skills. They're more than what they accomplish, or how well they succeed, or how much they do or don't struggle with academic skills.

The Context Counts

After that talk with Brandon's father, I met with Brandon and discussed his diagnosis with him. While I expected the talk to be a difficult one, I was surprised when Brandon said he was relieved. "I thought I wasn't smart," he told me. "I told myself I wasn't good at *anything*. But, really, it's just hard for me to read." Such diagnoses can give a name to struggles kids have had for years. With Brandon, I also focused on why his dyslexia mattered in the here and now—but it didn't matter everywhere, at all times. That helped to put dyslexia in its place.

Soon I asked him to try an experiment. Imagine himself a hundred and twenty years back.[60] Many men worked as laborers and could make a solid income without needing to read. Next, I asked him to imagine himself back before the printing press. Maybe he'd have struggled, if he'd been a monk, but what if he'd been a farmer or a craftsman?[61]

Next, I asked him to imagine himself in another *place*. Since English has many irregular words (such as "sign" and "womb"), its patterns are hard to master. But what if he lived in Spain? Since Spanish is a far less complicated language than English, kids with dyslexia typically read without much trouble, but often more slowly than kids who don't have dyslexia.[62] Spanish kids aren't different from American kids, but their *situation* is. Their difference from typically reading peers might not be as noticeable.

This thought experiment was inspired by my colleagues at Boston Children's Hospital, Deborah Waber and Ellen Boiselle, who write of the "child-world interaction."[63] We often think about a learning disability as something inherent to the child. Really, it has far more to do with an interaction between the child and his or her world; that is, a difference between what the world is asking of a child and what he or she is able to do at any one time. This model can bring powerful realizations. Brendan described realizing how his learning difference felt like a bigger challenge because of where and when he lived, in a society in which literacy skills are all-important. What's more, most of the kids in his class were strong readers, making his reading appear weaker in comparison. It wasn't only the general time and place that made the difference. It was also the *specific* world of his class. Conversations with those close to him could allow him to make sense of these ideas.

....

How, When, and Where: Talk for Differences

Helping kids understand differences—in learning and more generally—means shining a light on the context. *Ask kids: What about this place or time makes your "difference" matter more or less? How might this "problem" look, at another time or place, like a strength? Dyslexia is only one example. For these conversations, try the following:*

1. ***Expand on your child's thinking.*** *How is he making sense of a label or diagnosis? What has he noticed about differences between how he and others learn? If it's another child who seems "different," what has he seen that child doing or saying? Why might he be saying that? Watch for labels, like "dumb" or "useless." Challenge these labels with facts. If necessary, educate yourself.*

2. **Identify ways to accommodate.** *Ask your child: What has helped him learn? What's made things harder? Maybe it's having multiple assignments or longer books. Or maybe it's that his teacher now expects kids to read on their own. Explore actions to help. Try out a tracker for reading, if he tends to skip lines, or a bouncy chair, if he has trouble sitting still. Collaborate with his teachers, framing the conversation as a partnership.*

3. **Encourage action and evaluation.** *I've seen many kids thrive after opening up about their learning struggles. Explore smaller steps; say, talking to a friend. Afterward, ask how he felt and how his friend reacted. If he learns of a friend's challenges, evaluate how he feels after talking with that friend. What does he now understand? What does he still wonder about? That process can work for siblings equally well.*

To Build Openness: Start with Your Attitude

That's not to say these discussions are easy. We may push discomfort under the rug, at times to move kids along, and at times in order not to cause a fuss. I've found myself doing much the same—and not only in terms of learning differences. Questions of gender can feel especially fraught. When Sophie was four years old, she attended a friend's "princess" party, filled with ceramic teacups and pink candles. The girls had dressed up in sparkly outfits. Sophie, who'd never been much of a fan of glitter, pointed to a few pirate costumes stuffed on a rack.

"I want to wear one of those," she said.

"You want to be a *pirate*?"

She nodded.

"Well—okay." I started taking the pirate costume down. But soon, a woman wearing a store badge walked over.

"Those are for boys." She clicked her tongue, watching me with an impatient stare. "Your daughter wouldn't want to stand out."

As the other girls raced around, I asked the woman if she had extra pirate costumes. No, she said. I sensed my irritation rising. Sure, it would be simple to point Sophie to the princess costumes. But we'd already had conversations about what being a girl meant. She worried she wasn't a fan of dolls (a preference that would change) and she liked getting messy (one that would stick). We'd talked about how those preferences were fine.

Sophie kept insisting. Finally, the woman relented, and Sophie happily became a pirate for the next few hours. The incident reminded me of a broader point. Our gender stereotypes, influenced by the messages of our culture, come out in how kids play with one another and how they view one another and themselves. I've been startled to hear even young kids shame those who don't fit the mold. "That's a boy color" or a "girl color" are common complaints.

Over the past twenty years, these stereotypes have become more rigid and regressive than in the preceding thirty, likely due in part to marketing shifts since the early 1980s that emphasized these categories.[64] While the 1970s brought with it the second wave of feminism, and a corresponding flurry of ads challenging gender stereotypes, these challenges were short-lived. In 1984, as sociologist Elizabeth Sweet writes in *The Atlantic*, "the deregulation of children's television programming suddenly freed toy companies to create program-length advertisements for their products, and gender became an increasingly important differentiator of these shows and the toys advertised alongside them." By 1995, she notes, gendered toys composed around half of the offerings in the Sears catalog; the same proportion as that from many decades earlier. Compare that statistic with one from 1975, when less than *two* percent of Sears catalog toys were marketed to either boys or girls.

Advertisements aren't the only reason for kids liking one toy over another, of course. There's a complex mix of culture and biology over which scientists are still arguing. As one review of studies found, from young ages, children do tend to play with toys typed to their own gender. This held true in multiple countries and across the age span from age one through age eight.[65] That's not to say that kids *should* play with such toys, only that they often do. As study author John Barry of University College London argues, "In reality, gendered behavior is a mix of biology and social influence."[66] Both innate factors and social ones play a role.[67]

With all that in mind, it's worth thinking about how you respond to the type of toys and play your child chooses, and how he or she responds to the choices of friends. See if the conversation is one that leans toward openness and exploration, or toward dismissiveness or shame. If it's the latter—either on your part, or that of your child—notice *why* you or she might be feeling negatively about a specific kind of toy or type of play. See if you can start having more relaxed conversations, emphasizing the joy and creativity to be found in play more generally, rather than giving outsize attention to what exactly a child is playing with.

In these conversations, frame play as part of exploring what it means to be a human being. Which positive qualities is your child cultivating with her play—or could she? Emphasize that we all have multiple roles and qualities, and that these don't have to be in conflict. You can be a nurturing father *and* a competitive race-car driver, for example, or a brilliant research scientist *and* a woman who loves taking part in a theater group. Help your child shift from one role to the other freely, without feeling as though it has to be *only* this way, or only that.

This ability to shift is especially important as cultural messaging tends to perpetuate gender stereotypes: boys being more active, for example, and girls giggling and hiding their faces.[68] Such stereotypes can make children's thinking more rigid and prescriptive, as they start believing that things *should* be a certain way. For some kids, these links can seem set in stone. They first make *vertical* associations, linking a category to a habit or trait. For example, "boys like trucks." Later come *horizonal* associations: "Boys like trucks, so they also like monster cars and planes."[69] Rigid thinking tends to peak around ages five or six. Many kids pass through a phase of buying into common stereotypes, believing for example that it's "wrong" for a boy to wear nail polish or a girl to play football, but this unquestioning acceptance of cultural messaging often disappears by elementary school.[70]

Knowing where your child is in his development lets you notice if he's likely in a phase, while allowing you to question his assumptions. Keep in mind that stereotypes can be tough to change, once kids have developed them. You'll probably need multiple discussions over time.[71]

Luckily, in the preteen and teenage years, kids can learn to view categories through a far more nuanced and critical lens. Emphasize the need to refer to people as they refer to themselves. Whatever your perspective about the hot-button topic of gender identity in children, emphasize that it's a question of respect. Many teens have language and terminology for gender differences that simply weren't part of the conversation in earlier years—and many younger kids are already asking to explore the language they hear.[72] Navigating this language is critical not only for "questioning" kids, but all kids, to help friends feel accepted and cared for.

To Discuss Gender and Related Preferences, Use the Three Es:

1. *Expand on children's understanding of gender.* What does it mean to be a "tomboy"? What does a "girly" girl do?

2. *Explore: Where do these ideas come from?* Investigate counterexamples: Do they know anyone who shows a mix of more and less "girly" characteristics? Find examples in media or books.

3. *Help them evaluate their judgments.* Emphasize not leaping to conclusions. Notice when a child shows a preference for a stereotypically "girl" or "boy" activity. Maybe that tells you something about his or her gender identity, but maybe not. Keeping conversations open-ended lets kids test choices without feeling boxed in.

To Build Understanding: Encourage Real-Life Meetings

In the long run, to deepen their understanding, kids need more than talk. Real-life encounters matter—and not only onetime events.[73] Kids need to get to know others with a diverse range of backgrounds over time.

Simply bringing your child into contact with those who are "other"—in ability, race, ethnicity, religion, class, gender, and/or language—is a start. Emphasize positive activities like parties or outings where kids are already poised to get along. Answer questions about difference as objectively as possible, modeling a positive attitude.

Also, notice your own tendencies to tamp down questions or take a neutral question as a judgmental one (for instance, "Why does her hair look like that?"). Explore your child's understanding, with questions like "What language do you think he speaks?" *Expand* on his thinking, clarifying misconceptions. Say he complains about a child speaking English "badly," then clarifies, "He's always mixing English and Spanish. It makes no sense."

Start with active listening. As tempting as it might be to come at these discussions from a punitive angle, that's only likely to make a child defensive. Discuss "code-switching." Code-switching is the act of switching the language or dialogue you use based on your situation or your conversation partners.[74] For example, a child might speak Spanish at home and English at school. Or he might use a southern dialogue, for example saying "y'all," around his southern relatives, but not when he's with his relatives from the North.

Sometimes this code-switching happens even within a single conversation, or a single sentence, called "code-mixing."[75] For example, a bilingual child might shift from one language to another, or dialect to another, mid-sentence or phrase (say, "I like the *gato*"). Many teachers and parents I've met worry about this sort of code-mixing. Maybe, they say, it means the child isn't learning languages well. In fact, many studies have found that this code-mixing is very common, and that kids who do it are as proficient in each language as kids who don't. They're not "confused." They're simply developing skills in an uneven way, as all kids do.[76]

Maybe your family does this sort of code-switching or code-mixing, or a family you know does. Discuss how it's not "wrong" or "harmful," but shows skills in both languages. It's a form of linguistic creativity and a way of navigating social situations. As research has found, people often code-switch without even thinking about it. At other times, they do it as a way to fit in, say something in secret, or convey a thought more precisely.

What if your child is the recipient of negative comments about a perceived difference?

1. *Expand on the comments.* What exactly did the other child say?

2. *Explore your child's emotions.* Does he feel hurt, or embarrassed? Does he fear the comments have a grain of truth?

- Separate facts from assumptions. Maybe he does have an accent or looks different than his friends. But that doesn't mean anything's wrong.

- Search out positive role models. Maybe his uncles or cousins sound similar, or maybe he's heard people talk that way on his favorite show.

3. *Role-play responses, then evaluate how your child feels.* Simply stating, "That's not true," and changing the subject can be more effective than shouting back. The same goes for walking away. Emphasize that these aren't signs of weakness. Especially if a "friend" is consistently negative or critical, ask if he wants to stay friends with someone who makes comments like these.

To Raise Awareness: Use Privilege Talk

The simple fact of where kids are born gives some an advantage, based on the societies they live in. Discussing this privilege helps kids realize it's not a natural law, like "the sky is blue." You're given special treatment based on your membership in a group. And the consequences of this treatment can be huge.[77] Systemic racism and police brutality are one reason why many Black parents I know tell me they talk about race and being targeted "all the time."[78]

In other cases, issues of privilege and discrimination can be far subtler. Still, these issues can have lasting effects. For example, I know several Asian American students who've internalized "model minority" stereotypes. "I *have* to be good at math," one ninth-grader told me, after showing me a failing grade. "All Asian kids are." Such beliefs set them up for self-doubt or shame. When they *do* have trouble, teachers often miss it. They're also less likely to seek help for issues with their academics or mental health, which can lead to problems getting worse.[79,80,81]

If kids don't consider the source of these injustices or stereotypes, they're not likely to question them. To support them, try the following steps: **Notice, Counter, Personalize**:

Notice, Counter, Personalize: Undo Stereotypes

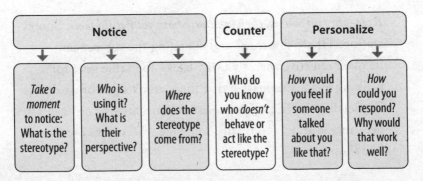

> **Talk Tip:** In discussing difference, focus on small steps and many conversations over time. Praise your child for his willingness to participate.

Privilege depends on the specifics of a child's family, school, and community. It looks and feels different, depending on who's experiencing it. Maybe being blond offers some advantage in your community, or having a British accent does. Encourage your child to keep context in mind.

More broadly, to raise global citizens, try out these habits:

Conversational Habit #1:
To Encourage Exploration, Try the "Swoop"

Focus on localized conversations, using your child's experiences as windows onto the broader world. Try the following:

- *Start with your immediate surroundings.* Move out in circles. Explore: How does your next-door neighbor live differently from you? The person in the next city? The next country? What about their lives is the same?

- *Explore your family history.* This lets your child learn about where he comes from, while recognizing that there may be more diversity within your family than he thought. What's more, preteens and teenagers who know more about their family's history show higher levels of well-being and stronger senses of themselves, as compared to those who know less.[82]

- *Take opportunities when they come*: Think weekends with grandparents, holidays, or family reunions. Discuss your family's journeys from one town to another, or one country to the next. Focus on how relatives managed challenges. This talk builds resilience, inspiring your child to learn from older generations and take on challenges in a similar way.

- *Examine generational changes in talk and behavior.* Why does your child's Hungarian grandmother still make borscht, or cabbage soup? Question how words and traditions evolve. Where did "cool" come from? What about "K-pop," or Korean pop? Knowing what makes their own language, culture, and society unique equips kids to explore other differences positively.

- *Emphasize specific, nonjudgmental language.* Ask not only "What do we call it?" but "What do *they* call it?" Say your neighbor likes empanadas, but you call it "pastry with meat." Discuss which cultures traditionally eat which foods. Focus on the people behind the food. Who first made pizza, and why? Was it Italian immigrants, or did pizza not come from Italy at all?

- *Explore differences within groups and similarities across groups.* Find examples of people not fitting the stereotype. Or use a map as a springboard. Investigate differences within a single country or region. Start with your own. Even in Boston, the North End is called the "Italian district," but many people from China also live there. Highlight differences and commonalities. Maybe your child and his friend from Bangladesh both like mac and cheese—but his friend also likes Bengali recipes.

- *Flip the conversation.* If your child says of a friend, "She likes weird stuff," ask playfully what's "weird" about what *your* child likes. What would a person who eats vegetable soup for lunch say about a Klondike bar? If your child is the recipient of "you're weird" comments, role-play answers that help him feel empowered. Emphasize that we're all "weird" or unique in some way, and there are less hurtful ways to talk about difference.

- *Focus on positive comments about groups,* especially if your child is being negative. At the same time, give yourself a break. Recognize that you're only one piece of the puzzle. When your child hears consistent negative messages about a group, it's not possible for a few conversations to change his whole attitude.[83]

To Celebrate Differences, Use Compare and Contrast

Talk about differences in a positive light. Ask: How do your family's traditions not look like those around you? Do friends celebrate different holidays, or have foods or music you don't recognize? Where does a friend's tradition come from? Move beyond broad guesses, like "I guess it's Asian." Is it from Singapore or Afghanistan? What part? Is it popular at birthdays, or with older or younger people?[84]

Help kids question the idea of cultures and traditions as unchanging. Maybe there are food trucks in Nepal, or the Thai restaurants in your city have been replaced with McDonald's. Maybe a friend's family from India doesn't cook Indian food. Why? These discussions raise awareness that difference is ever-evolving, and that people don't always behave as we might assume.

Conversational Habit #2:
To See the Complexities, Ask "How and Why"

Focusing on "how" and "why" questions about language, culture, and traditions lets your child see how difference is complex and evolving. Try:

- *Investigate present reasons and causes from the past.* Emphasize **cognates**, **links**, and **commonalities** among how you say or do things and how others do. Cognates are words that sound the same in multiple languages. True cognates have similar or identical meanings, such as the German word *essen* and the English *eat*, while false cognates sound the same but mean different things, such as *caliente* (meaning "hot" in Spanish) and *cold*.

- *Explore the "why" of language differences.* Why are there so many "m" words for "mother": *mama, maman, mère*? Which sounds feel comforting versus off-putting?

- *Use analogies to see how diverse traditions and habits have similar functions.* How are a sari and a dress alike? A turban and a hat? Recognize meaningful differences. Why is wearing a turban important? For whom? Ask people who participate in the traditions you're exploring. Emphasize the importance of hearing answers from the people involved.

- *Encourage kids to interview family, friends, and neighbors.* Use humor to help everyone feel welcome and open up. Let your child pretend to be a reporter.

- *Expand your child's "difference palate."* Sensory experiences— food, music, celebrations, and performances—can be a gateway to history and abstract ideas. Why do people eat black-eyed peas on New Year's day? Where does flamenco music come from? Afterward, discuss likes, dislikes, and surprises.

- *Use travel to broaden perspectives.* It doesn't have to be far. Drive around to different neighborhoods and talk about what you notice. You can also travel back in time. For older kids, investigate how your neighborhood has changed. Use maps and historic photos as starting points. Talk to older neighbors. Say you find out that your neighborhood used to house Eastern European immigrants. Do you see evidence of that history in restaurants or street signs? Return to the same places over weeks and months. Try noticing something new each time. Even the most familiar-seeming spots are brimming with history, variation, and change.

Conversations about difference aren't always easy. It can take a long time, and much discussion, for kids to make sense of these ideas and undo learned stereotypes. But if we want them to grow into compassionate, caring people, this process is critical. Think of attachment as going far beyond early childhood. Everyone's heritage is complex. We can be attached to so many people, concepts, and identities in ways that evolve over time. In learning to care for others who are different, kids build attachments that count. That's the secret to helping them collaborate, bridge differences, "play well with others," and ultimately, broaden the borders of their worlds.

CHAPTER 8

Conversations for Temperament: Bringing Out Your Child's Best

Some of our deepest awakenings happen through the intimate and loving connections that remind us most fully of who we are.

—TARA BRACH[1]

When I met Rosie, a friend's two-year-old, on a playground near Boston, she was in the midst of a full-on tantrum. I'd known her and her mother for years but had never seen her in such a state. She was scowling, fists clenched around the handles of an oversize scooter. From the looks of her stained dress and red face, it was obvious she'd been crying for a while.

"*I* do it." She pushed the scooter back and forth. "I *can.*"

"You're not ready," said her mother, Janine, gently trying to guide Rosie's hands onto the handles. "Danielle's scooter is too big for you. You can try, with some help, but not alone."

"*No* . . ." Rosie's wail went up so loudly, everyone on the playground could hear.

"It's not that I haven't let her," her mother said, groaning. "I have, trust me. But she just keeps falling. She's getting hurt. At some point, won't she give up?"

Grabbing the scooter, Rosie pushed off, then promptly fell once again. Soon she started sobbing, dirty and out of sorts. Sighing, Janine said they had to go home.

For a while after that, life got busy, and we didn't see each other. But six months later, after Rosie's third birthday, she came over with her parents and sister, Danielle. At first, I'd expected a similar tantrum or a version of it. But to my surprise, Rosie went directly to the playroom, asked for crayons and paper, and started coloring. Soon she was ordering Sophie's stuffed animals around, telling the elephant to sit and reminding the pony, "Make sure you don't neigh, okay?"

The difference was astounding. Even her body language had changed. No longer was she standing with clenched fists; instead, she gazed up, proud and content. Struck by the shift, I thought that it had perhaps just been a result of natural development or a new preschool. I knew enough not to expect a magic bullet. So I was surprised when Janine said, without missing a beat, "She definitely *has* grown up. But we've also learned to work with her style."

"What do you mean?"

"I used to give her the activities her sister liked." Janine glanced over. "Then I'd help her with them. Danielle always liked being helped, and I did too, as a child. Even now, I *like* getting direction. But Rosie always fought. It was *no no no*, nonstop. So I decided I wouldn't keep pushing."

Often, when Rosie tried to do her sister's activities by herself, she got frustrated. Janine noticed herself wanting to jump in as a parent and stop Rosie from trying. She'd tell Rosie the activity was too hard, and they should find something better to do. As a parent, Janine recognized *she* was getting frustrated with Rosie's frustration! Ever since childhood, Janine hadn't wanted to try things that felt too far out of her reach. She was surprised at how different Rosie was from herself as a child. Equally important, she noticed that those differences were rubbing up against each other in unhelpful ways. Rosie wanted to keep trying, even if she kept failing, and Janine wanted her to do something simpler and find easier success.

But, with her new philosophy, Janine noticed Rosie's persistence and realized that Rosie didn't mind the struggle. The next time Rosie wanted to do a "too-hard" activity, Janine agreed. Approaching the situation positively, she framed it—for herself and Rosie—as a challenge. She laid out a few ground rules: No hurting yourself or others. If you need help, ask. If you want to try it out alone, say, "I've got it," or something similar, and Janine wouldn't assist.

"It's made a huge difference," Janine told me, as Rosie continued her play school. "I think it's that she senses we know *her*, and how she's different from her sister. She sees we're adapting to her—and I think that makes her more willing to adapt to us."

All that hadn't made Rosie's tantrums disappear. But it *had* done something powerful. Rosie's independent, persistent temperament had been a problem when she was younger, and when much more had been out of her reach. Her temperament had also been *framed* as a problem—especially when Janine had kept trying to force a style that wasn't working. But Janine had started taking a more reflective stance. She noticed the differences in how well she and Rosie tolerated frustration and how much they wanted to persist. Then she made small shifts in response. She reflected on Rosie's actions and her own reactions, becoming more conscious of the mismatches between them. And she did so in a way that wasn't punitive or angry, but that highlighted how Rosie's willingness to keep trying was a positive.

In the past, Janine realized, she'd been calling Rosie "stubborn." She started thinking instead of her daughter as "persistent," and using that same word when speaking about Rosie to others. This shift allowed her to respond to Rosie's attempts more positively and helpfully, supporting Rosie just enough, but no more.

That's only one small example of how noticing a child's temperament can enhance your interactions. Most likely, you can find examples in your own life, in which child and parent benefit from taking temperament into account. Maybe you're far more active than your child, who usually wants to relax. On Saturday mornings, you're ready to head out early, and he wants to lounge around.

It's easy to assume our way is the natural way. But neither way is "right." Simply being slow to wake up doesn't make your child "lazy." Rather, when you notice the difference in a more neutral light, you can start using dialogue to find compromises. Even when kids are still young, noticing and working with their temperaments helps them blossom, while making your interactions far smoother, less stressful, and more fun.

Rosie's story reminded me of the work of the physicians Alexander Thomas and Stella Chess, who argued that the temperaments of kids and parents influence *each other*.[2] How well your temperaments fit together changes your interactions, in a dynamic called match and mismatch. Think about two puzzle pieces—or more than two, including siblings or other family. A good fit means a child's temperament meshes well with yours. A poor fit means you may have a clash.

But those clashes aren't inevitable. When we take the time

to see a child in all his or her fullness, we can make space for a different approach. That's especially important with mismatches. Talking with kids about temperament—their own, and ours—raises the issue into consciousness. This lets us evolve well together, celebrate both our similarities and our differences, and find ways to let each person thrive.

Rich Talk Is Individualized— the "No Recipe" Recipe

In the last chapter, we explored conversations about diversity among children. But so much diversity exists even *within* children, based on their underlying temperaments. How active is your child? How rambunctious or studious? How much does he embrace or fear risks? The answers differ for each child, and to some extent change over time.

On the surface, it might seem odd to go from the biggest possible topic (raising a global citizen) to the smallest (understanding each person's temperament). But these two dimensions are far more connected than they seem. No matter how global our conversations, we're all looking at the world from our own individualized, quirky perspectives. Dynamics shift unpredictably, as kids meet new friends, start new schools or activities, or simply grow up. Noticing how a child evolves over the short and long term is a powerful way to meet her needs and help her adapt to the world around her. Over time, in this process, she becomes more flexible, and our relationship becomes more seamless—or can. She also becomes far more self-aware, appreciating the positive sides of her quirks and finding ways to get along when she needs to.

Really, assumptions about a child "being" one way or the other miss the point. "He's shy," we might say, or "excitable," or "difficult." We often miss the nuances. We also tend to forget that it's *we* who perceive the temperament and assign a label. These labels shape our conversation and over time affect who our kids become. If Janine had kept redirecting, and Rosie's tantrums had worsened, their dynamic could have become truly negative. Rosie might have started seeing herself as a "bad kid," and Janine as the "nagging mother." Instead, Janine's shift primed them for a more positive dynamic. They each felt better about themselves and didn't feel stuck in their roles.

In this way, quality conversation lets you get to know your kids intimately, and lets *them* get to know *you*, not as a onetime process, but in an ongoing way. Especially in a culture so focused on efficiency and success, this knowledge lets you take another path. It encourages a different vision of success, focused on building an authentic, connected relationship in which you both thrive. That thriving looks different from child to child and family to family. And that's precisely the point. When you start from a perspective of knowing each child individually, you're primed to see how to help *him* thrive. All that starts with understanding the true nature of temperament.

What Is Temperament Anyway?

Temperament has to do with the strength of a child's reactions, as well as his typical emotional state and how easily he regulates himself.[3] How much does he startle at unfamiliar sights or sounds? When he gets upset, how long does it take to calm down? What's his overall energy level and mood? Think of it as the "how" of talk and behavior. It's different from *ability*, or how well a child performs, and from motivation, or *why* he acts as he does. Most scientists believe temperament starts showing up in infancy, has a biological basis, and remains somewhat stable over time.[4]

And thinking about temperament goes far back. In the second century, the philosopher Galen proposed four temperaments, based on the body's "humors."[5] *Melancholic* temperaments, with an excess of black bile, are quiet but analytical. *Sanguine* temperaments, related to an excess of blood, are hopeful and carefree. Having too much "phlegm" meant you'd have a *calm* temperament, while too much yellow bile meant you'd be *angry*. An ideal temperament meant a balance of the four.[6] These concepts, long ago debunked, likely sound medieval to our ears. Still, hints of Galen's philosophy remain in our language, as when we call someone "melancholic."[7]

Modern thinking about temperament took shape in the 1950s, when the physicians Alexander Thomas and Stella Chess studied more than one hundred infants. Some, they found, were "easy," some "difficult," and others "slow to warm."[8] As of 1970, they created a temperament model that's still popular today, with nine elements: how physically *active* a child is; how *regular* his biological functions, such as waking and sleeping, are; how *adaptable* he is; how much he *approaches or withdraws* from a new situation; how *sensitive* he is; how *intensely* he reacts; how *distractible* he is; how his *mood* typically is; and how long he *persists and pays attention.*[9] In later years, the psychologist Mary Rothbart consolidated their ideas down to three: how *extroverted* a child is, how *negative* his overall mood, and how easily he can *regulate* his behavior and feelings—for example, how well can he soothe himself?[10,11]

You can see those elements playing out in everyday ways. Think about a child whose school-bus route changes. He has to wake up early, then sit with a new group of kids. A year back, this happened to two ten-year-old girls I know, living a few doors apart. We met at a neighborhood park, and they started discussing how school had gone. One girl, Marie, said she'd had a terrible week. She'd woken up late every morning and had to rush. She'd arrived at the bus tired, then sat in silence, eating bread she hadn't had time to toast, and with no friends she knew. Rachel, standing beside her, told a different story. Her eyes brightened as she described leaving the house before her brother and sitting beside friendly teenagers on the bus.

What explained the difference in their perspectives? Rachel was more optimistic, true. But where did her optimism come from? I soon realized it had to do with temperament. Rachel had always been an early riser. Since toddlerhood, she'd had an easy time with transitions, such as starting preschool. She'd been more *adaptable*, at least when the challenge wasn't too far over her head.

For Marie, missing sleep left her in a terrible mood. Since infancy, she'd had trouble sleeping. She'd thrived with predictable routines and schedules. Preschool had been great, once she'd gotten used to going. But new situations could leave her feeling distressed, even overwhelmed.

While overall mood is one part of temperament, other factors play a role. Probably Rachel had an easier time *approaching* new people, while Marie often withdrew. Perhaps Marie was more *sensitive* to noise, so the bustle of bus passengers stressed her out. Most likely, Rachel was more *extroverted*, drawn to bigger groups, while Marie needed more quiet and downtime.

We don't often think about these factors. We only see the result—Marie complaining and Rachel talking excitedly—and end up drawing conclusions about who the girls are as people. An outsider might assume, "Marie isn't friendly," or ask her, "Why can't you be more like Rachel?" That's especially true if you're more like Rachel, and meeting new people seems simple.

Our talk often comes out of wanting to help kids adapt. We're well intended. But comments like the ones above aren't likely to help Marie—and probably won't do much for your relationship. Instead, becoming conscious of each child's temperament, as it plays out, lets you help her shine for who she is.

The Long Shadow of Temperament

Learning a child's temperament is like watching a mystery unfold— one you can see in glimmers, even as you can't know how it will turn out. It's not like having blue eyes, or some other quality that settles down early on. Instead, it's a constant evolution, stretching into adulthood. This process has enchanted me long before becoming a mother, and continues to as my kids grow. Traits stick with a child and *also* are open to evolution. Temperament casts a "long shadow," in the words of the prominent American psychologist Jerome Kagan.[12] The infant who keeps crying until he's changed may become a ten-year-old who reads for hours.

When Sophie was three years old, she begged to practice the monkey bars daily. She worked to reach for the first rung, falling dozens of times until she could make it across. Once she'd accomplished that, she kept going until she could *skip* a rung.

"I've got it!" she finally said, pumping her fist.

"Does she do gymnastics?" another mother asked me, and I shook my head. "She just likes to keep trying," I said.

Years later, as I sat with eight-year-old Sophie, watching her read the same book for the third time, I wondered if she was showing that same persistence from five years back, in another form. But she had changed, as had her circumstances. Her friends and teachers had begun to play a bigger role—and her interests were different, too. It's that change in the midst of stability that intrigues me: How does *that* baby become *this* child, then *this* teenager?

At times, these changes can be subtle and hard to see. It's a lot like height: you tend to notice changes more in kids you don't see much. I often laugh to see the changes in temperament in friends' kids from year to year. So often, what I expected surprises me, as a trait takes an unexpected turn, or one that once served a child well starts causing problems.

The beauty of temperament is also its challenge. Take a fifteen-year-old I know, Lisa, who's very diligent, completing her homework without being nagged and planning projects ahead of time. On the surface, she's primed for better academic achievement and even higher social skills.[13] The downside? Such kids may be perfectionistic, and less flexible and spontaneous.[14] I remember hearing that Lisa did her work even when it felt like drudgery, not noticing what she liked or didn't. But later, when given a choice of projects, she complained that she didn't know what interested her.

The psychiatrist David Rettew, author of the book *Child Temperament*, talked to me of the "and yet" phenomenon. We expect kids to be friendly "and yet" not too sociable or active "and yet" not too impulsive.[15,16] "We want it both ways," he says. But that's impossible. Worse, if you try to "fix" harder parts of a child's temperament, you may tamp down positives. If you insist a child calm down on playdates, he may become less sociable overall.

That's one example of how temperament isn't as fixed as it looks.

It evolves in a daily back-and-forth between kids and their environments. And we as adults play a fundamental role. Fearful, cautious infants, Kagan found, often become shy adults, especially when parents are overprotective. Yet, as he found in one study, when parents encouraged their infants to socialize, the infants became less inhibited as teenagers.[17] Early support set the stage for kids to make friends more easily. Talk that fits your child's tendencies lets you relate better in the moment. Long-term, it develops their strong suits and shores up their weaker sides. And all that starts in the earliest years.

Temperament Differences Start Early

"Who *is* this child?" more than one parent I know has wondered, peering into his baby's face in the early days of life. Indeed, elements of temperament do show up early. Traits play out as kids grow. From early on, biology puts some kids at risk. Preterm babies, by the time they're toddlers, tend to have more challenges regulating emotions, stronger reactions to new situations, and more trouble paying attention.[18] They're also at risk for speaking and listening problems, probably since they have shorter attention spans.[19,20] But these tendencies aren't universal and don't always last.[21] In my clinical work, I've been surprised to review a thick file—a difficult birth, a need for intensive care—and then see a dynamic, talkative child.

At the same time, even nine-month-old babies show vast differences in temperaments. Take any meetup of new parents; you'll likely find one eager infant and one sobbing uncontrollably. A happy babbler tends to attract more excited responses. She may also let you feel more successful as a parent. Your self-talk grows more positive. "I can do this," you think. Later, you might sense that your kids are opposite, temperament-wise, from you—or you're eerily similar. "I'll read for hours," one father of three kids said, "but they run around from morning to night." Or, as a mother of teens told me, "When they whine, I hear my mother's voice—and mine."[22,23]

It's true: the way kids talk gives a window into their temperaments. Some jump in eagerly, not worrying about mistakes. Others wait till they're sure of themselves. Temperament deeply affects how softly or quietly they speak, how quickly or slowly, whether in a boisterous or somber tone. It impacts how they interact with strangers, how much they sing or sit still, the kinds of friends they make, how teachers interact with them, and even how they perceive themselves.

What's more, as I've come to find, listening to kids talk can tell a lot about temperament. Preschool kids who stutter tend to have more negative moods and more trouble adapting than those who don't.[24] I've seen so many kids pinned as not smart or asocial, due to how readily they talk. We often hear silence as a lack of interest or apathy. "He doesn't talk" becomes "he doesn't *want* to."[25] Those assumptions affect how we relate to kids and how they see themselves. Our relationships with them change how they interact with others, and how they're treated, in a cycle that goes on and on.

Still, a complex interplay of nurture and nature affects how temperaments play out.[26] Some kids simply want to talk more than others do. Family structure also affects temperament—say, if a child is an "only" or has many siblings. One family I know, with six kids, has everyone vying for talk time. If a child doesn't push to be heard, he's likely to get left behind. Still, the effects differ for each child. Talk that challenges one may defeat another. The same message that builds one's confidence may break another down.

A More Complex Picture

As it turns out, the "long shadow" of temperament isn't always fixed. New situations can bring out new aspects or change how they look. Some aspects aren't even visible when kids are babies; for example, impulse control. Even most toddlers are still in the earliest—messy—stages of mastery. As Sophie diplomatically said of Paul, "He's doing well . . . *for his age*." He'd managed to wait a minute at the swings before shrieking, "My turn!"

Was Paul patient or impulsive? In fact, traits aren't all one way or the other. They come in a spectrum, or shades, and can shift over time, based on how kids come to interact with the world around them, and how others respond.[27] Maybe your son seems very inhibited at age four, but only slightly at seven. What's more, each aspect of temperament can affect the others, in ways that shape the child we eventually see.

Say two babies tend to be "difficult," or colicky, and often in negative moods. A few years later, the first baby, Matthew, has learned to control his impulses reasonably well; say, not throwing a toy when he's angry (at least sometimes). The second, Victor, hasn't been as successful. When he's excited, he tips over his chair. When he's upset, he pushes. By preschool, Matthew generally hears positive feedback from parents and teachers. Victor often gets called disruptive and put in time-out.[28] He doesn't get to see his friends as much as Victor does, and he doesn't spend as much time learning. Once curious and interested, he becomes withdrawn.

Using the terms of temperament, Matthew's negative affect has gone into hiding. Victor's is all the more evident. That difference will likely create a widening gap between the kids, in terms of their learning, relationships, and happiness. It's a spiral: the happier we are with a child's behavior, the more pleasantly we talk, and the more we highlight the positive aspects of his temperament. "Good job sharing," we might tell Matthew, which encourages him to share more. Or "You're always *acting out*," we may say to Victor, as we put him in his room. When he sits by himself, he doesn't learn skills to stop acting out, but only ruminates. The negative side of his temperament may win out.

Certainly some traits put kids at risk for physical and social challenges. Young kids who are more impulsive and extroverted tend to overestimate their abilities. They're prone to getting hurt more often. "I can do *that*," they think, seeing a tall fence that looks perfect for climbing.[29] As they reach adulthood, more impulsive kids are more likely to get into legal trouble, while very inhibited kids can be plagued by anxiety, depression, and phobias, leaving them in need of special attention and support.

Still, if we focus only on how our child acts, we're missing half the picture. A child's temperament, as it plays out, has as much to do with *us* as with him.[30]

That's especially true of temperament and sex. We tend to think of the two as related, and there's some truth to that. In one review of studies, girls on average had an easier time regulating their emotions than boys. Boys tended to be more active and less shy and were more likely to enjoy high-intensity experiences, like racing cars.[31] But there's a huge range. You're as likely to have a louder girl as a quiet, well-regulated boy. How surprised you are by your "loud" girl changes how you interact with her. Do you tamp her down, or encourage her spirit? How does she react—by quieting down or getting louder? Your reactions change how she behaves, which changes how you think of her—and on and on, in a spiral that powerfully shapes you both.

Temperament Talk Helps Kids
Come to Terms with Themselves

In earlier years, I didn't put much stock in temperament, or the importance of these spirals. It wasn't until I started my clinical work that I really noticed them playing out.

At one school meeting, a mother, Gabriella, spoke of worrying about her ninth-grade son, Jim, who seemed inhibited. As a child, she'd been equally shy. While she'd developed a successful career as a business consultant, she still found it hard to collaborate. As an adult, her severe trouble with public speaking had made aspects of her career extremely stressful, and had led her to turn down opportunities that could have benefitted her. "I don't want him to have my problems," she said, noting that she and Jim both had dyslexia.

Over the next weeks, I helped Jim come to terms with his diagnosis and also advocate for himself. I didn't want to "make" him extroverted. Instead, I wanted to honor his temperament while helping him test his limits. I recognized the trend Susan Cain describes in her 2012 book *Quiet*.[32] Schools in the United States often privilege extroversion, ignoring traits like thoughtfulness and creativity that introversion can bring. Indeed, while Jim had great ideas, he didn't want to draw attention to himself. His teacher complained that he didn't contribute, adding to his frustration and his negative evaluation of his abilities.

Using the Three Es, I began by *expanding* on his perspective, asking why he didn't want attention.

"I want to be sure I have something good to say first," he told me.

We discussed this feeling as natural, acceptable, and even helpful, in making sure he was prepared. We then *explored* ways to have that quality work for him. I asked him to describe his ideal way of responding. "I need a plan," he said. We decided on a system: He'd put Post-it notes on his desk. When he had ideas, he'd scribble them down, read them over, choose one, then raise his hand. Later, we'd discuss how well that worked, and change as needed.

This process let him see his own tendencies with compassion and recognize that they weren't "bad." His new system let him *evaluate* his ideas, raising his self-awareness about their quality. As a bonus, he got practice writing and reading, which was especially useful for a child with dyslexia. He could feel good about himself while adapting to the situation in a way that suited his temperament.

The Fit Between School and a Child's Temperament

My work with Jim confirmed the importance of context and "fit" that I'd sensed as a clinician in training, moving schools every few months. Those public schools enrolled kids from diverse ethnic and socioeconomic backgrounds but differed in a few key ways. In one school, the bell clanged every period, so loudly it shook the desks. Announcements buzzed frequently over the loudspeaker.

"Jose R. to the principal's office," the announcement crackled. Jose fake-hid under his desk. "Not me, okay?" He looked flushed when he reappeared.

Afternoons, the kids raced to the playground, voices echoing. The scramble left me with a sense of claustrophobia. I thought it was only me—a lifelong introvert, sensitive to sound—but soon, I saw Jose and a few other kids hanging back. When I asked if he was all right, he smiled bleakly and said, "I need some time for nothing, if that's okay."

At the time, I didn't think much of it. But upon reflection, his comment revealed a deeper issue. Many kids need "time for nothing" that our schools and homes frankly don't allow. When teachers speak at rapid-fire pace, kids with slower processing speeds and those with more reactive temperaments can get left behind. Our achievement culture only exacerbates the issue: kids are pushed to answer quickly, without much attention to learning styles or temperament needs.[33]

At another school in Winthrop, Massachusetts, I found a different story. On my subway ride to the school beside the ocean, I grew energized. In smaller classes, kids could work in groups, with more space in between them, or alone. Staggered lunchtimes let them talk with fewer friends. The bell rang, but without the same clanging. Even the hallways felt quieter.

Feeling calmer, I asked fewer but more pointed questions. Rather than asking, "Did that make sense?" I noticed their responses: Did they laugh at jokes? Did they read with expression?

Slowly, I recognized how much context changed how kids performed, even who they seemed to be. Some who stayed silent in groups retold stories perfectly one-on-one. Some jumped in before I'd finished my thought but solved puzzles carefully. These children became my teachers. Soon I began to focus on how they blossomed or shut down, based in part on how their teachers, their classmates, and I responded to them. I began making hypotheses about which sorts of conversational openings would have them talking a mile a minute, and which would have them responding with one-word answers, like "fine," or not at all. I also started to notice how *I* felt about my side of the conversation. When did I feel more stressed, I asked myself, or more at ease? And I started to pay attention to the context—the time of day, the season, even the weather—as it shaped children's moods, learning, and relationships. If kids were hungry before lunch, or restless before a snowstorm, I knew it would be harder to engage them. That held true for most kids, at least—and some were especially sensitive to any change in routine.

Focusing on temperament, I learned alongside those kids. Talk let me meet them where they were; not to transform them, but to highlight their quirks, preferences, and individual needs.

We don't always see our own role in these interactions. In fact, our temperaments affect our emotions and everyday language—the words we choose, when we use them, even our tone—and change how children react. For example, from young ages, kids who seem more irritable and anxious tend to draw more negative talk from us, and vice versa.[34] It's not the occasional upset, but the long-term pattern that matters most.[35] The same goes for a positive cycle.

Later, as a mother, the importance of these dynamics really hit home. For years, Sophie has been sensitive to sound. Even though I *know* that, it's still hard to remember—until that fact comes boomeranging back.

"Stop *screaming* at me," seven-year-old Sophie said one day when Philippe asked her (politely, for the third time) to get dressed. She *was* being melodramatic. But her reaction brought home the way a quiet request can sound, to some, like a roar.

Still, as I came to see, temperament isn't static. For years, Sophie's teachers had called her *quiet but independent*. She tended to hang back on playdates. Paul was different. At two years old, he waved to strangers and called the construction workers outside our window his "friends." It was tempting to call him "the social one."

But as soon as you see traits as static, kids will surprise you. With age, Sophie has become far more sociable and now trumps Paul in talking your ear off. At our last parent-teacher conference, her teachers said, "She always makes us laugh." She'd become more jokey at home, too. Reflecting on that comment, I saw how she'd changed and how my picture of her could as well.

As I watched her over time, I saw what I knew from the research: a child's temperament *draws* traits from his environment.[36],[37] The more you encourage a child's sociability or persistence, and highlight those traits, the more likely he'll tend that way. The opposite also holds true. He whines; your irritable mood worsens, and you nag him. He responds by whining more. If he starts sounding *less* whiny, you might not notice. You see what you expect to see.

The context matters. Take a quiet child in a very quiet family. At home, he seems ordinary, but at school, his friends tell him to speak up. The same goes for a very active child in a laid-back family: he stands out at home, but at rock-climbing camp, falls into line with the rest. Your temperament also influences how you see your child's traits. "Why don't you have more friends?" you ask, while he's content with those he has.[38]

That's why there's wisdom in not labeling kids too early—and to tread carefully if you do. It's natural to say, "That's the risk-taker" or "That's my joker," especially when you have more than one child. We often give kids labels to support them. "He'll need to be less impulsive," we might say. Those shortcuts aren't necessarily bad. The problem comes when we overly rely on them.

Indeed, a child's temperament is complex and multifaceted. He may be cooperative but moody, melancholic but materialistic. He's one way at home, one way at camp, another way at school. His brother's shyness may rub off on him, or he may get louder to prove he's the opposite. Later on, temperaments can go into "hiding," as kids may conceal their more vulnerable emotions. Your teen might seem laid-back to her friends, but to you, she's constantly stressed. Out of this complexity, it's impossible to create a single "box"— especially one that would account for the nuances of change over time.[39]

Different Parenting for Different Temperaments

Indeed, temperament develops as a two-way street. While it has genetic roots, it can evolve, in part based on how we and others respond. You can say the exact same words, in the same tone, to two kids. One will giggle, the other will dissolve into tears.[40]

You also change based on who your kids are, and who you see them becoming. Often, these changes are unconscious. As my friend Katie de Dominicis said, "My husband and I are each three different people to our three different kids." With her oldest, a boy—quieter, often empathetic—she often becomes less bubbly.

And that sort of change is a good thing. Kids don't need a one-size-fits-all approach. Noticing their nuances lets you parent more proactively. In one study, children with high self-control benefited from less structure and less oversight. Those with lower self-control did better with more structure. Another study of eight-to-twelve-year-olds found that, when the mother's style suited the child's temperament, the child experienced *half* the depression and anxiety, compared with a less ideal fit.[41] That is, kids who already have a lot of self-control don't need more controlling. They benefit from a more open-ended, looser approach, with less guidance and more chances to make choices. As one of the study's authors, the

University of Washington psychology professor Liliana Lengua, argues, "For kids who already have their own self-control, parents who offer a lot of guidance and structuring may be providing overcontrol or over-structuring."[42] But kids who don't have a lot of self-control need that additional guidance—at least until they develop more.

In this case, one size really doesn't fit all. It's most important to be able to adapt. And that back-and-forth dialogue, focused on knowing your kids and having them know you, is the key to adapting in a way that grows with your child.

In a world of Tiger Moms versus Free-Range Parents, it's important to remember that there is no one "right" parenting style. The best style is the one that works for both children and parents; that helps each individual family find their right "fits."

What about that good fit? At its best, it can feel seamless. You love reading the newspaper while your child sits coloring. Or you're both adventurous and enjoy testing out new snowboarding spots. With a good fit, a child tends to have higher self-esteem, more flexible thinking, and stronger feelings of belonging. A poor fit, on the other hand, can hurt a child's chances for thriving, *especially* if you're not conscious of it. This is especially true for children at risk of developing behavior problems, or those with developmental delays, as you may become less playful in response.[43] Unintentionally, he can get the message there's something wrong with him. He may try to hide or tamp down aspects of himself, or develop negative self-talk if he thinks he needs to "fix" himself, which can leave him anxious or depressed.

Say your child is very active and impulsive, while you're more cautious. You take a trip to a waterfall and see him leaning close to the edge.

"Be *careful*," you say, and he responds, "But I wasn't *doing* anything."

"Do you want to end up in the ER?" you ask, your voice rising as you clutch his jacket. "I can't believe how you *never think*."

He jumps, and you reprimand. The pattern repeats. Soon he asks to go home.

Sure, he needs to be careful—but you may be overly cautious.[44] That's where paying attention to mismatches, and to your reactions, can help.

That's especially true in times of developmental shifts. Say you're an early riser, while your child is slow to get started. You've always argued in the morning, but in his teenage years, your arguments have gotten worse. He naturally needs more sleep, but you can't help thinking, "He's so unmotivated."[45] But he's not more unmotivated than before. In fact, he was never "unmotivated." It's the label you gave him. Sure, he might have trouble getting out of bed. But the mismatch between you can make the situation worse. Reflecting on that mismatch can help. Instead of yelling, then beating yourself up, imagine how you might collaborate with him to get both your needs met. Notice how your own temperament makes it hard to understand his—and try to separate your emotions from the facts.

That same noticing can help with bigger-picture questions. In wanting a child to turn out one way or choose a certain career path, we may push aside his interests and natural temperament. "You're going to be a lawyer like your dad," I've heard parents say, or "I bet you'll be an engineer like your cousin." Maybe so—but what if your child doesn't have an argumentative temperament or isn't detail-oriented? Or what if he simply doesn't like the subjects? When we notice each child's evolving temperament and respond to it compassionately, we're far less likely to try to mold a child into someone he's not. We're more likely to nurture his natural qualities and support him in his weaker areas.

This echoes the psychologist Alison Gopnik's idea about two parenting styles: the "carpenter," who thinks children can be molded into what we like, versus the "gardener," who believes our role is to create space for them to blossom. As she writes, "Unlike a good chair, a good garden is constantly changing, as it adapts to the changing circumstances of weather and the seasons." A child who has room to be herself is "more robust and adaptable than the most carefully tended hothouse bloom."[46] When we work *with*, rather than *against*, her temperament, we acknowledge her individuality and empower her to build a life that's uniquely hers.

The Trouble with Our "Temperament Talk"

So if paying attention to temperament is so important, why don't we? Our default settings and the messages culture gives us often push us not to notice temperament. In a rush, we don't take the time to support kids in adapting to new situations. We miss the opportunity to help them turn their temperaments to their advantage. In part, we're responding to the achievement emphasis of many schools, which prioritizes forward motion over depth. When assessing or teaching, I often see kids who've been "helpfully" pushed ahead for years. They've learned to cope, but the nuances of their temperament get forgotten: *how* they approach tasks, how they learn and make friends, and what they need to feel comfortable. They end up feeling *helped*, but not always *heard*.

It's not only school structures that make it hard to know each child authentically. The consumer focus of modern society doesn't help. So many people talk about creating a "personal brand," or a statement or vision that sums you up. That often encourages us as adults to project a single identity. Are you an entrepreneur, a wellness guru, or a high-functioning engineer? This emphasis, and the related talk, trickles down to kids. Awash in videos of nine-year-old You-Tube stars, kids can understandably start believing that they should act "on brand." As Sophie told me after returning from a playdate, where she'd watched a few YouTubers perform, "Which one should I be like to be rich?" Why be authentic when there's a multimillion-dollar empire at stake? There's a big emphasis on performing well— and earning money for it—as opposed to being yourself.

At a more minor level, we often encourage kids to move ahead, simply in the interest of time. In the midst of things, we don't want to go overboard and do a deep dive into every single thought or worry. At times, that makes sense. It's important to encourage kids to take risks and show up in the face of fear—especially if you sense they can handle it. I've done much the same. When Sophie was three, I took her to a puppet show for the first time. Before the show, she started crying and said she was scared to go. She didn't like the darkness, she said.

"You'll get over it," I said. I took her hand, even as she whined, and we went in.

It wasn't the most friendly comment, but it was true. And, as soon as the show started, she was fine. If I'd rushed her home, we'd have missed the show—and she'd have missed the chance to chal-lenge her idea that puppet shows were scary. She'd have let her fear get the best of her.

Yes, kids are hearty and will "get over" a lot. We don't want to blow a small comment out of proportion, or teach them that, if they feel a hint of fear, they should turn around. But, even in the face of those minor challenges, it's helpful to reflect after the fact. Reflecting on what's hard and why develops their self-awareness, which lets them adapt. They learn to take chances, work with their worries, and if needed, stretch their understanding of what's "too risky" or "too hard."

When we focus on more trivial or mundane matters, we miss the chance to see how kids are making sense of the world: how they perceive others and how they're perceived. We lose the deeper meaning behind their words. Say you tell your two kids, "It'll be rainy tomorrow." They say, "Okay." One child feels excited, anticipating a cozy day inside, while his brother, who wants to play soccer, feels dread. If *you* were hoping for a sunny day, the first child's excitement might grate on you—and, by dinnertime, you find yourselves irritated, in opposite moods.

But being always on the go means we don't tend to notice these mismatches, at times due to qualities we can't easily help. Mary, a friend of mine, talked about needing downtime after a busy party, while her daughter Laurel wanted to chat about everything.

"Weren't Caroline's Converse cool?" Laurel asked, hardly stopping for a breath. "Did you like the hot dogs? And do you think we'll have another party soon?"

"I don't know, all right?" Mary snapped.

"Why are you so grumpy?" Laurel responded. "What did I *say*?"

Mary looked up and was surprised to see Laurel in tears. In the moment, Mary hadn't felt her irritation rising. By the time she *did*, it was too late. Even for adults, it's tricky to notice these patterns. For kids, it's harder—especially when emotions are running high. It would have been more effective for Mary to have said she needed a minute or suggest Laurel call a friend to chat.

At the same time, children's temperaments might look different, and play out differently, depending on their environments. It all depends on what we value and what we ask of them.

Our Environments Shape Our Temperaments

Take a quality like patience. Is it a virtue? Your answer depends in part on where you grew up. The same goes for risk-taking. In an individualistic, competitive society like the United States, we often see it as a positive, but that's not universal. These big-picture issues affect the temperaments kids develop, as they emphasize qualities they're praised for.

How do these patterns play out in different environments? To learn more, I called Dorsa Amir, a postdoctoral fellow at Boston College. While Amir focuses on studying the Shuar, an indigenous tribe in Ecuador, her research on temperament has taken her all over the world. When we spoke, she'd just returned from a trip and laughed at how everything in Boston seemed so "bright" and how grocery stores sold a dozen kinds of milk.[47]

We think of our stores as normal because that's what we grew up with. The same goes for temperament. It's easy to assume the qualities *we* value are the same ones everyone else does. Amir's work upends that idea. She traveled to four different countries to study patience in kids. As she found, Shuar kids—who lived in a very rural society—were more risk-averse and impatient than kids in industrialized countries, who had easier access to markets and stores. Couldn't that be a cultural difference?

To find out, she studied two rural Shuar groups, one even more isolated than the other. The more isolated group was more impatient and willing to take risks.[48]

"Patience, for these kids, wasn't helpful," she told me. When getting food isn't easy, you jump at the first chance you have. These kids weren't born with different temperaments. They were only responding to their circumstances. When you're isolated, without many chances to get food, taking a risk to make sure you eat is logical. But if you're sure you'll find food in a nearby store, risk-taking makes far less sense. These differences also held true for parental expectations. Many Shuar kids do "adult-like" tasks—cooking over fire, cutting with knives—with little supervision. To many middle-class parents living in Boston or New York, they might look quite independent. But to their parents, they're simply ordinary.

Of course, kids in Boston or New York obviously vary greatly as well, in terms of how many risks they're willing to take. In part, it's a question of individual temperament. But it also depends on what they're asked. A child is more likely, for example, to cut with knives if her parents expect her to—and if her parents are both working late, and dinner depends on her preparations.[49,50]

That is, temperaments depend on the environment and our assumptions.[51,52] Before assuming what qualities kids *should* have, look first at what you or others are asking of them. Think about temperament as a set of strategies, making it easier or harder to adapt.

How Conversation Helps

Each family has its own set of temperaments, with matches and mismatches that shift over time. If we don't notice and respond flexibly, we can get into ruts that create larger disconnects. Say your son has a relaxed temperament and works at his own pace. If you push him to finish his homework, he slows down. Frustrated, you might nag or lower your expectations. As the weeks pass, you come to *expect* the argument—or even start thinking of yourself as an irritable person. That is, your comments change how you think about yourself.

But that's not how things have to go. Recognizing and managing dynamics is the key to making positive shifts. Without forcing change, you can become more conscious of how your temperaments support and detract from each other. Your child learns to see traits not as bad or good, but as qualities he can work with, more independently as he grows.

Helping your child with this perspective means taking advantage of "temperament" talks. These talks highlight matches and work to smooth mismatches between you. Learning your child's temperament, and continuing to learn it, helps you tailor your conversations and compromise more effectively. It's not about letting him do whatever he wants or insisting he always adapts. Instead, if you reflect on *when* and *how* destructive temperament-based cycles get started, you can stop them before they become routine. This may mean changing his environment, encouraging him to shift his behavior, or changing the way you respond.

Equally important, these talks let a child not get stuck with a label. If you don't pay attention, it's easy to take a few instances as proof of an underlying trait. You might try to protect her in ways she doesn't need. I've done as much myself. When Sophie was four years old, I took her to the movies. As soon as the previews blared, she started squealing.

"I have to go, okay?" She held her hands to her ears. "It's way too loud."

"Why don't we watch for a few minutes?"

"No!" she sobbed.

Sensing the case was closed, I let it go, and we headed off. I told myself *she's just sensitive*—and assumed we'd probably be watching movies at home for a while. But a few months later, on a snowy morning, she begged me to go again.

"Movies are too loud for you there," I said, as if she didn't remember.

"It's different this time." She huffed. "Come on."

"Well, let's at least take headphones," I said. "Or sit in the back."

"I'm not a *baby*!"

To my surprise, when the previews came on—as loud as before—she only laughed.

· ·

To Help a Child Stretch: Notice Your Labels

It's easy to get into habits that don't suit where your kids are. You may talk to your second child the same as your first, or help him in ways he no longer needs. Notice if you've labeled your child as having a certain fixed trait. Ask yourself: Am I responding to the child in front of me today? Check your language. Do you say, "That's just how she is?" Look out for new choices she's making. Maybe she's no longer asking you to walk her up the stairs to school. Notice if it's you wanting her to need you. Try to let go and take a more open view.

· ·

Stay Open and Leave Behind Your Negative Associations

This open view especially helps change negative labels. One eighteen-year-old I knew, Tim, had dyslexia that had gone undiagnosed for years. *In need of significant remediation*, his file read. A high school senior, he had only basic reading skills. A prescription for disaster, I thought. But at our first meeting, he stood tall, shaking my hand with obvious assurance.

"I've been so busy." His eyes lit up. "I'm mentoring a fifth-grade soccer team."

In the literacy room, I apologized for the babyish books.

"I've got to practice." He shrugged. "Let's get to it."

Over the next few weeks, we worked on his reading while laying out a plan for him to graduate. He met with a school counselor. Through dialogue, linked to action, he took charge of his future, recognizing how much he had to give. His maturity helped, but so did his persistent temperament. His troubles hadn't worn him down. It was *my* frame that needed a shift, not his.

Four Steps for Temperament Talk

When a child comes with a question or problem, try these steps:

1. *Listen* with two questions in mind: "What role is his temperament playing?" and "What role does *mine* play?" We each have underlying tendencies. A child's norm might be different from his friend's. Say your typically easygoing child starts crying at camp. That's not a strange reaction, but strange for *him*. Recognizing that it's out of his norm means you're less likely to brush off his fears.

2. *Notice* how temperament mismatches can heighten existing problems. Say your inhibited child describes an argument with his more boisterous friend. At one point, his friend shouted,

"Why don't you ever *talk back*?" The friend interpreted your child's quietness as passivity, which upset him more.

3. *Expand* on his perceptions. Did arguing make him nervous? Or did he feel he had nothing to say?

4. *Explore* your reaction. Do you feel irritated he didn't argue back? Notice if you're "helping" in a way that doesn't align with his temperament. Maybe you want to offer solutions, but he'd prefer a listening ear.

....

Notice Temperament Triggers

Check how past experiences influence your reactions. Say a child pounds his fist the same way your ex-husband used to. Taking the time to notice triggers can keep you from overreacting. Bring your full attention to the current situation. Pause to breathe. Ask yourself: Who is this like? How did I feel in the earlier scenario? How does my body feel? Try to name those emotions. Notice tension or physical stress and shake it loose. Remind yourself, this isn't the same.

....

Making Small Shifts: Smooth Mismatches

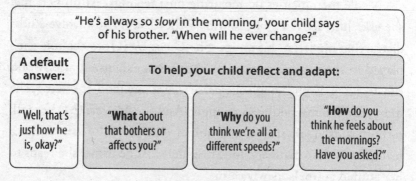

"He's always so *slow* in the morning," your child says of his brother. "When will he ever change?"			
A default answer:	**To help your child reflect and adapt:**		
"Well, that's just how he is, okay?"	"**What** about that bothers or affects you?"	"**Why** do you think we're all at different speeds?"	"**How** do you think he feels about the mornings? Have you asked?"

Try Making Room

Smoothing these mismatches means reflecting alongside your kids. One parent friend, Nicole, told me about her kids, Rudy and Julie, fighting at the dinner table, with squabbles that escalated as the evening went on. She ended up shouting, and Rudy, the younger, started throwing food. To help dinnertimes go more smoothly, Nicole uses a process I've called ROOM. It has four elements: *Recognize*, *Organize*, *Own Up*, and *Match Talk to Your Child*.

First, she *Recognizes* (**R**) the underlying issue. While she wanted to connect, she realized, she'd often focused on asking Julie about how she was doing in school. Julie, in a playful mood, ignored the questions, leaving them both frustrated. Nicole then *Organizes* (**O**) her response around three elements: connecting with her kids, reflecting with them on what happened, and repairing hurt feelings or misunderstandings. She starts with connecting. Before dinner the next evening, she sits and reads them a few stories. She moves to reflecting on the situation, discussing what could go better. Julie says she wants rules: no grabbing or throwing food. After some back-and-forth, Rudy agrees.

Nicole then focuses on repairing hurt feelings. At dinnertime, she asks Julie for her "joke routine." They laugh and involve Rudy, distracting him from his antics. She *Owns Up* (**O**) to the role she's played in the negative dynamic. She's often exhausted after work, she explains. Even though she *doesn't* want any food-throwing, she didn't need to react quite so strongly. And she *Matches* (**M**) her talk to both kids' ages, stages, and quirks. She playfully asks Julie to teach Rudy table manners. Julie brightens. At bedtime, she reads to her stuffed animals, newly calm.

In the above example, Rudy's clowning, active nature and Julie's quieter, more reflective one needed two different approaches. Reflection raised their self-awareness and led to less negativity all around.

Conversations for the Sensitive Child

Sensitive kids, who are more susceptible to stress and negative feedback, especially need these strategies. In his book *The Orchid and the Dandelion*, the UCSF professor of pediatrics W. Thomas Boyce describes around 80 percent of children as "dandelions," more adaptable to a range of situations, and around 20 percent as "orchids," more biologically sensitive to both good and bad environments. These "orchids" naturally need more encouragement and support. Overly competitive environments can stress them out. On the positive side, they benefit greatly from our attention and from awareness of each person's style.[53]

This idea is grounded in powerful research. In 2010, Jay Belsky, professor at University of California, Davis, and his colleague Kevin Beaver studied more than 1,500 teenagers, measuring how involved their mothers had been in their lives and how well the teens regulated their feelings, attention, and behavior. They analyzed the results based on genetic variants known to affect behavior and mood. Some of these variants were "plastic," meaning they could shift based on the environment (including the input of parents and caregivers). For the boys who carried more of these "plastic" variants, how well they regulated themselves depended more strongly on how engaged their mothers had been. For those with one or no variants, the mothers' engagement didn't have much effect.[54]

You might have or know an "orchid" child. Check the following:

- Does she have trouble coping with change or unexpected situations?
- Is she especially sensitive, thoughtful, and/or reactive?
- Does she seem easily startled by new noises, sights, tastes, or smells?
- Does she react strongly to schedule disruptions?

If so, find ways to stretch her, but not so much or so fast that you overwhelm her. Start by setting the stage. Boyce suggests rituals such as routine dinners.[55] Or set a regular check-in. Find time to be with your child one-on-one in nature, or somewhere calm. Quieter or more introspective kids especially need time to let deeper thoughts and feelings rise up.

Soon after talking to Belsky, I recognized Sophie as an "orchid" child.[56] I thought of the previous summer, on a weekend trip to the mountains. After dinner, we headed out to a playground, a delicious departure from our typical routine.

"What's this?" she asked, seeing a pole with a ball attached.

"Tetherball," I told her: a game from my childhood.

"Glow-in-the-dark tetherball," she clarified, as the sky darkened.

We began hitting the ball rhythmically. The hotel staff started up a fire for roasting marshmallows. The fatigue of the three-hour drive—punctuated with lots of "Can I have your phone?"—began falling away.

"I wonder what Paul's doing." Sophie inspected the stars. "Sleeping, I guess."

"Hopefully." I gave the ball a gentle slap.

"You know—" she spoke more slowly, meeting my gaze "—it's good to have times like this."

"I agree."

"Let's do this every year." She stopped the ball. "Come out here, have dinner together, put Paul to bed, and play."

"I'd like that."

"Sometimes, I miss the way things were," she said. "I love Paul and all, but I miss the time we used to spend like this."

Soon she headed to the fire, and I followed. Her face shone. Kids jostled for space in the warmth. Silence enveloped us. I felt the preciseness of that single moment in a way I hadn't for a while. We'd been so busy, with chaotic schedules. I resolved to make more time for the two of us. In the years to come, I imagined, it would be these moments she remembered—not the big trips, or the great joys, but the peaceful togetherness.

The key to such intimacy and bonding: do nothing, for long enough. Find an activity that's enjoyable, that you can relax into, and ideally, that comforts you both.

But you don't need a trip to check in, or even a whole afternoon. That's where conversational habits come in. Think of them as mini-breaks where you pause and take stock. These breaks build up. Over time, they can offer you and your kids a more expansive frame.

"Temp" Talk: Conversational Habits

To encourage adaptations, focus on *compassionate* and *nuanced* conversations. These explore the ways each person's temperament affects your dynamics and your evolving fit.

Conversational Habit #1:
To Manage Frustration, Check the Context

- *Start with a compassionate frame.* When your child acts in a
  way that's surprising or frustrating, ask: Why is he behaving
  this way *in this time and place*?

  Say his old school required uniforms, but his new school
  doesn't. Now, he's having trouble picking out clothes. Still,
  he may not be truly indecisive. The situation is just new
  to him.

- *Pay attention to changes in your family system.* This is
  especially true for "new" aspects of temperament. Say your
  toddler has become needier or—once typically calm—he's
  started shouting. What might have changed? Maybe your
  job has you traveling more, or maybe he's started day care.
  Before reacting, reflect: Is this a change in *him*, or in his
  environment or routines?

- *Let your child brainstorm alongside you. Use questions to:*
  - *Expand:* "Is it about your brother?" Bring in your own
    perspective; say, "It's been hard, with him needing so
    much attention."
  - *Explore* alternatives: say, "How would your ideal breakfast
    time look?" Maybe you can't have a one-on-one breakfast
    every morning but could cook pancakes together once a
    week. Or maybe each parent can make sure to have some
    one-on-one time with each child.
  - *Evaluate* how the changes make everyone feel. Check in to
    see what needs tweaking. Emphasize that adapting isn't a
    onetime event, and that everyone may need to compromise.

Conversational Habit #2:
To Support Self-Awareness, Discuss the Nuances

Think of each child as having a temperament comfort zone. For some, it may be wide, with fluctuating boundaries. They're as happy with strangers as with friends. For others, it's far narrower. Noticing and responding compassionately when he's stretched helps him feel comfortable and confident. Try the following:

- *After an activity, check in.* "I noticed you didn't want to talk at the party."

- *Start with open-ended questions.* For example, "What were you feeling?" If she doesn't know, move to a closed-ended version, like "Were there too many people, or were you tired?" Ask how his body feels. For example, "Did you feel shaky or jittery?" Connect sensations and emotion words.

Or test out the following strategies:

- *Use your child's words.* Take on the terms he uses in describing himself and others; for example, *quiet*. Explore when and how he behaved that way; say, "You acted quiet *when* the neighbors were around." Ask your child how he's changed from a month or a year ago. With siblings, try not to compare temperaments aloud; as in "That's my quiet child" and "That's my talkative one." That can cause kids to settle into their labels or shut off aspects of themselves (say, a child feels he can't be "talkative" because his older brother is). Instead, leave room for nuances and for each child to have more of a range.

- *See the hidden gems.* Say your child feels upset because his friends say he's too cautious and call him "scaredy-cat."

Explore the positives. Maybe being cautious keeps him out of trouble or lets him think before jumping in. Ask for his examples, and use your life as a model. Maybe your thoughtful, analytic nature makes it hard to brainstorm but helps you make good decisions. Maybe his "too loud" friend is a great companion at parties. Thinking this way builds self-compassion and empathy while teaching him to recognize the nuances.

- *Raise self-awareness.* Say your child struggles with some aspect of his temperament. Ask: What about being that way is making life hard? Instead of "fixing," think "adapting." Say your teenager chats constantly in dance class, which frustrates her teacher. Try these steps:

  - *Start with the gems;* say, she's lucky to have many close friends.

  - *Reflect* on when her chatty nature works against her, such as when she needs to pay attention quietly.

  - *Make a plan* to adapt while remaining true to her temperament. Maybe she can chat with friends for five minutes, then plan to meet up after class.

Conversational Habit #3:
To Smooth Mismatches, Meet Difference
with Compassion

Validate temperament differences within the family. Highlight ways your temperaments *don't* align. Make note of the ways siblings set each other off, and when temperaments give each other a positive boost. Maybe your more reactive daughter likes quieter dinnertimes, while your louder, more impulsive son wants to joke. Before you know it, there's a clash. Or maybe you find comfort in regular bedtimes, which also soothes your active toddler. Notice matches and mismatches between you and your partner or other family members. Labeling differences lets you find compromises. Also, recognize how differences complement one another. There's a reason why opposites attract. If you're impulsive and your partner is laid-back, you may end up—most of the time—with a good middle ground.

Use compassionate dialogue to meet everyone's "talk needs." Maybe you need quiet when you first walk in, while your two kids literally climb up your leg. Identify creative ways of meeting all your needs. Maybe your kids could have a ten-second silent contest or put on a pot of tea as quietly as possible. Maybe, after being super-quiet, they can see how loud they can be. Offer up options in a proactive way, *before* you're all stressed.

Or say you have a child who speaks far more slowly than his siblings and ends up frustrated at dinner. Rather than prompting a child to speak faster, or shaming him if he can't, help friends and family understand what he needs. Discuss "think time." Use the Three Es:

Expand on his feelings. *Explore* strategies for new situations; riffing on a comment, or using humor. Model compassion for those who speak differently. Move away from "better" and "worse" and toward "different." *Evaluate*: notice when *you* feel frustrated at a child's lack of engagement—or overengagement, if he's a nonstop talker. Ask: What triggers you and why? Take a deep breath. Separate his behavior from your reaction, if you can.

To Give Kids a Discussion Starter:
Use the Temperament Profile

Try this temperament profile as a jumping-off point. This profile raises kids' self-awareness about their traits, while highlighting that we're all on a spectrum.

- Ask your child to put an *x* on each line where he thinks he fits, then fill in the blanks: for example, "When am I more playful?" Specify: at school or on the playground? If the listed descriptions don't fit, try out others. And if reading and writing don't come easily, you can do this as a discussion just as well.

- Using that profile as a springboard, ask *exploratory* questions, such as:
  - Which qualities do you like most and least about yourself?
  - Which situations seem to bring out your best? Your worst?
  - Which situations feel easiest and hardest for you to manage?
  - Which qualities do you most admire in others?
  - Which qualities would you most like to develop?

- Fill out the chart yourself, then compare with your child and the rest of your family. Discuss the similarities and differences. Return to your charts over time. Which qualities have persisted? Which have changed?

The Temperament Profile

Where Do I Usually Fit?

Try placing yourself somewhere on each line.

1. *Playful* _____ *Serious*

2. *Risk-taking* _____ *Cautious*

3. *Excitable* _____ *Somber*

4. *Confident* _____ *Uncertain*

5. *Interested in novelty* _____ *Seeking consistency*

6. *Dominating conversations* _____ *Hanging back*

7. *Empathetic* _____ *Self-focused*

8. *Carefree* _____ *Worried*

9. *Agreeable* _____ *Argumentative*

10. *Impulsive* _____ *Reflective*

11. *Imaginative* _____ *Literal-minded or Down to earth*

When you master these strategies, you let kids know you respect their temperaments, but *also* their abilities to adapt and shift. You validate their temperaments without locking them down. Rather than asking them to conform to an imagined average, this talk leaves space for nuance and complexity. Instead of fearing or fleeing their own tendencies, kids can honor them, sticking to their guns or honing their reactions when they need to. Over time, they can learn to respond to society's demands and thrive within them without losing sight of themselves.

CONCLUSION

The Lasting Value of Rich Talk

*The meeting of two personalities is like
the contact of two chemical substances: if there is
any reaction, both are transformed.*

—CARL JUNG[1]

One day early in March 2020, Sophie came home from school and, at dinner, said casually, "We played a new kind of tag today."

"Oh?" I asked. "What did you call it?"

"Corona tag." She met my gaze. "It's like tag, but instead of saying, 'You're it,' the kids all say, 'You've got corona.'"

"And what happens after that?"

She shrugged. "You're sick, I guess. I haven't figured that part out."

That day, our conversation seemed forgettable. I'd heard of the coronavirus, a never-before-seen virus that first broke out in Wuhan, China, the prior year, and had heard of it migrating to the

States, but hadn't paid much attention to it otherwise. I figured that one of her school friends had a scientist parent and had learned about the virus that way. And I assumed that the game was one of the endless variety of "cooties" games that kids from time immemorial have played. Little did I sense that, over the course of the months to come, the word "coronavirus" would be on the lips of nearly everyone I met—that we'd soon be wearing face masks even outdoors, that our playdates would be reduced to zero, and that all schools in the state would be closed.[2,3]

Looking back, that conversation strikes me as an innocent but powerful forewarning, and a reminder: kids are listening. For more than you might think, they're paying attention to the signals around them. They quickly sense the rumbles of a coming storm.

I started writing this book as a mother, teacher, and clinician passionate about the art of talking to kids and wanting to share what I've learned. I'm ending it with the same goal, but from a vastly different perspective. Starting that March, as the number of coronavirus cases in Boston surged, my family stayed mostly inside, as the statewide advisory suggested. Schools and summer camps were canceled. We had no visits with friends, no vacations, no trips to see family. Over a single week, the local universities shut down, many sending the students home on a week's notice. My clinical work came to a grinding halt. My teaching skills went toward homeschooling, or rather "crisis schooling," Sophie, and to keeping Paul occupied.

No longer did I go to my office or a café to write in relative silence. No: I wrote in the midst of homeschooling video sessions, questions about two-digit addition, requests to play hide-and-seek, comments about spaghetti versus elbow pasta, bunk-bed renovations, Lego car races, pleas to use the "super-fun" vacuum, and fights over who got to use the single ladybug plate. Amid the laughter, questions, riddles, and jokes, I heard far more than the usual complaints, tantrums, and tears. And, through it all, there was conversation: more than I'd envisioned when planning to have kids, more even than I'd recalled from our family vacations. In our South End apartment, from morning to night, we were together—talking, squabbling, playing—*all* the time.

Like so many families, we all had frayed nerves and suffered from the isolation and stress. Amid the rising numbers of the sick and hospitalized, I struggled to shut the news off and not start conversations from a place of fear. There was the friend who'd lost three family members in a week, and an emergency room doctor who'd moved to a camper van, to avoid the risk of getting his family sick. As I soon heard, most friends and colleagues were attempting the impossible: full-time parent plus full-time employee. I sensed an echo of the "fight and flight" response I'd studied, in which the nervous system stays on heightened alert. That automatic response helped warn our ancestors of danger. But, for us, it can go on overdrive, leaving us and our kids anxious, unable to relate well, learn, or calm down.[4,5]

Soon Sophie began to whine, and Paul to regress; he started having tantrums and throwing food. I recognized how important the social aspects of school were to their health and well-being—and to ours. A few weeks later, Paul's preschool attempted virtual circle time. He hid under his comforter till we shut the computer off. With him, I saw in action what researchers call the "video deficit": young children often understand less through video than through real-life interactions. Many tire quickly of watching teachers on screens. They tend to focus on the visual elements of what they're watching, but have trouble with the spoken parts. As one review of studies found, this "video deficit" is most pronounced in babies and younger toddlers, and decreases as children approach age six.[6,7] Especially for younger children, technology is no replacement for in-person talk. Being close, in-person, lets you meet a child at his level of concreteness.

And yet the coronavirus pandemic, for me, served as a catalyst to see how much daily conversation could enhance our interactions. In the midst of the stress, loneliness, and anxiety we were all feeling, conversation could draw us together. It could help us find a deeper connection, and even give us the chance to laugh. At least, that was in the best of times. Or we could too easily get into ruts, as one child irritated the other, and as we parents—more harried and tired than usual—talked with less than our usual patience.

The quality of our conversations, I soon noticed, truly affected our daily lives. Without overstating it, I often felt that the difference between a bad and good day depended, in large part, on the conversations we had or didn't. Ideally, our conversations felt like buoys. More than ever, both kids needed comfort. They also needed talk that let them feel self-compassion, empathy, and a sense of control, when so much was out of their hands. Even the way we framed outings could shift them from "the worst ever," in Sophie's dramatic view, to chances to bond and laugh.

What's more, this extra time together let me pay closer attention and see both kids' language and thinking developing day by day. Over the course of a single month, Paul moved from speaking in simple sentences to regaling us with renditions of *Curious George* episodes. He started giving Sophie advice, such as his hairdresser's lesson: "You get a lollipop if you're good." ("Thanks, Paul," she said, with an extra dose of sarcasm.)

Of course, we didn't see independence or confidence sprout out of nowhere. That's not how development works. But we did start becoming more conscious of the details of our lived experiences, of the lack of structure and stimulation that made us crazy at times but also offered the chance for a new kind of attention.

And, over time, we *did* see new qualities developing. We saw the ways Paul and Sophie started creating their own mini-ecosystem. Amid all the squabbling, they grew to know and care for each other better, negotiating over whose Lego was whose, and whose turn it was to shower or tell their side of the story. We adjusted, as Paul picked up new words daily, exclaiming that "suddenly" there was a flash of lightning, or that he "recognized" a stray cat. His tantrums started lessening as he expressed himself more clearly, and as he and Sophie became more attuned. For her part, Sophie seemed to pay more attention and change her talk in response.

"Come on, little guy," Sophie told Paul one evening, as he screamed over having to wear pajamas. "I'm not very good at picking out pajamas," she added slyly. "Can you help?"

He was a good pajama-picker, he said, and calmed down. Choosing gave him a sense of control. "Helping" his older sister let him feel proud. And Sophie developed her sense of empathy. I reflected on her thoughtfulness with her, while trying not to praise her for every little thing. As I noticed, when we stopped saying "Great job" so much, both kids tended to do far more.

The time together also let us listen more closely, shifting our talk in response to each person's temperament; or, at least, trying to. I remember the night after we'd taken the crib rails off Paul's bed, he jumped up and down in his "big boy" bed.

"I don't want to sleep," he whined.

Years earlier, when we'd taken the rails off Sophie's bed, we'd told her, "Great, you're a big girl. You can sleep through the night." Without argument, she had. But Paul was different.

"Don't *leave* me," he said, voice rising. "I'm scared."

"You'll be fine," Philippe said. "Remember, you're a big boy now."

"I'm *two*," three-year-old Paul whined. "I won't sleep. Don't leave."

"Read him a boring book," Sophie suggested, running in. "He'll probably fall asleep."

"I doubt it," Philippe said, but headed back anyway. Sophie returned to bed. I could hear Philippe reading. Then: quiet. Twenty minutes later, Philippe emerged.

"What happened?" I asked.

"We read." He rubbed his eyes. "Then I held him. We talked about how everyone needs to sleep. Then we just sat there. He lay down. He knew I was there. I shut my eyes. Maybe I meditated, in my own way. It was nice to have a little quiet for once."

Their conversation was more powerful *because* it didn't have many words. It didn't involve convincing, punishments, or rewards. It instead had to do with attunement: noticing what the moment required, then responding in a way that suited them both. Paul didn't want dad to tell him how big he was. He wanted to be heard and held; to be comforted for the small person he still was. He needed to know his dad was nearby. For his part, Philippe needed a moment of calm. His solution gave them both what they needed. In the long run, I hoped, finding more such moments would help sustain us all.

As challenging as "pandemic life" has been, it has also been a constant lesson in listening, as well as a master class in navigating the unknown. How many ways can you say "I don't know"? I also came to realize that while the pandemic was new, these dynamics and opportunities had been there all along. It was only that the crisis had heightened them.

In the end, the true foundation of rich talk is silence, or the gaps we leave. Those gaps are what give kids the opportunity to drive the conversation: to ask their real questions, raise up their dreams, hopes, worries, and doubts, and give you a brief window into their inner worlds. Those worlds are often filled with ideas and questions we'd never have imagined—ideas that can startle us with their inventiveness—and in the best of times, it can be a pleasure and a privilege to be let inside.

In a society full of chatter, it can be rare to find quiet or time to think. It's even rarer when you have kids and so many schedules and demands. Still, during the months of shutdown, I found that the lack of outside activities gave us permission to focus on one another. We rode the waves of conversation as it connected us, taught us, and built us up. In conversation as in life, as I soon found, there was no perfect answer. Sometimes there wasn't even a good one. Having conversations go well means leaving space for them to go badly. Not every conversation will feel satisfying or have an "aha" moment. So often, it can feel like stumbling in the dark, searching for the "next right" thing to say, or trying to calm one child's nerves while not upsetting the other. But even then, it's that stumbling—and that deep listening—that can show you the way, if you're open to noticing.

For a while, every evening after dinner, Sophie started a series of questions I came to think of as "after corona," meaning after the coronavirus-related restrictions had ended, and we'd no longer fear getting the virus. A random sample: "After corona, can my old teachers come and babysit me?" "After corona, can we go to the biggest water park in the world, the day it opens?" "After corona, will you do cannonballs with me in the outdoor pool?"

One evening, as I cleaned up dishes, I gave her a careful look.

She and I both knew all that wouldn't be possible, at least not right away. But we'd had so much *"not right now"* and *"no"*—no playdates, no movie theaters, no trips—and we were both tired, I sensed. I was tired of saying no, and she was tired of hearing it. So I smiled, ruffled her hair, and answered her questions, one by one, "Yes" and "Yes."

It's that permission I hope this book offers: the chance to step back, look and listen closely, hear and be heard, in ways that aren't about efficiency, rightness, or success. It's the permission to relax the attempt for perfection, and instead give you and your kids what you need at any one time. And it's the chance to value your family's richness: your knowledge and passions, questions and curiosities, plans and fears, as they define you, bond you, and build you up. I hope this book invites you to bring your attention to the present moment and keep bringing it there; to let kids reveal what drives them; to share what you love.

True, quality conversation leaves no immediate trace. It can seem unproductive or inefficient, especially if you're exhausted or stressed. And yet it opens up the time and space to be truly responsive; the surest way to help your kids thrive.

In her 2019 book *How to Do Nothing,* Jenny Odell talks of the "attention economy." In a world where time is money, there isn't a moment to lose.[8] Social media, she argues, makes it hard to be present long enough for an involved conversation.[9] Shifting our attention lets us reengage in a new way, paying closer attention to what's in front of us.

Cultivating high-quality conversation means evolving in a moment-by-moment way. With it, we can let go of recipes, or scripts, or artificial lists like the "ten things to say to your child." Your child doesn't need those ten things. He needs you to sit with him as your interests evolve together. It's your *dialogue* that teaches what to do and say next. When you notice what's working smoothly and what's awkward, where your child freezes or opens up—and where you do—you have everything you need for your talk, and your child, to thrive.

This conversation doesn't need fancy words or complicated sentences—although it surely can have both. Its power lies in its simplicity and authenticity. It draws on your natural gifts and talents, even as you cultivate those of your child. At its best, it lets you move away from needing to *do* and lets you simply *be*. That's a tall order, with all the minor and major challenges of daily life, and in the face of long-term worries and fears. But truly being with your child is the key to deeper understanding. In your presence, your child can reveal himself as more complex and mysterious than you might have believed.

It's no accident that, in the past weeks, I put my phone down and brought out my camera. Looking and listening are deeply linked. As you see a child from multiple angles, you listen with a fresh perspective. You find ways to start from scratch after an argument. You make space between his behavior and your response. You notice when you're in a rut or a negative dynamic and pivot, or rethink. And you see the unexpected twists and turns in his development, and the surprising strangeness of *this* child becoming *that* adult.

To be sure, the chance to have these conversations is a privilege. Quality conversation requires some level of physical and emotional safety. If you're consumed by getting basic needs met, relaxed talk can't take priority. To take one example, a full 38 percent of Massachusetts families were "food insecure," or lacking reliable access to affordable, nutritious food, as of April 2020—up from 9 percent before the coronavirus crisis.[10] Even if you're not struggling with basic needs, too much stress can make it hard to find time or energy for relaxed conversation.

Still, in the face of our everyday challenges, we don't need to throw up our hands. There's room for an "yes and" perspective. Yes, these conversations require some energy and time, *and* they don't require a ton of it. In only a few minutes, you can start up these habits. When you get the ball rolling, you'll be surprised how much kids can take it from there.

Acknowledgments

As Sophie likes to say, "It's just so weird to think you can remember a time when I was a baby—and even before I was born!" I have an echo of that feeling in thinking back to a time when writing a book such as this one was no more than the vaguest dream. First and foremost, I'd like to thank my husband, Philippe, and our children, Sophie and Paul. It was the challenge of parenting, as much as the joys, that prompted me to pose the questions in this book. You have all enriched my life in countless ways, and it's the journey with you, in all its ups and downs, that has offered a chance to live more richly, love more deeply, and reflect.

My agent, Gillian MacKenzie, believed in and championed this book, in its many iterations, long past the time I could have expected her to. For her patience and engagement throughout, and her sure hand in editing, I am so appreciative. I hope we can continue to work together on many more projects. Also, to my editors, Shannon Welch and Anna Paustenbach at HarperOne, I cannot be more thankful. Shannon's insight and ability to see to the heart of a story inspire me, as I know it has many others. She had a sharp vision for this book that I only saw vaguely at first, and her guidance and feedback, from the big-picture to the smallest details, were invaluable. Her former assistant, Aidan Mahony, showed great enthusiasm for this book and was hugely helpful throughout. For her part, Anna has brought this book to completion with wonderful support and insight.

The development of this book was truly a collaborative process. Many thoughtful, creative, and deeply caring people contributed to it over the short and long term—showing great patience as I developed as a writer, teacher, and parent.

In terms of the writing, I benefitted greatly from the time, attention, advice, and thought of Pagan Kennedy and Ethan Gilsdorf at GrubStreet, and of my talented peers at the Nonfiction Career Lab. Kelly McMasters at Hofstra also supported this project in its early stages, as did editors Sandy Draper and Anna Bliss.

Over the years, I've been lucky to have so many generous writing teachers across the genres, including those at Lesley University's MFA program in fiction, particularly Michael Lowenthal, William Lychack, and Kyoko Mori, and Michelle Hoover at GrubStreet. At Harvard, I was lucky to learn poetry writing from Jorie Graham, fiction from Amy Hempel, and portraiture from Sara Lawrence-Lightfoot, whose lessons I still reflect on today. Back in high school, my English teacher Diana Lynn Farmer was inspirational in showing her care for poetry and her students. She served as a model for the way a caring teacher can affect generations.

My journey to writing this book was deeply shaped by my development as a scholar, teacher, and clinician. On the academic side, I'm hugely grateful for the mentorship and support of Nonie Lesaux at the Harvard Graduate School of Education, as well as the members of her Language Diversity and Literacy Development Research Group, with whom I collaborated and learned for many years. Especially Julie Russ Harris was a trusted and insightful sounding board, as well as a great companion as we made the weekly drive to western Massachusetts for a year together. Richard Weissbourd and Stephanie Jones served as members of my dissertation committee, and were extremely helpful as I focused my interests. With Rick, I dove into the complexities of adolescent romantic relationships, conducting research as the director of his research group over several years. Pamela Mason and Karen Brennan have been advocates of my teaching, guiding me to improve my practice. Robert Kegan, for whom I served as a Teaching Fellow, has deeply shaped my thinking about adult development and encouraged my pursuit of this path. Jenny Thomson also supported my development as a scholar and clinician and continues to offer valuable insight. Allison Pingree and Katherine Farrar of the Teaching and Learning Lab at Harvard have been warm, welcoming, and so helpful as I moved to teaching in the online format.

As a clinician, I so appreciate the deep learning journey and collaborative approach that working at an interdisciplinary clinic has allowed. Thank you to Deborah Waber and Ellen Boiselle, directors of the Boston Children's Hospital Learning Disabilities Program, and my fellow "OWLs," headed by Kristine Strand, including: Marie Chan, Kristin Canavan, and Margaret Pierce. I also greatly appreciate the support of KC Christopher of Harvard Medical School, as he has encouraged my thinking about the integration of multiple "hats."

In earlier years, in my journey to becoming a speech-language pathologist, I learned and benefitted from the mentorship of wonderful teachers at the MGH Institute of Health Professions in

Charlestown, Massachusetts, including: Charles Haynes, Pamela Hook, Lesley Maxwell, and Marjorie Nicholas.

In terms of this book's development, I have Helen Cohen and Jenny Gamson of Temple Israel/Frances Jacobson Early Childhood Center to thank, as well as the many outstanding teachers, parents, and staff. Under Helen's leadership, this school has been such a gift for our family, and has expanded my understanding of how a warm and open community can function, allowing both adults and children to thrive. Equally, Comer Yates and Sondra Mims of the Atlanta Speech School were profoundly generous with their time, attention, and support of these ideas. I have been continually impressed with their passion and the incredible schools they have built. "If only all our schools could function this way," as my students have said, after hearing Yates and Mims discuss their mission and philosophy. For showing models of progressive education, I am indebted to Debra Sullivan and the teachers at the Beacon Hill Nursery School, and to Nicole DuFauchard and the teachers at the Advent School.

Joan Kelley of Abound Parenting read drafts of this book and offered important insights, as did Sarah Westwood. Fabrice Jaumont at the French Embassy in New York provided important insight and advice about the publishing process. His passion for bilingual education is infectious. My writing groups, past and present, have been a huge source of encouragement, coping, and support, including: Rich Marcello, Marc Foster, Nancy Rubin Stuart, Deborah Good, Marc Guerin, Christine Giraud, and Robert Fernandes. I've also appreciated the sharing, insight, and sense of community from the Mother Artist Collaborative, including Nicole Lipson, Karen Winn, April Cowin, Rachel Barenbaum, Rebecca Roberts, Alison Judd, and Katherine Gergen Barnett. My fellow speech-language pathologists have equally provided a sense of community and understanding, especially in trying times, among them Kate Radville, Beth Cadogan, Rachel Coleman, Amy Lewis, Meghann Ridley, and Stacey Robarts.

Of course, I have learned perhaps the most from my students over the years, ranging from toddlers through adults in grad school. Thank you to the graduate students at the Harvard Graduate School of Education for their enthusiasm for and interest in educational assessment and to the physician-researchers working to improve their writing at the Harvard Medical School.

This book, for me, has represented a deep dive into so many profoundly complex and nuanced topics. On this journey, I've been informed, surprised, and humbled by the knowledge and experience of the many scholars, researchers, scientists, clinicians, and parents I interviewed. While not all of their insights made it into the text, each of their contributions has found its way into my thinking and framing. I truly am startled and moved by the time that so many people—many of whom are extremely busy—took to contribute to this book.

They include the following: Elias Aboujaoude, Dorsa Amir, Jay Belsky, Jean Berko Gleason, Debbie Blicher, Michele Borba, Marc Brackett, Fritz Breithaupt, Krista Byers-Heinlein, Jae Cody, Susan David, Liz Dawes Duraisingh, Cory Derby, Megha Deshpande, Laura DeThorne, Rory Devine, Sivan Einsohn, Michele Ferrari, Robyn Fivush, John Gabrieli, Michelle Garcia Winner, Susan Gelman, Melissa Giraud, Roberta Michnick Golinkoff, Andrew Grant-Thomas, Peter Gray, Megan-Brette Hamilton, Kathy Hirsh-Pasek, Erika Hoff, Fabrice Jaumont, Patrick Ishizuka, Carrie James, Robin Jarrett, Gary Karlson, Evan Kidd, Jessica Lahey, Eli Lebowitz, Sabine Little, Bronwen Low, Gigi Luk, Mandy Maguire, Lesley Maxwell, Jane McGonigal, Kate McLean, Gigliana Melzi, Sondra Mims, Vita Murrow, Sarah Myruski, Elizabeth Norton, Ingrid Piller, Elaine Reese, David Rettew, Rachel Romeo, Meredith Rowe, Iben Sandahl, Kiran Singh Sirah, Lenore Skenazy, Lori Koerner, Deena Skolnick Weisberg, Linda Smith, Catherine Snow, Lulu Song, Douglas Sperry, Maria Spinelli, Sarah Surrain, Dana Suskind, Yalda Uhls, Penny Van Bergen, Karen Winn, Maryanne Wolf, Evelyn Wright Fogle, Comer Yates, and Ana Zentella.

Thank you to all those who have cared for and loved my children, in countless unsung but significant ways, especially Lizzette and Linda. They have made it possible to take time away to teach and write, and have provided comfort and care to us all.

Thank you to my parents and sister and to my extended family. Also, thank you to Katie and Bikram for their decades-long friendships.

Most deeply, I thank all the parents and children I have met along this journey, and those I will meet. Your curiosity, patience, passion, and hope are inspiring—and I hope to continue learning alongside you for many years.

Appendix

Talk by Ages and Stages: Tailored Tips

The principles in this book apply to all ages, but many parents find it helpful to hear how they might look in action, based on age and stage. Think of these tips as general guides. Use the prompts as inspiration. Tailor and tweak them as you see fit.

Chapter 2: Conversations for Learning

Try these conversation starters:

Early Childhood Through Preschool

For a child just starting to talk:

- Help her make predictions. Roll a ball toward a table edge. Ask:
    - Can you point to where you think it'll land?
    - Can you try making it go slower? Faster?

- Notice when your child seems surprised and what the surprise is about. Ask:
    - Can you point to what seems funny [or silly, or strange]?

- Pay attention to what she's drawn to in her environment: say, a cloud or a ray of sunlight. Point out what seems special or unusual to you about it. Ask:
    - Can you show me the part you like best?

- With a drawing she's made, ask:
    - Can you show me which part took the longest? Which was the most fun to make? Which part are you the proudest of?
    - Which of these materials would you like to use next?
    - Let's see if you can make a bigger version [or tinier version, or one in chalk instead of paint]. Afterward, ask: Which one is your favorite? Can you tell me why?

Once your child is speaking in longer phrases or sentences:

- Discuss what she predicts will happen, versus what you think. Ask:
    - Does it look like it'll be warm outside? Why or why not?
    - What signs do you see? When have you seen those signs before?

- Make connections about how one thing causes another. Ask:
    - How did reaching for the ball make you tip out of your chair?
    - How did the birthday cake make you feel extra hyper?

Starting in Elementary School

Ask about information she's missing and how she could find it. Starting with her ideas, try:

- Do you know if we could (build a stage out of wood, start our own pretend café)? Who might be able to help us? What steps would help make those goals a reality?

Encourage "citizen scientists," who answer questions from their communities. Ask:

- How many salmon are spawning in that river? What tools would we need to find out?

Support her to think critically about news stories. Ask:

- How can you tell if that story is "true"? What source does it come from? Is the writer giving an opinion or sticking to the facts? How do you know?

Starting in Middle and High School

Ask her to consider different versions of what she reads or hears. Try:

- Which of those news stories seems most logical? Why? What holes in the logic do you see?

Help her see how her thinking and learning can still surprise her. Try:

- What about that book ending did you not expect? How would you have written it? What do you wish would have happened?

Support her to make connections between different opinions or arguments. Try:

- How do you and your friend feel similarly about animals, even if you disagree about keeping dogs on leashes?

- Do you agree with part of my argument, even if you mostly disagree? If so, why?

- How did hearing your friend's opinion change your thinking, if at all? How did your thinking stay the same?

Try this today:

Have a "mistake" conversation. Ask and answer:

1. What mistake or slip-up did you make today?

2. How did you try to fix it, and how well did that work?

3. What strategy might you test the next time?

Chapter 3: Conversations for Empathy

Try these conversation starters:

Early Childhood and PreK

Start with what children hear or see. Try:

- When you see another child, ask: What is his face or body telling you?

- What does it feel like when you do that with your body (clench fists, or jump up high)?

- Try saying what your friend said, like he said it. How do you feel?

Discuss how everyone wants help differently. Say a friend seems upset. Ask:

- Do you think your friend wants a hug, or quiet time? How would you know?

- What would you want if that happened to you? Do you think he wants the same?

Elementary School Kids

Focus on understanding others in nuanced ways. Ask:

- How might your friend feel if he misses summer camp but gets to see his grandparents?

Ask about moral or ethical dilemmas based on topics they bring up. Try:

- Say a child is sick but doesn't want to go to the doctor. What should his parents do?

Support them to think from different perspectives. Ask:

- Who would get hurt or helped if your school stopped selling lunches?
- What do you think about having birds kept as pets in cages? Who would be helped or hurt if it became illegal to do so?

Middle and High School Kids

Explore more complex feelings, dilemmas, and perspectives that don't fit the mold. Ask:

- What if you saw your best friend being bullied by other friends of yours?
- What if your friend found out that his father had committed a crime?

Help kids consider issues from multiple competing perspectives. Ask:

- How might climate change affect you in the United States, versus your cousin in Brazil?
- Why might a company decide to stop selling video games to kids under eighteen? How would that affect kids versus parents, versus the video game company?

Try this today:

Have an "empathy-building" conversation. Ask and answer:

1. What do you wish other people "got" about you?

2. When you feel angry/sad/disappointed, what most helps you feel better?

3. How can you help your friend or relative the next time she feels down?

Chapter 4: Conversations for Confidence and Independence

Try these conversation starters:

Early Childhood and PreK

Start with what your child is drawn to or already engaged in. Say he's trying to put a tablecloth on a table. Ask:

- What should we try next? Could we bring the table lower or higher?

- You've gotten the tablecloth halfway over the table. What do you need to finish?

- That table looks too high for you. What safe ways can we find to raise you up?

Encourage celebration of small successes:

- What part of that project were you proudest of?

- How did it feel to do so many drawings?

Elementary School Kids

Emphasize persisting through failure. Ask:

- What if your first plan doesn't work? What else could you try?

- How do you know if something is too hard, versus a goal you could meet with practice?

- What about meeting that goal makes you most excited?

Explore what kids are feeling about their own progress:

- Which part of that project did you most enjoy? What haven't you worked out yet?

- How will you know you're finished? How do you expect the end result to look?

Middle and High School Kids

Encourage reflection on persistent challenges:

- Why do you think that skill/task keeps posing a problem? How could you help yourself succeed?

- If your friend was having that problem, what would you tell him to do?

Support them to see the long-term utility:

- How will achieving that goal help you next month? Next year?

- Why does finishing that project/task matter to you?

- If you gain skills in that area, how might you be able to help someone else?

Try this today:

Have a "confidence-boosting" conversation. Ask and answer:

1. What's a goal you think you could reach by the end of this week, month, or year?

2. How would you know you were getting there? Identify in-between steps.

3. When you reach your goal, how would you like to celebrate?

Chapter 5: Conversations for Building Relationships

Try these conversation starters:

Early Childhood and PreK

Focus on concrete qualities of good friends. Ask:

- I see your friend looks disappointed. How could you help her feel better?

- That argument sounded hard. How can you make up?

- Your sister still looks angry. How could you show her you're really sorry?

Encourage kids to stretch their social skills:

- I see you feel nervous to talk to her. How else could you say hello?

- How can you help your new friend feel included? To help, think about what you would like a friend to do.

Elementary School Kids

Emphasize thinking through social dilemmas. Use questions such as:

- What if a friend tells you a secret and asks you not to tell, but then your best friend wants to know?

- What if a new student joins your class, and your friends start being mean to him?

- How can you tell your friend you want time alone without hurting his feelings?

Explore how kids feel about their friendships:

- Do you think you have enough friends? Close enough friends? Why or why not?

- If you could have the perfect friendship, what would it look like?

Middle and High School Kids

Encourage discussion of more complex dilemmas:

- What if your friend starts dating a boy you can't stand?

- What if your best friend says her brother started doing drugs, but not to tell anyone?

Support them to evaluate their own friendships and friendship skills:

- Why are you so close to that friend? What do you most appreciate about her?

- What could make you stop being friends with someone? Why?

- How would you know if a friendship wasn't good for you?

Try this today:
Have a "relationship-building" conversation. Ask and answer:

1. What are your best qualities as a friend? Where could you improve?

2. What do you appreciate most about your best or closest friends?

3. How do you want people to see you? What do you want them to remember?

Chapter 6: Conversations for—and Through—Play

Try these conversation starters:

Early Childhood and PreK

Start with his or her play. Say he's playing with a rubber band.

- How might we knot it so there's no flat part left?

- What might happen if you knotted it many times?

- How might we turn it into a bird or dinosaur? What else could it become?

Explore using natural materials:

- How many ways can you use that stick?

- How could we build a boat in the sand, using only our hands?

- What's the coolest thing you could build out of dirt and rocks?

Elementary School Kids

Start with what he or she is learning in school or is curious about. Try:

- How might a bucket become a rocket ship?

- How might a ball bounce on the moon, or on a distant planet?

- How might we design a better crate for eggs?

Explore the limits of materials and situations:

- How might we design a suitcase that pushes itself?

- How might we make a tasty breakfast that won't spoil after a week?

Middle and High School Kids

Explore hypotheticals, or situations that aren't real:

- How might you build a house differently if you had no electricity?

- How might you design a car that works using voice commands?

Investigate futuristic or historical ideas:

- How might basketball look if played in virtual reality?

- What might happen if an asteroid hit our planet?

- How might we design a museum for people who can't hear or see well?

Try this today:

Have a "play-based" conversation. Ask and answer:

1. What games, toys, or hobbies are most fun for you? Why do you think that is?

2. If you could invent a new game, what would it be?

3. Say you had a full day to do nothing but play. How would you use it?

Chapter 7: Conversations for Openness

Try these conversation starters:

Early Childhood and PreK

Start with what he or she sees in the world. Ask:

- What's the same about how you and your friend look or speak? What's different?

- Do you know anyone else who says (a word or phrase) like that?

Discuss the histories and cultures of familiar people. Ask:

- Where does your friend's family come from? Who else do we know from there?

- Which of the same holidays do we celebrate? Which different ones? Why do you think that is?

Elementary School Kids

Explore more abstract histories and cultures. Start with people he or she knows. Ask:

- What culture does that food come from? What other foods are popular there?

- How do different cultures celebrate birthdays? Ask friends in your class or neighborhood.

- Why does our family celebrate the holidays we do?

Support an attitude of open curiosity:

- Which new language would you most like to learn?

- If you could spend a month in another country, where would you go? Why?

Middle and High School Kids

Explore differences that aren't easily apparent:

- How do you and your friend learn differently? What about your opinions or beliefs is different?

- What might be making it hard for you (or your friend) to fit in? How could you help your friend be accepted?

Emphasize compassion and celebration of differences:

- How could you help others understand why that skill is hard for you or your friend?

- What could make your neighborhood or classroom more welcoming of differences?

- How does that difference between you and your friend make your relationship richer?

Try this today:

Have an "openness-building" conversation. Ask and answer:

1. Has anyone gotten the wrong idea about you when first meeting you? How?

2. Have you ever gotten the wrong idea when first meeting someone? How?

3. How did your ideas about a person change over time? Why do you think that happened?

Chapter 8: Conversations for Temperament

Try these conversation starters:

Early Childhood and PreK

Start with experiences he or she is familiar with. Ask:

- What does your body feel like when you're (tired, angry, lonely)?

- What can you do when you feel like that? How can I help you best?

Discuss concrete signs of temperament matches and mismatches. Ask:

- When do you and your brother get along best? When does it feel hard to get along? Why?

- What can you do when you see you're starting to argue?

Kindergarten and Elementary School Kids

Discuss ways that temperament affects their daily lives. Ask:

- When do friends or family make you feel calmer or more hyper?

- Why might your friend or sibling be acting that way? How would you act in her place?

- When you feel upset or stressed, what strategies help you feel calmer? How is that different for your friends, siblings, and other relatives?

Support an attitude of welcoming diverse temperaments:

- Which family member or friend do you feel most similar to, in terms of how you act or react to the world around you? Which friends or family member are you most different from?

- What can you do to help you and your most "different" friend/ family member get along? How can you meet in the middle?

Middle and High School Kids

Explore adapting your and their temperaments to relate more smoothly:

- What times or circumstances make it hardest for you to be your best self? Are you sensitive to loud noises, places with a lot of distractions, or a lack of sleep?

- When you get into a circumstance like that, how can you help yourself adapt? Which strategies have worked in the past?

Encourage kids to see the "good and bad" of each aspect of temperament:

- What about being like that (very active, very inhibited) do you and your friends appreciate? What about it makes it hard to get along or succeed in school?

- When you notice yourself feeling out of control, anxious, overwhelmed, or stressed, what "menu" of activities can help you relax or feel more in control?

- Which aspects of yourself are you most proud of or like the most? Which aspects do you struggle with or feel embarrassed by?

- How could you highlight those positive aspects and develop the less positive ones? What's one step you could take (today, this week, this month)?

Try this today:
Have an "understand me" conversation. Ask and answer:

1. In what ways are you like and unlike others in our family?

2. What places, people, and situations bring out your best self?

3. What one thing would you change about how we relate? How and why?

Notes

Introduction: Why Conversation Matters

1 Kim Parker and Eileen Patten, "The Sandwich Generation," Pew Research Center's Social & Demographic Trends Project, January 30, 2013, http://www.pewresearch.org/social-trends/2013/01/30/the-sandwich-generation.

2 As one 2019 study found, parenting-related exhaustion had a negative effect on the quality of the parent-child relationship for both mothers and fathers. See: Aurélie Gillis and Isabelle Roskam, "Daily Exhaustion and Support in Parenting: Impact on the Quality of the Parent–Child Relationship," *Journal of Child and Family Studies* 28, no. 7 (2019): 2007–16, https://doi.org/10.1007/s10826-019-01428-2.

3 For a broader overview, see: Jennifer Senior, *All Joy and No Fun: The Paradox of Modern Parenthood* (New York: Ecco, 2014).

4 There is interesting early research suggesting that parent guilt and burnout is related to feelings of fear (for example, fear of not being a "good enough" mother and fear related to lack of control). See: Sarah Hubert and Isabelle Aujoulat, "Parental Burnout: When Exhausted Mothers Open Up," *Frontiers in Psychology* 9 (2018), https://doi.org/10.3389/fpsyg.2018.01021. Research has also linked parental burnout and depression, see: Susan Roxburgh, "Parental Time Pressures and Depression among Married Dual-Earner Parents," *Journal of Family Issues* 33, no. 8 (September 2011): 1027–53, https://doi.org/10.1177/0192513x11425324.

5 National Scientific Council on the Developing Child, "Supportive Relationships and Active Skill-Building Strengthen the Foundations of Resilience: Working Paper No. 13," 2015. https://developingchild.harvard.edu/resources/supportive-relationships-and-active-skill-building-strengthen-the-foundations-of-resilience/. See also: "Resilience," Center on the Developing

Child at Harvard Univ., accessed August 17, 2020, https://developingchild
.harvard.edu/science/key-concepts/resilience/.

6 For a helpful set of resources, see: "5 Steps for Brain-Building Serve and
Return," Center on the Developing Child at Harvard Univ., accessed
October 29, 2020, https://developingchild.harvard.edu/resources/5-steps
-for-brain-building-serve-and-return/. See also research from Jack Shonkoff,
e.g., Jack P. Shonkoff and Linda Richter, "The Powerful Reach of Early
Childhood Development," in *Handbook of Early Childhood Development
Research and Its Impact on Global Policy*, eds. Pia Rebello Britto, Patrice L.
Engle, and Charles M. Super (New York: Oxford Univ. Press, 2013), 24–34,
https://doi.org/10.1093/acprof:oso/9780199922994.003.0002.

7 For more on the power of these everyday exchanges, see the work of the
developmental psychologist Junlei Li and the Simple Interactions initiative:
"Simple Interactions," Fred Rogers Center for Early Learning & Children's
Media, accessed June 4, 2021, https://www.fredrogerscenter.org/what-we
-do/simple-interactions/.

8 Catherine E. Snow, "Conversations with Children," in *Language Acquisition:
Studies in First Language Development,* eds. Paul Fletcher and Michael
Garman (New York: Cambridge Univ. Press, 1986), 69–89, https://doi.org
/10.1017/cbo9780511620683.006.

9 For a discussion of these ideas for adolescents, see: William Nagy and
Dianna Townsend, "Words as Tools: Learning Academic Vocabulary as
Language Acquisition," *Reading Research Quarterly* 47, no. 1 (2012): 91–108,
https://doi.org/10.1002/rrq.011. For an intervention study, see: Nonie K.
Lesaux, Julie Russ Harris, and Phoebe Sloane, "Adolescents' Motivation in
the Context of an Academic Vocabulary Intervention in Urban Middle
School Classrooms," *Journal of Adolescent & Adult Literacy* 56, no. 3 (2012):
231–40, https://doi.org/10.1002/jaal.00132.

10 MindShift, "The Role of Metacognition in Learning and Achievement,"
KQED, August 10, 2016, http://www.kqed.org/mindshift/46038/the-role
-of-metacognition-in-learning-and-achievement.

11 Mark Richard Dadds et al., "Outcomes, Moderators, and Mediators of
Empathic-Emotion Recognition Training for Complex Conduct Problems
in Childhood," *Psychiatry Research* 199, no. 3 (2012): 201–7, https://doi.org
/10.1016/j.psychres.2012.04.033.

12 Robyn Fivush and Jessica McDermott Sales, "Coping, Attachment, and
Mother-Child Narratives of Stressful Events," *Merrill-Palmer Quarterly* 52,
no. 1 (2006): 125–50, https://doi.org/10.1353/mpq.2006.0003.

13 Sarah D. Sparks, "Want More Creativity? Help Children See Themselves
Differently," Education Week, July 10, 2019, http://blogs.edweek
.org/edweek/inside-school-research/2019/07/helping_children_see
_themselves_differently_boosts_creativity.html?override=web.

14 Matthias R. Mehl et al., "Eavesdropping on Happiness: Well-Being Is
Related to Having Less Small Talk and More Substantive Conversations,"

Psychological Science 21, no. 4 (2010): 539–41, https://www.ncbi.nlm.nih.gov /pmc/articles/PMC2861779/.

15 Much has been made of a "30-million-word gap" between children from richer and poorer families, in which children from poorer families are said to hear 30 million words fewer, on average, by age three than their richer counterparts; see: Betty Hart and Todd Risley, *Meaningful Differences in the Everyday Experience of Young American Children* (Baltimore, MD: Brookes Publishing Co., 1995). The size of this gap may be overstated, but the gap is real—and impacts learning and school achievement for years; see: Roberta Michnick Golinkoff et al., "Language Matters: Denying the Existence of the 30-Million-Word Gap Has Serious Consequences," *Child Development* 90, no. 3 (2018): 985–92, https://doi.org/10.1111/cdev.13128. However, it's also quite controversial, in that it's been unfairly used to suggest that less well-off families "talk worse" than their richer counterparts. In my view, that gap deserves attention, especially as poverty and other factors impact the quality of talk, and luckily has been the focus of over two decades of research. Still, this book focuses less on words and more on conversations: how back-and-forth talk helps kids with far more than word learning, well beyond the early years. For related research, see: Rachel R. Romeo et al., "Beyond the 30-Million-Word Gap: Children's Conversational Exposure Is Associated with Language-Related Brain Function," *Psychological Science* 29, no. 5 (2018): 700–10, https://doi.org/10.1177/0956797617742725. Also, for the first study relating conversational turns to changes in brain structure, see: Rachel R. Romeo et al., "Language Exposure Relates to Structural Neural Connectivity in Childhood," *Journal of Neuroscience* 38, no. 36 (2018): 7870–77, https://doi.org/10.1523/jneurosci.0484-18.2018.

16 Donald W. Winnicott, "Communication between Infant and Mother, and Mother and Infant, Compared and Contrasted," in *The Collected Works of D. W. Winnicott*, eds. Lesley Caldwell and Helen Taylor Robinson (New York: Oxford Univ. Press, 2016), 227–38, https://doi.org/10.1093/med:psych /9780190271404.003.0040.

17 Brenda Salley et al., "Preverbal Communication Complexity in Infants," *Infancy* 25, no. 1 (2019): 4–21, https://doi.org/10.1111/infa.12318. See also: Hui-Chin Hsu and Alan Fogel, "Infant Vocal Development in a Dynamic Mother-Infant Communication System," *Infancy* 2, no. 1 (January 2001): 87–109, https://doi.org/10.1207/s15327078in0201_6; and Carolyn Brockmeyer Cates et al., "Infant Communication and Subsequent Language Development in Children from Low-Income Families," *Journal of Developmental & Behavioral Pediatrics* 33, no. 7 (2012): 577–85, https:// doi.org/10.1097/dbp.0b013e318264c10f.

18 Cynthia L. Crown et al., "The Cross-Modal Coordination of Interpersonal Timing: Six-Week-Olds Infants' Gaze with Adults' Vocal Behavior," *Journal of Psycholinguistic Research* 31, no. 1 (January 2002): 1–23, https://doi.org /10.1023/a:1014301303616.

19 Ruth Feldman, "Parent-Infant Synchrony: A Biobehavioral Model of Mutual Influences in the Formation of Affiliative Bonds," *Monographs of the Society for Research in Child Development* 77, no. 2 (2012): 42–51, https://doi.org/10.1111/j.1540-5834.2011.00660.x.

20 Baby talk doesn't hurt children's language skills. In fact, this talk—with its slowed speech, high pitch, and simpler words—helps with social communication and allows children the time and opportunity to babble or talk. More practice means better language skills, more positive feelings for us both when we interact, and stronger connections between our kids and ourselves. With coaching, parents can learn to use more "parentese," otherwise known as "baby talk," with infants, which links to stronger language skills on their part. The same thing goes for gesturing: pointing at objects, for young babies, and saying what those objects are. When parents use more of these gestures, kids use more in response, allowing them to point out what excites them, and what they notice around them in the moment. This sets the foundation for quality conversation early on. See: Meredith L. Rowe and Kathryn A. Leech, "A Parent Intervention with a Growth Mindset Approach Improves Children's Early Gesture and Vocabulary Development," *Developmental Science* 22, no. 4 (2018), https://doi.org/10.1111/desc.12792.

Chapter 1: What Rich Talk Is, and Why We're Missing Out

1 David Whyte, "10 Questions That Have No Right to Go Away," Oprah.com, June 15, 2011, https://www.oprah.com/oprahs-lifeclass/poet-david-whytes-questions-that-have-no-right-to-go-away_1.

2 Amanda Ruggeri, "The Dangerous Downsides of Perfectionism," BBC Future, February 20, 2018, http://www.bbc.com/future/story/20180219-toxic-perfectionism-is-on-the-rise.

3 "Statistics," National Institute of Mental Health (US Department of Health and Human Services), accessed June 4, 2021, https://www.nimh.nih.gov/health/statistics/.

4 See especially the research on maladaptive perfectionism, for example: Lisa A. Turner and Paul E. Turner, "The Relation of Behavioral Inhibition and Perceived Parenting to Maladaptive Perfectionism in College Students," *Personality and Individual Differences* 50, no. 6 (2011): 840–44, https://doi.org/10.1016/j.paid.2011.01.006.

5 In fact, everyday moments may be all the "quality time" kids need. In 2007, researchers Tamar Kremer-Sadlik at UCLA and Amy L. Paugh published their interview and video study of 32 parents, with the results suggesting that "everyday activities (like household chores or running errands) may afford families quality moments, unplanned, unstructured instances of social interaction that serve the important relationship-building functions that parents seek from 'quality time.'" See: Tamar Kremer-Sadlik and Amy L.

Paugh, "Everyday Moments," *Time & Society* 16, no. 2-3 (2007): 287–308, https://doi.org/10.1177/0961463x07080276.

6 Sara H. Konrath, Edward H. O'Brien, and Courtney Hsing, "Changes in Dispositional Empathy in American College Students Over Time: A Meta-Analysis," *Personality and Social Psychology Review* 15, no. 2 (May 2010): 180–98, https://doi.org/10.1177/1088868310377395.

7 For a review of the issues with empathy in our contemporary culture, see: Michele Borba, *UnSelfie: Why Empathetic Kids Succeed in Our All-About-Me World* (New York: Touchstone, 2016).

8 Oscar Ybarra et al., "Friends (and Sometimes Enemies) with Cognitive Benefits," *Social Psychological and Personality Science* 2, no. 3 (2010): 253–61, https://doi.org/10.1177/1948550610386808.

9 Gillian M. Sandstrom and Elizabeth W. Dunn, "Social Interactions and Well-Being," *Personality and Social Psychology Bulletin* 40, no. 7 (2014): 910–22, https://doi.org/10.1177/0146167214529799.

10 Carol S. Dweck and Ellen L. Leggett, "A Social-Cognitive Approach to Motivation and Personality," *Psychological Review* 95, no. 2 (1988): 256–73, https://doi.org/10.1037/0033-295x.95.2.256.

11 Céline Darnon et al., "The Interplay of Mastery and Performance Goals in Social Comparison: A Multiple-Goal Perspective," *Journal of Educational Psychology* 102, no. 1 (2010): 212–22, https://doi.org/10.1037/a0018161.

12 Rebecca Givens Rolland, "Synthesizing the Evidence on Classroom Goal Structures in Middle and Secondary Schools," *Review of Educational Research* 82, no. 4 (2012): 396–435, https://doi.org/10.3102/003465431 2464909.

13 Nonie K. Lesaux et al., "The Regulated Learning Environment: Supporting Adults to Support Children," *Young Children* 70, no. 5 (2015): 20–27, https://www.jstor.org/stable/ycyoungchildren.70.5.20. See also: "The Rigorous and Regulated Learning Environment," RWJF, accessed March 10, 2014, https://www.rwjf.org/en/library/research/2014/03/the-rigorous-and -regulated-learning-environment.html.

14 For more on the relationship between adverse early experiences, learning, and social-emotional functioning, see: Jack P. Shonkoff, "Leveraging the Biology of Adversity to Address the Roots of Disparities in Health and Development," *Proceedings of the National Academy of Sciences* 109, no. Supplement_2 (August 2012): 17302–7, https://doi.org/10.1073/pnas .1121259109.

15 School-level poverty may be one factor affecting the ways teacher stress and children's executive function relate. See: Regula Neuenschwander et al., "Teacher Stress Predicts Child Executive Function: Moderation by School Poverty," *Early Education and Development* 28, no. 7 (2017): 880–900, https://doi.org/10.1080/10409289.2017.1287993.

16 Andres S. Bustamante and Kathy Hirsh-Pasek, "Are Our Preschool Teachers Worth More Than They Were Two Months Ago?," Brookings,

April 13, 2020, https://www.brookings.edu/blog/education-plus
-development/2020/04/13/are-our-preschool-teachers-worth-more-than
-they-were-two-months-ago/; Rachel D. McKinnon et al., "Teacher–Child
Relationships in the Context of Poverty: The Role of Frequent School
Mobility," *Journal of Children and Poverty* 24, no. 1 (February 2018): 25–46,
https://doi.org/10.1080/10796126.2018.1434761.

17 Rebecca Givens Rolland, "Exploring Early Childhood Teachers'
Professional Experiences in a High-Risk Setting: Generating Hypotheses
for Enhanced Professional Development" (PhD diss., Harvard Univ., 2014).

18 For more on the stresses faced by early childhood teachers in Head Start
classrooms in the United States, and the links to their abilities to use
effective strategies with young children, see: Christine Li Grining et al.,
"Understanding and Improving Classroom Emotional Climate and Behavior
Management in the 'Real World': The Role of Head Start Teachers'
Psychosocial Stressors," *Early Education & Development* 21, no. 1 (2010):
65–94, https://doi.org/10.1080/10409280902783509.

19 For research into how the "stress mindset" of preschool teachers relates to
their job turnover, see: Joungyoun Kim et al., "Stress Mindset Predicts Job
Turnover among Preschool Teachers," *Journal of School Psychology* 78 (2020):
13–22, https://doi.org/10.1016/j.jsp.2019.11.002. For related research, see:
Jennifer Wallace Jacoby and Nonie K. Lesaux, "Language and Literacy
Instruction in Preschool Classes That Serve Latino Dual Language
Learners," *Early Childhood Research Quarterly* 40 (2017): 77–86, https://doi
.org/10.1016/j.ecresq.2016.10.001.

20 Stephanie M. Jones, Suzanne M. Bouffard, and Richard Weissbourd,
"Educators' Social and Emotional Skills Vital to Learning," *Phi Delta
Kappan* 94, no. 8 (2013): 62–65, https://doi.org/10.1177/0031721713
09400815.

21 John D. Bransford, Rodney R. Cocking, and Ann L. Brown, *How People
Learn: Brain, Mind, Experience, and School*, Expanded Edition (Washington,
DC: National Academies Press, 2000), 26.

22 Senior, *All Joy and No Fun*, 179.

23 Adele Faber et al., *How to Talk So Kids Will Listen & Listen So Kids Will Talk*
(New York: Simon & Schuster, 2012).

24 Jean Piaget, "The Role of Action in the Development of Thinking," in
Knowledge and Development, eds. Willis F. Overton and Jeanette M. Gallagher
(Boston: Springer, 1977), 17–42, https://doi.org/10.1007/978-1-4684-2547-5_2.

25 Jean Piaget, *The Origins of Intelligence in Children* (New York: International
Universities Press, 1952).

26 Jean Piaget and Barbel Inhelder, *The Growth of Logical Thinking from
Childhood to Adolescence: An Essay on the Construction of Formal Operational
Structures* (New York: Basic Books, 1958).

27 L. S. Vygotsky et al., *Mind in Society: The Development of Higher Psychological
Processes* (Cambridge, MA: Harvard Univ. Press, 1978).

28 The Zone of Proximal Development, in Vygotsky's words, translated from Russian, is defined as "the distance between the actual developmental level as determined by independent problem solving and the level of potential development as determined through problem solving under adult guidance or in collaboration with more capable peers." See: L. S. Vygotsky, "Volume 1: Problems of General Psychology, Including the Volume Thinking and Speech," in *The Collected Works of L.S. Vygotsky*, eds. Robert W. Rieber and Aaron S. Carton (New York: Plenum Press, 1987).

29 "Zone of Proximal Development," in *Encyclopedia of Evolutionary Psychological Science*, eds. Todd K. Shackelford and Viviana A. Weekes-Shackelford (Cham, Switzerland: Springer, 2021), https://doi.org/10.1007 /978-3-319-19650-3_305625.

30 Rob Wass and Clinton Golding, "Sharpening a Tool for Teaching: The Zone of Proximal Development," *Teaching in Higher Education* 19, no. 6 (2014): 671–84, https://doi.org/10.1080/13562517.2014.901958.

31 For a critique of Piaget and Vygotsky, see: Eugene Matusov and Renee Hayes, "Sociocultural Critique of Piaget and Vygotsky," *New Ideas in Psychology* 18, no. 2-3 (2000): 215–39, https://doi.org/10.1016/s0732-118x(00)00009-x.

32 See, for example, in terms of the early years: Beverly J. Dodici, Dianne C. Draper, and Carla A. Peterson, "Early Parent—Child Interactions and Early Literacy Development," *Topics in Early Childhood Special Education* 23, no. 3 (2003): 124–36, https://doi.org/10.1177/02711214030230030301; and Meredith L. Rowe, "A Longitudinal Investigation of the Role of Quantity and Quality of Child-Directed Speech in Vocabulary Development," *Child Development* 83, no. 5 (2012): 1762–74, https://doi.org/10.1111/j.1467-8624 .2012.01805.x. For research on the role of parental interactions with older children and adolescents, see, for example: B. Bradford Brown and Jeremy P. Bakken, "Parenting and Peer Relationships: Reinvigorating Research on Family-Peer Linkages in Adolescence," *Journal of Research on Adolescence* 21, no. 1 (2011): 153–65, https://doi.org/10.1111/j.1532-7795.2010.00720.x; and Campbell Leaper et al., "Adolescent-Parent Interactions in Relation to Adolescents' Gender and Ego Development Pathway," *Journal of Early Adolescence* 9, no. 3 (1989): 335–61, https://doi.org/10.1177/02724316 89093009. For related research on the importance of the family emotional climate, see: Sabina Kapetanovic and Therése Skoog, "The Role of the Family's Emotional Climate in the Links between Parent-Adolescent Communication and Adolescent Psychosocial Functioning," *Research on Child and Adolescent Psychopathology* 49, no. 2 (2020): 141–54, https://doi .org/10.1007/s10802-020-00705-9.

33 In fact, Vygotsky conceived interaction as a highly dynamic, social process, which the term "scaffolding" doesn't fully capture; for a critique, see: Jiao Xi and James P. Lantolf, "Scaffolding and the Zone of Proximal Development: A Problematic Relationship," *Journal for the Theory of Social Behaviour* 51, no. 1 (2020): 25–48, https://doi.org/10.1111/jtsb.12260.

34 Sarah J. Tracy, "Let's Talk: Conversation as a Defining Moment for the Communication Discipline," *Health Communication* 35, no. 7 (2019): 910–16, https://doi.org/10.1080/10410236.2019.1593081.

35 Tanya L. Chartrand and John A. Bargh, "The Chameleon Effect: The Perception–Behavior Link and Social Interaction," *Journal of Personality and Social Psychology* 76, no. 6 (1999): 893–910, https://doi.org/10.1037/0022-3514 .76.6.893; Jessica L. Lakin and Tanya L. Chartrand, "Using Nonconscious Behavioral Mimicry to Create Affiliation and Rapport," *Psychological Science* 14, no. 4 (2003): 334–39, https://doi.org/10.1111/1467-9280.14481.

36 Elaine Hatfield, John T. Cacioppo, and Richard L. Rapson, "Emotional Contagion," *Current Directions in Psychological Science* 2, no. 3 (1993): 96–100, https://doi.org/10.1111/1467-8721.ep10770953.

37 David Jacobson, "Interpreting Instant Messaging: Context and Meaning in Computer-Mediated Communication," *Journal of Anthropological Research* 63, no. 3 (2007): 359–81, https://doi.org/10.3998/jar.0521004.0063.303.

38 Barbara A. Wasik and Charlene Iannone-Campbell, "Developing Vocabulary through Purposeful, Strategic Conversations," *The Reading Teacher* 66, no. 4 (2012): 321–32, https://doi.org/10.1002/trtr.01095.

39 Kathy Hirsh-Pasek, Rebecca M. Alper, and Roberta Michnick Golinkoff, "Living in Pasteur's Quadrant: How Conversational Duets Spark Language at Home and in the Community," *Discourse Processes* 55, no. 4 (March 2018): 338–45, https://doi.org/10.1080/0163853x.2018.1442114.

40 Jacobson, "Interpreting Instant Messaging: Context and Meaning in Computer-Mediated Communication," 359–81.

41 Stefan Kopp, "Social Resonance and Embodied Coordination in Face-to-Face Conversation with Artificial Interlocutors," *Speech Communication* 52, no. 6 (2010): 587–97, https://doi.org/10.1016/j.specom.2010.02.007.

42 Ipke Wachsmuth, Manuela Lenzen, and Günther Knoblich, "Embodied Communication in Humans and Machines," *Oxford Scholarship Online*, March 2012, https://doi.org/10.1093/acprof:oso/9780199231751.001.0001.

43 Piaget used a now-famous example of pouring a single large glass of water into two cups. You ask your child to watch, and then ask her whether the amount of water is the same. Before age seven or so, a child will say there is more or less water, depending on how it looks. It's not until they understand the principle of "conservation" that they will say the correct answer. See: Jean Piaget, "Quantification, Conservation, and Nativism," *Science* 162, no. 3857 (1968): 976–79, https://doi.org/10.1126/science.162.3857.976; and Frank H. Hooper, "Piaget's Conservation Tasks: The Logical and Development Priority of Identity Conservation," *Journal of Experimental Child Psychology* 8, no. 2 (1969): 234–49, https://doi.org/10.1016/00220965 (69)90098-8.

44 Martin J. Pickering and Simon Garrod, "Toward a Mechanistic Psychology of Dialogue," *Behavioral and Brain Sciences* 27, no. 2 (2004), https://doi.org /10.1017/s0140525x04000056.

45 Hirsh-Pasek, Alper, and Golinkoff, "Living in Pasteur's Quadrant," 338–45.

46 Martin J. Pickering and Simon Garrod, "Alignment as the Basis for Successful Communication," *Research on Language and Computation* 4, no. 2-3 (2006): 203–28, https://doi.org/10.1007/s11168-006-9004-0.

47 Dana Shai and Jay Belsky, "Parental Embodied Mentalizing: How the Nonverbal Dance between Parents and Infants Predicts Children's Socio-Emotional Functioning," *Attachment & Human Development* 19, no. 2 (2016): 191–219, https://doi.org/10.1080/14616734.2016.1255653.

48 Shai and Belsky, "Parental Embodied Mentalizing."

49 These ideas are inspired in part by the work of the infant specialist Magda Gerber, the founder of RIE (Resources for Infant Educarers). As Gerber writes in *Dear Parent: Caring for Infants with Respect*, "We have a basic trust in the infant to be an initiator . . . we provide the infant with only enough help necessary to allow the child to enjoy mastery of her own actions" (2). See: Magda Gerber, *Dear Parent: Caring for Infants with Respect* (Los Angeles: Resources for Infant Educarers (RIE), 2003).

50 Jay Belsky and Sara R. Jaffee, "The Multiple Determinants of Parenting," in *Developmental Psychopathology*, eds. Dante Cicchetti and Donald J. Cohen (New York: John Wiley & Sons, 2015), 38–85, https://doi.org/10.1002/9780470939406.ch2.

51 Megan-Brette Hamilton, interview with the author, November 27, 2019. For more on Hamilton's research, see: Megan-Brette Hamilton, Eusabia V. Mont, and Cameron McLain, "Deletion, Omission, Reduction: Redefining the Language We Use to Talk About African American English," *Perspectives of the ASHA Special Interest Groups* 3, no. 1 (2018): 107–17, https://doi.org/10.1044/persp3.sig1.107.

52 Kopp, "Social Resonance and Embodied Coordination in Face-to-Face Conversation with Artificial Interlocutors," 587–97.

53 Cheri Foster Triplett and Mary Alice Barksdale, "Third through Sixth Graders' Perceptions of High-Stakes Testing," *Journal of Literacy Research* 37, no. 2 (2005): 237–60, https://doi.org/10.1207/s15548430jlr3702_5.

54 Brett D. Jones, "The Unintended Outcomes of High-Stakes Testing," in *High Stakes Testing: New Challenges and Opportunities for School Psychology*, eds. Louis J. Kruger and David Shriberg (New York: Routledge, 2007), 65–86, https://doi.org/10.4324/9780203836583-5.

55 David Berliner, "Rational Responses to High Stakes Testing: The Case of Curriculum Narrowing and the Harm That Follows," *Cambridge Journal of Education* 41, no. 3 (2011): 287–302, https://doi.org/10.1080/0305764x.2011.607151.

56 As Scott G. Isaksen and John P. Gaulin argue, "Brainstorming can result in improved coordination, better understanding of the ideas generated, and faster implementation of those ideas. In addition, individuals learn the importance of a climate conducive to creativity, the value of diverse thinking and problem-solving styles, and that creative thinking is enjoyable and

powerful" (326). See: Scott G. Isaksen and John P. Gaulin, "A Reexamination of Brainstorming Research: Implications for Research and Practice," *Gifted Child Quarterly* 49, no. 4 (2005): 315–29, https://doi.org/10.1177 /001698620504900405.

57 Claire Cain Miller, "The Relentlessness of Modern Parenting," *New York Times*, December 25, 2018, https://www.nytimes.com/2018/12/25/upshot /the-relentlessness-of-modern-parenting.html.

58 Patrick Ishizuka surveyed more than 3,600 parents across the country, from a range of income brackets. See: Patrick Ishizuka, "Social Class, Gender, and Contemporary Parenting Standards in the United States: Evidence from a National Survey Experiment," *Social Forces* 98, no. 1 (2019): 31–58, https:// doi.org/10.1093/sf/soy107.

59 Sonja Haller, "'Intensive' Parenting Is Here for 2019 and It's Taking Helicopter Parenting to the Next Level," *USA Today*, January 17, 2019, https://www.usatoday.com/story/life/allthemoms/2019/01/17/intensive -parents-taking-helicopter-parenting-next-level/2602652002/.

60 This didn't account for multitasking—so if a child was watching a video while texting, that counted twice.

61 "The Common Sense Census: Media Use by Tweens and Teens, 2019: Common Sense Media," Common Sense Media, October 28, 2019, https:// www.commonsensemedia.org/research/the-common-sense-census-media -use-by-tweens-and-teens-2019.

62 Elroy Boers et al., "Association of Screen Time and Depression in Adolescence," *JAMA Pediatrics* 173, no. 9 (January 2019): 853, https://doi .org/10.1001/jamapediatrics.2019.1759.

63 Sarah Myruski et al., "Digital Disruption? Maternal Mobile Device Use Is Related to Infant Social-Emotional Functioning," *Developmental Science* 21, no. 4 (2017), https://doi.org/10.1111/desc.12610.

64 NPR Staff, "Making the Case for Face to Face in an Era of Digital Conversation," NPR, September 26, 2015, https://www.npr.org/2015/09 /26/443480452/making-the-case-for-face-to-face-in-an-era-of-digital -conversation.

Chapter 2: Conversations for Learning: Sparking Your Child's Lifelong Curiosity

1 Maria Montessori, *The Advanced Montessori Method. Spontaneous Activity in Education* (Cambridge, MA: R. Bentley, 1964).

2 Carol S. Dweck, *Mindset: The New Psychology of Success* (New York: Ballantine Books, 2008).

3 Christine Gross-Loh, "How Praise Became a Consolation Prize," *The Atlantic*, December 16, 2016, https://www.theatlantic.com/education /archive/2016/12/how-praise-became-a-consolation-prize/510845/.

4 Carol Dweck, "The Power of Believing That You Can Improve," TED,

November 2014, https://www.ted.com/talks/carol_dweck_the_power_of
_believing_that_you_can_improve.

5 Jennifer Paley, "Praising Intelligence: Costs to Children's Self-Esteem and
   Motivation," Bing Nursery School, October 1, 2011, https://bingschool
   .stanford.edu/news/praising-intelligence-costs-childrens-self-esteem-and
   -motivation.

6 Paley, "Praising Intelligence."

7 Paley, "Praising Intelligence."

8 For a review, see: Charlotte Dignath and Gerhard Büttner, "Components of
   Fostering Self-Regulated Learning among Students. A Meta-Analysis on
   Intervention Studies at Primary and Secondary School Level," *Metacognition
   and Learning* 3, no. 3 (January 2008): 231–64, https://doi.org/10.1007
   /s11409-008-9029-x. For a study specifically for students with learning
   difficulties, see: Mélanie S. Bosson et al., "Strategy Acquisition by Children
   with General Learning Difficulties through Metacognitive Training,"
   Australian Journal of Learning Difficulties 15, no. 1 (2010): 13–34, https://doi
   .org/10.1080/19404150903524523.

9 Ken Robinson and Lou Aronica, *The Element: How Finding Your Passion
   Changes Everything* (New York: Random House, 2009), 222.

10 Patterning refers to finding the rule in a predictable series of items (e.g., red,
   blue, green, red, blue, ___). See: Robert Pasnak, "Empirical Studies of
   Patterning," *Psychology* 08, no. 13 (2017): 2276–93, https://doi.org/10.4236
   /psych.2017.813144. Indeed, young children's patterning skills in early
   preschool are a predictor for their later math skills. See: Bethany Rittle-
   Johnson, Erica L. Zippert, and Katherine L. Boice, "The Roles of
   Patterning and Spatial Skills in Early Mathematics Development," *Early
   Childhood Research Quarterly* 46 (2019): 166–78, https://doi.org/10.1016
   /j.ecresq.2018.03.006.

11 For more on how children use questions to drive their cognitive development,
   see: Michael M. Chouinard, "Children's Questions: A Mechanism for
   Cognitive Development," *Monographs of the Society for Research in Child
   Development* 72, no. 1 (March 2007): vii–ix, 1–112; discussion 113–26.

12 For more on this phenomenon, known as the "Matthew effect" in reading,
   see: Keith E. Stanovich, "Matthew Effects in Reading: Some Consequences
   of Individual Differences in the Acquisition of Literacy," *Reading Research
   Quarterly* 21, no. 4 (1986): 360–407, https://doi.org/10.1177/00220574091
   89001-204. For a more recent study, see: Kate Cain and Jane Oakhill,
   "Matthew Effects in Young Readers," *Journal of Learning Disabilities* 44,
   no. 5 (2011): 431–43, https://doi.org/10.1177/0022219411410042.

13 J. Ricardo García and Kate Cain, "Decoding and Reading Comprehension,"
   Review of Educational Research 84, no. 1 (2014): 74–111, https://doi.org/10
   .3102/0034654313499616. For more on the influence of working memory
   on children's comprehension, see: Alix Seigneuric and Marie-France
   Ehrlich, "Contribution of Working Memory Capacity to Children's Reading

Comprehension: A Longitudinal Investigation," *Reading and Writing* 18, no. 7-9 (2005): 617–56, https://doi.org/10.1007/s11145-005-2038-0.

14 While decoding skills clearly affect comprehension, some children still struggle to comprehend text even with adequate decoding skills, often referred to as a specific comprehension deficit (SCD). For a review of SCD, as well as an overview of the main theories of reading comprehension, see: Mercedes Spencer and Richard K. Wagner, "The Comprehension Problems of Children with Poor Reading Comprehension Despite Adequate Decoding: A Meta-Analysis," *Review of Educational Research* 88, no. 3 (March 2018): 366–400, https://doi.org/10.3102/0034654317749187. It is estimated that approximately 10 to 15 percent of seven-to-eight-year-old children have adequate decoding skills but struggle to comprehend text; see: Kate Nation and Margaret Snowling, "Assessing Reading Difficulties: The Validity and Utility of Current Measures of Reading Skill," *British Journal of Educational Psychology* 67, no. 3 (1997): 359–70, https://doi.org/10.1111/j.2044-8279.1997.tb01250.x; and Susan E. Stothard and Charles Hulme, "A Comparison of Phonological Skills in Children with Reading Comprehension Difficulties and Children with Decoding Difficulties," *Journal of Child Psychology and Psychiatry* 36, no. 3 (1995): 399–408, https://doi.org/10.1111/j.1469-7610.1995.tb01298.x.

15 For more information, see: "Atlanta Speech School: Homepage," Atlanta Speech School, accessed April 9, 2021, https://www.atlantaspeechschool.org/.

16 For the most part, schools that prioritize conversation are an exception and typically serve primarily children with specific special needs. What should be a universal focus in our schools and families becomes something to seek out—often in ways that go against the flow of typical schooling.

17 Maryanne Wolf, *Reader, Come Home: The Reading Brain in a Digital World* (New York: Harper, 2019).

18 Thomas A. Edison and Dagobert D. Runes, *The Diary and Observations of Thomas Alva Edison* (New York: Philosophical Library, 1976), 43.

19 Seth Godin, *The Dip: A Little Book That Teaches You When to Quit (and When to Stick)* (New York: Portfolio, 2007).

20 Jill K. Fahy, "Language and Executive Functions: Self-Talk for Self-Regulation," *Perspectives on Language Learning and Education* 21, no. 2 (2014): 61–71, https://doi.org/10.1044/lle21.2.61.

21 That study, of students in grades four through six, asked some students to take a math test while engaging in "effort" self-talk, such as saying, "I will do my very best." Other students were asked to use "ability" self-talk, such as saying, "I am very good at this," and others weren't asked to do any self-talk at all. The "effort" self-talk was linked to better performance for those students who held negative beliefs about their math skills. See: Sander Thomaes et al., "Effort Self-Talk Benefits the Mathematics Performance of Children with Negative Competence Beliefs," *Child Development* 91, no. 6 (2019): 2211–20, https://srcd.onlinelibrary.wiley.com/doi/full/10.1111/cdev.13347.

22 Nadya Pancsofar, Lynne Vernon-Feagans, and The Family Life Project Investigators, "Fathers' Early Contributions to Children's Language Development in Families from Low-Income Rural Communities," *Early Childhood Research Quarterly* 25, no. 4 (October 1, 2010): 450–63, https://www.ncbi.nlm.nih.gov/pmc/articles/PMC2967789/.

23 This use of "because" is only the first stage. As kids develop, these connections become more nuanced and abstract. For example, "The peasants revolted because they were oppressed," or "The beaker exploded because those chemicals mixed." When kids start using other connection words and phrases, such as "however" or "even though," they can make new logical leaps. Such words and phrases, or "connectives," tend to appear more in text than in our everyday speech; thus, reading is an important way of introducing children to these leaps. For more on connectives, see: Amy C. Crosson and Nonie K. Lesaux, "Connectives," *The Reading Teacher* 67, no. 3 (2013): 193–200, https://doi.org/10.1002/trtr.1197.

24 See: Hart and Risley, *Meaningful Differences in the Everyday Experience of Young American Children*; Kathy Hirsh-Pasek et al., "The Contribution of Early Communication Quality to Low-Income Children's Language Success," *Psychological Science* 26, no. 7 (May 2015): 1071–83, https://doi.org/10.1177/0956797615581493; and Erika Hoff, "The Specificity of Environmental Influence: Socioeconomic Status Affects Early Vocabulary Development Via Maternal Speech," *Child Development* 74, no. 5 (2003): 1368–78, https://doi.org/10.1111/1467-8624.00612. For a set of strategies for interacting with young children based on this research, see: Dana Suskind, *Thirty Million Words: Building a Child's Brain* (New York: Dutton, 2016).

25 Catherine E. Snow, "The Theoretical Basis for Relationships between Language and Literacy in Development," *Journal of Research in Childhood Education* 6, no. 1 (1991): 5–10, https://doi.org/10.1080/02568549109594817.

26 As Meredith Rowe, a Harvard professor and researcher, has found, the more parents used decontextualized language and many different kinds of words with preschoolers, the stronger the children's vocabularies were one year later. See: Rowe, "A Longitudinal Investigation of the Role of Quantity and Quality of Child-Directed Speech in Vocabulary Development."

27 In one study, a child's decontextualized language at thirty months predicted how much higher-level language she used as a teenager. See: Paola Uccelli et al., "Children's Early Decontextualized Talk Predicts Academic Language Proficiency in Midadolescence," *Child Development* 90, no. 5 (2018): 1650–63, https://doi.org/10.1111/cdev.13034.

28 Dorothy Varygiannes, "The Impact of Open-Ended Tasks," *Teaching Children Mathematics* 20, no. 5 (2013): 277–80, https://doi.org/10.5951/teacchilmath.20.5.0277.

29 Nanci Bell, "Gestalt Imagery: A Critical Factor in Language Comprehension," *Annals of Dyslexia* 41, no. 1 (1991): 246–60, https://doi.org/10.1007

/bf02648089. See also: Nanci Bell, *Visualizing and Verbalizing: For Language Comprehension and Thinking* (Avila Beach, CA: Gander, 2007).

30 Adele Diamond et al., "The Early Years: Preschool Program Improves Cognitive Control," *Science* 318, no. 5855 (2007): 1387–88, https://doi.org /10.1126/science.1151148.

31 Dale H. Schunk, "Verbalization and Children's Self-Regulated Learning," *Contemporary Educational Psychology* 11, no. 4 (1986): 347–69, https://doi .org/10.1016/0361-476x(86)90030-5.

32 Nanci Bell, "Visualizing and Verbalizing: Q and A with Nanci Bell of Lindamood-Bell," Reading Rockets, accessed October 15, 2019, https:// www.readingrockets.org/article/visualizing-and-verbalizing-q-and-nanci -bell-lindamood-bell.

33 Relatedly, verbalizing a promise not to cheat (or "peek") was found to significantly reduce cheating among three-to-five-year-olds; see: Angela D. Evans, Alison M. O'Connor, and Kang Lee, "Verbalizing a Commitment Reduces Cheating in Young Children," *Social Development* 27, no. 1 (2017): 87–94, https://doi.org/10.1111/sode.12248.

34 For more on this perspective, see: Marlene Scardamalia and Carl Bereiter, "Child as Coinvestigator: Helping Children Gain Insight into Their Own Mental Processes," in *Learning and Motivation in the Classroom*, eds. Scott G. Paris, Gary M. Olson, and Harold W. Stevenson (London: Routledge, 2017), 61–82, https://doi.org/10.4324/9781315188522-4.

35 Brandy N. Frazier, Susan A. Gelman, and Henry M. Wellman, "Preschoolers' Search for Explanatory Information within Adult-Child Conversation," *Child Development* 80, no. 6 (2009): 1592–1611, https://www.ncbi.nlm.nih .gov/pmc/articles/PMC2784636/.

36 Frazier, Gelman, and Wellman, "Preschoolers' Search for Explanatory Information within Adult-Child Conversation."

37 Brandy N. Frazier, Susan A. Gelman, and Henry M. Wellman, "Young Children Prefer and Remember Satisfying Explanations," *Journal of Cognition and Development* 17, no. 5 (2016): 718–36, https://doi.org/10 .1080/15248372.2015.1098649.

38 Virginia Salo et al., "Father Input and Child Vocabulary Development: The Importance of *Wh* Questions and Clarification Requests," *Seminars in Speech and Language* 34, no. 04 (February 2013): 249–59, https://doi.org/10.1055/s -0033-1353445. For related work, see also: Rowe and Leech, "A Parent Intervention with a Growth Mindset Approach Improves Children's Early Gesture and Vocabulary Development."

39 Mai Stafford et al., "Parent–Child Relationships and Offspring's Positive Mental Wellbeing from Adolescence to Early Older Age," *Journal of Positive Psychology* 11, no. 3 (2015): 326–37, https://doi.org/10.1080/17439760.2015 .1081971.

40 Barbara A. Wasik and Mary Alice Bond, "Beyond the Pages of a Book: Interactive Book Reading and Language Development in Preschool

Classrooms," *Journal of Educational Psychology* 93, no. 2 (2001): 243–50, https://doi.org/10.1037/0022-0663.93.2.243. For recent studies on the effectiveness of dialogic reading, see: Anne C. Hargrave and Monique Sénéchal, "A Book Reading Intervention with Preschool Children Who Have Limited Vocabularies: The Benefits of Regular Reading and Dialogic Reading," *Early Childhood Research Quarterly* 15, no. 1 (2000): 75–90, https://doi.org/10.1016/s0885-2006(99)00038-1; and Christan Grygas Coogle et al., "A Comparison of Dialogic Reading, Modeling, and Dialogic Reading Plus Modeling," *Infants & Young Children* 33, no. 2 (2020): 119–31, https://doi.org/10.1097/iyc.0000000000000162.

41 Paul L. Morgan and Catherine R. Meier, "Dialogic Reading's Potential to Improve Children's Emergent Literacy Skills and Behavior," *Preventing School Failure: Alternative Education for Children and Youth* 52, no. 4 (2008): 11–16, https://doi.org/10.3200/psfl.52.4.11-16.

42 Also, consider which book-reading format engages you and your child the most and leads to the warmest interaction. Research has found, for example, differences in warmth and engagement when parents use screen reading versus paper books. See: Nicola Yuill and Alex F. Martin, "Curling Up with a Good E-Book: Mother-Child Shared Story Reading on Screen or Paper Affects Embodied Interaction and Warmth," *Frontiers in Psychology* 7 (2016), https://doi.org/10.3389/fpsyg.2016.01951. In another study of parents and toddlers, parents showed more dialogic reading, and toddlers verbalized more, when reading print books than when they read electronic or animated books. See: Tiffany G. Munzer et al., "Differences in Parent-Toddler Interactions with Electronic versus Print Books," American Academy of Pediatrics, April 1, 2019, https://pediatrics.aappublications.org/content/143/4/e20182012. However, every family is different; simply noticing whether your interactions change and how is an important start.

43 Rollanda E. O'Connor, Annika White, and H. Lee Swanson, "Repeated Reading versus Continuous Reading: Influences on Reading Fluency and Comprehension," *Exceptional Children* 74, no. 1 (2007): 31–46, https://doi.org/10.1177/001440290707400102; Elizabeth A. Stevens, Melodee A. Walker, and Sharon Vaughn, "The Effects of Reading Fluency Interventions on the Reading Fluency and Reading Comprehension Performance of Elementary Students with Learning Disabilities: A Synthesis of the Research from 2001 to 2014," *Journal of Learning Disabilities* 50, no. 5 (November 2016): 576–90, https://doi.org/10.1177/0022219416638028; William J. Therrien, "Fluency and Comprehension Gains as a Result of Repeated Reading," *Remedial and Special Education* 25, no. 4 (2004): 252–61, https://doi.org/10.1177/07419325040250040801.

44 Ulrike E. Nett et al., "Metacognitive Strategies and Test Performance: An Experience Sampling Analysis of Students' Learning Behavior," *Education Research International* 2012 (November 1, 2012), https://www.hindawi.com/journals/edri/2012/958319/.

45 However, younger children can also benefit from using metacognitive strategies and are capable of metacognition far earlier than previously thought. For more on research into young children's metacognition, see for example: Elena Escolano-Pérez, Maria Luisa Herrero-Nivela, and M. Teresa Anguera, "Preschool Metacognitive Skill Assessment in Order to Promote Educational Sensitive Response from Mixed-Methods Approach: Complementarity of Data Analysis," *Frontiers in Psychology* 10 (2019), https://doi.org/10.3389/fpsyg.2019.01298.

46 Patricia Chen et al., "Strategic Resource Use for Learning: A Self-Administered Intervention That Guides Self-Reflection on Effective Resource Use Enhances Academic Performance," *Psychological Science* 28, no. 6 (2017): 774–85, https://doi.org/10.1177/0956797617696456.

47 Youki Terada, "How Metacognition Boosts Learning," Edutopia, November 21, 2017, https://www.edutopia.org/article/how-metacognition-boosts-learning.

48 These standards were written partly in response to the Bush-era No Child Left Behind Act, which was later replaced in 2015 by the Every Student Succeeds Act (ESSA). For an overview, see: "The Common Core FAQ," NPR, May 27, 2014, https://www.npr.org/sections/ed/2014/05/27/307755798 /the-common-core-faq#q4; and Allie Bidwell, "The History of Common Core State Standards," *U.S. News & World Report*, February 27, 2014, https:// www.usnews.com/news/special-reports/articles/2014/02/27/the-history-of -common-core-state-standards. Also, for related research on whether the Common Core standards "worked," see: Morgan S. Polikoff, "Is Common Core 'Working'? And Where Does Common Core Research Go from Here?," *AERA Open* 3, no. 1 (2017), https://doi.org/10.1177/2332858417691749.

49 Dana Goldstein, "After 10 Years of Hopes and Setbacks, What Happened to the Common Core?," *New York Times*, December 6, 2019, https://www .nytimes.com/2019/12/06/us/common-core.html.

50 Liana Loewus, "For Parents Confused by Common-Core Math, Ask the Teacher for Help," Education Week, January 7, 2016, https://www .edweek.org/teaching-learning/for-parents-confused-by-common-core -math-ask-the-teacher-for-help/2016/01.

51 As the writer Kathleen Lucadamo notes in a 2016 *Hechinger Report* article; see Kathleen Lucadamo, "Back Off Parents: It's Not Your Job to Teach Common Core Math When Helping with Homework," *Hechinger Report*, January 5, 2016, https://hechingerreport.org/back-off-parents-its -not-your-job-to-teach-common-core-math-when-helping-with-homework/.

52 According to the Univ. of Chicago psychologist Sian Beilock, a study author, "If a parent is walking around saying 'Oh, I don't like math' or 'This stuff makes me nervous,' kids pick up on this messaging and it affects their success." See: Susie Allen, "Parents' Math Anxiety Can Undermine Children's Math Achievement," Univ. of Chicago News, August 10, 2015, https://news.uchicago.edu/story/parents-math-anxiety-can-undermine -childrens-math-achievement.

53 Erin A. Maloney et al., "Intergenerational Effects of Parents' Math Anxiety on Children's Math Achievement and Anxiety," *Psychological Science* 26, no. 9 (July 2015): 1480–88, https://doi.org/10.1177/0956797615592630.

54 Research has also found that conversational strategies can help parents become less directive and more collaborative with their kids when learning math. See: Lee Shumow, "Promoting Parental Attunement to Children's Mathematical Reasoning Through Parent Education," *Journal of Applied Developmental Psychology* 19, no. 1 (1998): 109–27, https://doi.org/10.1016 /s0193-3973(99)80031-8.

55 Even children in elementary school can contribute to research as "citizen scientists," conducting tasks in support of larger research projects. For research in this area, see: Victoria L. Miczajka, Alexandra-Maria Klein, and Gesine Pufal, "Elementary School Children Contribute to Environmental Research as Citizen Scientists," *PLOS ONE* 10, no. 11 (2015), https://doi .org/10.1371/journal.pone.0143229.

56 In many research studies, a child's level of curiosity is defined in part as to the degree of uncertainty with which he or she is comfortable. See: Jamie Jirout and David Klahr, "Children's Scientific Curiosity: In Search of an Operational Definition of an Elusive Concept," *Developmental Review* 32, no. 2 (2012): 125–60, https://doi.org/10.1016/j.dr.2012.04.002.

57 Athanasia Chatzipanteli, Vasilis Grammatikopoulos, and Athanasios Gregoriadis, "Development and Evaluation of Metacognition in Early Childhood Education," *Early Child Development and Care* 184, no. 8 (2013): 1223–32, https://doi.org/10.1080/03004430.2013.861456.

58 This metacognition is not only found in older children but also, at least at basic levels, in children at surprisingly young ages. For example, one study found children from ages five to six years old were aware of a range of metacognitive strategies and could recommend them. See: Elizabeth L. Davis et al., "Metacognitive Emotion Regulation: Children's Awareness That Changing Thoughts and Goals Can Alleviate Negative Emotions," *Emotion* 10, no. 4 (2010): 498–510, https://doi.org/10.1037/a0018428.

59 Kathrin Lockl and Wolfgang Schneider, "Precursors of Metamemory in Young Children: The Role of Theory of Mind and Metacognitive Vocabulary," *Metacognition and Learning* 1, no. 1 (September 2006): 15–31, https://doi.org/10.1007/s11409-006-6585-9.

Chapter 3: Conversations for Empathy: Fostering Your Child's Understanding of Others

1 Cressida Leyshon, "This Week in Fiction: Mohsin Hamid," *The New Yorker*, September 16, 2012, https://www.newyorker.com/books/page-turner/this -week-in-fiction-mohsin-hamid.

2 Fabrizio Mafessoni and Michael Lachmann, "The Complexity of Understanding Others as the Evolutionary Origin of Empathy and

Emotional Contagion," *Scientific Reports* 9, no. 5794 (2019), https://www
.nature.com/articles/s41598-019-41835-5.

3 Daniel Goleman, "Hot to Help," *Greater Good*, March 1, 2008, https://
greatergood.berkeley.edu/article/item/hot_to_help.

4 J. Robinson, "Empathy and Prosocial Behavior," in *Encyclopedia of Infant and
Early Childhood Development*, eds. Marshall M. Haith and Janette B. Benson
(Cambridge: Academic Press, 2008), 441–50, https://doi.org/10.1016/b978
-012370877-9.00056-6.

5 Mark R. Dadds et al., "A Measure of Cognitive and Affective Empathy in
Children Using Parent Ratings," *Child Psychiatry and Human Development*
39, no. 2 (2007): 111–22, https://doi.org/10.1007/s10578-007-0075-4.

6 See the work of Univ. of Kansas professor Patricia Hawley and Univ. of
Connecticut professor Antonius Cillessen, as discussed in Po Bronson and
Ashley Merryman's book *NurtureShock: New Thinking about Children* (New
York: Twelve, 2009), 191–93. For representative studies, see, for example,
Hawley's work: Patricia H. Hawley, Todd D. Little, and Noel A. Card, "The
Allure of a Mean Friend: Relationship Quality and Processes of Aggressive
Adolescents with Prosocial Skills," *International Journal of Behavioral
Development* 31, no. 2 (2007): 170–80, https://doi.org/10.1177/0165
025407074630; Patricia H. Hawley, "Prosocial and Coercive Configurations
of Resource Control in Early Adolescence: A Case for the Well-Adapted
Machiavellian," *Merrill-Palmer Quarterly* 49, no. 3 (2003): 279–309, https://
doi.org/10.1353/mpq.2003.0013; and Patricia H. Hawley, "Social Dominance
and Prosocial and Coercive Strategies of Resource Control in Preschoolers,"
International Journal of Behavioral Development 26, no. 2 (2002): 167–76,
https://doi.org/10.1080/01650250042000726. For the work of Cillessen, see
for example: Antonius H. Cillessen and Lara Mayeux, "From Censure to
Reinforcement: Developmental Changes in the Association between
Aggression and Social Status," *Child Development* 75, no. 1 (2004): 147–63,
https://doi.org/10.1111/j.1467-8624.2004.00660.x; and Antonius H.N.
Cillessen and Amanda J. Rose, "Understanding Popularity in the Peer
System," *Current Directions in Psychological Science* 14, no. 2 (2005): 102–5,
https://doi.org/10.1111/j.0963-7214.2005.00343.x.

7 Luciano Gasser and Monika Keller, "Are the Competent the Morally
Good? Perspective Taking and Moral Motivation of Children Involved in
Bullying," *Social Development* 18, no. 4 (2009): 798–816, https://doi.org/10
.1111/j.1467-9507.2008.00516.x. In this study, only victims showed a deficit
in perspective-taking, while children who were more aggressive showed a
deficit in moral motivation.

8 Holly E. Recchia et al., "The Construction of Moral Agency in Mother–
Child Conversations about Helping and Hurting across Childhood and
Adolescence," *Developmental Psychology* 50, no. 1 (2014): 34–44, https://doi
.org/10.1037/a0033492.

9 Veronica Ornaghi, Elisabetta Conte, and Ilaria Grazzani, "Empathy in

Toddlers: The Role of Emotion Regulation, Language Ability, and Maternal Emotion Socialization Style," *Frontiers in Psychology* 11 (2020), https://doi .org/10.3389/fpsyg.2020.586862.

10 For the role of caregiver interactions and trauma on the development of empathy, see: Jonathan Levy, Abraham Goldstein, and Ruth Feldman, "The Neural Development of Empathy Is Sensitive to Caregiving and Early Trauma," *Nature Communications* 10, no. 1 (2019), https://doi.org/10.1038 /s41467-019-09927-y.

11 Research shows that parents and caregivers *can* enhance children's theory of mind, in part by telling stories, having conversations about events in the future and past, and talking about "mental states"—that is, how we feel, and how other people might feel. See: Paul L. Harris, Marc de Rosnay, and Francisco Pons, "Language and Children's Understanding of Mental States," *Current Directions in Psychological Science* 14, no. 2 (2005): 69–73, https://doi .org/10.1111/j.0963-7214.2005.00337.x.

12 Indeed, building children's language skills seems to help build their theory of mind. See studies including: Courtney Melinda Hale and Helen Tager-Flusberg, "The Influence of Language on Theory of Mind: A Training Study," *Developmental Science* 6, no. 3 (2003): 346–59, https://doi.org/10.1111 /1467-7687.00289.

13 Becky Friedman and Jason Fruchter, *Daniel Tiger's Neighborhood: Daniel's New Friend* (New York: Simon Spotlight, 2015).

14 Grace B. Martin and Russell D. Clark, "Distress Crying in Neonates: Species and Peer Specificity," *Developmental Psychology* 18, no. 1 (1982): 3–9, https://doi.org/10.1037/0012-1649.18.1.3.

15 Other research has found some signs of cognitive and emotional empathy appearing even earlier, in babies from eight to ten months old. It takes slightly longer for kids to show prosocial or caring behavior. See, for example: Sara R. Nichols, Margarita Svetlova, and Celia A. Brownell, "Toddlers' Responses to Infants' Negative Emotions," *Infancy* 20, no. 1 (April 2014): 70–97, https://doi.org/10.1111/infa.12066.

16 Ronit Roth-Hanania, Maayan Davidov, and Carolyn Zahn-Waxler, "Empathy Development from 8 to 16 Months: Early Signs of Concern for Others," *Infant Behavior and Development* 34, no. 3 (2011): 447–58, https:// doi.org/10.1016/j.infbeh.2011.04.007. For additional discussion, see also: Ariel Knafo et al., "The Developmental Origins of a Disposition toward Empathy: Genetic and Environmental Contributions.," *Emotion* 8, no. 6 (2008): 737–52, https://doi.org/10.1037/a0014179; and Carolyn Zahn-Waxler et al., "Development of Concern for Others," *Developmental Psychology* 28, no. 1 (1992): 126–36, https://doi.org/10.1037/0012-1649 .28.1.126.

17 Over the past decade, significant links have been found between empathy and prosocial behavior in children. For example, in one study, both five-year-old children and three-year-old children showed increased prosocial

(helping) behavior for others when they had been primed to show empathy for them. See: Amanda Williams, Kelly O'Driscoll, and Chris Moore, "The Influence of Empathic Concern on Prosocial Behavior in Children," *Frontiers in Psychology* 5 (December 2014), https://doi.org/10.3389/fpsyg .2014.00425.

18 Margarita Svetlova, Sara R. Nichols, and Celia A. Brownell, "Toddlers' Prosocial Behavior: From Instrumental to Empathic to Altruistic Helping," *Child Development* 81, no. 6 (2010): 1814–27, https://doi.org/10.1111/j .1467-8624.2010.01512.x. For an overview of empathy by stages, see: Carla Poole, Susan A. Miller, and Ellen Booth Church, "Ages & Stages: Empathy," Scholastic, accessed May 26, 2021, https://www.scholastic.com /teachers/articles/teaching-content/ages-stages-empathy/.

19 Leïla Bensalah, Stéphanie Caillies, and Marion Anduze, "Links among Cognitive Empathy, Theory of Mind, and Affective Perspective Taking by Young Children," *Journal of Genetic Psychology* 177, no. 1 (2016): 17–31, https://doi.org/10.1080/00221325.2015.1106438.

20 Ruth T. Zajdel et al., "Children's Understanding and Experience of Mixed Emotions: The Roles of Age, Gender, and Empathy," *Journal of Genetic Psychology* 174, no. 5 (2013): 582–603, https://doi.org/10.1080/00221325 .2012.732125.

21 Poole, Miller, and Church, "Ages & Stages: Empathy."

22 So Yeon Shin, Kathryn A. Leech, and Meredith L. Rowe, "Examining Relations between Parent-Child Narrative Talk and Children's Episodic Foresight and Theory of Mind," *Cognitive Development* 55 (2020): 100910, https://doi.org/10.1016/j.cogdev.2020.100910.

23 Kimberly A. Schonert-Reichl et al., "Promoting Children's Prosocial Behaviors in School: Impact of the 'Roots of Empathy' Program on the Social and Emotional Competence of School-Aged Children," *School Mental Health* 4, no. 1 (April 2011): 1–21, https://doi.org/10.1007/s12310-011 -9064-7.

24 Suparna Choudhury, Sarah-Jayne Blakemore, and Tony Charman, "Social Cognitive Development during Adolescence," *Social Cognitive and Affective Neuroscience* 1, no. 3 (January 2006): 165–74, https://doi.org/10.1093/scan /nsl024.

25 Marc A. Brackett, *Permission to Feel: Unlocking the Power of Emotions to Help Our Kids, Ourselves, and Our Society Thrive* (New York: Celadon Books, 2019).

26 See "Emotions Matter," RULER Approach, accessed June 1, 2021, https:// www.rulerapproach.org/. For research on the program, see: Jessica D. Hoffmann et al., "Teaching Emotion Regulation in Schools: Translating Research into Practice with the RULER Approach to Social and Emotional Learning," *Emotion* 20, no. 1 (2020): 105–9, https://doi.org/10.1037 /emo0000649; and Marc A. Brackett et al., "Enhancing Academic Performance and Social and Emotional Competence with the RULER

Feeling Words Curriculum," *Learning and Individual Differences* 22, no. 2 (2012): 218–24, https://doi.org/10.1016/j.lindif.2010.10.002.

27 Anna Ratka, "Empathy and the Development of Affective Skills," *American Journal of Pharmaceutical Education* 82, no. 10 (December 2018): 7192, https://www.ncbi.nlm.nih.gov/pmc/articles/PMC6325458/.

28 Rebecca Brewer and Jennifer Murphy, "People with Autism Can Read Emotions, Feel Empathy" *Scientific American*, July 13, 2016, https://www.scientificamerican.com/article/people-with-autism-can-read-emotions-feel-empathy1/.

29 Roy Pea et al., "Media Use, Face-to-Face Communication, Media Multitasking, and Social Well-Being among 8- to 12-Year-Old Girls," *Developmental Psychology* 48, no. 2 (2012): 327–36, https://doi.org/10.1037/a0027030.

30 Yalda T. Uhls et al., "Five Days at Outdoor Education Camp without Screens Improves Preteen Skills with Nonverbal Emotion Cues," *Computers in Human Behavior* 39 (2014): 387–92, https://doi.org/10.1016/j.chb.2014.05.036.

31 Robert Thornberg et al., "Bystander Motivation in Bullying Incidents: To Intervene or Not to Intervene?," *Western Journal of Emergency Medicine* 13, no. 3 (January 2012): 247–52, https://doi.org/10.5811/westjem.2012.3.11792.

32 Based on the books *How Full Is Your Bucket?* and *Have You Filled a Bucket Today?* See: Tom Rath and Audra Wallace, *How Full Is Your Bucket?* (New York: Scholastic, 2019); and Carol McCloud, *Have You Filled a Bucket Today?: A Guide to Daily Happiness* (Chicago: Bucket Fillers, 2015). For more information, see: Bucket Fillers, accessed May 11, 2021, https://bucketfillers101.com/.

33 Kristin D. Neff and Daniel J. Faso, "Self-Compassion and Well-Being in Parents of Children with Autism," *Mindfulness* 6, no. 4 (August 2014): 938–47, https://doi.org/10.1007/s12671-014-0359-2. As the mother of a child with autism, she found that "self-compassion pulled me back from the precipice of despair"; see: Kristin Neff, *Self-Compassion: The Proven Power of Being Kind to Yourself* (New York: William Morrow, 2015), 105.

34 Simon Baron-Cohen, Alan M. Leslie, and Uta Frith, "Does the Autistic Child Have a 'Theory of Mind'?," *Cognition* 21, no. 1 (1985): 37–46, https://doi.org/10.1016/0010-0277(85)90022-8.

35 Brad M. Farrant et al., "Empathy, Perspective Taking and Prosocial Behaviour: The Importance of Parenting Practices," *Infant and Child Development* 21, no. 2 (June 2011): 175–88, https://doi.org/10.1002/icd.740.

36 As the Swedish psychologist Elia Psouni argues, building perspective-taking skills with young kids starts with focusing on the same information at the same time. It helps if you're actively engaged. See: Elia Psouni et al., "Together I Can! Joint Attention Boosts 3- to 4-Year-Olds' Performance in a Verbal False-Belief Test," *Child Development* 90, no. 1 (2018): 35–50, https://doi.org/10.1111/cdev.13075.

37 Psouni et al., "Together I Can!"

38 Gleason is best known for her invention of the Wug Test, in which she used nonsense words to judge young children's knowledge of linguistic rules. See: Jean Berko, "The Child's Learning of English Morphology," *Word* 14, no. 2-3 (1958): 150–77, https://doi.org/10.1080/00437956.1958.11659661. See also: Jean Berko Gleason and Sandra Weintraub, "The Acquisition of Routines in Child Language," *Language in Society* 5, no. 2 (1976): 129–36, https://doi.org/10.1017/s0047404500006977.

39 Richard Ely and Jean Berko Gleason, "*I'm Sorry I Said That:* Apologies in Young Children's Discourse," *Journal of Child Language* 33, no. 3 (2006): 599–620, https://doi.org/10.1017/s0305000906007446.

40 Richard Ely et al., "Attention to Language: Lessons Learned at the Dinner Table," *Social Development* 10, no. 3 (2001): 355–73, https://doi.org/10.1111/1467-9507.00170.

41 See: Gerber, *Dear Parent: Caring for Infants with Respect.*

42 Catherine A. McMahon and Elizabeth Meins, "Mind-Mindedness, Parenting Stress, and Emotional Availability in Mothers of Preschoolers," *Early Childhood Research Quarterly* 27, no. 2 (2012): 245–52, https://doi.org/10.1016/j.ecresq.2011.08.002; Katherine L. Rosenblum et al., "Reflection in Thought and Action: Maternal Parenting Reflectivity Predicts Mind-Minded Comments and Interactive Behavior," *Infant Mental Health Journal* 29, no. 4 (2008): 362–76, https://doi.org/10.1002/imhj.20184.

43 "Building Emotional Intelligence Playfully," Generation Mindful, accessed June 6, 2021, https://genmindful.com/.

44 For research on the role of mutual help in adolescent friendships, see: Loes G. Rijsewijk et al., "The Interplay Between Adolescents' Friendships and the Exchange of Help: A Longitudinal Multiplex Social Network Study," *Journal of Research on Adolescence* 30, no. 1 (October 2019): 63–77, https://doi.org/10.1111/jora.12501.

45 Larissa G. Duncan, J. Douglas Coatsworth, and Mark T. Greenberg, "A Model of Mindful Parenting: Implications for Parent–Child Relationships and Prevention Research," *Clinical Child and Family Psychology Review* 12, no. 3 (February 2009): 255–70, https://doi.org/10.1007/s10567-009-0046-3.

46 Neil Katz and Kevin McNulty, "Reflective Listening - Syracuse University," 1994, https://www.maxwell.syr.edu/uploadedFiles/parcc/cmc/Reflective%20Listening%20NK.pdf .

47 These two names are pseudonyms.

48 As the psychiatrist Daniel Siegel argues, "Parents reflect to us what they see going on in our inner world, not just noticing our behaviors but, for example, reflecting to us about our feelings, what we might be thinking, remembering, perceiving. All of these are ways we get signals back from our caregivers that help us see the internal world with clarity." See: "What Is Mindsight? An Interview with Dr. Dan Siegel," PsychAlive, September 15, 2017, https://www.psychalive.org/what-is-mindsight-an-interview-with-dr

-dan-siegel/. For further information on Siegel's approach, focused on parental presence, see: Daniel J. Siegel, *Mindsight: The New Science of Personal Transformation* (New York: Bantam Books, 2011); and Daniel J. Siegel and Tina Payne Bryson, *The Power of Showing Up: How Parental Presence Shapes Who Our Kids Become and How Their Brains Get Wired* (New York: Ballantine Books, 2021).

49 Penny Van Bergen et al., "The Effects of Mother Training in Emotion-Rich, Elaborative Reminiscing on Children's Shared Recall and Emotion Knowledge," *Journal of Cognition and Development* 10, no. 3 (2009): 162–87, https://doi.org/10.1080/15248370903155825.

50 Susan David, interview with the author, March 21, 2019.

51 Robyn Fivush et al., "Family Reminiscing Style: Parent Gender and Emotional Focus in Relation to Child Well-Being," *Journal of Cognition and Development* 10, no. 3 (2009): 210–35, https://doi.org/10.1080/1524837 0903155866.

52 Deborah Laible, "Mother-Child Discourse in Two Contexts: Links with Child Temperament, Attachment Security, and Socioemotional Competence," *Developmental Psychology* 40, no. 6 (2004): 979–92, https:// doi.org/10.1037/0012-1649.40.6.979.

53 Paola Corsano and Laura Guidotti, "Parents' Reminiscing Training in Typically Developing and 'at-Risk' Children: A Review," *Early Child Development and Care* 189, no. 1 (2017): 143–56, https://doi.org/10.1080 /03004430.2017.1289518.

54 Charles Derber, *The Pursuit of Attention: Power and Ego in Everyday Life* (New York: Oxford Univ. Press, 2001).

55 Bronson and Merryman, *NurtureShock*, 239.

Chapter 4: Conversations for Confidence and Independence: Encouraging Your Child to Embrace Challenges

1 Louisa May Alcott, *Little Women*, ed. John Escott (Oxford: Oxford Univ. Press, 2008), Chapter 44, p. 1.

2 Viviana A. Zelizer, *Pricing the Priceless Child: The Changing Social Value of Children* (New York: Basic Books, 1985), 14.

3 Albert Bandura, "Perceived Self-Efficacy in the Exercise of Personal Agency," *Journal of Applied Sport Psychology* 2, no. 2 (1990): 128–63, https:// doi.org/10.1080/10413209008406426; Albert Bandura, *Social Foundations of Thought and Action: A Social Cognitive Theory* (Englewood Cliffs, NJ: Prentice Hall, 1995).

4 Frank Pajares, "Self-Efficacy Beliefs in Academic Settings," *Review of Educational Research* 66, no. 4 (1996): 543–78, https://doi.org/10.3102/003 46543066004543.

5 Karen D. Multon, Steven D. Brown, and Robert W. Lent, "Relation of Self-Efficacy Beliefs to Academic Outcomes: A Meta-Analytic

Investigation," *Journal of Counseling Psychology* 38, no. 1 (1991): 30–38, https://doi.org/10.1037/0022-0167.38.1.30.

6 Anthony R. Artino, "Academic Self-Efficacy: from Educational Theory to Instructional Practice," *Perspectives on Medical Education* 1, no. 2 (November 2012): 76–85, https://doi.org/10.1007/s40037-012-0012-5.

7 Deborah Perkins-Gough, "The Significance of Grit: A Conversation with Angela Lee Duckworth," *Education Leadership*, September 1, 2013, http://www.ascd.org/publications/educational-leadership/scpt13/vol71/num01/The-Significance-of-Grit@-A-Conversation-with-Angela-Lee-Duckworth.aspx.

8 Angela Duckworth, *Grit: The Power of Passion and Perseverance* (New York: Scribner, 2016).

9 Angela L. Duckworth et al., "Grit: Perseverance and Passion for Long-Term Goals," *Journal of Personality and Social Psychology* 92, no. 6 (2007): 1087–1101, https://doi.org/10.1037/0022-3514.92.6.1087.

10 As Yeager and Walton found in 2011, seemingly small interventions related to mindset can have large effects on academic achievement; see: David S. Yeager and Gregory M. Walton, "Social-Psychological Interventions in Education: They're Not Magic," *Review of Educational Research* 81, no. 2 (June 1, 2011): 267–301, https://doi.org/10.3102/0034654311405999. However, this link may not hold true for all students. Notably, a 2018 review of studies found less support for growth mindset practices in impacting students' academic achievement than had been previously thought. However, children at highest risk for academic failure and those from low socio-economic backgrounds benefitted most from a growth mindset, and adolescents and children benefitted more than adults. See: Victoria F. Sisk et al., "To What Extent and Under Which Circumstances Are Growth Mind-Sets Important to Academic Achievement? Two Meta-Analyses," *Psychological Science* 29, no. 4 (May 2018): 549–71, https://doi.org/10.1177/0956797617739704.

11 As one 2017 study of high school and college students found, the "persistence" element of grit related significantly to students' grades, more so than did the consistency of their interests. See: Katherine Muenks et al., "How True Is Grit? Assessing Its Relations to High School and College Students' Personality Characteristics, Self-Regulation, Engagement, and Achievement," *Journal of Educational Psychology* 109, no. 5 (2017): 599–620, https://doi.org/10.1037/edu0000153.

12 See: John Bowlby, "The Growth of Independence in the Young Child," *Journal (Royal Society of Health)* 76, no. 9 (1955): 587–91, https://doi.org/10.1177/146642405507600912; and Glen Heathers, "Emotional Dependence and Independence in Nursery School Play," *Journal of Genetic Psychology* 87, no. 1 (1955): 37–57, https://doi.org/10.1080/00221325.1955.10532914. For more recent research, see: Andreas B. Neubauer et al., "A Little Autonomy Support Goes a Long Way: Daily Autonomy-Supportive Parenting, Child Well-Being, Parental Need Fulfillment, and Change in Child, Family, and

Parent Adjustment Across the Adaptation to the COVID-19 Pandemic," *Child Development* (2021), https://doi.org/10.1111/cdev.13515.

13 Ryan F. Lei et al., "Children Lose Confidence in Their Potential to 'Be Scientists,' but Not in Their Capacity to 'Do Science,'" *Developmental Science* 22, no. 6 (August 2019), https://doi.org/10.1111/desc.12837.

14 Linda S. Siegel, "Perspectives on Dyslexia," *Paediatrics & Child Health* 11, no. 9 (2006): 581–87, https://doi.org/10.1093/pch/11.9.581.

15 Rory Devine, interview with the author, May 30, 2019. For more on Devine's research in this and related areas, especially the role of parents' "mental state" talk and mind-mindness, see: Rory T. Devine and Claire Hughes, "Let's Talk: Parents' Mental Talk (Not Mind-Mindedness or Mindreading Capacity) Predicts Children's False Belief Understanding," *Child Development* 90, no. 4 (August 2017): 1236–53, https://doi.org/10 .1111/cdev.12990; and Claire Hughes, Rory T. Devine, and Zhenlin Wang, "Does Parental Mind-Mindedness Account for Cross-Cultural Differences in Preschoolers' Theory of Mind?," *Child Development* 89, no. 4 (March 2017): 1296–1310, https://doi.org/10.1111/cdev.12746.

16 Having an internal locus of control doesn't mean kids think *everything* is in their power. It also doesn't mean ignoring unfairness, like being cut from a team because you weren't close friends with the coach. Clearly, some kids *do* have an external advantage. They may be stronger or come from wealthier families, or naturally shine at academic tasks. It would be silly to ignore all that. Indeed, an overfocus on grit as an individual quality can ignore the structural factors, such as poverty, racism, and sexism, that are at play and that keep children from reaching their full potential. See, for example: David Denby, "The Limits of 'Grit,'" *The New Yorker*, June 21, 2016, https:// www.newyorker.com/culture/culture-desk/the-limits-of-grit. As Dr. Jack Shonkoff of Harvard's Center on the Developing Child argues, "A lot of it [i.e., lack of success] has to do with problems of focusing attention, working memory, and cognitive flexibility. And you may not have developed those capacities because of what happened to you early on in your life," as found in Paul Tough, *Helping Children Succeed: What Works and Why* (Boston: Houghton Mifflin Harcourt, 2016), 51. Still, within the bounds of these limitations, you can encourage kids to notice all that they can do, and all they can control, through the ways you discuss their efforts, plans, and goals. Equally important, you can encourage them to notice and discuss these structural factors, including the ways their circumstances offer them more or fewer opportunities. Through talk, you can set the foundations for their understanding of these abstract issues and even support them to think through ways of creating more equal societies.

17 Erin C. Tully et al., "Family Correlates of Daughter's and Son's Locus of Control Expectancies during Childhood," *Early Child Development and Care* 186, no. 12 (June 2016): 1939–51, https://doi.org/10.1080/03004430.2015 .1137562.

18 Donald A. Gordon, Richard H. Jones, and Nancy L. Short, "Task Persistence and Locus of Control in Elementary School Children," *Child Development* 48, no. 4 (1977): 1716, https://doi.org/10.2307/1128543.

19 Susan Nolen-Hoeksema, Joan S. Girgus, and Martin E. Seligman, "Learned Helplessness in Children: A Longitudinal Study of Depression, Achievement, and Explanatory Style," *Journal of Personality and Social Psychology* 51, no. 2 (1986): 435–42, https://doi.org/10.1037/0022-3514.51.2.435.

20 Dweck, *Mindset: The New Psychology of Success*; Claudia M. Mueller and Carol S. Dweck, "Praise for Intelligence Can Undermine Children's Motivation and Performance," *Journal of Personality and Social Psychology* 75, no. 1 (1998): 33–52, https://doi.org/10.1037/0022-3514.75.1.33.

21 Dweck, "The Power of Believing That You Can Improve."

22 Carol S. Dweck, "Beliefs Are Central to Understanding Human Motivation," *PsycEXTRA Dataset*, 2014, https://doi.org/10.1037/e515492014-004.

23 Andrew J. Elliot and Carol S. Dweck, *Handbook of Competence and Motivation* (New York: Guilford Press, 2007).

24 This may be in part because of how children attend to and interpret feedback about their learning and performance. Children with a fixed mindset, for example, may see constructive feedback as a threat to their sense of competence, rather than as information from which they can learn. See: Jennifer A. Mangels et al., "Why Do Beliefs about Intelligence Influence Learning Success? A Social Cognitive Neuroscience Model," *Social Cognitive and Affective Neuroscience* 1, no. 2 (January 2006): 75–86, https://doi.org/10.1093/scan/nsl013.

25 Carol S. Dweck, "Messages That Motivate: How Praise Molds Students' Beliefs, Motivation, and Performance (in Surprising Ways)," in *Improving Academic Achievement*, ed. Joshua Aronson (New York: Academic Press, 2002), 37–60, https://doi.org/10.1016/b978-012064455-1/50006-3.

26 With cortical blindness, part of the brain is damaged, leading to a total or partial vision loss—even though there's nothing wrong with the eye itself. See: Sasha Mansukhani et al., "Accelerated Visual Recovery from Protracted Hypoxic Cortical Blindness in a Child," *American Journal of Ophthalmology Case Reports* 16 (2019): 100534, https://doi.org/10.1016/j.ajoc.2019.100534.

27 Edward L. Deci and Richard M. Ryan, "Self-Determination," in *The Corsini Encyclopedia of Psychology*, eds. Irving R. Weiner and W. Edward Craighead (New York: John Wiley & Sons, 2010), https://doi.org/10.1002/9780470 479216.corpsy0834.

28 Edward L. Deci and Richard M. Ryan, "Self-Determination Theory: A Macrotheory of Human Motivation, Development, and Health," *Canadian Psychology/Psychologie Canadienne* 49, no. 3 (2008): 182–85, https://doi .org/10.1037/a0012801.

29 Garth Sundem, "Kids with Low Self-Esteem: The Parental Praise Paradox," *Wired*, March 6, 2013, https://www.wired.com/2013/03/kids-with-low-self -esteem-the-parental-praise-paradox/.

30 Sundem, "Kids with Low Self-Esteem.

31 Eddie Brummelman et al., "'That's Not Just Beautiful—That's Incredibly Beautiful!': The Adverse Impact of Inflated Praise on Children with Low Self-Esteem," *Psychological Science* 25, no. 3 (2014): 728–35, https://doi.org/10.1177/0956797613514251.

32 Jessica Lahey, *The Gift of Failure: How the Best Parents Learn to Let Go So Their Children Can Succeed* (New York: Harper, 2015), 187.

33 "The Let Grow Project," Let Grow, accessed April 13, 2021, https://letgrow.org/program/the-let-grow-project/.

34 Lenore Skenazy, interview with the author June 22, 2019.

35 Gary Karlson, interview with the author, June 26, 2019.

36 Denise Civiletti, "New Assistant Principal Named at Aquebogue Elementary School," Riverhead LOCAL, September 14, 2019, https://riverheadlocal.com/2019/09/14/new-assistant-principal-nam-ed-at-aquebogue-elementary-school/.

37 Jessica Joelle Alexander and Iben Dissing Sandahl, *The Danish Way of Parenting: What the Happiest People in the World Know about Raising Confident, Capable Kids* (New York: TarcherPerigee, 2016).

38 "Resilience," Center on the Developing Child at Harvard Univ.

39 Nolen-Hoeksema, Girgus, and Seligman, "Learned Helplessness in Children."

40 Raymond B. Flannery and Mary R. Harvey, "Psychological Trauma and Learned Helplessness: Seligman's Paradigm Reconsidered," *Psychotherapy: Theory, Research, Practice, Training* 28, no. 2 (1991): 374–78, https://doi.org/10.1037/0033-3204.28.2.374.

41 Karin Neijenhuis et al., "An Evidence-Based Perspective on 'Misconceptions' Regarding Pediatric Auditory Processing Disorder," *Frontiers in Neurology* 10 (March 2019), https://doi.org/10.3389/fneur.2019.00287.

42 Huseyin Yaratan and Rusen Yucesoylu, "Self-Esteem, Self-Concept, Self-Talk and Significant Others' Statements in Fifth Grade Students: Differences According to Gender and School Type," *Procedia - Social and Behavioral Sciences* 2, no. 2 (2010): 3506–18, https://doi.org/10.1016/j.sbspro.2010.03.543.

43 David A. Cole et al., "Targeted Peer Victimization and the Construction of Positive and Negative Self-Cognitions: Connections to Depressive Symptoms in Children," *Journal of Clinical Child & Adolescent Psychology* 39, no. 3 (2010): 421–35, https://doi.org/10.1080/15374411003691776.

44 Thomas M. Brinthaupt and Christian T. Dove, "Differences in Self-Talk Frequency as a Function of Age, Only-Child, and Imaginary Childhood Companion Status," *Journal of Research in Personality* 46, no. 3 (2012): 326–33, https://doi.org/10.1016/j.jrp.2012.03.003.

45 For more about this learning cycle, see: "Anticipation-Action-Reflection Cycle—OECD Future of Education and Skills 2030," OECD, accessed

June 1, 2021, https://www.oecd.org/education/2030-project/teaching-and
-learning/learning/aar-cycle/.

46 Known as the *gradual release of responsibility*, this model lets your child develop
skills *in interaction* with you. The more they do, the less you do yourself. Based
on the work of Lev Vygotsky, the term was coined in 1983 by Pearson and
Gallagher to describe an instructional approach; see: P. David Pearson and
Margaret C. Gallagher, "The Instruction of Reading Comprehension,"
Contemporary Educational Psychology 8, no. 3 (1983): 317–44, https://doi.org/10
.1016/0361-476x(83)90019-x. For a detailed exploration of this approach as
applied to parenting, and the related model known as scaffolding, see the
psychiatrist Harold Koplewicz's work; for example, Harold S. Koplewicz, *The
Scaffold Effect* (New York: Harmony Books, 2021).

47 Carol Dweck, "Carol Dweck Revisits the 'Growth Mindset' (Opinion),"
Education Week, September 22, 2015, https://www.edweek.org/leadership
/opinion-carol-dweck-revisits-the-growth-mindset/2015/09.

48 Psychologist Angela Duckworth, author of the 2016 book *Grit*, talks of the
"hard thing rule" she has put in place with her family—for both adults and
kids. The rule has three parts: it needs to require "daily deliberate practice,"
it can't be stopped until a "natural" stopping point is reached, and each
person gets to choose their own "hard thing." See: Duckworth, *Grit: The
Power of Passion and Perseverance*, 241–42. Also, for a commentary, see:
David Burkus, "Want Your Kids (or Employees) to Have More Grit? Add
This Rule," Inc.com, August 22, 2016, https://www.inc.com/david-burkus
/want-your-kids-or-employees-to-have-more-grit-add-this-rule.html.

49 Richard M. Ryan and Edward L. Deci, *Self-Determination Theory: Basic
Psychological Needs in Motivation, Development, and Wellness* (New York:
Guilford Press, 2018).

50 Thanasis Georgakopoulos, "Semantic Maps," *Linguistics*, 2019, https://doi
.org/10.1093/obo/9780199772810-0229.

51 David Burns, *Feeling Good: The New Mood Therapy* (New York: Morrow, 1980).

52 Katerina Rnic, David J.A. Dozois, and Rod A. Martin, "Cognitive
Distortions, Humor Styles, and Depression," *Europe's Journal of Psychology* 12,
no. 3 (2016): 348–62, https://doi.org/10.5964/ejop.v12i3.1118.

Chapter 5: Conversations for Building Relationships: Cultivating Your Child's Social Skills

1 C.S. Lewis, *The Four Loves* (San Francisco: HarperOne, 2017).

2 R. Chris Fraley, "A Brief Overview of Adult Attachment Theory and
Research," accessed May 25, 2021, http://labs.psychology.illinois.edu
/~rcfraley/attachment.htm.

3 Charles A. Nelson, Kathleen M. Thomas, and Michelle de Haan, "Neural
Bases of Cognitive Development," in *Handbook of Child Psychology*, eds.
Deanna Kuhn and Robert S. Siegler (New York: John Wiley & Sons, 2007),

https://doi.org/10.1002/9780470147658.chpsy0201; Steven D. Stagg, Karina J. Linnell, and Pamela Heaton, "Investigating Eye Movement Patterns, Language, and Social Ability in Children with Autism Spectrum Disorder," *Development and Psychopathology* 26, no. 2 (December 2014): 529–37, https://doi.org/10.1017/s0954579414000108.

4 Dale F. Hay, Alexandra Payne, and Andrea Chadwick, "Peer Relations in Childhood," *Journal of Child Psychology and Psychiatry* 45, no. 1 (2004): 84–108, https://doi.org/10.1046/j.0021-9630.2003.00308.x.

5 Keshia B. Wagers and Elizabeth J. Kiel, "The Influence of Parenting and Temperament on Empathy Development in Toddlers," *Journal of Family Psychology* 33, no. 4 (2019): 391–400, https://doi.org/10.1037/fam0000505.

6 Jenny M. Cundiff and Karen A. Matthews, "Friends with Health Benefits: The Long-Term Benefits of Early Peer Social Integration for Blood Pressure and Obesity in Midlife," *Psychological Science* 29, no. 5 (2018): 814–23, https://doi.org/10.1177/0956797617746510.

7 Haridhan Goswami, "Social Relationships and Children's Subjective Well-Being," *Social Indicators Research* 107, no. 3 (2011): 575–88, https://doi.org/10.1007/s11205-011-9864-z. For research on older children and adolescents, see: Lixian Cui et al., "Longitudinal Links between Maternal and Peer Emotion Socialization and Adolescent Girls' Socioemotional Adjustment," *Developmental Psychology* 56, no. 3 (2020): 595–607, https://doi.org/10.1037/dev0000861; and Catherine L. Bagwell, Andrew F. Newcomb, and William M. Bukowski, "Preadolescent Friendship and Peer Rejection as Predictors of Adult Adjustment," *Child Development* 69, no. 1 (1998): 140–53, https://doi.org/10.2307/1132076.

8 Mark D. Holder and Ben Coleman, "The Contribution of Social Relationships to Children's Happiness," *Journal of Happiness Studies* 10, no. 3 (2007): 329–49, https://doi.org/10.1007/s10902-007-9083-0.

9 Peiqi Lu et al., "Friendship Importance Around the World: Links to Cultural Factors, Health, and Well-Being," *Frontiers in Psychology* 11 (2021), https://doi.org/10.3389/fpsyg.2020.570839.

10 Michael J. Guralnick et al., "Linkages between Delayed Children's Social Interactions with Mothers and Peers," *Child Development* 78, no. 2 (2007): 459–73, https://doi.org/10.1111/j.1467-8624.2007.01009.x.

11 Peter Gray, interview with the author, August 12, 2019.

12 Lydia Denworth, *Friendship: The Evolution, Biology, and Extraordinary Power of Life's Fundamental Bond* (New York: W.W. Norton, 2020).

13 Gary C. Glick and Amanda J. Rose, "Prospective Associations between Friendship Adjustment and Social Strategies: Friendship as a Context for Building Social Skills," *Developmental Psychology* 47, no. 4 (2011): 1117–32, https://doi.org/10.1037/a0023277.

14 Robert M. Seyfarth and Dorothy L. Cheney, "The Evolutionary Origins of Friendship," *Annual Review of Psychology* 63, no. 1 (October 2012): 153–77, https://doi.org/10.1146/annurev-psych-120710-100337.

15 Bennett Helm, "Friendship," Stanford Encyclopedia of Philosophy (Stanford Univ.) July 30, 2021, https://plato.stanford.edu/entries/friendship /#1.1.

16 Seyfarth and Cheney, "The Evolutionary Origins of Friendship."

17 Helm, "Friendship."

18 Amy C. Hartl et al., "Dyadic Instruction for Middle School Students: Liking Promotes Learning," *Learning and Individual Differences* 44 (2015): 33–39, https://doi.org/10.1016/j.lindif.2015.11.002.

19 Catherine L. Bagwell, Andrew F. Newcomb, and William M. Bukowski, "Preadolescent Friendship and Peer Rejection as Predictors of Adult Adjustment," in *Interpersonal Development*, eds. Brett Laursen and Rita Žukauskienė (London: Routledge, 2017), 267–80, https://doi.org/10 .4324/9781351153683-16.

20 Mark D. Holder and Ben Coleman, "Children's Friendships and Positive Well-Being," *Friendship and Happiness* (2015): 81–97, https://doi.org/10 .1007/978-94-017-9603-3_5.

21 Kathryn R. Wentzel, Carolyn McNamara Barry, and Kathryn A. Caldwell, "Friendships in Middle School: Influences on Motivation and School Adjustment," *Journal of Educational Psychology* 96, no. 2 (2004): 195–203, https://doi.org/10.1037/0022-0663.96.2.195.

22 Barbara Menting, Pol A.C. van Lier, and Hans M. Koot, "Language Skills, Peer Rejection, and the Development of Externalizing Behavior from Kindergarten to Fourth Grade," *Journal of Child Psychology and Psychiatry* 52, no. 1 (2010): 72–9, https://doi.org/10.1111/j.1469-7610.2010.02279.x.

23 This is especially true if children start becoming chronically bullied or victimized; see: Becky Kochenderfer-Ladd and James L. Wardrop, "Chronicity and Instability of Children's Peer Victimization Experiences as Predictors of Loneliness and Social Satisfaction Trajectories," *Child Development* 72, no. 1 (2001): 134–51, https://doi.org/10.1111/1467-8624 .00270.

24 Viviana Amati et al., "Social Relations and Life Satisfaction: The Role of Friends," *Genus* 74, no. 1 (April 2018), https://doi.org/10.1186/s41118-018 -0032-z.

25 Cheuk Yin Ho, "Better Health with More Friends: The Role of Social Capital in Producing Health," *Health Economics* 25, no. 1 (2014): 91–100, https://doi.org/10.1002/hec.3131.

26 A.-L. van Harmelen et al., "Adolescent Friendships Predict Later Resilient Functioning across Psychosocial Domains in a Healthy Community Cohort," *Psychological Medicine* 47, no. 13 (November 2017): 2312–22, https://doi.org/10.1017/s0033291717000836.

27 Karen E. Clark and Gary W. Ladd, "Connectedness and Autonomy Support in Parent–Child Relationships: Links to Children's Socioemotional Orientation and Peer Relationships," *Developmental Psychology* 36, no. 4 (2000): 485–98, https://doi.org/10.1037/0012-1649.36.4.485.

28 Sheri Overton and John L. Rausch, "Peer Relationships as Support for Children with Disabilities," *Focus on Autism and Other Developmental Disabilities* 17, no. 1 (2002): 11–29, https://doi.org/10.1177/1088357 60201700102.

29 Rebecca Graber, Rhiannon Turner, and Anna Madill, "Best Friends and Better Coping: Facilitating Psychological Resilience through Boys' and Girls' Closest Friendships," *British Journal of Psychology* 107, no. 2 (2015): 338–58, https://doi.org/10.1111/bjop.12135.

30 Basil B. Bernstein, *Class, Codes and Control* (London: Routledge, 2009).

31 Eleanor E. Maccoby, "Gender and Relationships: A Developmental Account," *American Psychologist* 45, no. 4 (1990): 513–20, https://doi.org /10.1037/0003-066x.45.4.513.

32 Marjorie Harness Goodwin, "Exclusion in Girls' Peer Groups: Ethnographic Analysis of Language Practices on the Playground," *Human Development* 45, no. 6 (2002): 392–415, https://doi.org/10.1159/000066260.

33 Linda Gillespie, "Rocking and Rolling—It Takes Two: The Role of Co-Regulation in Building Self-Regulation Skills," Zero to Three, July 2015, https://www.zerotothree.org/resources/1777-it-takes-two-the-role-of-co -regulation-in-building-self-regulation-skills.

34 Robert L. Selman, *The Growth of Interpersonal Understanding: Developmental and Clinical Analyses* (San Diego: Academic Press, 1980).

35 Sidsel Vive Jensen, "Difference and Closeness: Young Children's Peer Interactions and Peer Relations in School," *Childhood* 25, no. 4 (November 2018): 501–15, https://doi.org/10.1177/0907568218803437.

36 Marjorie J. Kostelnik et al., *Guiding Children's Social Development & Learning: Theory and Skills* (Boston: Cengage Learning, 2018).

37 Jayne O'Donnell, "Teens Aren't Socializing in the Real World. And That's Making Them Super Lonely," *USA Today*, March 20, 2019, https://www .usatoday.com/story/news/health/2019/03/20/teen-loneliness-social-media -cell-phones-suicide-isolation-gaming-cigna/3208845002/.

38 The nature of these "obligations" is often deeply linked to socioeconomic status. In wealthier families, overscheduling often means multiple afterschool activities designed to get kids ahead. For related research, see: Suniya S. Luthar and Shawn J. Latendresse, "Children of the Affluent: Challenges to Well-Being," *Current Directions in Psychological Science* 14, no. 1 (2005): 49–53, https://doi.org/10.1111/j.0963-7214.2005.00333.x.

39 These tendencies can also lead, in part, to children disliking or hating school; see: Valerie Strauss, "In a Liberal Boston Suburb, Kindergarten Teachers Say Their Students Are Learning to 'Hate' School," *Washington Post*, June 13, 2019, https://www.washingtonpost.com/education/2019/06/13/liberal-boston -suburb-kindergarten-teachers-say-their-students-are-learning-hate-school/.

40 Erin R. Ottmar et al., "Does the Responsive Classroom Approach Affect the Use of Standards-Based Mathematics Teaching Practices?," *Elementary School Journal* 113, no. 3 (2013): 434–57, https://doi.org/10.1086/668768.

41 Pamela Druckerman, *Bringing Up Bébé: One American Mother Discovers the Wisdom of French Parenting* (New York: Penguin Books, 2012).

42 Cal Newport, *Digital Minimalism: Choosing a Focused Life in a Noisy World* (London: Penguin Business, 2020).

43 As many studies have found, it's easier to make negative or bullying comments online than in person, and the anonymity of cyberbullying can make it more difficult to catch; see: Tracy Vaillancourt, Robert Faris, and Faye Mishna, "Cyberbullying in Children and Youth: Implications for Health and Clinical Practice," *Canadian Journal of Psychiatry* 62, no. 6 (2016): 368–73, https://doi.org/10.1177/0706743716684791.

Combine that finding with frequent social media use, and you have a recipe for kids saying hurtful things on the spur of the moment, leaving "friends" to deal with the aftermath. However, there is a good deal of overlap between cyberbullying and in-person bullying, as a 2016 national study in the US found. That is, those who are bullied online are also likely to be bullied in person, and vice versa. See: Justin W. Patchin, "New National Bullying and Cyberbullying Statistics," Cyberbullying Research Center, October 10, 2016, https://cyberbullying.org/new-national-bullying -cyberbullying-data.

44 Jennifer LaBounty et al., "Mothers' *and* Fathers' Use of Internal State Talk with Their Young Children," *Social Development* 17, no. 4 (2008): 757–75, https://doi.org/10.1111/j.1467-9507.2007.00450.x.

45 Cheryl Slomkowski and Judy Dunn, "Young Children's Understanding of Other People's Beliefs and Feelings and Their Connected Communication with Friends," *Developmental Psychology* 32, no. 3 (1996): 442–47, https:// doi.org/10.1037/0012-1649.32.3.442.

46 Menting, van Lier, and Koot, "Language Skills, Peer Rejection, and the Development of Externalizing Behavior from Kindergarten to Fourth Grade."

47 Pearl L. Mok et al., "Longitudinal Trajectories of Peer Relations in Children With Specific Language Impairment," *Journal of Child Psychology and Psychiatry* 55, no. 5 (November 2014): 516–27, https://doi.org/10.1111 /jcpp.12190.

48 Lara Mayeux, Amy D. Bellmore, and Antonius H. Cillessen, "Predicting Changes in Adjustment Using Repeated Measures of Sociometric Status," *Journal of Genetic Psychology* 168, no. 4 (January 2007): 401–24, https://doi .org/10.3200/gntp.168.4.401-424.

49 Luis J. Martín-Antón et al., "Problematic Social Situations for Peer-Rejected Students in the First Year of Elementary School," *Frontiers in Psychology* 7 (2016), https://doi.org/10.3389/fpsyg.2016.01925.

50 Doran C. French and Jody Conrad, "School Dropout as Predicted by Peer Rejection and Antisocial Behavior," *Journal of Research on Adolescence* 11, no. 3 (2001): 225–44, https://doi.org/10.1111/1532-7795.00011.

51 Rachel Maunder and Claire P. Monks, "Friendships in Middle Childhood:

Links to Peer and School Identification, and General Self-Worth," *British Journal of Developmental Psychology* 37, no. 2 (2018): 211–29, https://doi.org /10.1111/bjdp.12268.

52 The same goes for adolescents and romantic relationships; kids often don't receive the support or discussion that would help them navigate these relationships well. See: Richard Weissbourd and Rebecca Givens Rolland, "Learning about Love: How Schools Can Better Prepare Students for Romantic Relationships," *Harvard Education Letter* 29, no. 2 (March/April 2013), https://www.hepg.org/hel-home/issues/29_2/helarticle/learning -about-love.

53 Heather S. Lonczak, "Catastrophizing and Decatastrophizing: A PositivePsychology.com Guide," PositivePsychology.com, October 7, 2020, https://positivepsychology.com/catastrophizing/.

54 As I discussed with Jessica Lahey, author of *The Gift of Failure.* Interview with the author, May 15, 2019.

55 LaBounty et al., "Mothers' *and* Fathers' Use of Internal State Talk with Their Young Children."

56 Slomkowski and Dunn, "Young Children's Understanding of Other People's Beliefs and Feelings and Their Connected Communication with Friends."

57 Susan David, interview by author, March 21, 2019.

58 Eli Lebowitz, interview with the author, August 15, 2019.

59 "Social Communication," American Speech-Language-Hearing Association, accessed May 26, 2021, https://www.asha.org/public/speech/development /social-communication/.

60 Anat Ninio and Catherine E. Snow, *Pragmatic Development* (New York: Routledge, 1996), https://doi.org/10.4324/9780429498053-7.

61 Michelle Garcia Winner and Pamela J. Crooke, "Social Communication Strategies for Adolescents with Autism," *The ASHA Leader* 16, no. 1 (2011): 8–11, https://doi.org/10.1044/leader.ftr1.16012011.8.

62 National Center for Educational Statistics, "Student Reports of Bullying and Cyber-bullying: Results from the 2017 School Crime Supplement to the National Victimization Survey," US Department of Education, April 30, 2015, from http://nces.ed.gov/pubsearch/pubsinfo.asp?pubid=2015056.

63 Vaillancourt, Fari, and Mishna, "Cyberbullying in Children and Youth."

64 Elias Aboujaoude et al., "Cyberbullying: Review of an Old Problem Gone Viral," *Journal of Adolescent Health* 57, no. 1 (2015): 10–18, https://doi.org /10.1016/j.jadohealth.2015.04.011. I also spoke over the phone to Aboujaoude about these topics; Elias Aboujaoude, interview with the author, March 14, 2019.

65 Michele P. Hamm et al., "Prevalence and Effect of Cyberbullying on Children and Young People," *JAMA Pediatrics* 169, no. 8 (January 2015): 770–77, https://doi.org/10.1001/jamapediatrics.2015.0944.

66 For a systematic review of parents' perceptions on bullying, including the need for more targeted support, see: Susan Harcourt, Marieke Jasperse, and

Vanessa A. Green, "'We Were Sad and We Were Angry': A Systematic Review of Parents' Perspectives on Bullying," *Child & Youth Care Forum* 43, no. 3 (2014): 373–91, https://doi.org/10.1007/s10566-014-9243-4.

67 Sara Mota Bottino et al., "Cyberbullying and Adolescent Mental Health: A Systematic Review," *Cadernos De Saúde Pública* 31, no. 3 (2015): 463–75, https://doi.org/10.1590/0102-311x00036114.

68 Louise Arseneault, "Annual Research Review: The Persistent and Pervasive Impact of Being Bullied in Childhood and Adolescence: Implications for Policy and Practice," *Journal of Child Psychology and Psychiatry* 59, no. 4 (2017): 405–21, https://doi.org/10.1111/jcpp.12841.

69 Douglas Vanderbilt and Marilyn Augustyn, "The Effects of Bullying," *Paediatrics and Child Health* 20, no. 7 (2010): 315–20, https://doi.org/10.1016/j.paed.2010.03.008.

70 Antti Kärnä et al., "A Large-Scale Evaluation of the KiVa Antibullying Program: Grades 4-6," *Child Development* 82, no. 1 (2011): 311–330, https://doi.org/10.1111/j.1467-8624.2010.01557.x.

71 Christina Salmivalli, Antti Kärnä, and Elisa Poskiparta, "Counteracting Bullying in Finland: The KiVa Program and Its Effects on Different Forms of Being Bullied," *International Journal of Behavioral Development* 35, no. 5 (2011): 405–11, https://doi.org/10.1177/0165025411407457.

72 "Why Kids Become Bullies," Yale Medicine, February 28, 2017, https://www.yalemedicine.org/stories/understanding-bullying/.

73 As my colleague the Harvard psychologist Richard Weissbourd argues in his 2009 book *The Parents We Mean to Be*, "The parent-child relationship is at the center of the development of all the most important moral qualities" (1–2). See: Richard Weissbourd, *The Parents We Mean to Be: How Well-Intentioned Adults Undermine Children's Moral and Emotional Development* (Boston: Houghton Mifflin Harcourt, 2009). Also, for more research and initiatives to support children's caring, see the Making Caring Common Project at the Harvard Graduate School of Education, for which Weissbourd is faculty director, at: https://mcc.gse.harvard.edu/.

74 Peter Elbow, "Bringing the Rhetoric of Assent and the Believing Game Together—and into the Classroom," *College English* 67, no. 4 (January 2005): 388–99, https://doi.org/10.2307/30044680.

75 Bronnie Ware, *The Top Five Regrets of the Dying: A Life Transformed by the Dearly Departing* (Alexandria, NSW: Hay House Australia, 2019).

76 Aristotle, *Aristotle: Nicomachean Ethics*, eds., Christopher Rowe and Sarah Broadie (New York: Oxford Univ. Press, 2002). See also: A. W. Price, "Perfect Friendship in Aristotle," in *Love and Friendship in Plato and Aristotle* (New York: Oxford Univ. Press, 1990), 103–30, https://doi.org/10.1093/acprof:oso/9780198248996.003.0004.

77 Meera Senthilingam, "This Is the Age When You Start Losing Friends," CNN, June 6, 2016, https://www.cnn.com/2016/06/06/health/losing-friends-mid-twenties/.

78 Kunal Bhattacharya et al., "Sex Differences in Social Focus across the Life Cycle in Humans," *Royal Society Open Science* 3, no. 4 (2016): 160097, https://doi.org/10.1098/rsos.160097.

Chapter 6: Conversations for—and Through—Play: Promoting Your Child's Joy and Creativity

1 Michel de Montaigne and Marvin Lowenthal, *The Autobiography of Michel De Montaigne* (London: Routledge, 1935), 165.

2 Douglas Fuchs and Lynn S. Fuchs, "Introduction to Response to Intervention: What, Why, and How Valid Is It?," *Reading Research Quarterly* 41, no. 1 (March 2006): 93–9, https://doi.org/10.1598/rrq.41.1.4.

3 David R. Hill et al., "Fidelity of Implementation and Instructional Alignment in Response to Intervention Research," *Learning Disabilities Research & Practice* 27, no. 3 (2012): 116–24, https://doi.org/10.1111/j .1540-5826.2012.00357.x.

4 "No Time for Recess, No Need for Nap," FairTest, accessed June 9, 2021, https://www.fairtest.org/no-time-recess-no-need-nap.

5 Robert Murray and Catherine Ramstetter, "The Crucial Role of Recess in School," *Pediatrics* 131, no. 1 (January 2013): 11–88, http://pediatrics .aappublications.org/content/131/1/183.

6 Jianghong Liu et al., "Midday Napping in Children: Associations between Nap Frequency and Duration across Cognitive, Positive Psychological Well-Being, Behavioral, and Metabolic Health Outcomes," *Sleep* 42, no. 9 (2019), https://doi.org/10.1093/sleep/zsz126.

7 Erika Christakis, *The Importance of Being Little: What Young Children Really Need from Grownups* (New York: Penguin Putnam, 2016), 165.

8 For further discussion, from a Vygotskian perspective, see: Elena Bodrova, "Make-Believe Play versus Academic Skills: A Vygotskian Approach to Today's Dilemma of Early Childhood Education," *European Early Childhood Education Research Journal* 16, no. 3 (2008): 357–69, https://doi.org/10.1080 /13502930802291777.

9 Katharine Schwab, "Will Toys Ever Go Beyond Blue and Pink?," *The Atlantic*, May 5, 2016, https://www.theatlantic.com/entertainment/archive /2016/05/beyond-blue-and-pink-the-rise-of-gender-neutral-toys/480624/.

10 This play, along with mindfulness activities, has been linked to increased happiness and playfulness; see, for example, Regina Lee et al., "Effects of an Unstructured Free Play and Mindfulness Intervention on Wellbeing in Kindergarten Students," *International Journal of Environmental Research and Public Health* 17, no. 15 (2020): 5382, https://doi.org/10.3390/ijerph 17155382.

11 Stuart L. Brown and Christopher C. Vaughan, *Play: How It Shapes the Brain, Opens the Imagination, and Invigorates the Soul* (New York: Avery, 2010).

12 Deena Skolnick Weisberg, Kathy Hirsh-Pasek, and Roberta Michnick

Golinkoff, "Guided Play: Where Curricular Goals Meet a Playful Pedagogy," *Mind, Brain, and Education* 7, no. 2 (2013): 104–12, https://doi.org/10.1111/mbe.12015.

13 Deena Skolnick Weisberg et al., "Guided Play: Principles and Practices," *Current Directions in Psychological Science* 25, no. 3 (2016): 177–82, https://doi.org/10.1177/0963721416645512.

14 Miguel Sicart, *Play Matters* (Cambridge, MA: MIT Press, 2017).

15 Gwen Goodwin, "Well Played: The Origins and Future of Playfulness," *American Journal of Play* 6, no. 2 (Winter 2014): 234–66.

16 Elian Fink, Silvana Mareva, and Jenny L. Gibson, "Dispositional Playfulness in Young Children: A Cross-Sectional and Longitudinal Examination of the Psychometric Properties of a New Child Self-Reported Playfulness Scale and Associations with Social Behaviour," *Infant and Child Development* 29, no. 4 (2020), https://doi.org/10.1002/icd.2181.

17 René T. Proyer et al., "The Positive Relationships of Playfulness with Indicators of Health, Activity, and Physical Fitness," *Frontiers in Psychology* 9 (2018), https://doi.org/10.3389/fpsyg.2018.01440.

18 The psychologist Lynn A. Barnett, a professor at the Univ. of Illinois, defines playfulness as "the predisposition to frame (or reframe) a situation in such a way as to provide oneself (and possibly others) with amusement, humour, and/or entertainment." See: L.A. Barnett, "The Nature of Playfulness in Young Adults," *Personality and Individual Differences* 43, no. 4 (2007): 949–58, https://doi.org/10.1016/j.paid.2007.02.018.

19 Rebecca Winthrop, "How Playful Learning Can Help Leapfrog Progress in Education," Brookings, April 2, 2019, https://www.brookings.edu/research/how-playful-learning-can-help-leapfrog-progress-in-education/.

20 René T. Proyer, "The Well-Being of Playful Adults: Adult Playfulness, Subjective Well-Being, Physical Well-Being, and the Pursuit of Enjoyable Activities," *European Journal of Humour Research* 1, no. 1 (2013): 84–98, https://doi.org/10.7592/ejhr2013.1.1.proyer.

21 Timothy Butterfield, "The Power of Playful Learning," Harvard Graduate School of Education, October 22, 2019, https://www.gse.harvard.edu/news/19/10/power-playful-learning.

22 Sandra Russ and Larissa Niec, *Play in Clinical Practice Evidence-Based Approaches* (New York: Guilford Press, 2011); Astrida L. Seja and Sandra W. Russ, "Children's Fantasy Play and Emotional Understanding," *Journal of Clinical Child Psychology* 28, no. 2 (1999): 269–77, https://doi.org/10.1207/s15374424jccp2802_13; Kyle D. Pruett, "Children at Play: Clinical and Developmental Approaches to Meaning and Representation," *Journal of the American Academy of Child & Adolescent Psychiatry* 34, no. 9 (1995): 1249, https://doi.org/10.1097/00004583-199509000-00027.

23 Kathy Hirsh-Pasek et al., *A Mandate for Playful Learning in Preschool* (New York: Oxford Univ. Press, 2008, https://doi.org/10.1093/acprof:oso/9780195382716.001.0001.

24 UNICEF, "Learning through Play," October 2018, https://www.unicef.org/sites/default/files/2018-12/UNICEF-Lego-Foundation-Learning-through-Play.pdf.

25 Mihaly Csikszentmihalyi, *Flow: The Psychology of Optimal Experience* (New York: Harper Perennial, 2008).

26 Sandra W. Russ, "Pretend Play, Affect, and Creativity," in *New Directions in Aesthetics, Creativity, and the Arts*, eds. Paul Locher, Colin Martindale, and Leonid Dorfman (New York: Routledge, 2020), 239–50, https://doi.org/10.4324/9781315224084-19.

27 Jerome L. Singer and Dorothy G. Singer, "Preschoolers' Imaginative Play as Precursor of Narrative Consciousness," *Imagination, Cognition and Personality* 25, no. 2 (2005): 97–117, https://doi.org/10.2190/0kqu 9a2v-yam2-xd8j.

28 Michele M. Root-Bernstein, "The Creation of Imaginary Worlds," in *The Oxford Handbook of the Development of Imagination*, ed. Marjorie Taylor (New York: Oxford Univ. Press, 2013), 417–37, http://doi.org/10.1093/oxfordhb/9780195395761.013.0027. For further discussion, see also: Michele Root-Bernstein, *Inventing Imaginary Worlds: From Childhood Play to Adult Creativity across the Arts and Sciences* (Lanham, MD: Rowman & Littlefield Education, 2014).

29 Kyung Hee Kim, "The Creativity Crisis: The Decrease in Creative Thinking Scores on the Torrance Tests of Creative Thinking," *Creativity Research Journal* 23, no. 4 (2011): 285–95, https://doi.org/10.1080/10400419.2011.627805.

30 Rachael Rettner, "Are Today's Youth Less Creative & Imaginative?," LiveScience, August 12, 2011, https://www.livescience.com/15535-children-creative.html.

31 Ronald A. Beghetto and Maciej Karwowski, "Educational Consequences of Creativity: A Creative Learning Perspective," *Creativity. Theories – Research – Applications* 5, no. 2 (January 2018): 146–54, https://doi.org/10.1515/ctra-2018-0011.

32 Sandra W. Russ, *Pretend Play in Childhood: Foundation of Adult Creativity* (Washington, DC: American Psychological Association, 2014), https://doi.org/10.1037/14282-003.

33 Hirsh-Pasek et al., *A Mandate for Playful Learning in Preschool*.

34 There has been pushback: as of 2017, Germany banned My Friend Cayla from store shelves, and the Federal Trade Commission in the United States has investigated it as an illegal surveillance device. See Soraya Sarhaddi Nelson, "Germany Bans 'My Friend Cayla' Doll Over Spying Concerns," NPR, February 20, 2017, https://www.npr.org/2017/02/20/516292295/germany-bans-my-friend-cayla-doll-over-spying-concerns.

35 See Grant Clauser, "Amazon's Alexa Never Stops Listening to You. Should You Worry?," *New York Times*, August 8, 2019, https://www.nytimes.com/wirecutter/blog/amazons-alexa-never-stops-listening-to-you/.

36 The same goes for "playmates" like Siri and Alexa, and the "Echo Dot Kids Edition," with messages and stories targeted at kids. No matter that reports suggest that Alexa, and Amazon, hold on to records of your child's conversations, even after you delete the audio clip. Apparently, since there's a command now, "Alexa, delete everything I said today," everything's all right. For an analysis, see: Jeb Su, "Why Amazon Alexa Is Always Listening to Your Conversations: Analysis," *Forbes*, May 16, 2019, https://www.forbes .com/sites/jeanbaptiste/2019/05/16/why-amazon-alexa-is-always-listening -to-your-conversations-analysis/?sh=108f020d2378. See also: Sophie-Charlotte Lemmer, "Alexa, Are You Friends with My Kid? Smart Speakers and Children's Privacy Under the GDPR," *SSRN Electronic Journal*, 2020, https://doi.org/10.2139/ssrn.3627478.

37 Clearly, issues of social class play a role; for a review, see the seminal work of Annette Lareau, who distinguishes between "concerted cultivation" of children in middle-class families, and the "accomplishment of natural growth" in working-class and poor families. These two tendencies have effects on children's time use and play. As she writes, for example, "Working class and poor families organize their time differently from middle-class families. Children's organized activities do not set the pace of life." See: Annette Lareau, *Unequal Childhoods: Class, Race, and Family Life* (Berkeley: Univ. of California Press, 2003), 72–73. Also, see: Annette Lareau, "Social Class and the Daily Lives of Children," *Childhood* 7, no. 2 (2000): 155–71, https://doi.org/10.1177/0907568200007002003.

38 Kathy Hirsh-Pasek, Roberta M. Golinkoff, and Diane E. Eyer, *Einstein Never Used Flash Cards: How Our Children Really Learn—And Why They Need to Play More and Memorize Less* (New York: Rodale, 2004).

39 Elly Singer, "Play and Playfulness, Basic Features of Early Childhood Education," *European Early Childhood Education Research Journal* 21, no. 2 (2013): 172–84, https://doi.org/10.1080/1350293x.2013.789198.

40 Linda Kaye et al., "The Conceptual and Methodological Mayhem of 'Screen Time,'" *International Journal of Environmental Research and Public Health* 17, no. 10 (2020): 3661, https://doi.org/10.3390/ijerph17103661.

41 Amy Orben and Andrew K. Przybylski, "The Association between Adolescent Well-Being and Digital Technology Use," *Nature Human Behaviour* 3, no. 2 (2019): 173–82, https://doi.org/10.1038/s41562-018 -0506.

42 Diankun Gong et al., "Enhanced Functional Connectivity and Increased Gray Matter Volume of Insula Related to Action Video Game Playing," *Scientific Reports* 5, no. 9763 (2015), https://www.nature.com/articles /srep09763.

43 Gregor R. Szycik et al., "Lack of Evidence That Neural Empathic Responses Are Blunted in Excessive Users of Violent Video Games: An FMRI Study," *Frontiers in Psychology* 8 (August 2017), https://doi.org/10.3389/fpsyg.2017 .00174.

44 Ossy Dwi Wulansari et al., "Video Games and Their Correlation to Empathy," *Advances in Intelligent Systems and Computing*, 2020, 151–63, https://doi.org/10.1007/978-3-030-40274-7_16.

45 Andrew Perrin, "5 Facts about Americans and Video Games," Pew Research Center, September 17, 2018, https://www.pewresearch.org/fact-tank/2018 /09/17/5-facts-about-americans-and-video-games/.

46 Jane E. Brody, "How to Avoid Burnout in Youth Sports," *New York Times*, May 7, 2018, https://www.nytimes.com/2018/05/07/well/how-to-avoid -burnout-in-youth-sports.html.

47 Ajay S. Padaki et al., "Quantifying Parental Influence on Youth Athlete Specialization: A Survey of Athletes' Parents," *Orthopedic Journal of Sports Medicine* 5, no. 9 (September 21, 2017), https://www.ncbi.nlm.nih.gov /pubmed/28975135.

48 Diana Shmukler, "Preschool Imaginative Play Predisposition and Its Relationship to Subsequent Third Grade Assessment," *Imagination, Cognition and Personality* 2, no. 3 (1983): 231–40, https://doi.org/10.2190/17ed-bkur -ybky-elew.; Jerome L. Singer, "Enhancing Elementary School Children's Achievement and Creativity through Imaginative Play in the Classroom," *PsycEXTRA Dataset*, 2011, https://doi.org/10.1037/e659042011-001.

49 Bernd Remmele and Nicola Whitton, "Disrupting the Magic Circle: The Impact of Negative Social Gaming Behaviours," in *Psychology, Pedagogy, and Assessment in Serious Games*, ed. Thomas M. Connolly et al. (Hershey, PA: IGI Global, 2014), 111–26, https://doi.org/10.4018/978-1-4666-4773-2.ch006.

50 Rikke Toft Nørgård, Claus Toft-Nielsen, and Nicola Whitton, "Playful Learning in Higher Education: Developing a Signature Pedagogy," *International Journal of Play* 6, no. 3 (February 2017): 272–82, https://doi .org/10.1080/21594937.2017.1382997.

51 A significant body of research, over decades, has shown this relationship; for a review, see: Catherine E. Snow, M. Susan Burns, and Peg Griffin, *Preventing Reading Difficulties in Young Children* (Washington, DC: National Academies Press, 1998). There is evidence of a causal link; see, for example, Joseph K. Torgesen, Richard K. Wagner, and Carol A. Rashotte, "Longitudinal Studies of Phonological Processing and Reading," *Journal of Learning Disabilities* 27, no. 5 (1994): 276–86, https://doi.org/10.1177/002 221949402700503. For a study on the relationship between phonological awareness and early reading, see: Tiffany P. Hogan, Hugh W. Catts, and Todd D. Little, "The Relationship between Phonological Awareness and Reading," *Language, Speech, and Hearing Services in Schools* 36, no. 4 (2005): 285–93, https://doi.org/10.1044/0161-1461(2005/029). See also: Rebecca Treiman, "Phonological Awareness and Its Roles in Learning to Read and Spell," in *Phonological Awareness in Reading*, eds. Diane J. Sawyer and Barbara J. Fox (New York: Springer, 1991), 159–89, https://doi.org/10 .1007/978-1-4612-3010-6_6.

52 Cohen speaks of "playing at the edge of the child's development." See:

Lawrence J. Cohen, *Playful Parenting* (New York: Ballantine Books, 2002), 82, 112.

53 For research on the significant problems associated with an excessive pressure to succeed, see: Suniya S. Luthar, Nina L. Kumar, and Nicole Zillmer, "High-Achieving Schools Connote Risks for Adolescents: Problems Documented, Processes Implicated, and Directions for Interventions," *American Psychologist* 75, no. 7 (2020): 983–95, https://doi .org/10.1037/amp0000556.

54 Jane McGonigal, interview with the author, September 16, 2019. See also: Jane McGonigal, *SuperBetter: A Revolutionary Approach to Getting Stronger, Happier, Braver and More Resilient* (London: HarperThorsons, 2016).

55 David Hammer and Emily van Zee, *Seeing the Science in Children's Thinking: Case Studies of Student Inquiry in Physical Science* (Portsmouth, NH: Heinemann, 2006).

56 "Playful Science," *Playful Science*, accessed June 3, 2021, https://web .stanford.edu/group/playfulscience/cgi-bin/about.php.

57 As Cohen writes, "If [kids] don't think we will play, they may not even ask. They just go about their business, and we go about ours, and we all miss chance after chance to reconnect." In Cohen, *Playful Parenting*, 17.

58 Dorothy G. Singer and Jerome L. Singer, *The House of Make-Believe: Children's Play and the Developing Imagination* (Cambridge, MA: Harvard Univ. Press, 1990).

59 In a study of mothers in sixteen nations, researchers found a surprising agreement that the lack of play was eroding children's sense of childhood. See: Dorothy G. Singer et al., "Children's Pastimes and Play in Sixteen Nations: Is Free-Play Declining?," *American Journal of Play* 1, no. 3 (Winter 2009): 283–312, https://eric.ed.gov/?id=EJ1069041. See also: Jerome L. Singer and Dorothy G. Singer, "Professional Paths over Six Decades Researching and Practicing Play," *International Journal of Play* 4, no. 2 (April 2015): 190–202, https://doi.org/10.1080/21594937.2015.1060570.

60 Maria Montessori and Claude Albert Claremont, *The Absorbent Mind* (New York: Dell, 1967).

Chapter 7: Conversations for Openness: Raising a Global Citizen

1 George Bernard Shaw, *Everybody's Political What's What?* (London: Constable and Company Limited, 1944), Chapter XXXVII: Creed and Conduct.

2 Marguerite A. Wright, *I'm Chocolate, You're Vanilla: Raising Healthy Black and Biracial Children in a Race-Conscious World* (San Francisco: Jossey-Bass, 2000).

3 Michelle F. Wright, Sebastian Wachs, and Zheng Huang, "Adolescents' Popularity-Motivated Aggression and Prosocial Behaviors: The Roles of Callous-Unemotional Traits and Social Status Insecurity," *Frontiers in Psychology* 12 (2021), https://doi.org/10.3389/fpsyg.2021.606865.

4 Adabel Lee and Benjamin L. Hankin, "Insecure Attachment, Dysfunctional Attitudes, and Low Self-Esteem Predicting Prospective Symptoms of Depression and Anxiety During Adolescence," *Journal of Clinical Child & Adolescent Psychology* 38, no. 2 (December 2009): 219–31, https://doi.org/10.1080/15374410802698396.

5 Yan Li and Michelle F. Wright, "Adolescents' Social Status Goals: Relationships to Social Status Insecurity, Aggression, and Prosocial Behavior," *Journal of Youth and Adolescence* 43, no. 1 (2013): 146–60, https://doi.org/10.1007/s10964-013-9939-z.

6 Kristen M. Klein and Mo Wang, "Deep-Level Diversity and Leadership," *American Psychologist* 65, no. 9 (2010): 932–34, https://doi.org/10.1037/a0021355. See also: Seong Wook Chae, Young Wook Seo, and Kun Chang Lee, "Task Difficulty and Team Diversity on Team Creativity: Multi-Agent Simulation Approach," *Computers in Human Behavior* 42 (2015): 83–92, https://doi.org/10.1016/j.chb.2014.03.032.

7 Judy Singer, *Neurodiversity: The Birth of an Idea* (Lexington, KY: Judy Singer, 2017). See also: Jenara Nerenberg, *Divergent Mind: Thriving in a World That Wasn't Designed for You* (New York: HarperOne, 2021).

8 Hua-Yu Sebastian Cherng, "If They Think I Can: Teacher Bias and Youth of Color Expectations and Achievement," *Social Science Research* 66 (2017): 170–86, https://doi.org/10.1016/j.ssresearch.2017.04.001.

9 Ingrid W. Schutte et al., "Preparing Students for Global Citizenship: The Effects of a Dutch Undergraduate Honors Course," *Education Research International*, 2017 (2017): 1–12, https://www.hindawi.com/journals/edri/2017/3459631/.

10 Sonia Nieto, *Language, Culture, and Teaching*, (New York: Routledge, 2017).

11 Nieto, *Language, Culture, and Teaching*, 163–80.

12 Mia Yee and Rupert Brown, "The Development of Gender Differentiation in Young Children," *British Journal of Social Psychology* 33, no. 2 (1994): 183–96, https://doi.org/10.1111/j.2044-8309.1994.tb01017.x.

13 Margaret L. Signorella, Rebecca S. Bigler, and Lynn S. Liben, "Developmental Differences in Children's Gender Schemata about Others: A Meta-Analytic Review," *Developmental Review* 13, no. 2 (1993): 147–83, https://doi.org/10.1006/drev.1993.1007.

14 Jessica W. Giles and Gail D. Heyman, "Young Children's Beliefs about the Relationship between Gender and Aggressive Behavior," *Child Development* 76, no. 1 (2005): 107–21, https://doi.org/10.1111/j.1467-8624.2005.00833.x.

15 G. E. Miller et al., "Low Early-Life Social Class Leaves a Biological Residue Manifested by Decreased Glucocorticoid and Increased Proinflammatory Signaling," *Proceedings of the National Academy of Sciences* 106, no. 34 (2009): 14716–21, https://doi.org/10.1073/pnas.0902971106.

16 P.A. Katz and J.A. Kofkin, "Race, Gender, and Young Children," in *Developmental Psychopathology: Perspectives on Adjustment, Risk, and Disorder*, eds. S. S. Luthar et al. (New York: Cambridge Univ. Press, 1997), 51–74.

17 Marc H. Bornstein and Martha E. Arterberry, "The Development of Object Categorization in Young Children: Hierarchical Inclusiveness, Age, Perceptual Attribute, and Group versus Individual Analyses," *Developmental Psychology* 46, no. 2 (2010): 350–65, https://doi.org/10.1037/a0018411.

18 Yee and Brown, "The Development of Gender Differentiation in Young Children."

19 Ed Yong, "Five-Month-Old Babies Prefer Their Own Languages and Shun Foreign Accents," *National Geographic*, June 14, 2009, https://www.nationalgeographic.com/science/phenomena/2009/06/14/five-month-old-babies-prefer-their-own-languages-and-shun-foreign-accents/.

20 David Buttelmann et al., "Selective Imitation of In-Group Over Out-Group Members in 14-Month-Old Infants," *Child Development* 84, no. 2 (2012): 422–28, https://doi.org/10.1111/j.1467-8624.2012.01860.x.

21 Marilynn B. Brewer, "The Psychology of Prejudice: Ingroup Love and Outgroup Hate?," *Journal of Social Issues* 55, no. 3 (1999): 429–44, https://doi.org/10.1111/0022-4537.00126.

22 Norman B. Anderson and Rodolfo A. Bulatao, *Understanding Racial and Ethnic Differences in Health in Late Life: A Research Agenda* (Washington, DC: National Academies Press, 2004).

23 John Baldwin, "Culture, Prejudice, Racism, and Discrimination," Oxford Research Encyclopedia of Communication, January 25, 2017, https://oxfordre.com/communication/view/10.1093/acrefore/9780190228613.001.0001/acrefore-9780190228613-e-164.

24 Gordon W. Allport, *The Nature of Prejudice* (Garden City, NY: Doubleday, 1958).

25 Sheri R. Levy and Melanie Killen, *Intergroup Attitudes and Relations in Childhood Through Adulthood* (New York: Oxford Univ. Press, 2010).

26 Marjorie Rhodes and Lisa Chalik, "Social Categories as Markers of Intrinsic Interpersonal Obligations," *Psychological Science* 24, no. 6 (2013): 999–1006, https://doi.org/10.1177/0956797612466267.

27 Kristin Shutts, "Young Children's Preferences: Gender, Race, and Social Status," *Child Development Perspectives* 9, no. 4 (2015): 262–66, https://doi.org/10.1111/cdep.12154.

28 Interestingly, as research with college students has found, "mere exposure" to faces of other racial categories increases liking for new faces of that race. See: Leslie A. Zebrowitz, Benjamin White, and Kristin Wieneke, "Mere Exposure and Racial Prejudice: Exposure to Other-Race Faces Increases Liking for Strangers of That Race," *Social Cognition* 26, no. 3 (2008): 259–75, https://doi.org/10.1521/soco.2008.26.3.259.

29 Frances E. Aboud, "The Formation of In-Group Favoritism and Out-Group Prejudice in Young Children: Are They Distinct Attitudes?," *Developmental Psychology* 39, no. 1 (2003): 48–60, https://doi.org/10.1037/0012-1649.39.1.48.

30 For a nuanced discussion of issues relating to disability and social interaction,

see: Rebekah Taussig, *Sitting Pretty: The View from My Ordinary Resilient Disabled Body* (New York: HarperOne, 2020).

31 Adia Harvey Wingfield, "Color Blindness Is Counterproductive," *The Atlantic*, September 13, 2015, https://www.theatlantic.com/politics/archive/2015/09/color-blindness-is-counterproductive/405037/.

32 Vernita Mayfield, "Learning to Challenge Racial 'Colorblindness,'" *Educational Leadership*, February 1, 2021, https://www.ascd.org/el/articles/learning-to-challenge-racial-colorblindness.

33 Jenny Gordon, "Inadvertent Complicity: Colorblindness in Teacher Education," *Educational Studies* 38, no. 2 (2005): 135–53, https://doi.org/10.1207/s15326993es3802_5.

34 Suman Fernando, *Mental Health, Race and Culture*, third ed. (London: Red Globe Press, 2010).

35 For a review of the concept of intersectionality, see: Evelyn M. Simien, "Doing Intersectionality Research: From Conceptual Issues to Practical Examples," *Politics & Gender* 3, no. 2 (2007), https://doi.org/10.1017/s1743923x07000086. Specifically, as Simien argues, "such identity categories as gender, age, race, ethnicity, class, and sexuality are mutually constituted and cannot be added together" (265). The term "intersectionality" was likely first used by Kimberlé Crenshaw in 1991; see: Kimberlé Crenshaw, "Mapping the Margins: Intersectionality, Identity Politics, and Violence against Women of Color," *Stanford Law Review* 43, no. 6 (1991): 1241–99, https://doi.org/10.2307/1229039. According to the concept of intersectionality, social constructs such as race have material impacts on the ways we live and relate to one another. For more on the ideas of intersectionality and the development of youth identity, see: Ursula Moffitt, Linda P. Juang, and Moin Syed, "Intersectionality and Youth Identity Development Research in Europe," *Frontiers in Psychology* 11 (2020), https://doi.org/10.3389/fpsyg.2020.00078. Also, for more on the ways using this framework can help us understand diversity as a positive and avoid a "deficit" approach, see: Meryl Alper, Vikki S. Katz, and Lynn Schofield Clark, "Researching Children, Intersectionality, and Diversity in the Digital Age," *Journal of Children and Media* 10, no. 1 (February 2016): 107–14, https://doi.org/10.1080/17482798.2015.1121886. Also, see the work of Robin Jarrett, with whom I spoke on October 17, 2019, about these issues. For example: Robin L. Jarrett and Sarai Coba-Rodriguez, "'If You Have a Kid That's Ready to Learn': The Kindergarten Transition Experiences of Urban, Low-Income, African-American Preschoolers," *Journal of Poverty* 23, no. 3 (2018): 229–52, https://doi.org/10.1080/10875549.2018.1555729.

36 For an accessible discussion of these topics, see: Erin Blakemore, "Race and Ethnicity: How Are They Different?" *National Geographic*, February 22, 2019, https://www.nationalgeographic.com/culture/article/race-ethnicity.

37 "EmbraceRace," EmbraceRace, accessed June 8, 2021, https://www.embracerace.org/.

38 Melissa Giraud and Andrew Grant-Thomas, interview with the author, April 9, 2019.

39 Madeleine Rogin, "Seeing, Noticing, and Talking about Differences with Young Children," EmbraceRace, accessed June 10, 2021, https://www .embracerace.org/resources/seeing-noticing-talking-about-difference-with -young-children.

40 Anya Kamenetz, "6 Potential Brain Benefits of Bilingual Education," NPR, November 29, 2016, https://www.npr.org/sections/ed/2016/11/29 /497943749/6-potential-brain-benefits-of-bilingual-education. Luk and I also discussed these ideas in a phone interview on September 10, 2019. For more on her research, especially on the complexities of the bilingual experience, see: Gigi Luk and Ellen Bialystok, "Bilingualism Is Not a Categorical Variable: Interaction between Language Proficiency and Usage," *Journal of Cognitive Psychology* 25, no. 5 (2013): 605–21, https://doi .org/10.1080/20445911.2013.795574.

41 Peggy J. Goetz, "The Effects of Bilingualism on Theory of Mind Development," *Bilingualism: Language and Cognition* 6, no. 1 (2003): 1–15, https://doi.org/10.1017/s1366728903001007.

42 Clearly, understanding the effect of bilingualism on children's learning and development is no simple matter, as their language use shapes their experiences, and vice versa. For an exploration of these complexities, see: Ellen Bialystok, "The Bilingual Adaptation: How Minds Accommodate Experience," *Psychological Bulletin* 143, no. 3 (2017): 233–62, https://doi .org/10.1037/bul0000099. For more on the potential role of bilingualism long-term, especially in protecting against cognitive decline, see: Ellen Bialystok, Fergus I.M. Craik, and Gigi Luk, "Bilingualism: Consequences for Mind and Brain," *Trends in Cognitive Sciences* 16, no. 4 (2012): 240–50, https://doi.org/10.1016/j.tics.2012.03.001.

43 He jumped from a neutral behavior—the men standing outside—to a negative personality trait—"Lazy." And he jumped from his single wrong conclusion to an even bigger generalization.

44 Carlos Alberto Torres and Emiliano Bosio, "Global Citizenship Education at the Crossroads: Globalization, Global Commons, Common Good, and Critical Consciousness," *Prospects* 48, no. 3-4 (2020): 99–113, https://doi .org/10.1007/s11125-019-09458-w.

45 "What Is Global Citizenship Education?," IDEAS for Global Citizenship, accessed May 26, 2021, https://www.ideas-forum.org.uk/what-is-global -citizenship-education.

46 Joel Westheimer and Joseph Kahne, "What Kind of Citizen? The Politics of Educating for Democracy," *American Educational Research Journal* 41, no. 2 (2004): 237–69, https://doi.org/10.3102/00028312041002237. The authors discuss three elements of a "good" citizen in a democratic society; that is, personally responsible, participatory, and justice oriented.

47 Alan K. Goodboy, Matthew M. Martin, and Christine E. Rittenour, "Bullying

as an Expression of Intolerant Schemas," *Journal of Child & Adolescent Trauma* 9, no. 4 (2016): 277–82, https://doi.org/10.1007/s40653-016-0089-9.

48 Megan Polanin and Elizabeth Vera, "Bullying Prevention and Social Justice," *Theory Into Practice* 52, no. 4 (February 2013): 303–10, https://doi .org/10.1080/00405841.2013.829736.

49 See: Cheryl Jones-Walker, "Being Constructed as Different, While Teaching about Difference," *PsycEXTRA Dataset*, 2010, https://doi.org /10.1037/e626412011-001; and Vlad Glăveanu, "Creativity and Global Citizenship Education," in *Global Citizenship Education*, eds. Abdeljalil Akkari and Kathrine Maleq (Cham, Switzerland: Springer, 2020), 191–202, https://doi.org/10.1007/978-3-030-44617-8_14.

50 Todd Rose, *The End of Average: How We Succeed in a World That Values Sameness* (New York: HarperOne, 2016).

51 Joan Richardson, "Can We Talk about Race? An Interview with Beverly Daniel Tatum," *Phi Delta Kappan*, November 13, 2017, https://www .kappanonline.org/richardson-race-interview-beverly-daniel-tatum/.

52 Richardson, "Can We Talk about Race?"

53 Beverly Daniel Tatum, *Why Are All the Black Kids Sitting Together in the Cafeteria?* Revised Edition (New York: Basic Books, 2017).

54 "The State of Learning Disabilities: Understanding the 1 in 5," National Center for Learning Disabilities, February 1, 2017, https://www.ncld.org /wp-content/uploads/2017/03/1-in-5-Snapshot.Fin_.03142017.pdf.

55 Margaret J. Snowling, Charles Hulme, and Kate Nation, "Defining and Understanding Dyslexia: Past, Present and Future," *Oxford Review of Education* 46, no. 4 (March 2020): 501–13, https://doi.org/10.1080 /03054985.2020.1765756.

56 For an overview, see: "Dyslexia Basics," International Dyslexia Association, March 10, 2020, https://dyslexiaida.org/dyslexia-basics/; and "Frequently Asked Questions," Dyslexia Help at the University of Michigan, accessed May 29, 2021, http://dyslexiahelp.umich.edu/answers/faq

57 See: "List of Dyslexic Achievers," Dyslexia the Gift, accessed May 29, 2021, https://www.dyslexia.com/about-dyslexia/dyslexic-achievers/all-achievers/.

58 See: "The Yale Center for Dyslexia & Creativity" (website), accessed May 29, 2021, https://dyslexia.yale.edu/ and related research; see, for example: Zoï Kapoula et al., "Education Influences Creativity in Dyslexic and Non-Dyslexic Children and Teenagers," *PLOS ONE* 11, no. 3 (July 2016), https:// doi.org/10.1371/journal.pone.0150421.

59 Anne Castles, Kathleen Rastle, and Kate Nation, "Ending the Reading Wars: Reading Acquisition from Novice to Expert," *Psychological Science in the Public Interest* 19, no. 1 (2018): 5–51, https://doi.org/10.1177/1529100618772271.

60 For a review of the emotional impacts of dyslexia, see: Emily M. Livingston, Linda S. Siegel, and Urs Ribary, "Developmental Dyslexia: Emotional Impact and Consequences," *Australian Journal of Learning Difficulties* 23, no. 2 (2018): 107–35, https://doi.org/10.1080/19404158.2018.1479975.

61 As we discussed, over the course of history, people have learned to read and write at different ages and stages, for a variety of reasons. Say, a craftsman needed to learn to read and write the names of tools in order to buy the ones he needed. It was only at the start of the twentieth century that people considered reading and writing critical skills to master in early elementary school. See: Max Roser and Esteban Ortiz-Ospina, "Literacy," Our World in Data, September 20, 2018, https://ourworldindata.org/literacy.

62 Paz Suárez-Coalla and Fernando Cuetos, "Reading Strategies in Spanish Developmental Dyslexics," *Annals of Dyslexia* 62, no. 2 (April 2012): 71–81, https://doi.org/10.1007/s11881-011-0064-y.

63 Deborah P. Waber, *Rethinking Learning Disabilities: Understanding Children Who Struggle in School* (New York: Guilford Press, 2011).

64 Elizabeth Sweet, "Toys Are More Divided by Gender Now Than They Were 50 Years Ago," *The Atlantic*, December 9, 2014, https://www.theatlantic .com/business/archive/2014/12/toys-are-more-divided-by-gender-now -than-they-were-50-years-ago/383556/.

65 Brenda K. Todd et al., "Sex Differences in Children's Toy Preferences: A Systematic Review, Meta-Regression, and Meta-Analysis," *Infant and Child Development* 27, no. 2 (March/April 2018), https://onlinelibrary.wiley.com /doi/abs/10.1002/icd.2064.

66 Eric W. Dolan, "Study Finds Robust Sex Differences in Children's Toy Preferences across a Range of Ages and Countries," PsyPost, December 30, 2017, https://www.psypost.org/2017/12/study-finds-robust-sex-differences -childrens-toy-preferences-across-range-ages-countries-50488.

67 Interestingly, Barry found that boys tended to play less with "boy"-typed toys when at home than when in the laboratory, and that girls played less with "girl"-typed toys in more recent studies than in older ones. Both the small-scale context (the playmates and setting) and the larger one (the cultural messaging) likely influence the types of toys and play that children choose.

68 Aysen Bakir and Kay M. Palan, "How Are Children's Attitudes toward Ads and Brands Affected by Gender-Related Content in Advertising?," *Journal of Advertising* 39, no. 1 (2010): 35–48, https://doi.org/10.2753/joa00913367 390103.

69 Kay Deaux and Laurie L. Lewis, "Structure of Gender Stereotypes: Interrelationships among Components and Gender Label," *Journal of Personality and Social Psychology* 46, no. 5 (1984): 991–1004, https://doi .org/10.1037/0022-3514.46.5.991.

70 Diane N. Ruble et al., "The Role of Gender Constancy in Early Gender Development," *Child Development* 78, no. 4 (2007): 1121–36, https://doi .org/10.1111/j.1467-8624.2007.01056.x.

71 Taylor, Marianne G., Marjorie Rhodes, and Susan A. Gelman. "Boys Will Be Boys; Cows Will Be Cows: Children's Essentialist Reasoning about Gender Categories and Animal Species," *Child Development* 80, no 2 (March/ April 2009): 461–81, https://doi.org/10.1111/j.1467-8624.2009.01272.x.

72 Gordon Nore, "This Is Why Young Children Need to Explore Gender Identity in the Classroom," Today's Parent, August 23, 2019, https://www.todaysparent.com/kids/school-age/young-children-need-to-learn-gender-identity/. For related research, see: Selin Gülgöz et al., "Similarity in Transgender and Cisgender Children's Gender Development," *Proceedings of the National Academy of Sciences* 116, no. 49 (2019): 24480–85, https://doi.org/10.1073/pnas.1909367116.

73 Schutte et al., "Preparing Students for Global Citizenship: The Effects of a Dutch Undergraduate Honors Course."

74 Matt Thompson, "Five Reasons Why People Code-Switch," NPR, April 13, 2013, https://www.npr.org/sections/codeswitch/2013/04/13/177126294/five-reasons-why-people-code-switch.

75 W. Quin Yow, Ferninda Patrycia, and Suzanne Flynn, "Code-Switching in Childhood," in *Bilingualism Across the Lifespan: Factors Moderating Language Proficiency*, eds. Elena Nicoladis and Simona Montanari (Washington, DC: American Psychological Association, 2016), 81–100, https://doi.org/10.1037/14939-006.

76 Leni Amelia Suek, "Code Switching and the Development of the Linguistic System of Simultaneous Bilingual Children," *Englisia* 5, no. 1 (January 2017): 1, https://doi.org/10.22373/ej.v5i1.1311.

77 In many parts of the United States, being Caucasian gives kids this status, while kids of color face bias and lowered expectations from majority Caucasian teachers. For more on the potential relationship between teacher bias and academic outcomes, see the results of a nationwide study conducted by Mark Chin and colleagues; see: Mark J. Chin et al., "Bias in the Air: A Nationwide Exploration of Teachers' Implicit Racial Attitudes, Aggregate Bias, and Student Outcomes," *Educational Researcher* 49, no. 8 (2020): 566–78, https://doi.org/10.3102/0013189x20937240. Most troubling, kids of color also face threats of violence and suspicion for innocuous acts. The February 2020 case of Ahmaud Arbery, a twenty-five-year-old Black man shot to death in Georgia while out for a jog, and the May 2020 murder of the forty-six-year-old Black man George Floyd, brutally killed at the hands of the police, are only the most flagrant cases. See: Riham Feshir, "Remembering George Floyd, the Man," MPR News, March 8, 2021, https://www.mprnews.org/story/2021/03/08/remembering-george-floyd; and Zak Cheney-Rice, "Never Stop Running," Intelligencer, May 8, 2020, https://nymag.com/intelligencer/2020/05/ahmaud-arbery-death-and-joy.html. For helpful resources, see: Dominique Parris, Victor St. John, and Jessica Dym Bartlett, "Resources to Support Children's Emotional Well-Being Amid Anti-Black Racism, Racial Violence, and Trauma," Child Trends, June 23, 2020, https://www.childtrends.org/publications/resources-to-support-childrens-emotional-well-being-amid-anti-black-racism-racial-violence-and-trauma; and Allison Briscoe-Smith and Sandra Chapman, "Supporting Kids of Color in the Wake of Racialized Violence: Part One,"

EmbraceRace, accessed June 3, 2021, https://www.embracerace.org
/resources/supporting-kids-of-color-in-the-wake-of-racialized-violenc
-part-one.

78 See, for example: David W. Janey, "Black Parents Give Their Kids 'The
Talk.' What If White Parents Did, Too?," WBUR, April 12, 2021, https://
www.wbur.org/cognoscenti/2021/04/12/the-talk-racism-black-parents
-children-david-w-janey; and Sam Sanders and Kenya Young, "A Black
Mother Reflects on Giving Her 3 Sons 'The Talk' . . . Again and Again,"
NPR, June 28, 2020, https://www.npr.org/2020/06/28/882383372
/a-black-mother-reflects-on-giving-her-3-sons-the-talk-again-and-again.

79 Arpana Gupta, Dawn M. Szymanski, and Frederick T. Leong, "The
'Model Minority Myth': Internalized Racialism of Positive Stereotypes as
Correlates of Psychological Distress, and Attitudes toward Help-Seeking,"
Asian American Journal of Psychology 2, no. 2 (2011): 101–14, https://doi.org
/10.1037/a0024183.

80 Paul Youngbin Kim and Donghun Lee, "Internalized Model Minority
Myth, Asian Values, and Help-Seeking Attitudes among Asian American
Students," *Cultural Diversity and Ethnic Minority Psychology* 20, no. 1 (2014):
98–106, https://doi.org/10.1037/a0033351.

81 Alice W. Cheng et al., "Model Minority Stereotype: Influence on Perceived
Mental Health Needs of Asian Americans," *Journal of Immigrant and
Minority Health* 19, no. 3 (2016): 572–81, https://doi.org/10.1007/s10903
-016-0440-0.

82 Robyn Fivush, Jennifer G. Bohanek, and Kelly Marin, "Patterns of Family
Narrative Co-Construction in Relation to Adolescent Identity and Well-
Being," in *Narrative Development in Adolescence*, eds. Kate C. McLean and
Monisha Pasupathi (Boston: Springer, 2010), 45–63, https://doi.org/10.1007
/978-0-387-89825-4_3.

83 Allison L. Skinner and Andrew N. Meltzoff, "Childhood Experiences and
Intergroup Biases among Children," *Social Issues and Policy Review* 13, no. 1
(2018): pp. 211–40, https://doi.org/10.1111/sipr.12054.

84 I've seen this token mention in classrooms, where one principal told me,
"We do different 'language days' every week: one week Arabic, then
Spanish, then French." Without any follow-up, these days risk becoming yet
another forgettable experience. Your talk, as it evolves from day to day, has
the chance to do more.

Chapter 8: Conversations for Temperament: Bringing Out Your Child's Best

1 Tara Brach, *Radical Acceptance: Embracing Your Life with the Heart of a
Buddha* (New York: Bantam Dell, 2003).

2 Sandra Graham McClowry, Eileen T. Rodriguez, and Robyn Koslowitz,
"Temperament-Based Intervention: Re-Examining Goodness of Fit,"

European Journal of Developmental Science 2, no. 1-2 (June 2008), 120–35, https://www.ncbi.nlm.nih.gov/pmc/articles/PMC2846651/.

3 Maria A. Gartstein et al., "Temperament and Personality," in *The Oxford Handbook of Treatment Processes and Outcomes in Psychology*, eds. Sara Maltzman (New York: Oxford Unive. Press, 2016), 11–41 https://doi.org/10.1093/oxfordhb/9780199739134.013.2; Mary K. Rothbart et al., "Developing Mechanisms of Temperamental Effortful Control," *Journal of Personality* 71, no. 6 (2003): 1113–44, https://doi.org/10.1111/1467-6494.7106009.

4 Ruth Feldman, "The Intrauterine Environment, Temperament, and Development: Including the Biological Foundations of Individual Differences in the Study of Psychopathology and Wellness," *Journal of the American Academy of Child & Adolescent Psychiatry* 47, no. 3 (2008): 233–35, https://doi.org/10.1097/chi.0b013e3181613a92.

5 Jerome Kagan, *Galen's Prophecy: Temperament in Human Nature* (New York: Routledge, 2019).

6 Robert M. Stelmack and Anastasios Stalikas, "Galen and the Humour Theory of Temperament," *Personality and Individual Differences* 12, no. 3 (1991): 255–63, https://doi.org/10.1016/0191-8869(91)90111 n.

7 The ancient Chinese also distinguished between *yin* and *yang*: a distinction that's lasted in our talk about being more withdrawn versus more approachable. See C. Robert Cloninger et al., "The Complex Genetics and Biology of Human Temperament: A Review of Traditional Concepts in Relation to New Molecular Findings," *Translational Psychiatry* 9, no. 1 (November 2019), https://doi.org/10.1038/s41398-019-0621-4; and Soo Jin Lee, Soo Hyun Park, and Han Chae, "Biopsychological Structure of Yin-Yang Using Cloninger's Temperament Model and Carver and White's BIS/BAS Scale," *PeerJ* 4 (2016), https://doi.org/10.7717/peerj.2021.

8 That is, uneasy at first, but growing more comfortable over time.

9 Alexander Thomas and Stella Chess's model from 1970; see Alexander Thomas, Stella Chess, and Herbert G. Birch, "The Origin of Personality," *Scientific American* 223, no. 2 (1970): 102–9, https://doi.org/10.1038/scientificamerican0870-102.

10 Mary Klevjord Rothbart, "Measurement of Temperament in Infancy," *Child Development* 52, no. 2 (1981): 569–78, https://doi.org/10.2307/1129176. See also: Samuel P. Putnam and Cynthia A. Stifter, "Reactivity and Regulation: The Impact of Mary Rothbart on the Study of Temperament," *Infant and Child Development* 17, no. 4 (2008): 311–20, https://doi.org/10.1002/icd.583.

11 Mary K. Rothbart and John E. Bates, "Temperament," in *Handbook of Child Psychology*, ed. Nancy Eisenberg (New York: John Wiley & Sons, 2007), https://doi.org/10.1002/9780470147658.chpsy0303.

12 Jerome Kagan and Nancy Snidman, *The Long Shadow of Temperament* (Cambridge, MA: Belknap Press of Harvard Univ. Press, 2004).

13 Sandra Graham McClowry, *Your Child's Unique Temperament: Insights and Strategies for Responsive Parenting* (Champaign, IL: Research Press, 2003).

14 McClowry, Rodriguez, and Koslowitz, "Temperament-Based Intervention."

15 David Rettew, *Child Temperament: New Thinking about the Boundary between Traits and Illness* (New York: W.W. Norton, 2013).

16 David Rettew, interview with the author, September 23, 2019.

17 Amy Novotney, "Understanding Our Personalities Requires a Lesson in History," *Monitor on Psychology* 39, no. 11 (December 2008), https://www.apa.org/monitor/2008/12/kagan.

18 Diane L. Langkamp and John M. Pascoe, "Temperament of Pre-Term Infants at 9 Months of Age," *Ambulatory Child Health* 7, no. 3-4 (2001): 203–12, https://doi.org/10.1046/j.1467-0658.2001.00131.x.; N. Sajaniemi et al., "Cognitive Performance and Attachment Patterns at Four Years of Age in Extremely Low Birth Weight Infants after Early Intervention," *European Child & Adolescent Psychiatry* 10, no. 2 (2001): 122–29, https://doi.org/10.1007/s007870170035.

19 Frédérique Gayraud and Sophie Kern, "Influence of Preterm Birth on Early Lexical and Grammatical Acquisition," *First Language* 27, no. 2 (2007): 159–73, https://doi.org/10.1177/0142723706075790; Alessandra Sansavini, Annalisa Guarini, and Maria Cristina Caselli, "Preterm Birth: Neuropsychological Profiles and Atypical Developmental Pathways," *Developmental Disabilities Research Reviews* 17, no. 2 (2011): 102–13, https://doi.org/10.1002/ddrr.1105; Alessandra Sansavini et al., "Longitudinal Trajectories of Gestural and Linguistic Abilities in Very Preterm Infants in the Second Year of Life," *Neuropsychologia* 49, no. 13 (2011): 3677–88, https://doi.org/10.1016/j.neuropsychologia.2011.09.023.

20 There are significant links between early language markers and later language skills. As one study found, early gestures in very low birth weight infants from nine months to a year and three months were linked significantly to language skills at five years old. See: S. Stolt et al., "Do the Early Development of Gestures and Receptive and Expressive Language Predict Language Skills at 5;0 in Prematurely Born Very-Low-Birth-Weight Children?," *Journal of Communication Disorders* 61 (2016): 16–28, https://doi.org/10.1016/j.jcomdis.2016.03.002.

21 Langkamp and Pascoe, "Temperament of Pre-Term Infants at 9 Months of Age"; Nina Sajaniemi et al., "Cognitive Development, Temperament and Behavior at 2 Years as Indicative of Language Development at 4 Years in Pre-Term Infants," *Child Psychiatry and Human Development* 31, no. 4 (2001): 329–46, https://doi.org/10.1023/a:1010238523628.

22 Nancy Eisenberg et al., "Parental Reactions to Children's Negative Emotions: Longitudinal Relations to Quality of Children's Social Functioning," *Child Development* 70, no. 2 (1999): 513–34, https://doi.org/10.1111/1467-8624.00037; Liliana J. Lengua and Erica A. Kovacs, "Bidirectional Associations between Temperament and Parenting and the Prediction of Adjustment Problems in Middle Childhood," *Journal of Applied Developmental Psychology* 26, no. 1 (2005): 21–38, https://doi.org/10.1016/j.appdev.2004.10.001.

23 John E. Bates et al., "Interaction of Temperamental Resistance to Control and Restrictive Parenting in the Development of Externalizing Behavior," *Developmental Psychology* 34, no. 5 (1998): 982–95, https://doi.org/10.1037/0012-1649.34.5.982.

24 For research into the links between temperament, anxiety, and stuttering, see: Elaina Kefalianos et al., "Early Stuttering, Temperament and Anxiety: Two Hypotheses," *Journal of Fluency Disorders* 37, no. 3 (2012): 151–63, https://doi.org/10.1016/j.jfludis.2012.03.002.

25 Robert J. Coplan et al., "Do You 'Want' to Play? Distinguishing between Conflicted Shyness and Social Disinterest in Early Childhood," *Developmental Psychology* 40, no. 2 (2004): 244–58, https://doi.org/10.1037/0012-1649.40.2.244.

26 Marc H. Bornstein et al., "Infant Temperament: Stability by Age, Gender, Birth Order, Term Status, and Socioeconomic Status," *Child Development* 86, no. 3 (December 2015): 844–63, https://doi.org/10.1111/cdev.12367.

27 See, for example, Erica H. Lee et al., "Bidirectional Relations between Temperament and Parenting Styles in Chinese Children," *International Journal of Behavioral Development* 37, no. 1 (November 2012): 57–67, https://doi.org/10.1177/0165025412460795.

28 Putnam and Stifter, "Reactivity and Regulation: the Impact of Mary Rothbart on the Study of Temperament."

29 David C. Schwebel and Jodie M. Plumert, "Longitudinal and Concurrent Relations among Temperament, Ability Estimation, and Injury Proneness," *Child Development* 70, no. 3 (1999): 700–12, https://doi.org/10.1111/1467-8624.00050.

30 For more on the ways parenting influences infant temperament and vice versa, see: David J. Bridgett et al, "Maternal and Contextual Influences and the Effect of Temperament Development during Infancy on Parenting in Toddlerhood," *Infant Behavior and Development* 32, no. 1 (2009): 103–16, https://doi.org/10.1016/j.infbeh.2008.10.007. In this study, infants who had more negative moods and were less self-regulated from four to twelve months tended to have parents who showed more negative parenting at eighteen months; those infants who showed the strongest changes in moods and/or behavior had parents who displayed the most negative parenting.

31 Nicole M. Else-Quest et al., "Gender Differences in Temperament: A Meta-Analysis," *Psychological Bulletin* 132, no. 1 (2006): 33–72, https://doi.org/10.1037/0033-2909.132.1.33.

32 Susan Cain, *Quiet: The Power of Introverts in a World That Can't Stop Speaking* (New York: Crown Publishers, 2012).

33 Indeed, a child's temperament—particularly the ability to self-regulate—may play a role in his or her school success or challenges; see, for example: Purificación Checa and Alicia Abundis-Gutierrez, "Parenting and Temperament Influence on School Success in 9–13 Year Olds," *Frontiers in Psychology* 8 (December 2017), https://doi.org/10.3389/fpsyg.2017.00543.

34 Eisenberg et al., "Parental Reactions to Children's Negative Emotions: Longitudinal Relations to Quality of Children's Social Functioning"; Lengua Kovacs, "Bidirectional Associations between Temperament and Parenting and the Prediction of Adjustment Problems in Middle Childhood."

35 Bates et al., "Interaction of Temperamental Resistance to Control and Restrictive Parenting in the Development of Externalizing Behavior."

36 Melanie R. Klein et al., "Bidirectional Relations between Temperament and Parenting Predicting Preschool-Age Children's Adjustment," *Journal of Clinical Child & Adolescent Psychology* 47, no. sup1 (November 2016), https://doi.org/10.1080/15374416.2016.1169537.

37 Nan Chen, Kirby Deater-Deckard, and Martha Ann Bell, "The Role of Temperament by Family Environment Interactions in Child Maladjustment," *Journal of Abnormal Child Psychology* 42, no. 8 (March 2014): 1251–62, https://doi.org/10.1007/s10802-014-9872-y.

38 These patterns also hold true in the classroom. I've talked to teachers who prefer a child shouting out to one needing coaxing. The shouting child meshes with some teachers' extroverted personalities. They may perceive him as more engaged, even if he's not.

39 Robert Cloninger, professor at the Washington University School of Medicine, created a model including four dimensions: how much a person tends to *persist, avoid harm, seek novelty,* and *depend on rewards.* One aspect may not predict another. See: C. Robert Cloninger, "A Psychobiological Model of Temperament and Character," *Archives of General Psychiatry* 50, no. 12 (January 1993): 975, https://doi.org/10.1001/archpsyc.1993.01820240059008. For related research, see: Nathan A Gillespie et al., "The Genetic and Environmental Relationship between Cloninger's Dimensions of Temperament and Character," *Personality and Individual Differences* 35, no. 8 (2003): 1931–46, https://doi.org/10.1016/s0191-8869(03)00042-4.

40 Edward G. Conture, Ellen M. Kelly, and Tedra A. Walden, "Temperament, Speech and Language: An Overview," *Journal of Communication Disorders* 46, no. 2 (2013): 125–42, https://www.ncbi.nlm.nih.gov/pmc/articles/PMC3630249/.

41 Cara J. Kiff, Liliana J. Lengua, and Nicole R. Bush, "Temperament Variation in Sensitivity to Parenting: Predicting Changes in Depression and Anxiety," *Journal of Abnormal Child Psychology* 39, no. 8 (2011): 1199–212, https://doi.org/10.1007/s10802-011-9539-x.

42 Stacey Schultz, "Your Child's Temperament: Finding the Right Parenting Style to Match," ParentMap, April 28, 2012, https://www.parentmap.com/article/your-childs-temperament-finding-the-right-parenting-style.

43 Rebecca P. Newland and Keith A. Crnic, "Developmental Risk and Goodness of Fit in the Mother-Child Relationship: Links to Parenting Stress and Children's Behaviour Problems," *Infant and Child Development* 26, no. 2 (October 2016), https://doi.org/10.1002/icd.1980.

44 This negative pattern may be especially apparent in children who have impulsive tendencies, irritability, or trouble regulating themselves. As Cara Kiff and colleagues argue in a 2011 paper, "children high in frustration, impulsivity and low in effortful control are more vulnerable to the adverse effects of negative parenting, while in turn, many negative parenting behaviors predict increases in these characteristics." Thus, they may elicit more negative responses from their parents, and then be more impacted by those negative responses. See: Cara J. Kiff, Liliana J. Lengua, and Maureen Zalewski, "Nature and Nurturing: Parenting in the Context of Child Temperament," *Clinical Child and Family Psychology Review* 14, no. 3 (February 2011): 251–301, https://doi.org/10.1007/s10567-011-0093-4.

45 For more on the research on teens and sleep, see: Paul Kelley et al., "Synchronizing Education to Adolescent Biology: 'Let Teens Sleep, Start School Later,'" *Learning, Media and Technology* 40, no. 2 (2014): 210–26, https://doi.org/10.1080/17439884.2014.942666.

46 Alison Gopnik, *The Gardener and the Carpenter* (New York: Farrar, Straus & Giroux, 2016), 19.

47 Dorsa Amir, interview with the author, September 24, 2019.

48 Dorsa Amir et al., "The Developmental Origins of Risk and Time Preferences across Diverse Societies.," *Journal of Experimental Psychology: General* 149, no. 4 (2020): 650–61, https://doi.org/10.1037/xge0000675.

49 For more on this model, called an "adaptation-based" approach, see: Bruce J. Ellis et al., "Beyond Risk and Protective Factors: An Adaptation-Based Approach to Resilience," *Perspectives on Psychological Science* 12, no. 4 (2017): 561–87, https://doi.org/10.1177/1745691617693054.

50 Really, as Michelle Ann Kline and others note, we should see variation as the only universal; see: Michelle Ann Kline, Rubeena Shamsudheen, and Tanya Broesch, "Variation Is the Universal: Making Cultural Evolution Work in Developmental Psychology," *Philosophical Transactions of the Royal Society B: Biological Sciences* 373, no. 1743 (February 2018): 20170059, https://doi.org/10.1098/rstb.2017.0059.

51 While we need more studies to confirm these ideas, the implication is a powerful one.

52 Culture shapes the lens through which we view children's behavior and temperaments, and those temperaments depend, at least in part, on their environments. From one perspective, temperament acts to influence developmental change; for example, more extroverted infants tend to receive more interactions from caregivers, which supports their further extroversion. See: Ann Sanson, Sheryl A. Hemphill, and Diana Smart, "Connections between Temperament and Social Development: A Review," *Social Development* 13, no. 1 (2004): 142–70, https://doi.org/10.1046/j.1467-9507.2004.00261.x. For research into cross-cultural differences in temperament, see for example: Chamarrita Farkas and Claire Vallotton, "Differences in Infant Temperament between Chile and the US," *Infant*

Behavior and Development 44 (2016): 208–18, https://doi.org/10.1016/j
.infbeh.2016.07.005. There is also interesting research on the links between
temperament and parenting styles in a number of cultural contexts; see, for
example, Lee et al., "Bidirectional Relations between Temperament and
Parenting Styles in Chinese Children."

53 W. Thomas Boyce, *The Orchid and the Dandelion: Why Sensitive Children Face
Challenges and How All Can Thrive* (New York: Vintage, 2019), 157.

54 Jay Belsky and Kevin M. Beaver, "Cumulative-Genetic Plasticity, Parenting
and Adolescent Self-Regulation," *Journal of Child Psychology and Psychiatry*
52, no. 5 (May 2011): 619–26, https://doi.org/10.1111/j.1469-7610.2010
.02327.x.

55 Boyce, *The Orchid and the Dandelion*, 159–60.

56 Jay Belsky, interview with the author, September 26, 2019.

Conclusion: The Lasting Value of Rich Talk

1 Carl G. Jung, *Modern Man in Search of a Soul* (London: Routledge and
Kegan Paul, 1933).

2 AJMC Staff, "A Timeline of COVID-19 Developments in 2020," AJMC,
January 1, 2021, https://www.ajmc.com/view/a-timeline-of-covid19
-developments-in-2020.

3 Thiago Carvalho, Florian Krammer, and Akiko Iwasaki, "The First 12
Months of COVID-19: A Timeline of Immunological Insights," *Nature
Reviews Immunology* 21, no. 4 (2021): 245–56, https://doi.org/10.1038
/s41577-021-00522-1.

4 Monica Bucci et al., "Toxic Stress in Children and Adolescents," *Advances
in Pediatrics* 63, no. 1 (2016): 403–28, https://doi.org/10.1016/j.yapd.2016
.04.002.

5 Karen Yirmiya et al., "Human Attachment Triggers Different Social
Buffering Mechanisms under High and Low Early Life Stress Rearing,"
International Journal of Psychophysiology 152 (2020): 72–80, https://doi.org
/10.1016/j.ijpsycho.2020.04.001. The effects of a consistently heightened
stress response on development can be seen dramatically in children who
have experienced neglect and then have been placed into foster care; see
Katie A. McLaughlin et al., "Causal Effects of the Early Caregiving
Environment on Development of Stress Response Systems in Children,"
Proceedings of the National Academy of Sciences 112, no. 18 (2015): 5637–42,
https://doi.org/10.1073/pnas.1423363112.

6 Daniel R. Anderson and Katherine G. Hanson, "From Blooming, Buzzing
Confusion to Media Literacy: The Early Development of Television
Viewing," *Developmental Review* 30, no. 2 (June 2010): 239–55, https://doi
.org/10.1016/j.dr.2010.03.004.

7 Gabrielle A. Strouse and Jennifer E. Samson, "Learning from Video: A
Meta-Analysis of the Video Deficit in Children Ages 0 to 6 Years," *Child*

Development 92, no. 1 (January/February 2021): e20–e38, https://doi.org
/10.1111/cdev.13429.

8 Jenny Odell, *How to Do Nothing: Resisting the Attention Economy* (New York:
Melville House, 2019). Also, see the discussion at: Ellie Shechet, "How to
Do Nothing: The New Guide to Refocusing on the Real World," *The
Guardian*, April 2, 2019, https://www.theguardian.com/lifeandstyle/2019
/apr/02/jenny-odell-how-to-do-nothing-attention.

9 Odell speaks, importantly, of the distinction between connectivity and
sensitivity, and the need for what she describes as two linked forms of
listening: "1) listening in the Deep Listening, bodily sense, and 2) listening,
as in me understanding your perspective." See Odell, *How to Do Nothing*, 23.

10 Ainslie Cromar, "'A Real Fragile State': How COVID 19 Threatens
Massachusetts' Hunger Relief Efforts," Boston.com, April 20, 2020, https://
www.boston.com/news/local-news/2020/04/20/how-covid-19-threatens
-massachusetts-hunger-relief-efforts.

Selected Bibliography

Aboujaoude, Elias, Matthew W. Savage, Vladan Starcevic, and Wael O. Salame. "Cyberbullying: Review of an Old Problem Gone Viral." *Journal of Adolescent Health* 57, no. 1 (2015): 10–18. https://doi.org/10.1016/j.jadohealth.2015.04.011.

AJMC Staff. "A Timeline of COVID-19 Developments in 2020." AJMC, January 1, 2021. https://www.ajmc.com/view/a-timeline-of-covid19-developments-in-2020.

Alcott, Louisa May. *Little Women*. Edited by John Escott. Oxford Univ. Press, 2008.

Alexander, Jessica Joelle, and Iben Dissing Sandahl. *The Danish Way of Parenting: What the Happiest People in the World Know about Raising Confident, Capable Kids*. New York: TarcherPerigee, 2016.

Allen, Susie. "Parents' Math Anxiety Can Undermine Children's Math Achievement." Univ. of Chicago News, August 10, 2015. https://news.uchicago.edu/story/parents-math-anxiety-can-undermine-childrens-math-achievement.

Allport, Gordon W. *The Nature of Prejudice*. Garden City, NY: Doubleday, 1958.

Alper, Meryl, Vikki S. Katz, and Lynn Schofield Clark. "Researching Children, Intersectionality, and Diversity in the Digital Age." *Journal of Children and Media* 10, no. 1 (February 2016): 107–14. https://doi.org/10.1080/17482798.2015.1121886.

Amati, Viviana, Silvia Meggiolaro, Giulia Rivellini, and Susanna Zaccarin. "Social Relations and Life Satisfaction: The Role of Friends." *Genus* 74, no. 7 (2018). https://doi.org/10.1186/s41118-018-0032-z.

Amir, Dorsa, Matthew R. Jordan, Katherine McAuliffe, Claudia R. Valeggia,

Lawrence S. Sugiyama, Richard G. Bribiescas, J. Josh Snodgrass, and Yarrow Dunham. "The Developmental Origins of Risk and Time Preferences across Diverse Societies." *Journal of Experimental Psychology: General* 149, no. 4 (2020): 650–61. https://doi.org/10.1037/xge0000675.

Anderson, Norman B., and Rodolfo A. Bulatao. *Understanding Racial and Ethnic Differences in Health in Late Life: A Research Agenda.* Washington, DC: National Academies Press, 2004.

"Anticipation-Action-Reflection Cycle—OECD Future of Education and Skills 2030." OECD. Accessed June 1, 2021. https://www.oecd.org/education/2030-project/teaching-and-learning/learning/aar-cycle/.

Aristotle. *Aristotle: Nicomachean Ethics.* Edited by Sarah Broadie and Christopher Rowe. Oxford: Oxford Univ. Press, 2002.

Arseneault, Louise. "Annual Research Review: The Persistent and Pervasive Impact of Being Bullied in Childhood and Adolescence: Implications for Policy and Practice." *Journal of Child Psychology and Psychiatry* 59, no. 4 (2017): 405–21. https://doi.org/10.1111/jcpp.12841.

Artino, Anthony R. "Academic Self-Efficacy: From Educational Theory to Instructional Practice." *Perspectives on Medical Education* 1, no. 2 (November 2012): 76–85. https://doi.org/10.1007/s40037-012-0012-5.

"Atlanta Speech School: Homepage." Atlanta Speech School, accessed April 9, 2021. https://www.atlantaspeechschool.org/.

Bagwell, Catherine L., Andrew F. Newcomb, and William M. Bukowski. "Preadolescent Friendship and Peer Rejection as Predictors of Adult Adjustment." In *Interpersonal Development.* Edited by Brett Laursen and Rita Žukauskienė, 267–80. London: Routledge, 2017.

Bandura, Albert. "Perceived Self-Efficacy in the Exercise of Personal Agency." *Journal of Applied Sport Psychology* 2, no. 2 (1990): 128–63. https://doi.org/10.1080/10413209008406426.

Bandura, Albert. *Social Foundations of Thought and Action: A Social Cognitive Theory.* Englewood Cliffs, NJ: Prentice Hall, 1995.

Barnett, L.A. "The Nature of Playfulness in Young Adults." *Personality and Individual Differences* 43, no. 4 (2007): 949–58. https://doi.org/10.1016/j.paid.2007.02.018.

Baron-Cohen, Simon, Alan M. Leslie, and Uta Frith. "Does the Autistic Child Have a 'Theory of Mind'?" *Cognition* 21, no. 1 (1985): 37–46. https://doi.org/10.1016/0010-0277(85)90022-8.

Bates, John E., Gregory S. Pettit, Kenneth A. Dodge, and Beth Ridge. "Interaction of Temperamental Resistance to Control and Restrictive Parenting in the Development of Externalizing Behavior." *Developmental Psychology* 34, no. 5 (1998): 982–95. https://doi.org/10.1037/0012-1649.34.5.982.

Beghetto, Ronald A., and Maciej Karwowski. "Educational Consequences of Creativity: A Creative Learning Perspective." *Creativity. Theories – Research*

- Applications 5, no. 2 (January 2018): 146–54. https://doi.org/10.1515/ctra -2018-0011.

Bell, Nanci. "Gestalt Imagery: A Critical Factor in Language Comprehension." *Annals of Dyslexia* 41, no. 1 (1991): 246–60. https://doi.org/10.1007/bf02648089.

Bell, Nanci. *Visualizing and Verbalizing: For Language Comprehension and Thinking.* Avila Beach, CA: Gander, 2007.

Bell, Nanci. "Visualizing and Verbalizing: Q and A with Nanci Bell of Lindamood-Bell." Reading Rockets. Accessed October 15, 2019. https:// www.readingrockets.org/article/visualizing-and-verbalizing-q-and-nanci -bell-lindamood-bell.

Belsky, Jay, and Kevin M. Beaver. "Cumulative-Genetic Plasticity, Parenting and Adolescent Self Regulation." *Journal of Child Psychology and Psychiatry* 52, no. 5 (May 2011): 619–26. https://doi.org/10.1111/j.1469 -7610.2010.02327.x.

Belsky, Jay, and Sara R. Jaffee. "The Multiple Determinants of Parenting." In *Developmental Psychopathology.* Edited by Dante Cicchetti and Donald J. Cohen, 38–85. New York: John Wiley & Sons, 2015. https://doi.org /10.1002/9780470939406.ch2.

Bensalah, Leïla, Stéphanie Caillies, and Marion Anduze. "Links among Cognitive Empathy, Theory of Mind, and Affective Perspective Taking by Young Children." *Journal of Genetic Psychology* 177, no. 1 (2016): 17–31. https://doi.org/10.1080/00221325.2015.1106438.

Berko, Jean. "The Child's Learning of English Morphology." *Word* 14, no. 2-3 (1958): 150–77. https://doi.org/10.1080/00437956.1958.11659661.

Berliner, David. "Rational Responses to High Stakes Testing: The Case of Curriculum Narrowing and the Harm That Follows." *Cambridge Journal of Education* 41, no. 3 (2011): 287–302. https://doi.org/10.1080/0305764x .2011.607151.

Bernstein, Basil B. *Class, Codes and Control.* London: Routledge, 2009.

Bhattacharya, Kunal, Asim Ghosh, Daniel Monsivais, Robin I.M. Dunbar, and Kimmo Kaski. "Sex Differences in Social Focus across the Life Cycle in Humans." *Royal Society Open Science* 3, no. 4 (2016): 160097. https://doi.org /10.1098/rsos.160097.

Bialystok, Ellen. "The Bilingual Adaptation: How Minds Accommodate Experience." *Psychological Bulletin* 143, no. 3 (2017): 233–62. https://doi.org /10.1037/bul0000099.

Bialystok, Ellen, Fergus I.M. Craik, and Gigi Luk. "Bilingualism: Consequences for Mind and Brain." *Trends in Cognitive Sciences* 16, no. 4 (2012): 240–50. https://doi.org/10.1016/j.tics.2012.03.001.

Bidwell, Allie. "The History of Common Core State Standards." *U.S. News & World Report,* February 27, 2014. https://www.usnews.com/news/special -reports/articles/2014/02/27/the-history-of-common-core-state-standards.

Birch, S.A.J., V. Li, T. Haddock, S.E. Ghrear, P. Brosseau-Liard, A. Baimel, and M. Whyte. "Perspectives on Perspective Taking." In *Advances in Child*

Development and Behavior. Edited by Janette B. Benson, 185–226. Vancouver: Univ. of British Columbia, 2017. https://doi.org/10.1016/bs .acdb.2016.10.005.

Blakemore, Erin. "Race and Ethnicity: How Are They Different?" *National Geographic*, February 22, 2019. https://www.nationalgeographic.com/culture /article/race-ethnicity.

Bodrova, Elena. "Make-Believe Play versus Academic Skills: A Vygotskian Approach to Today's Dilemma of Early Childhood Education." *European Early Childhood Education Research Journal* 16, no. 3 (2008): 357–69. https:// doi.org/10.1080/13502930802291777.

Boers, Elroy, Mohammad H. Afzali, Nicola Newton, and Patricia Conrod. "Association of Screen Time and Depression in Adolescence." *JAMA Pediatrics* 173, no. 9 (January 2019): 853–59. https://doi.org/10.1001 /jamapediatrics.2019.1759.

Borba, Michele. *UnSelfie: Why Empathetic Kids Succeed in Our All-About-Me World*. New York: Touchstone, 2016.

Bornstein, Marc H., and Martha E. Arterberry. "The Development of Object Categorization in Young Children: Hierarchical Inclusiveness, Age, Perceptual Attribute, and Group versus Individual Analyses." *Developmental Psychology* 46, no. 2 (2010): 350–65. https://doi.org/10.1037/a0018411.

Bosson, Mélanie S., Marco G.P. Hessels, Christine Hessels-Schlatter, Jean-Louis Berger, Nadine M. Kipfer, and Fredi P. Büchel. "Strategy Acquisition by Children with General Learning Difficulties through Metacognitive Training." *Australian Journal of Learning Difficulties* 15, no. 1 (2010): 13–34. https://doi.org/10.1080/19404150903524523.

Bottino, Sara Mota Borges, Cássio M.C. Bottino, Caroline Gomez Regina, Aline Villa Lobo Correia, and Wagner Silva Ribeiro. "Cyberbullying and Adolescent Mental Health: Systematic Review." *Cadernos de Saúde Pública* 31, no. 3 (2015): 463–75. https://doi.org/10.1590/0102-311x000 36114.

Bowlby, John. "The Growth of Independence in the Young Child." *Journal (Royal Society of Health)* 76, no. 9 (1955): 587–91. https://doi.org/10.1177 /146642405507600912.

Boyce, W. Thomas. *The Orchid and the Dandelion: Why Sensitive Children Face Challenges and How All Can Thrive*. New York: Vintage, 2019.

Brach, Tara. *Radical Acceptance: Embracing Your Life With the Heart of a Buddha*. New York: Bantam Dell, 2003.

Brackett, Marc A. *Permission to Feel: Unlocking the Power of Emotions to Help Our Kids, Ourselves, and Our Society Thrive*. New York: Celadon Books, 2019.

Brackett, Marc A., Susan E. Rivers, Maria R. Reyes, and Peter Salovey. "Enhancing Academic Performance and Social and Emotional Competence with the RULER Feeling Words Curriculum." *Learning and Individual Differences* 22, no. 2 (2012): 218–24. https://doi.org/10.1016/j.lindif.2010 .10.002.

Bransford, John D., Rodney R. Cocking, and Ann L. Brown. *How People Learn: Brain, Mind, Experience, and School*, Expanded Edition. Washington, DC: National Academies Press, 2000.

Brewer, Rebecca, and Jennifer Murphy. "People with Autism Can Read Emotions, Feel Empathy." *Scientific American*, July 13, 2016. https://www .scientificamerican.com/article/people-with-autism-can-read-emotions-feel -empathy1/.

Bridgett, David J., Maria A. Gartstein, Samuel P. Putnam, Talia McKay, Erin Iddins, Christopher Robertson, Kristin Ramsay, and Anna Rittmueller. "Maternal and Contextual Influences and the Effect of Temperament Development during Infancy on Parenting in Toddlerhood." *Infant Behavior and Development* 32, no. 1 (2009): 103–16. https://doi.org/10.1016/j.infbeh .2008.10.007.

Brinthaupt, Thomas M., and Christian T. Dove. "Differences in Self-Talk Frequency as a Function of Age, Only-Child, and Imaginary Childhood Companion Status." *Journal of Research in Personality* 46, no. 3 (2012): 326–33. https://doi.org/10.1016/j.jrp.2012.03.003.

Briscoe-Smith, Allison, and Sandra Chapman. "Supporting Kids of Color in the Wake of Racialized Violence: Part One." EmbraceRace. Accessed June 3, 2021. https://www.embracerace.org/resources/supporting-kids-of-color -in-the-wake-of-racialized-violenc-part-one.

Brody, Jane E. "How to Avoid Burnout in Youth Sports." *New York Times*, May 7, 2018. https://www.nytimes.com/2018/05/07/well/how-to-avoid -burnout-in-youth-sports.html.

Bronson, Po, and Ashley Merryman. *NurtureShock: New Thinking About Children*. New York: Twelve, 2009.

Brown, B. Bradford, and Jeremy P. Bakken. "Parenting and Peer Relationships: Reinvigorating Research on Family-Peer Linkages in Adolescence." *Journal of Research on Adolescence* 21, no. 1 (2011): 153–65. https://doi.org/10.1111/j .1532-7795.2010.00720.x.

Brown, Stuart L., and Christopher C. Vaughan. *Play: How It Shapes the Brain, Opens the Imagination, and Invigorates the Soul*. New York: Avery, 2010.

Bucci, Monica, Sara Silvério Marques, Debora Oh, and Nadine Burke Harris. "Toxic Stress in Children and Adolescents." *Advances in Pediatrics* 63, no. 1 (2016): 403–28. https://doi.org/10.1016/j.yapd.2016.04.002.

Bucket Fillers. Accessed May 11, 2021. https://bucketfillers101.com/.

"Building Emotional Intelligence Playfully." Generation Mindful. Accessed June 6, 2021. https://genmindful.com/.

Burkus, David. "Want Your Kids (or Employees) to Have More Grit? Add This Rule." Inc.com., August 22, 2016. https://www.inc.com/david-burkus /want-your-kids-or-employees-to-have-more-grit-add-this-rule.html.

Burns, David D. *Feeling Good: The New Mood Therapy*. New York: Morrow, 1980.

Bustamante, Andres S., and Kathy Hirsh-Pasek. "Are Our Preschool Teachers

Worth More Than They Were Two Months Ago?" Brookings. April 13, 2020. https://www.brookings.edu/blog/education-plus-development/2020/04/13 /are-our-preschool-teachers-worth-more-than-they-were-two-months-ago/.

Buttelmann, David, Norbert Zmyj, Moritz Daum, and Malinda Carpenter. "Selective Imitation of In-Group Over Out-Group Members in 14-Month-Old Infants." *Child Development* 84, no. 2 (2012): 422–28. https://doi.org /10.1111/j.1467-8624.2012.01860.x.

Cain, Kate, and Jane Oakhill. "Matthew Effects in Young Readers: Reading Comprehension and Reading Experience Aid Vocabulary Development." *Journal of Learning Disabilities* 44, no. 5 (2011): 431–43. https://doi.org/10.1177/0022219411410042.

Cain, Susan. *Quiet: The Power of Introverts in a World That Can't Stop Speaking.* New York: Crown Publishers, 2012.

Carvalho, Thiago, Florian Krammer, and Akiko Iwasaki. "The First 12 Months of COVID-19: A Timeline of Immunological Insights." *Nature Reviews Immunology* 21, no. 4 (2021): 245–56. https://doi.org/10.1038/s41577-021 -00522-1.

Castles, Anne, Kathleen Rastle, and Kate Nation. "Ending the Reading Wars: Reading Acquisition from Novice to Expert." *Psychological Science in the Public Interest* 19, no. 1 (2018): 5–51. https://doi.org/10.1177/1529100618772271.

Cates, Carolyn Brockmeyer, Benard P. Dreyer, Samantha B. Berkule, Lisa J. White, Jenny A. Arevalo, and Alan L. Mendelsohn. "Infant Communication and Subsequent Language Development in Children from Low-Income Families." *Journal of Developmental & Behavioral Pediatrics* 33, no. 7 (2012): 577–85. https://doi.org/10.1097/dbp.0b013e318264c10f.

Chae, Seong Wook, Young Wook Seo, and Kun Chang Lee. "Task Difficulty and Team Diversity on Team Creativity: Multi-Agent Simulation Approach." *Computers in Human Behavior* 42 (2015): 83–92. https://doi.org /10.1016/j.chb.2014.03.032.

Chartrand, Tanya L., and John A. Bargh. "The Chameleon Effect: The Perception–Behavior Link and Social Interaction." *Journal of Personality and Social Psychology* 76, no. 6 (1999): 893–910. https://doi.org/10.1037/0022 -3514.76.6.893.

Chatzipanteli, Athanasia, Vasilis Grammatikopoulos, and Athanasios Gregoriadis. "Development and Evaluation of Metacognition in Early Childhood Education." *Early Child Development and Care* 184, no. 8 (2013): 1223–32. https://doi.org/10.1080/03004430.2013.861456.

Checa, Purificación, and Alicia Abundis-Gutierrez. "Parenting and Temperament Influence on School Success in 9–13 Year Olds." *Frontiers in Psychology* 8 (December 2017). https://doi.org/10.3389/fpsyg.2017.00543.

Chen, Nan, Kirby Deater-Deckard, and Martha Ann Bell. "The Role of Temperament by Family Environment Interactions in Child Maladjustment." *Journal of Abnormal Child Psychology* 42, no. 8 (March 2014): 1251–62. https://doi.org/10.1007/s10802-014-9872-y.

Chen, Patricia, Omar Chavez, Desmond C. Ong, and Brenda Gunderson. "Strategic Resource Use for Learning: A Self-Administered Intervention That Guides Self-Reflection on Effective Resource Use Enhances Academic Performance." *Psychological Science* 28, no. 6 (2017): 774–85. https://doi.org/10.1177/0956797617696456.

Cheney-Rice, Zak. "Never Stop Running." *Intelligencer*, May 8, 2020. https://nymag.com/intelligencer/2020/05/ahmaud-arbery-death-and-joy.html.

Cheng, Alice W., Janet Chang, Janine O'Brien, Marc S. Budgazad, and Jack Tsai. "Model Minority Stereotype: Influence on Perceived Mental Health Needs of Asian Americans." *Journal of Immigrant and Minority Health* 19, no. 3 (2016): 572–81. https://doi.org/10.1007/s10903-016-0440-0.

Cherng, Hua-Yu Sebastian. "If They Think I Can: Teacher Bias and Youth of Color Expectations and Achievement." *Social Science Research* 66 (2017): 170–86. https://doi.org/10.1016/j.ssresearch.2017.04.001.

Chin, Mark J., David M. Quinn, Tasminda K. Dhaliwal, and Virginia S. Lovison. "Bias in the Air: A Nationwide Exploration of Teachers' Implicit Racial Attitudes, Aggregate Bias, and Student Outcomes." *Educational Researcher* 49, no. 8 (2020): 566–78. https://doi.org/10.3102/0013189x20937240.

Chouinard, Michael M. "Children's Questions: A Mechanism for Cognitive Development." *Monographs of the Society for Research in Child Development* 72, no. 1 (March 2007): vii–ix, 1-112; discussion 113-26. https://doi.org/10.1111/j.1540-5834.2007.00412.x.

Choudhury, Suparna, Sarah-Jayne Blakemore, and Tony Charman. "Social Cognitive Development during Adolescence." *Social Cognitive and Affective Neuroscience* 1, no. 3 (January 2006): 165–74. https://doi.org/10.1093/scan/nsl024.

Christakis, Erika. *The Importance of Being Little: What Young Children Really Need from Grownups.* New York: Penguin Putnam, 2016.

Cillessen, Antonius H.N., and Lara Mayeux. "From Censure to Reinforcement: Developmental Changes in the Association between Aggression and Social Status." *Child Development* 75, no. 1 (2004): 147–63. https://doi.org/10.1111/j.1467-8624.2004.00660.x.

Cillessen, Antonius H.N., and Amanda J. Rose. "Understanding Popularity in the Peer System." *Current Directions in Psychological Science* 14, no. 2 (2005): 102–5. https://doi.org/10.1111/j.0963-7214.2005.00343.x.

Civiletti, Denise. "New Assistant Principal Named at Aquebogue Elementary School." RiverheadLOCAL, September 14, 2019. https://riverheadlocal.com/2019/09/14/new-assistant-principal-nam-ed-at-aquebogue-elementary-school/.

Clark, Karen E., and Gary W. Ladd. "Connectedness and Autonomy Support in Parent–Child Relationships: Links to Children's Socioemotional Orientation and Peer Relationships." *Developmental Psychology* 36, no. 4 (2000): 485–98. https://doi.org/10.1037/0012-1649.36.4.485.

Clauser, Grant. "Amazon's Alexa Never Stops Listening to You. Should You Worry?" *New York Times*, August 8, 2019. https://www.nytimes.com /wirecutter/blog/amazons-alexa-never-stops-listening-to-you/.

Cloninger, C. Robert. "A Psychobiological Model of Temperament and Character." *Archives of General Psychiatry* 50, no. 12 (January 1993): 975. https://doi.org/10.1001/archpsyc.1993.01820240059008.

Cloninger, C. Robert, Kevin M. Cloninger, Igor Zwir, and Liisa Keltikangas-Järvinen. "The Complex Genetics and Biology of Human Temperament: A Review of Traditional Concepts in Relation to New Molecular Findings." *Translational Psychiatry* 9, no. 1 (November 2019). https://doi.org/10.1038 /s41398-019-0621-4.

Cohen, Lawrence J. *Playful Parenting*. New York: Ballantine Books, 2002.

Cole, David A., Melissa A. Maxwell, Tammy L. Dukewich, and Rachel Yosick. "Targeted Peer Victimization and the Construction of Positive and Negative Self-Cognitions: Connections to Depressive Symptoms in Children." *Journal of Clinical Child & Adolescent Psychology* 39, no. 3 (2010): 421–35. https://doi.org/10.1080/15374411003691776.

"The Common Core FAQ." NPR, May 27, 2014. https://www.npr.org/sections /ed/2014/05/27/307755798/the-common-core-faq#q4.

"The Common Sense Census: Media Use by Tweens and Teens, 2019: Common Sense Media." Common Sense Media, October 28, 2019. https:// www.commonsensemedia.org/research/the-common-sense-census-media -use-by-tweens-and-teens-2019.

Coogle, Christan Grygas, Allison Ward Parsons, Leslie La Croix, and Jennifer R. Ottley. "A Comparison of Dialogic Reading, Modeling, and Dialogic Reading Plus Modeling." *Infants & Young Children* 33, no. 2 (2020): 119–31. https://doi.org/10.1097/iyc.0000000000000162.

Coplan, Robert J., Kavita Prakash, Kim O'Neil, and Mandana Armer. "Do You 'Want' to Play? Distinguishing Between Conflicted Shyness and Social Disinterest in Early Childhood." *Developmental Psychology* 40, no. 2 (2004): 244–58. https://doi.org/10.1037/0012-1649.40.2.244.

Crenshaw, Kimberlé. "Mapping the Margins: Intersectionality, Identity Politics, and Violence against Women of Color." *Stanford Law Review* 43, no. 6 (1991): 1241–99. https://doi.org/10.2307/1229039.

Crosson, Amy C., and Nonie K. Lesaux. "Connectives." *The Reading Teacher* 67, no. 3 (2013): 193–200. https://doi.org/10.1002/trtr.1197.

Crown, Cynthia L., Stanley Feldstein, Michael D. Jasnow, Beatrice Beebe, and Joseph Jaffe. "The Cross-Modal Coordination of Interpersonal Timing: Six-Week-Olds Infants' Gaze with Adults' Vocal Behavior." *Journal of Psycholinguistic Research* 31, no. 1 (January 2002): 1–23. https://doi.org/10 .1023/a:1014301303616.

Csikszentmihalyi, Mihaly. *Flow: The Psychology of Optimal Experience*. New York: Harper Perennial, 2008.

Cui, Lixian, Michael M. Criss, Erin Ratliff, Zezhen Wu, Benjamin J.

Houltberg, Jennifer S. Silk, and Amanda Sheffield Morris. "Longitudinal Links between Maternal and Peer Emotion Socialization and Adolescent Girls' Socioemotional Adjustment." *Developmental Psychology* 56, no. 3 (2020): 595–607. https://doi.org/10.1037/dev0000861.

Cundiff, Jenny M., and Karen A. Matthews. "Friends with Health Benefits: The Long-Term Benefits of Early Peer Social Integration for Blood Pressure and Obesity in Midlife." *Psychological Science* 29, no. 5 (2018): 814–23. https://doi.org/10.1177/0956797617746510.

Dadds, Mark R., Kirsten Hunter, David J.D. Hawes, Aaron D. Frost, Shane Vassallo, Paul Bunn, Sabine Merz, and Yasmeen El Masry. "A Measure of Cognitive and Affective Empathy in Children Using Parent Ratings." *Child Psychiatry and Human Development* 39, no. 2 (2007): 111–22. https://doi.org/10.1007/s10578-007-0075-4.

Dadds, Mark Richard, Avril Jessica Cauchi, Subodha Wimalaweera, David John Hawes, and John Brennan. "Outcomes, Moderators, and Mediators of Empathic-Emotion Recognition Training for Complex Conduct Problems in Childhood." *Psychiatry Research* 199, no. 3 (2012): 201–7. https://doi.org/10.1016/j.psychres.2012.04.033.

Darnon, Céline, Benoît Dompnier, Ophélie Gilliéron, and Fabrizio Butera. "The Interplay of Mastery and Performance Goals in Social Comparison: A Multiple-Goal Perspective." *Journal of Educational Psychology* 102, no. 1 (2010): 212–22. https://doi.org/10.1037/a0018161.

Davis, Elizabeth L., Linda J. Levine, Heather C. Lench, and Jodi A. Quas. "Metacognitive Emotion Regulation: Children's Awareness That Changing Thoughts and Goals Can Alleviate Negative Emotions." *Emotion* 10, no. 4 (2010): 498–510. https://doi.org/10.1037/a0018428.

Deaux, Kay, and Laurie L. Lewis. "Structure of Gender Stereotypes: Interrelationships among Components and Gender Label." *Journal of Personality and Social Psychology* 46, no. 5 (1984): 991–1004. https://doi.org/10.1037/0022-3514.46.5.991.

Deci, Edward L., and Richard M. Ryan. "Self-Determination Theory: A Macrotheory of Human Motivation, Development, and Health." *Canadian Psychology/Psychologie Canadienne* 49, no. 3 (2008): 182–85. https://doi.org/10.1037/a0012801.

Deci, Edward L., and Richard M. Ryan. "Self-Determination." In *The Corsini Encyclopedia of Psychology*. Edited by Irving R. Weiner and W. Edward Craighead. New York: John Wiley & Sons, 2010. https://doi.org/10.1002/9780470479216.corpsy0834.

Denby, David. "The Limits of 'Grit.'" *The New Yorker*, June 21, 2016. https://www.newyorker.com/culture/culture-desk/the-limits-of-grit.

Denworth, Lydia. *Friendship: The Evolution, Biology, and Extraordinary Power of Life's Fundamental Bond*. New York: W.W. Norton, 2020.

Derber, Charles. *The Pursuit of Attention: Power and Ego in Everyday Life*. New York: Oxford Univ. Press, 2001.

Devine, Rory T., and Claire Hughes. "Let's Talk: Parents' Mental Talk (Not Mind-Mindedness or Mindreading Capacity) Predicts Children's False Belief Understanding." *Child Development* 90, no. 4 (August 2017): 1236–53. https://doi.org/10.1111/cdev.12990.

Diamond, Adele, W. Steven Barnett, Jessica Thomas, and Sarah Munro. "The Early Years: Preschool Program Improves Cognitive Control." *Science* 318, no. 5855 (2007): 1387–88. https://doi.org/10.1126/science.1151148.

Dignath, Charlotte, and Gerhard Büttner. "Components of Fostering Self-Regulated Learning among Students. A Meta-Analysis on Intervention Studies at Primary and Secondary School Level." *Metacognition and Learning* 3, no. 3 (January 2008): 231–64. https://doi.org/10.1007/s11409-008-9029-x.

Dodici, Beverly J., Dianne C. Draper, and Carla A. Peterson. "Early Parent—Child Interactions and Early Literacy Development." *Topics in Early Childhood Special Education* 23, no. 3 (2003): 124–36. https://doi.org/10.1177/02711214030230030301.

Druckerman, Pamela. *Bringing Up Bébé: One American Mother Discovers the Wisdom of French Parenting*. New York: Penguin Books, 2012.

Duckworth, Angela L., Christopher Peterson, Michael D. Matthews, and Dennis R. Kelly. "Grit: Perseverance and Passion for Long-Term Goals." *Journal of Personality and Social Psychology* 92, no. 6 (2007): 1087–1101. https://doi.org/10.1037/0022-3514.92.6.1087.

Duckworth, Angela. *Grit: The Power of Passion and Perseverance*. New York: Scribner, 2016.

Duncan, Larissa G., J. Douglas Coatsworth, and Mark T. Greenberg. "A Model of Mindful Parenting: Implications for Parent–Child Relationships and Prevention Research." *Clinical Child and Family Psychology Review* 12, no. 3 (February 2009): 255–70. https://doi.org/10.1007/s10567-009-0046-3.

Dweck, Carol S. "Beliefs Are Central to Understanding Human Motivation." *PsycEXTRA Dataset*, 2014. https://doi.org/10.1037/e515492014-004.

Dweck, Carol S. "Messages That Motivate: How Praise Molds Students' Beliefs, Motivation, and Performance (in Surprising Ways)." In *Improving Academic Achievement*. Edited by Joshua Aronson, 37–60. New York: Academic Press, 2002. https://doi.org/10.1016/b978-012064455-1/50006-3.

Dweck, Carol S. *Mindset: The New Psychology of Success*. New York: Ballantine Books, 2008.

Dweck, Carol S., and Ellen L. Leggett. "A Social-Cognitive Approach to Motivation and Personality." *Psychological Review* 95, no. 2 (1988): 256–73. https://doi.org/10.1037/0033-295x.95.2.256.

Dweck, Carol. "Carol Dweck Revisits the 'Growth Mindset' (Opinion)." Education Week, September 22, 2015. https://www.edweek.org/leadership/opinion-carol-dweck-revisits-the-growth-mindset/2015/09.

Dweck, Carol. "The Power of Believing That You Can Improve." TED, November 2014. https://www.ted.com/talks/carol_dweck_the_power_of_believing_that_you_can_improve.

"Dyslexia Basics." International Dyslexia Association, March 10, 2020. https:// dyslexiaida.org/dyslexia-basics/.

Edison, Thomas A., and Dagobert D. Runes. *The Diary and Observations of Thomas Alva Edison*. New York: Philosophical Library, 1976.

Eisenberg, Nancy, Richard A. Fabes, Stephanie A. Shepard, Ivanna K. Guthrie, Bridget C. Murphy, and Mark Reiser. "Parental Reactions to Children's Negative Emotions: Longitudinal Relations to Quality of Children's Social Functioning." *Child Development* 70, no. 2 (1999): 513–34. https://doi.org/10.1111/1467-8624.00037.

Elbow, Peter. "Bringing the Rhetoric of Assent and the Believing Game Together—and into the Classroom." *College English* 67, no. 4 (January 2005): 388–399. https://doi.org/10.2307/30044680.

Elliot, Andrew J., and Carol S. Dweck. *Handbook of Competence and Motivation*. New York: Guilford Press, 2007.

Ellis, Bruce J., JeanMarie Bianchi, Vladas Griskevicius, and Willem E. Frankenhuis. "Beyond Risk and Protective Factors: An Adaptation-Based Approach to Resilience." *Perspectives on Psychological Science* 12, no. 4 (2017): 561–87. https://doi.org/10.1177/1745691617693054.

Else-Quest, Nicole M., Janet Shibley Hyde, H. Hill Goldsmith, and Carol A. Van Hulle. "Gender Differences in Temperament: A Meta-Analysis." *Psychological Bulletin* 132, no. 1 (2006): 33–72. https://doi.org/10.1037/0033 2909.132.1.33.

Ely, Richard, and Jean Berko Gleason. "*I'm Sorry I Said That:* Apologies in Young Children's Discourse." *Journal of Child Language* 33, no. 3 (2006): 599–620. https://doi.org/10.1017/s0305000906007446.

Ely, Richard, Jean Berko Gleason, Ann MacGibbon, and Elena Zaretsky. "Attention to Language: Lessons Learned at the Dinner Table." *Social Development* 10, no. 3 (2001): 355–73. https://doi.org/10.1111/1467-9507 .00170.

EmbraceRace. "EmbraceRace." Accessed June 8, 2021. https://www.embracerace .org/.

"Emotions Matter." RULER Approach. Accessed June 1, 2021. https://www .rulerapproach.org/.

Escolano-Pérez, Elena, Maria Luisa Herrero-Nivela, and M. Teresa Anguera. "Preschool Metacognitive Skill Assessment in Order to Promote Educational Sensitive Response from Mixed-Methods Approach: Complementarity of Data Analysis." *Frontiers in Psychology* 10 (2019). https://doi.org/10.3389 /fpsyg.2019.01298.

Evans, Angela D., Alison M. O'Connor, and Kang Lee. "Verbalizing a Commitment Reduces Cheating in Young Children." *Social Development* 27, no. 1 (2017): 87–94. https://doi.org/10.1111/sode.12248.

Faber, Adele, Elaine Mazlish, Joanna Faber, Kimberly Ann Coe, and Kimberly Ann Coe. *How to Talk so Kids Will Listen & Listen so Kids Will Talk*. New York: Simon & Schuster, 2012.

Fahy, Jill K. "Language and Executive Functions: Self-Talk for Self-Regulation." *Perspectives on Language Learning and Education* 21, no. 2 (2014): 61–71. https://doi.org/10.1044/lle21.2.61.

Farkas, Chamarrita, and Claire Vallotton. "Differences in Infant Temperament between Chile and the US." *Infant Behavior and Development* 44 (2016): 208–18. https://doi.org/10.1016/j.infbeh.2016.07.005.

Farrant, Brad M., Tara A.J. Devine, Murray T. Maybery, and Janet Fletcher. "Empathy, Perspective Taking and Prosocial Behaviour: The Importance of Parenting Practices." *Infant and Child Development* 21, no. 2 (June 2011): 175–88. https://doi.org/10.1002/icd.740.

Feldman, Ruth. "Parent-Infant Synchrony: A Biobehavioral Model of Mutual Influences in the Formation of Affiliative Bonds." *Monographs of the Society for Research in Child Development* 77, no. 2 (2012): 42–51. https://doi.org/10.1111/j.1540-5834.2011.00660.x.

Feldman, Ruth. "The Intrauterine Environment, Temperament, and Development: Including the Biological Foundations of Individual Differences in the Study of Psychopathology and Wellness." *Journal of the American Academy of Child & Adolescent Psychiatry* 47, no. 3 (2008): 233–35. https://doi.org/10.1097/chi.0b013e3181 613a92.

Ferjan Ramírez, Naja, Sarah Roseberry Lytle, and Patricia K. Kuhl. "Parent Coaching Increases Conversational Turns and Advances Infant Language Development." *Proceedings of the National Academy of Sciences* 117, no. 7 (2020): 3484–91. https://doi.org/10.1073/pnas.1921653117.

Fernando, Suman. *Mental Health, Race and Culture*, third ed. London: Red Globe Press, 2010.

Feshir, Riham. "Remembering George Floyd, the Man." MPR News, March 8, 2021. https://www.mprnews.org/story/2021/03/08/remembering-george-floyd.

Fink, Elian, Silvana Mareva, and Jenny L. Gibson. "Dispositional Playfulness in Young Children: A Cross-Sectional and Longitudinal Examination of the Psychometric Properties of a New Child Self-Reported Playfulness Scale and Associations with Social Behaviour." *Infant and Child Development* 29, no. 4 (2020). https://doi.org/10.1002/icd.2181.

"Five Steps for Brain-Building Serve and Return." Center on the Developing Child at Harvard University, October 29, 2020. https://developingchild .harvard.edu/resources/5-steps-for-brain-building-serve-and-return/.

Fivush, Robyn, and Jessica McDermott Sales. "Coping, Attachment, and Mother-Child Narratives of Stressful Events." *Merrill–Palmer Quarterly* 52, no. 1 (2006): 125–50. https://doi.org/10.1353/mpq.2006.0003.

Fivush, Robyn, Jennifer G. Bohanek, and Kelly Marin. "Patterns of Family Narrative Co-Construction in Relation to Adolescent Identity and Well-Being." In *Narrative Development in Adolescence*. Edited by Kate C. McLean and Monisha Pasupathi 45–63. Boston: Springer, 2010. https://doi.org/10 .1007/978-0-387-89825-4_3.

Fivush, Robyn, Kelly Marin, Kelly McWilliams, and Jennifer G. Bohanek. "Family Reminiscing Style: Parent Gender and Emotional Focus in Relation to Child Well-Being." *Journal of Cognition and Development* 10, no. 3 (2009): 210–35. https://doi.org/10.1080/15248370903155866.

Flannery, Raymond B., and Mary R. Harvey. "Psychological Trauma and Learned Helplessness: Seligman's Paradigm Reconsidered." *Psychotherapy: Theory, Research, Practice, Training* 28, no. 2 (1991): 374–78. https://doi.org/10.1037/0033-3204.28.2.374.

Frazier, Brandy N., Susan A. Gelman, and Henry M. Wellman. "Young Children Prefer and Remember Satisfying Explanations." *Journal of Cognition and Development* 17, no. 5 (2016): 718–36. https://doi.org/10.1080/15248372.2015.1098649.

French, Doran C., and Jody Conrad. "School Dropout as Predicted by Peer Rejection and Antisocial Behavior." *Journal of Research on Adolescence* 11, no. 3 (2001): 225–44. https://doi.org/10.1111/1532-7795.00011.

"Frequently Asked Questions." Dyslexia Help at the University of Michigan. Accessed May 29, 2021. http://dyslexiahelp.umich.edu/answers/faq.

Friedman, Becky, and Jason Fruchter. *Daniel Tiger's Neighborhood: Daniel's New Friend*. New York: Simon Spotlight, 2015.

Fuchs, Douglas, and Lynn S. Fuchs. "Introduction to Response to Intervention: What, Why, and How Valid Is It?" *Reading Research Quarterly* 41, no. 1 (March 2006): 93–9. https://doi.org/10.1598/rrq.41.1.4.

García, J. Ricardo, and Kate Cain. "Decoding and Reading Comprehension." *Review of Educational Research* 84, no. 1 (2014): 74–111. https://doi.org/10.3102/0034654313499616.

Gartstein, Maria A., Samuel P. Putnam, Elaine N. Aron, and Mary K. Rothbart. "Temperament and Personality." In *The Oxford Handbook of Treatment Processes and Outcomes in Psychology*. Edited by Sara Maltzman, 11–14. New York: Oxford Univ. Press, 2016, 2016. https://doi.org/10.1093/oxfordhb/9780199739134.013.2.

Gasser, Luciano, and Monika Keller. "Are the Competent the Morally Good? Perspective Taking and Moral Motivation of Children Involved in Bullying." *Social Development* 18, no. 4 (2009): 798–816. https://doi.org/10.1111/j.1467-9507.2008.00516.x.

Gayraud, Frédérique, and Sophie Kern. "Influence of Preterm Birth on Early Lexical and Grammatical Acquisition." *First Language* 27, no. 2 (2007): 159–73. https://doi.org/10.1177/0142723706075790.

Georgakopoulos, Thanasis. "Semantic Maps." *Linguistics*, 2019. https://doi.org/10.1093/obo/9780199772810-0229.

Gerber, Magda. *Dear Parent: Caring for Infants with Respect*. Los Angeles: Resources for Infant Educarers (RIE), 2003.

Giles, Jessica W., and Gail D. Heyman. "Young Children's Beliefs about the Relationship between Gender and Aggressive Behavior." *Child Development* 76, no. 1 (2005): 107–21. https://doi.org/10.1111/j.1467-8624.2005.00833.x.

Gillespie, Nathan A, C. Robert Cloninger, Andrew C. Heath, and Nicholas G. Martin. "The Genetic and Environmental Relationship between Cloninger's Dimensions of Temperament and Character." *Personality and Individual Differences* 35, no. 8 (2003): 1931–46. https://doi.org/10.1016/s0191 -8869(03)00042-4.

Gillis, Aurélie, and Isabelle Roskam. "Daily Exhaustion and Support in Parenting: Impact on the Quality of the Parent–Child Relationship." *Journal of Child and Family Studies* 28, no. 7 (2019): 2007–16. https://doi.org/10.1007 /s10826-019-01428-2.

Givens Rolland, Rebecca. "Synthesizing the Evidence on Classroom Goal Structures in Middle and Secondary Schools." *Review of Educational Research* 82, no. 4 (2012): 396–435. https://doi.org/10.3102/003465431 2464909.

Glăveanu, Vlad. "Creativity and Global Citizenship Education." In *Global Citizenship Education*. Edited by Abdeljalil Akkari and Kathrine Maleq, 191–202. Cham, Switzerland: Springer, 2020. https://doi.org/10.1007/978 -3-030-44617-8_14.

Gleason, Jean Berko, and Sandra Weintraub. "The Acquisition of Routines in Child Language." *Language in Society* 5, no. 2 (1976): 129–36. https://doi .org/10.1017/s0047404500006977.

Glick, Gary C., and Amanda J. Rose. "Prospective Associations between Friendship Adjustment and Social Strategies: Friendship as a Context for Building Social Skills." *Developmental Psychology* 47, no. 4 (2011): 1117–32. https://doi.org/10.1037/a0023277.

Godin, Seth. *The Dip: A Little Book That Teaches You When to Quit (and When to Stick)*. New York: Portfolio, 2007.

Goetz, Peggy J. "The Effects of Bilingualism on Theory of Mind Development." *Bilingualism: Language and Cognition* 6, no. 1 (2003): 1–15. https://doi.org/10.1017/s1366728903001007.

Goleman, Daniel. "Hot to Help." *Greater Good*, March 1, 2008. https:// greatergood.berkeley.edu/article/item/hot_to_help.

Golinkoff, Roberta Michnick, Erika Hoff, Meredith L. Rowe, Catherine S. Tamis-LeMonda, and Kathy Hirsh-Pasek. "Language Matters: Denying the Existence of the 30-Million-Word Gap Has Serious Consequences." *Child Development* 90, no. 3 (2018): 985–92. https://doi.org/10.1111 /cdev.13128.

Golinkoff, Roberta Michnick, Kathy Hirsh-Pasek, Laura E. Berk, and Dorothy Singer. "Sharing the Science: From the Lab to the Classroom." *PsycEXTRA Dataset*, 2009. https://doi.org/10.1037/e516472011-003.

Gong, Diankun, Hui He, Dongbo Liu, Weiyi Ma, Li Dong, Cheng Luo, and Dezhong Yao. "Enhanced Functional Connectivity and Increased Gray Matter Volume of Insula Related to Action Video Game Playing." *Scientific Reports* 5, no. 9763 (2015). https://www.nature.com/articles /srep09763.

Goodboy, Alan K., Matthew M. Martin, and Christine E. Rittenour. "Bullying as an Expression of Intolerant Schemas." *Journal of Child & Adolescent Trauma* 9, no. 4 (2016): 277–82. https://doi.org/10.1007/s40653 -016-0089-9.

Goodwin, Gwen. "Well Played: The Origins and Future of Playfulness." *American Journal of Play* 6, no. 2 (Winter 2014): 234-66.

Gopnik, Alison. *The Gardener and the Carpenter.* New York: Farrar, Straus & Giroux, 2016.

Gordon, Jenny. "Inadvertent Complicity: Colorblindness in Teacher Education." *Educational Studies* 38, no. 2 (2005): 135–53. https://doi.org/10.1207/s153 26993es3802_5.

Goswami, Haridhan. "Social Relationships and Children's Subjective Well-Being." *Social Indicators Research* 107, no. 3 (2011): 575–88. https://doi.org /10.1007/s11205-011-9864-z.

Graber, Rebecca, Rhiannon Turner, and Anna Madill. "Best Friends and Better Coping: Facilitating Psychological Resilience through Boys' and Girls' Closest Friendships." *British Journal of Psychology* 107, no. 2 (2015): 338–58. https://doi.org/10.1111/bjop.12135.

Gülgöz, Selin, Jessica J. Glazier, Elizabeth A. Enright, Daniel J. Alonso, Lily J. Durwood, Anne A. Fast, Riley Lowe, et al. "Similarity in Transgender and Cisgender Children's Gender Development." *Proceedings of the National Academy of Sciences* 116, no. 49 (2019): 24480–85. https://doi.org/10.1073 /pnas.1909367116.

Gupta, Arpana, Dawn M. Szymanski, and Frederick T. Leong. "The 'Model Minority Myth': Internalized Racialism of Positive Stereotypes as Correlates of Psychological Distress, and Attitudes toward Help-Seeking." *Asian American Journal of Psychology* 2, no. 2 (2011): 101–14. https://doi.org /10.1037/a0024183.

Guralnick, Michael J., Brian Neville, Mary A. Hammond, and Robert T. Connor. "Linkages between Delayed Children's Social Interactions with Mothers and Peers." *Child Development* 78, no. 2 (2007): 459–73. https:// doi.org/10.1111/j.1467-8624.2007.01009.x.

Hale, Courtney Melinda, and Helen Tager-Flusberg. "The Influence of Language on Theory of Mind: a Training Study." *Developmental Science* 6, no. 3 (2003): 346–59. https://doi.org/10.1111/1467-7687.00289.

Hamilton, Megan-Brette, Eusabia V. Mont, and Cameron McLain. "Deletion, Omission, Reduction: Redefining the Language We Use to Talk About African American English." *Perspectives of the ASHA Special Interest Groups* 3, no. 1 (2018): 107–17. https://doi.org/10.1044/persp3.sig1.107.

Hamm, Michele P., Amanda S. Newton, Annabritt Chisholm, Jocelyn Shulhan, Andrea Milne, Purnima Sundar, Heather Ennis, Shannon D. Scott, and Lisa Hartling. "Prevalence and Effect of Cyberbullying on Children and Young People." *JAMA Pediatrics* 169, no. 8 (January 2015): 770–77. https://doi.org/10.1001/jamapediatrics.2015.0944.

Hammer, David, and Emily van Zee. *Seeing the Science in Children's Thinking: Case Studies of Student Inquiry in Physical Science.* Portsmouth, NH: Heinemann, 2006.

Harcourt, Susan, Marieke Jasperse, and Vanessa A. Green. "'We Were Sad and We Were Angry': A Systematic Review of Parents' Perspectives on Bullying." *Child & Youth Care Forum* 43, no. 3 (2014): 373–91. https://doi .org/10.1007/s10566-014-9243-4.

Hargrave, Anne C., and Monique Sénéchal. "A Book Reading Intervention with Preschool Children Who Have Limited Vocabularies: the Benefits of Regular Reading and Dialogic Reading." *Early Childhood Research Quarterly* 15, no. 1 (2000): 75–90. https://doi.org/10.1016/s0885-2006(99)00038-1.

Harness Goodwin, Marjorie. "Exclusion in Girls' Peer Groups: Ethnographic Analysis of Language Practices on the Playground." *Human Development* 45, no. 6 (2002): 392–415. https://doi.org/10.1159/000066260.

Harris, Paul L., Marc de Rosnay, and Francisco Pons. "Language and Children's Understanding of Mental States." *Current Directions in Psychological Science* 14, no. 2 (2005): 69–73. https://doi.org/10.1111/j.0963-7214.2005.00337.x.

Hart, Betty, and Todd Risley. *Meaningful Differences in the Everyday Experience of Young American Children.* Baltimore, MD: Brookes Publishing Co., 1995.

Hartl, Amy C., Dawn DeLay, Brett Laursen, Jill Denner, Linda Werner, Shannon Campe, and Eloy Ortiz. "Dyadic Instruction for Middle School Students: Liking Promotes Learning." *Learning and Individual Differences* 44 (2015): 33–39. https://doi.org/10.1016/j.lindif.2015.11.002.

Hartman, Sarah, and Jay Belsky. "Prenatal Programming of Postnatal Plasticity." *Prenatal Stress and Child Development*, 2021, 349–85. https://doi .org/10.1007/978-3-030-60159-1_13.

Hatfield, Elaine, John T. Cacioppo, and Richard L. Rapson. "Emotional Contagion." *Current Directions in Psychological Science* 2, no. 3 (1993): 96–100. https://doi.org/10.1111/1467-8721.ep10770953.

Hawley, Patricia H. "Social Dominance and Prosocial and Coercive Strategies of Resource Control in Preschoolers." *International Journal of Behavioral Development* 26, no. 2 (2002): 167–76. https://doi.org/10.1080/0165025 0042000726.

Hawley, Patricia. "Prosocial and Coercive Configurations of Resource Control in Early Adolescence: A Case for the Well-Adapted Machiavellian." *Merrill-Palmer Quarterly* 49, no. 3 (2003): 279–309. https://doi.org/10.1353/mpq .2003.0013.

Hawley, Patricia H., Todd D. Little, and Noel A. Card. "The Allure of a Mean Friend: Relationship Quality and Processes of Aggressive Adolescents with Prosocial Skills." *International Journal of Behavioral Development* 31, no. 2 (2007): 170–80. https://doi.org/10.1177/0165025407074630.

Heathers, Glen. "Emotional Dependence and Independence in Nursery School Play." *Journal of Genetic Psychology* 87, no. 1 (1955): 37–57. https://doi.org/10 .1080/00221325.1955.10532914.

Helm, Bennett. "Friendship." Stanford Encyclopedia of Philosophy (Stanford University), July 30, 2021. https://plato.stanford.edu/entries/friendship/#1.1.

Hill, David R., Seth A. King, Christopher J. Lemons, and Jane N. Partanen. "Fidelity of Implementation and Instructional Alignment in Response to Intervention Research." *Learning Disabilities Research & Practice* 27, no. 3 (2012): 116–24. https://doi.org/10.1111/j.1540-5826.2012.00357.x.

Hirsh-Pasek, Kathy, Lauren B. Adamson, Roger Bakeman, Margaret Tresch Owen, Roberta Michnick Golinkoff, Amy Pace, Paula K.S. Yust, and Katharine Suma. "The Contribution of Early Communication Quality to Low-Income Children's Language Success." *Psychological Science* 26, no. 7 (May 2015): 1071–83. https://doi.org/10.1177/0956797615581493.

Hirsh-Pasek, Kathy, Rebecca M. Alper, and Roberta Michnick Golinkoff. "Living in Pasteur's Quadrant: How Conversational Duets Spark Language at Home and in the Community." *Discourse Processes* 55, no. 4 (March 2018): 338–45. https://doi.org/10.1080/0163853x.2018.1442114.

Hirsh-Pasek, Kathy, Roberta M. Golinkoff, and Diane E. Eyer. *Einstein Never Used Flash Cards: How Our Children Really Learn—And Why They Need to Play More and Memorize Less.* New York: Rodale, 2004.

Hirsh-Pasek, Kathy, Roberta Michnick Golinkoff, Laura E, Berk, and Dorothy Singer. *A Mandate for Playful Learning in Preschool.* Oxford: Oxford University Press, 2008. https://doi.org/10.1093/acprof:oso/9780195382716.001.0001.

Ho, Cheuk Yin. "Better Health with More Friends: The Role of Social Capital in Producing Health." *Health Economics* 25, no. 1 (2014): 91–100. https://doi.org/10.1002/hec.3131.

Hoff, Erika. "The Specificity of Environmental Influence: Socioeconomic Status Affects Early Vocabulary Development Via Maternal Speech." *Child Development* 74, no. 5 (2003): 1368–78. https://doi.org/10.1111/1467-8624.00612.

Hoffmann, Jessica D., Marc A. Brackett, Craig S. Bailey, and Cynthia J. Willner. "Teaching Emotion Regulation in Schools: Translating Research into Practice with the RULER Approach to Social and Emotional Learning." *Emotion* 20, no. 1 (2020): 105–9. https://doi.org/10.1037/emo0000649.

Hogan, Tiffany P., Hugh W. Catts, and Todd D. Little. "The Relationship Between Phonological Awareness and Reading." *Language, Speech, and Hearing Services in Schools* 36, no. 4 (2005): 285–93. https://doi.org/10.1044/0161-1461(2005/029).

Holder, Mark D., and Ben Coleman. "Children's Friendships and Positive Well-Being." *Friendship and Happiness* (2015): 81–97. https://doi.org/10.1007/978-94-017-9603-3_5.

Holder, Mark D., and Ben Coleman. "The Contribution of Social Relationships to Children's Happiness." *Journal of Happiness Studies* 10, no. 3 (2007): 329–49. https://doi.org/10.1007/s10902-007-9083-0.

Hooper, Frank H. "Piaget's Conservation Tasks: The Logical and Development Priority of Identity Conservation." *Journal of Experimental*

Child Psychology 8, no. 2 (1969): 234–49. https://doi.org/10.1016/0022
-0965(69)90098-8.

Hsu, Hui-Chin, and Alan Fogel. "Infant Vocal Development in a Dynamic
Mother-Infant Communication System." *Infancy* 2, no. 1 (January 2001):
87–109. https://doi.org/10.1207/s15327078in0201_6.

Hubert, Sarah, and Isabelle Aujoulat. "Parental Burnout: When Exhausted
Mothers Open Up." *Frontiers in Psychology* 9 (2018). https://doi.org/10.3389
/fpsyg.2018.01021.

Hughes, Claire, Rory T. Devine, and Zhenlin Wang. "Does Parental Mind-
Mindedness Account for Cross-Cultural Differences in Preschoolers'
Theory of Mind?" *Child Development* 89, no. 4 (March 2017): 1296–1310.
https://doi.org/10.1111/cdev.12746.

Isaksen, Scott G., and John P. Gaulin. "A Reexamination of Brainstorming
Research: Implications for Research and Practice." *Gifted Child Quarterly* 49,
no. 4 (2005): 315–29. https://doi.org/10.1177/001698620504900405.

Ishizuka, Patrick. "Social Class, Gender, and Contemporary Parenting
Standards in the United States: Evidence from a National Survey
Experiment." *Social Forces* 98, no. 1 (2019): 31–58. https://doi.org/10.1093
/sf/soy107.

Jacobson, David. "Interpreting Instant Messaging: Context and Meaning
in Computer-Mediated Communication." *Journal of Anthropological
Research* 63, no. 3 (2007): 359–81. https://doi.org/10.3998/jar.0521004
.0063.303.

Jacoby, Jennifer Wallace, and Nonie K. Lesaux. "Language and Literacy
Instruction in Preschool Classes That Serve Latino Dual Language
Learners." *Early Childhood Research Quarterly* 40 (2017): 77–86. https://doi
.org/10.1016/j.ecresq.2016.10.001.

Janey, David W. "Black Parents Give Their Kids 'The Talk.' What If White
Parents Did, Too?" WBUR, April 12, 2021. https://www.wbur.org
/cognoscenti/2021/04/12/the-talk-racism-black-parents-children-david
-w-janey.

Jarrett, Robin L., and Sarai Coba-Rodriguez. "'If You Have a Kid That's Ready
to Learn:' The Kindergarten Transition Experiences of Urban, Low-Income,
African-American Preschoolers." *Journal of Poverty* 23, no. 3 (2018):
229–52. https://doi.org/10.1080/10875549.2018.1555729.

Jensen, Sidsel Vive. "Difference and Closeness: Young Children's Peer
Interactions and Peer Relations in School." *Childhood* 25, no. 4 (November
2018): 501–15. https://doi.org/10.1177/0907568218803437.

Jirout, Jamie, and David Klahr. "Children's Scientific Curiosity: In Search of an
Operational Definition of an Elusive Concept." *Developmental Review* 32,
no. 2 (2012): 125–60. https://doi.org/10.1016/j.dr.2012.04.002.

Jones, Brett D. "The Unintended Outcomes of High-Stakes Testing." In *High
Stakes Testing: New Challenges and Opportunities for School Psychology*. Edited
by Louis J. Kruger and David Shriberg. New York: Routledge, 2007. https://
doi.org/10.4324/9780203836583-5.

Jones, Stephanie M., Suzanne M. Bouffard, and Richard Weissbourd. "Educators' Social and Emotional Skills Vital to Learning." *Phi Delta Kappan* 94, no. 8 (2013): 62–65. https://doi.org/10.1177/003172171309400815.

Jones-Walker, Cheryl. "Being Constructed as Different, While Teaching about Difference." *PsycEXTRA Dataset*, 2010. https://doi.org/10.1037 /e626412011-001.

Jung, Carl G. *Modern Man in Search of a Soul*. London: Routledge and Kegan Paul, 1933.

Kagan, Jerome. *Galen's Prophecy: Temperament in Human Nature*. New York: Routledge, 2019.

Kagan, Jerome, and Nancy Snidman. *The Long Shadow of Temperament*. Cambridge, MA: The Belknap Press of Harvard Univ. Press, 2004.

Kamenetz, Anya. "6 Potential Brain Benefits Of Bilingual Education." NPR, November 29, 2016. https://www.npr.org/sections/ed/2016/11/29/497943749 /6-potential-brain-benefits-of-bilingual-education.

Kapetanovic, Sabina, and Thérése Skoog. "The Role of the Family's Emotional Climate in the Links between Parent-Adolescent Communication and Adolescent Psychosocial Functioning." *Research on Child and Adolescent Psychopathology* 49, no. 2 (2020): 141–54. https://doi.org/10.1007/s10802 -020-00705-9.

Kapoula, Zoï, Sarah Ruiz, Lisa Spector, Marion Mocorovi, Chrystal Gaertner, Catherine Quilici, and Marine Vernet. "Education Influences Creativity in Dyslexic and Non-Dyslexic Children and Teenagers." *PLOS ONE* 11, no. 3 (July 2016). https://doi.org/10.1371/journal.pone.0150421.

Kärnä, Antti, Marinus Voeten, Todd D. Little, Elisa Poskiparta, Anne Kaljonen, and Christina Salmivalli. "A Large-Scale Evaluation of the KiVa Antibullying Program: Grades 4-6." *Child Development* 82, no. 1 (2011): 311–30. https://doi.org/10.1111/j.1467-8624.2010.01557.x.

Katz, Neil, and Kevin McNulty. "Reflective Listening - Syracuse University," 1994. https://www.maxwell.syr.edu/uploadedFiles/parcc/cmc/Reflective %20Listening%20NK.pdf.

Katz, P.A., and J.A. Kofkin. "Race, Gender, and Young Children." *Developmental Psychopathology: Perspectives on Adjustment, Risk, and Disorder*. Edited by S.S. Luthar, J.A. Burack, D. Cicchetti, and J.R. Weisz, 51–74. New York: Cambridge Univ. Press, 1997.

Kaye, Linda, Amy Orben, David A. Ellis, Simon C. Hunter, and Stephen Houghton. "The Conceptual and Methodological Mayhem of 'Screen Time.'" *International Journal of Environmental Research and Public Health* 17, no. 10 (2020): 3661. https://doi.org/10.3390/ijerph17103661.

Kefalianos, Elaina, Mark Onslow, Susan Block, Ross Menzies, and Sheena Reilly. "Early Stuttering, Temperament and Anxiety: Two Hypotheses." *Journal of Fluency Disorders* 37, no. 3 (2012): 151–63. https:// doi.org/10.1016/j.jfludis.2012.03.002.

Kelley, Paul, Steven W. Lockley, Russell G. Foster, and Jonathan Kelley. "Synchronizing Education to Adolescent Biology: 'Let Teens Sleep, Start

School Later.'" *Learning, Media and Technology* 40, no. 2 (2014): 210–26. https://doi.org/10.1080/17439884.2014.942666.

Kiff, Cara J., Liliana J. Lengua, and Maureen Zalewski. "Nature and Nurturing: Parenting in the Context of Child Temperament." *Clinical Child and Family Psychology Review* 14, no. 3 (February 2011): 251–301. https://doi.org/10.1007/s10567-011-0093-4.

Kiff, Cara J., Liliana J. Lengua, and Nicole R. Bush. "Temperament Variation in Sensitivity to Parenting: Predicting Changes in Depression and Anxiety." *Journal of Abnormal Child Psychology* 39, no. 8 (2011): 1199–212. https://doi.org/10.1007/s10802-011-9539-x.

Kim, Joungyoun, Yeoul Shin, Eli Tsukayama, and Daeun Park. "Stress Mindset Predicts Job Turnover among Preschool Teachers." *Journal of School Psychology* 78 (2020): 13–22. https://doi.org/10.1016/j.jsp.2019.11.002.

Kim, Kyung Hee. "The Creativity Crisis: The Decrease in Creative Thinking Scores on the Torrance Tests of Creative Thinking." *Creativity Research Journal* 23, no. 4 (2011): 285–95. https://doi.org/10.1080/10400419.2011.627805.

Kim, Paul Youngbin, and Donghun Lee. "Internalized Model Minority Myth, Asian Values, and Help-Seeking Attitudes among Asian American Students." *Cultural Diversity and Ethnic Minority Psychology* 20, no. 1 (2014): 98–106. https://doi.org/10.1037/a0033351.

Klein, Kristen M., and Mo Wang. "Deep-Level Diversity and Leadership." *American Psychologist* 65, no. 9 (2010): 932–34. https://doi.org/10.1037/a0021355.

Klein, Melanie R., Liliana J. Lengua, Stephanie F. Thompson, Lyndsey Moran, Erika J. Ruberry, Cara Kiff, and Maureen Zalewski. "Bidirectional Relations between Temperament and Parenting Predicting Preschool-Age Children's Adjustment." *Journal of Clinical Child & Adolescent Psychology* 47, no. sup1 (November 2016). https://doi.org/10.1080/15374416.2016.1169537.

Kline, Michelle Ann, Rubeena Shamsudheen, and Tanya Broesch. "Variation Is the Universal: Making Cultural Evolution Work in Developmental Psychology." *Philosophical Transactions of the Royal Society B: Biological Sciences* 373, no. 1743 (February 2018): 20170059. https://doi.org/10.1098/rstb.2017.0059.

Knafo, Ariel, Carolyn Zahn-Waxler, Carol Van Hulle, JoAnn L. Robinson, and Soo Hyun Rhee. "The Developmental Origins of a Disposition toward Empathy: Genetic and Environmental Contributions." *Emotion* 8, no. 6 (2008): 737–52. https://doi.org/10.1037/a0014179.

Kochenderfer-Ladd, Becky, and James L. Wardrop. "Chronicity and Instability of Children's Peer Victimization Experiences as Predictors of Loneliness and Social Satisfaction Trajectories." *Child Development* 72, no. 1 (2001): 134–51. https://doi.org/10.1111/1467-8624.00270.

Konrath, Sara H., Edward H. O'Brien, and Courtney Hsing. "Changes in Dispositional Empathy in American College Students Over Time: A

Meta-Analysis." *Personality and Social Psychology Review* 15, no. 2 (May 2010): 180–98. https://doi.org/10.1177/1088868310377395.

Koplewicz, Harold S. *The Scaffold Effect*. New York: Harmony Books, 2021.

Kopp, Stefan. "Social Resonance and Embodied Coordination in Face-to-Face Conversation with Artificial Interlocutors." *Speech Communication* 52, no. 6 (2010): 587–97. https://doi.org/10.1016/j.specom.2010.02.007.

Kostelnik, Marjorie J., Alice Phipps Whiren, Anne Keil Soderman, and Michelle Rupiper. *Guiding Children's Social Development & Learning: Theory and Skills*. Boston: Cengage Learning, 2018.

Kremer-Sadlik, Tamar, and Amy L. Paugh. "Everyday Moments." *Time & Society* 16, no. 2-3 (2007): 287–308. https://doi.org/10.1177/0961463x07080276.

LaBounty, Jennifer, Henry M. Wellman, Sheryl Olson, Kristin Lagattuta, and David Liu. "Mothers' *and* Fathers' Use of Internal State Talk with Their Young Children." *Social Development* 17, no. 4 (2008): 757–75. https://doi.org/10.1111/j.1467-9507.2007.00450.x.

Laible, Deborah. "Mother-Child Discourse in Two Contexts: Links with Child Temperament, Attachment Security, and Socioemotional Competence." *Developmental Psychology* 40, no. 6 (2004): 979–92. https://doi.org/10.1037/0012-1649.40.6.979.

Lakin, Jessica L., and Tanya L. Chartrand. "Using Nonconscious Behavioral Mimicry to Create Affiliation and Rapport." *Psychological Science* 14, no. 4 (2003): 334–39. https://doi.org/10.1111/1467-9280.14481.

Langkamp, Diane L., and John M. Pascoe. "Temperament of Pre Term Infants at 9 Months of Age." *Ambulatory Child Health* 7, no. 3-4 (2001): 203–12. https://doi.org/10.1046/j.1467-0658.2001.00131.x.

Lareau, Annette. "Social Class and the Daily Lives of Children." *Childhood* 7, no. 2 (2000): 155–71. https://doi.org/10.1177/0907568200007002003.

Lareau, Annette. *Unequal Childhoods: Class, Race, and Family Life*. Berkeley: Univ. of California Press, 2003.

Leaper, Campbell, Stuart T. Hauser, Adam Kremen, Sally I. Powers, Alan M. Jacobson, Gil G. Noam, Bedonna Weiss-Perry, and Donna Follansbee. "Adolescent-Parent Interactions in Relation to Adolescents' Gender and Ego Development Pathway." *Journal of Early Adolescence* 9, no. 3 (1989): 335–61. https://doi.org/10.1177/0272431689093009.

Lee, Adabel, and Benjamin L. Hankin. "Insecure Attachment, Dysfunctional Attitudes, and Low Self-Esteem Predicting Prospective Symptoms of Depression and Anxiety During Adolescence." *Journal of Clinical Child & Adolescent Psychology* 38, no. 2 (December 2009): 219–31. https://doi.org/10.1080/15374410802698396.

Lee, Erica H., Qing Zhou, Nancy Eisenberg, and Yun Wang. "Bidirectional Relations between Temperament and Parenting Styles in Chinese Children." *International Journal of Behavioral Development* 37, no. 1 (2012): 57–67. https://doi.org/10.1177/0165025412460795.

Lee, Regina, Shelly Lane, Anson Tang, Cynthia Leung, Stephen Kwok, Lobo

Louie, Graeme Browne, and Sally Chan. "Effects of an Unstructured Free Play and Mindfulness Intervention on Wellbeing in Kindergarten Students." *International Journal of Environmental Research and Public Health* 17, no. 15 (2020): 5382. https://doi.org/10.3390/ijerph17155382.

Lee, Soo Jin, Soo Hyun Park, and Han Chae. "Biopsychological Structure of Yin-Yang Using Cloninger's Temperament Model and Carver and White's BIS/BAS Scale." *PeerJ* 4 (2016). https://doi.org/10.7717/peerj.2021.

Lei, Ryan F., Emily R. Green, Sarah-Jane Leslie, and Marjorie Rhodes. "Children Lose Confidence in Their Potential to 'Be Scientists,' but Not in Their Capacity to 'Do Science.'" *Developmental Science* 22, no. 6 (August 2019). https://doi.org/10.1111/desc.12837.

Lemmer, Sophie-Charlotte. "Alexa, Are You Friends with My Kid? Smart Speakers and Children's Privacy Under the GDPR." *SSRN Electronic Journal*, 2020. https://doi.org/10.2139/ssrn.3627478.

Lengua, Liliana J., and Erica A. Kovacs. "Bidirectional Associations between Temperament and Parenting and the Prediction of Adjustment Problems in Middle Childhood." *Journal of Applied Developmental Psychology* 26, no. 1 (2005): 21–38. https://doi.org/10.1016/j.appdev.2004.10.001.

Lesaux, Nonie K., Julie Russ Harris, and Phoebe Sloane. "Adolescents' Motivation in the Context of an Academic Vocabulary Intervention in Urban Middle School Classrooms." *Journal of Adolescent & Adult Literacy* 56, no. 3 (2012): 231–40. https://doi.org/10.1002/jaal.00132.

Lesaux, Nonie K., Stephanie Jones, Kristen Paratore Bock, and Julie Russ Harris. "The Regulated Learning Environment: Supporting Adults to Support Children." *Young Children* 70, no. 5 (2015): 20–27. https://www.jstor.org/stable/ycyoungchildren.70.5.20.

"The Let Grow Project." Let Grow. Accessed April 13, 2021. https://letgrow.org/program/the-let-grow-project/.

Levy, Jonathan, Abraham Goldstein, and Ruth Feldman. "The Neural Development of Empathy Is Sensitive to Caregiving and Early Trauma." *Nature Communications* 10, no. 1 (2019). https://doi.org/10.1038/s41467-019-09927-y.

Levy, Sheri R., and Melanie Killen. *Intergroup Attitudes and Relations in Childhood Through Adulthood.*: Oxford Univ. Press, 2010.

Lewis, C.S. *The Four Loves.* San Francisco: HarperOne, 2017.

Leyshon, Cressida. "This Week in Fiction: Mohsin Hamid." *The New Yorker*, September 16, 2012. https://www.newyorker.com/books/page-turner/this-week-in-fiction-mohsin-hamid.

Li, Yan, and Michelle F. Wright. "Adolescents' Social Status Goals: Relationships to Social Status Insecurity, Aggression, and Prosocial Behavior." *Journal of Youth and Adolescence* 43, no. 1 (2013): 146–60. https://doi.org/10.1007/s10964-013-9939-z.

Li Grining, Christine, C. Cybele Raver, Kina Champion, Latriese Sardin, Molly Metzger, and Stephanie M. Jones. "Understanding and Improving

Classroom Emotional Climate and Behavior Management in the 'Real World': The Role of Head Start Teachers' Psychosocial Stressors." *Early Education & Development* 21, no. 1 (2010): 65–94. https://doi.org/10.1080/10409280902783509.

Liu, Jianghong, Rui Feng, Xiaopeng Ji, Naixue Cui, Adrian Raine, and Sara C Mednick. "Midday Napping in Children: Associations between Nap Frequency and Duration across Cognitive, Positive Psychological Well-Being, Behavioral, and Metabolic Health Outcomes." *Sleep* 42, no. 9 (2019). https://doi.org/10.1093/sleep/zsz126.

Lindsey, Eric W., and Yvonne M. Caldera. "Shared Affect and Dyadic Synchrony among Secure and Insecure Parent-Toddler Dyads." *Infant and Child Development* 24, no. 4 (2014): 394–413. https://doi.org/10.1002/icd.1893.

"List of Dyslexic Achievers." Dyslexia the Gift. Accessed May 29, 2021. https://www.dyslexia.com/about-dyslexia/dyslexic-achievers/all-achievers/.

Livingston, Emily M., Linda S. Siegel, and Urs Ribary. "Developmental Dyslexia: Emotional Impact and Consequences." *Australian Journal of Learning Difficulties* 23, no. 2 (2018): 107–35. https://doi.org/10.1080/19404158.2018.1479975.

Lockl, Kathrin, and Wolfgang Schneider. "Precursors of Metamemory in Young Children: The Role of Theory of Mind and Metacognitive Vocabulary." *Metacognition and Learning* 1 (2006): 15–31. https://doi.org/10.1007/s11409-006-6585-9.

Loewus, Liana. "For Parents Confused by Common-Core Math, Ask the Teacher for Help." Education Week, January 7, 2016. https://www.edweek.org/teaching-learning/for-parents-confused-by-common-core-math-ask-the-teacher-for-help/2016/01.

Lonczak, Heather S. "Catastrophizing and Decatastrophizing: A PositivePsychology.com Guide." PositivePsychology.com, October 7, 2020. https://positivepsychology.com/catastrophizing/.

Lu, Peiqi, Jeewon Oh, Katelin E. Leahy, and William J. Chopik. "Friendship Importance Around the World: Links to Cultural Factors, Health, and Well-Being." *Frontiers in Psychology* 11 (2021). https://doi.org/10.3389/fpsyg.2020.570839.

Lucadamo, Kathleen. "Back off Parents: It's Not Your Job to Teach Common Core Math When Helping with Homework." *Hechinger Report*, January 5, 2016. https://hechingerreport.org/back-off-parents-its-not-your-job-to-teach-common-core-math-when-helping-with-homework/.

Luk, Gigi, and Ellen Bialystok. "Bilingualism Is Not a Categorical Variable: Interaction Between Language Proficiency and Usage." *Journal of Cognitive Psychology* 25, no. 5 (2013): 605–21. https://doi.org/10.1080/20445911.2013.795574.

Luthar, Suniya S., and Shawn J. Latendresse. "Children of the Affluent: Challenges to Well-Being." *Current Directions in Psychological Science* 14, no. 1 (2005): 49–53. https://doi.org/10.1111/j.0963-7214.2005.00333.x.

Luthar, Suniya S., Nina L. Kumar, and Nicole Zillmer. "High-Achieving Schools Connote Risks for Adolescents: Problems Documented, Processes Implicated, and Directions for Interventions." *American Psychologist* 75, no. 7 (2020): 983–95. https://doi.org/10.1037/amp0000556.

Maccoby, Eleanor E. "Gender and Relationships: A Developmental Account." *American Psychologist* 45, no. 4 (1990): 513–20. https://doi.org/10.1037/0003 -066x.45.4.513.

Mafessoni, Fabrizio, and Michael Lachmann. "The Complexity of Understanding Others as the Evolutionary Origin of Empathy and Emotional Contagion." *Scientific Reports* 9, no. 5794 (2019). https://www.nature.com/articles /s41598-019-41835-5.

Making Caring Common. Accessed June 7, 2021. https://mcc.gse.harvard.edu/.

Mangels, Jennifer A., Brady Butterfield, Justin Lamb, Catherine Good, and Carol S. Dweck. "Why Do Beliefs About Intelligence Influence Learning Success? A Social Cognitive Neuroscience Model." *Social Cognitive and Affective Neuroscience* 1, no. 2 (January 2006): 75–86. https://doi.org/10.1093 /scan/nsl013.

Mansukhani, Sasha, Mai-Lan Ho, Elizabeth A. Bradley, and Michael C. Brodsky. "Accelerated Visual Recovery from Protracted Hypoxic Cortical Blindness in a Child." *American Journal of Ophthalmology Case Reports* 16 (2019): 100534. https://doi.org/10.1016/j.ajoc.2019.100534.

Martin, Grace B., and Russell D. Clark. "Distress Crying in Neonates: Species and Peer Specificity." *Developmental Psychology* 18, no. 1 (1982): 3–9. https:// doi.org/10.1037/0012-1649.18.1.3.

Martín-Antón, Luis J., María Inés Monjas, Francisco J. García Bacete, and Irene Jiménez-Lagares. "Problematic Social Situations for Peer-Rejected Students in the First Year of Elementary School." *Frontiers in Psychology* 7 (2016). https://doi.org/10.3389/fpsyg.2016.01925.

Matusov, Eugene, and Renee Hayes. "Sociocultural Critique of Piaget and Vygotsky." *New Ideas in Psychology* 18, no. 2-3 (2000): 215–39. https://doi .org/10.1016/s0732-118x(00)00009-x.

Maunder, Rachel, and Claire P. Monks. "Friendships in Middle Childhood: Links to Peer and School Identification, and General Self-Worth." *British Journal of Developmental Psychology* 37, no. 2 (2018): 211–29. https://doi.org /10.1111/bjdp.12268.

Mayeux, Lara, Amy D. Bellmore, and Antonius H.N. Cillessen. "Predicting Changes in Adjustment Using Repeated Measures of Sociometric Status." *Journal of Genetic Psychology* 168, no. 4 (January 2007): 401–24. https://doi .org/10.3200/gntp.168.4.401-424.

Mayfield, Vernita. "Learning to Challenge Racial 'Colorblindness.'" *Educational Leadership*, February 1, 2021. https://www.ascd.org/el/articles /learning-to-challenge-racial-colorblindness.

McAdams, Dan P. *The Redemptive Self: Stories Americans Live By.* New York: Oxford Univ. Press, 2013.

McCloud, Carol. *Have You Filled a Bucket Today?: A Guide to Daily Happiness.* Chicago: Bucket Fillers, Inc., 2015.

McClowry, Sandra Graham. *Your Child's Unique Temperament: Insights and Strategies for Responsive Parenting.* Champaign, IL: Research Press, 2003.

McGonigal, Jane. *SuperBetter: How a Gameful Life Can Make You Stronger, Happier, Braver and More Resilient.* London: HarperThorsons, 2016.

McKinnon, Rachel D., Allison Friedman-Krauss, Amanda L. Roy, and C. Cybele Raver. "Teacher–Child Relationships in the Context of Poverty: The Role of Frequent School Mobility." *Journal of Children and Poverty* 24, no. 1 (February 2018): 25–46. https://doi.org/10.1080/10796126.2018.1434761.

McLaughlin, Katie A., Margaret A. Sheridan, Florin Tibu, Nathan A. Fox, Charles H. Zeanah, and Charles A. Nelson. "Causal Effects of the Early Caregiving Environment on Development of Stress Response Systems in Children." *Proceedings of the National Academy of Sciences* 112, no. 18 (2015): 5637–42. https://doi.org/10.1073/pnas.1423363112.

McMahon, Catherine A., and Elizabeth Meins. "Mind Mindedness, Parenting Stress, and Emotional Availability in Mothers of Preschoolers." *Early Childhood Research Quarterly* 27, no. 2 (2012): 245–52. https://doi.org/10.1016/j.ecresq.2011.08.002.

Menting, Barbara, Pol A.C. van Lier, and Hans M. Koot. "Language Skills, Peer Rejection, and the Development of Externalizing Behavior from Kindergarten to Fourth Grade." *Journal of Child Psychology and Psychiatry* 52, no. 1 (2010): 72–9. https://doi.org/10.1111/j.1469-7610.2010.02279.x.

Miczajka, Victoria L., Alexandra-Maria Klein, and Gesine Pufal. "Elementary School Children Contribute to Environmental Research as Citizen Scientists." *PLOS ONE* 10, no. 11 (2015). https://doi.org/10.1371/journal.pone.0143229.

Milkie, Melissa A., Kei M. Nomaguchi, and Kathleen E. Denny. "Does the Amount of Time Mothers Spend With Children or Adolescents Matter?" *Journal of Marriage and Family* 77, no. 2 (2015): 355–72. https://doi.org/10.1111/jomf.12170.

Miller, G.E., E. Chen, A.K. Fok, H. Walker, A. Lim, E.F. Nicholls, S. Cole, and M.S. Kobor. "Low Early-Life Social Class Leaves a Biological Residue Manifested by Decreased Glucocorticoid and Increased Proinflammatory Signaling." *Proceedings of the National Academy of Sciences* 106, no. 34 (2009): 14716–21. https://doi.org/10.1073/pnas.0902971106.

Moffitt, Ursula, Linda P. Juang, and Moin Syed. "Intersectionality and Youth Identity Development Research in Europe." *Frontiers in Psychology* 11 (2020). https://doi.org/10.3389/fpsyg.2020.00078.

Mok, Pearl L.H., Andrew Pickles, Kevin Durkin, and Gina Conti-Ramsden. "Longitudinal Trajectories of Peer Relations in Children With Specific Language Impairment." *Journal of Child Psychology and Psychiatry* 55, no. 5 (November 2014): 516–27. https://doi.org/10.1111/jcpp.12190.

Montaigne, Michel de, and Marvin Lowenthal. *The Autobiography of Michel De Montaigne.* London: Routledge, 1935.

Montessori, Maria. *The Advanced Montessori Method. Spontaneous Activity in Education*. Cambridge, MA: R. Bentley, 1964.

Montessori, Maria, and Claude Albert Claremont. *The Absorbent Mind*. New York: Dell, 1967.

Morgan, Paul L., and Catherine R. Meier. "Dialogic Reading's Potential to Improve Children's Emergent Literacy Skills and Behavior." *Preventing School Failure: Alternative Education for Children and Youth* 52, no. 4 (2008): 11–16. https://doi.org/10.3200/psfl.52.4.11-16.

Mueller, Claudia M., and Carol S. Dweck. "Praise for Intelligence Can Undermine Children's Motivation and Performance." *Journal of Personality and Social Psychology* 75, no. 1 (1998): 33–52. https://doi.org/10.1037/0022 -3514.75.1.33.

Muenks, Katherine, Allan Wigfield, Ji Seung Yang, and Colleen R. O'Neal. "How True Is Grit? Assessing Its Relations to High School and College Students' Personality Characteristics, Self-Regulation, Engagement, and Achievement." *Journal of Educational Psychology* 109, no. 5 (2017): 599–620. https://doi.org/10.1037/edu0000153.

Multon, Karen D., Steven D. Brown, and Robert W. Lent. "Relation of Self-Efficacy Beliefs to Academic Outcomes: A Meta-Analytic Investigation." *Journal of Counseling Psychology* 38, no. 1 (1991): 30–38. https://doi.org/10.1037/0022-0167.38.1.30.

Munzer, Tiffany G., Alison L. Miller, Heidi M. Weeks, Niko Kaciroti, and Jenny Radesky. "Differences in Parent-Toddler Interactions With Electronic versus Print Books." American Academy of Pediatrics, April 1, 2019. https://pediatrics.aappublications.org/content/143/4/e20182012.

Myruski, Sarah, Olga Gulyayeva, Samantha Birk, Koraly Pérez-Edgar, Kristin A. Buss, and Tracy A. Dennis-Tiwary. "Digital Disruption? Maternal Mobile Device Use Is Related to Infant Social-Emotional Functioning." *Developmental Science* 21, no. 4 (2017). https://doi.org/10.1111/desc.12610.

Nagy, William, and Dianna Townsend. "Words as Tools: Learning Academic Vocabulary as Language Acquisition." *Reading Research Quarterly* 47, no. 1 (2012): 91–108. https://doi.org/10.1002/rrq.011.

Nation, Kate, and Margaret Snowling. "Assessing Reading Difficulties: the Validity and Utility of Current Measures of Reading Skill." *British Journal of Educational Psychology* 67, no. 3 (1997): 359–70. https://doi.org/10.1111/j .2044-8279.1997.tb01250.x.

National Scientific Council on the Developing Child. "Supportive Relationships and Active Skill-Building Strengthen the Foundations of Resilience: Working Paper No. 13." 2015. https://developingchild.harvard .edu/resources/supportive-relationships-and-active-skill-building-strengthen -the-foundations-of-resilience/.

Neff, Kristin. *Self-Compassion: The Proven Power of Being Kind to Yourself*. New York: William Morrow, 2015.

Neff, Kristin D., and Daniel J. Faso. "Self-Compassion and Well-Being in

Parents of Children with Autism." *Mindfulness* 6, no. 4 (August 2014): 938–47. https://doi.org/10.1007/s12671-014-0359-2.

Neijenhuis, Karin, Nicole G. Campbell, Martin Cromb, Margreet R. Luinge, David R. Moore, Stuart Rosen, and Ellen de Wit. "An Evidence-Based Perspective on 'Misconceptions' Regarding Pediatric Auditory Processing Disorder." *Frontiers in Neurology* 10 (March 2019). https://doi.org/10.3389 /fneur.2019.00287.

Nelson, Soraya Sarhaddi. "Germany Bans 'My Friend Cayla' Doll Over Spying Concerns." NPR, February 20, 2017. https://www.npr.org/2017/02/20 /516292295/germany-bans-my-friend-cayla-doll-over-spying-concerns.

Nerenberg, Jenara. *Divergent Mind: Thriving in a World That Wasn't Designed for You*. New York: HarperOne, 2021.

Nett, Ulrike E., Thomas Goetz, Nathan C. Hall, and Anne C. Frenzel. "Metacognitive Strategies and Test Performance: An Experience Sampling Analysis of Students' Learning Behavior." *Education Research International 2012*, November 1, 2012. https://www.hindawi.com/journals/edri/2012/958319/.

Neubauer, Andreas B., Andrea Schmidt, Andrea C. Kramer, and Florian Schmiedek. "A Little Autonomy Support Goes a Long Way: Daily Autonomy-Supportive Parenting, Child Well-Being, Parental Need Fulfillment, and Change in Child, Family, and Parent Adjustment Across the Adaptation to the COVID-19 Pandemic." *Child Development*, 2021. https://doi.org/10.1111/cdev.13515.

Neuenschwander, Regula, Allison Friedman-Krauss, Cybele Raver, and Clancy Blair. "Teacher Stress Predicts Child Executive Function: Moderation by School Poverty." *Early Education and Development* 28, no. 7 (2017): 880–900. https://doi.org/10.1080/10409289.2017.1287993.

Newland, Rebecca P., and Keith A. Crnic. "Developmental Risk and Goodness of Fit in the Mother-Child Relationship: Links to Parenting Stress and Children's Behaviour Problems." *Infant and Child Development* 26, no. 2 (October 2016). https://doi.org/10.1002/icd.1980.

Newport, Cal. *Digital Minimalism: Choosing a Focused Life in a Noisy World*. London: Penguin Business, 2020.

Nichols, Sara R., Margarita Svetlova, and Celia A. Brownell. "Toddlers' Responses to Infants' Negative Emotions." *Infancy* 20, no. 1 (April 2014): 70–97. https://doi.org/10.1111/infa.12066.

Nieto, Sonia. *Language, Culture, and Teaching*. New York: Routledge, 2017.

Ninio, Anat, and Catherine E. Snow. *Pragmatic Development*. New York: Routledge, 1996. https://doi.org/10.4324/9780429498053-7.

"No Time for Recess, No Need for Nap." FairTest. Accessed June 9, 2021. https://www.fairtest.org/no-time-recess-no-need-nap.

Nolen-Hoeksema, Susan, Joan S. Girgus, and Martin E. Seligman. "Learned Helplessness in Children: A Longitudinal Study of Depression, Achievement, and Explanatory Style." *Journal of Personality and Social Psychology* 51, no. 2 (1986): 435–42. https://doi.org/10.1037/0022-3514.51.2.435.

Nore, Gordon. "This Is Why Young Children Need to Explore Gender Identity in the Classroom." Today's Parent, August 23, 2019. https://www.todaysparent .com/kids/school-age/young-children-need-to-learn-gender-identity/.

Nørgård, Rikke Toft, Claus Toft-Nielsen, and Nicola Whitton. "Playful Learning in Higher Education: Developing a Signature Pedagogy." *International Journal of Play* 6, no. 3 (February 2017): 272–82. https://doi .org/10.1080/21594937.2017.1382997.

Novotney, Amy. "Understanding Our Personalities Requires a Lesson in History." *Monitor on Psychology* 39, no. 11 (December 2008). https://www .apa.org/monitor/2008/12/kagan.

O'Connor, Rollanda E., Annika White, and H. Lee Swanson. "Repeated Reading versus Continuous Reading: Influences on Reading Fluency and Comprehension." *Exceptional Children* 74, no. 1 (2007): 31–46. https://doi .org/10.1177/001440290707400102.

Odell, Jenny. *How to Do Nothing: Resisting the Attention Economy*. New York: Melville House, 2019.

Orben, Amy, and Andrew K. Przybylski. "The Association between Adolescent Well-Being and Digital Technology Use." *Nature Human Behaviour* 3, no. 2 (2019): 173–82. https://doi.org/10.1038/s41562-018-0506-1.

Ornaghi, Veronica, Elisabetta Conte, and Ilaria Grazzani. "Empathy in Toddlers: The Role of Emotion Regulation, Language Ability, and Maternal Emotion Socialization Style." *Frontiers in Psychology* 11 (2020). https://doi .org/10.3389/fpsyg.2020.586862.

Ottmar, Erin R., Sara E. Rimm-Kaufman, Robert Q. Berry, and Ross A. Larsen. "Does the Responsive Classroom Approach Affect the Use of Standards-Based Mathematics Teaching Practices?" *Elementary School Journal* 113, no. 3 (2013): 434–57. https://doi.org/10.1086/668768.

Overton, Sheri, and John L. Rausch. "Peer Relationships as Support for Children with Disabilities." *Focus on Autism and Other Developmental Disabilities* 17, no. 1 (2002): 11–29. https://doi.org/10.1177/108835760201700102.

Pajares, Frank. "Self-Efficacy Beliefs in Academic Settings." *Review of Educational Research* 66, no. 4 (1996): 543–78. https://doi.org/10.3102 /00346543066004543.

Paley, Jennifer. "Praising Intelligence: Costs to Children's Self-Esteem and Motivation." Bing Nursery School, October 1, 2011. https://bingschool .stanford.edu/news/praising-intelligence-costs-childrens-self-esteem-and -motivation.

Parris, Dominique, Victor St. John, and Jessica Dym Bartlett. "Resources to Support Children's Emotional Well-Being Amid Anti-Black Racism, Racial Violence, and Trauma." Child Trends, June 23, 2020. https://www .childtrends.org/publications/resources-to-support-childrens-emotional -well-being-amid-anti-black-racism-racial-violence-and-trauma.

Pasnak, Robert. "Empirical Studies of Patterning." *Psychology* 08, no. 13 (2017): 2276–93. https://doi.org/10.4236/psych.2017.813144.

Patchin, Justin W. "New National Bullying and Cyberbullying Statistics." Cyberbullying Research Center, October 10, 2016. https://cyberbullying .org/new-national-bullying-cyberbullying-data.

Pea, Roy, Clifford Nass, Lyn Meheula, Marcus Rance, Aman Kumar, Holden Bamford, Matthew Nass, et al. "Media Use, Face-to-Face Communication, Media Multitasking, and Social Well-Being among 8- to 12-Year-Old Girls." *Developmental Psychology* 48, no. 2 (2012): 327–36. https://doi.org /10.1037/a0027030.

Pearson, P. David, and Margaret C. Gallagher. "The Instruction of Reading Comprehension." *Contemporary Educational Psychology* 8, no. 3 (1983): 317–44. https://doi.org/10.1016/0361-476x(83)90019-x.

Perrin, Andrew. "5 Facts about Americans and Video Games." Pew Research Center, September 17, 2018. https://www.pewresearch.org/fact-tank/2018 /09/17/5-facts-about-americans-and-video-games/.

Piaget, Jean. "Quantification, Conservation, and Nativism." *Science* 162, no. 3857 (1968): 976–79. https://doi.org/10.1126/science.162.3857.976.

Piaget, Jean. *The Origins of Intelligence in Children*. New York: International Universities Press, 1952.

Piaget, Jean. "The Role of Action in the Development of Thinking." In *Knowledge and Development*. Edited by Willis F. Overton and Jeanette M. Gallagher, 17–42. Boston: Springer, 1977. https://doi.org/10.1007/978-1-4684-2547-5_2.

Piaget, Jean, and Barbel Inhelder. *The Growth of Logical Thinking from Childhood to Adolescence: An Essay on the Construction of Formal Operational Structures*. New York: Basic Books, 1958.

Pickering, Martin J., and Simon Garrod. "Alignment as the Basis for Successful Communication." *Research on Language and Computation* 4, no. 2-3 (2006): 203–28. https://doi.org/10.1007/s11168-006-9004-0.

Pickering, Martin J., and Simon Garrod. "Toward a Mechanistic Psychology of Dialogue." *Behavioral and Brain Sciences* 27, no. 2 (2004). https://doi.org /10.1017/s0140525x04000056.

Playful Science. Accessed June 3, 2021. https://web.stanford.edu/group /playfulscience/cgi-bin/about.php.

Polanin, Megan, and Elizabeth Vera. "Bullying Prevention and Social Justice." *Theory Into Practice* 52, no. 4 (February 2013): 303–10. https://doi .org/10.1080/00405841.2013.829736.

Polikoff, Morgan S. "Is Common Core 'Working'? And Where Does Common Core Research Go From Here?" *AERA Open* 3, no. 1 (2017): 233285841769174. https://doi.org/10.1177/2332858417691749.

Poole, Carla, Susan A. Miller, and Ellen Booth Church. "Ages & Stages: Empathy." Scholastic. Accessed May 26, 2021. https://www.scholastic.com /teachers/articles/teaching-content/ages-stages-empathy/.

Price, A.W. "Perfect Friendship in Aristotle." In *Love and Friendship in Plato and Aristotle*. Oxford: Oxford Univ. Press, 1990. https://doi.org/10.1093 /acprof:oso/9780198248996.003.0004.

Proyer, René T. "The Well-Being of Playful Adults: Adult Playfulness, Subjective Well-Being, Physical Well-Being, and the Pursuit of Enjoyable Activities." *European Journal of Humour Research* 1, no. 1 (2013): 84–98. https://doi.org/10.7592/ejhr2013.1.1.proyer.

Proyer, René T., Fabian Gander, Emma J. Bertenshaw, and Kay Brauer. "The Positive Relationships of Playfulness with Indicators of Health, Activity, and Physical Fitness." *Frontiers in Psychology* 9 (2018). https://doi.org/10.3389/fpsyg.2018.01440.

Pruett, Kyle D. "Children at Play: Clinical and Developmental Approaches to Meaning and Representation." *Journal of the American Academy of Child & Adolescent Psychiatry* 34, no. 9 (1995): 1249. https://doi.org/10.1097/00004583-199509000-00027.

Psouni, Elia, Andreas Falck, Leni Boström, Martin Persson, Lisa Sidén, and Maria Wallin. "Together I Can! Joint Attention Boosts 3- to 4-Year-Olds' Performance in a Verbal False-Belief Test." *Child Development* 90, no. 1 (2018): 35–50. https://doi.org/10.1111/cdev.13075.

Rath, Tom, and Audra Wallace. *How Full Is Your Bucket?* New York: Scholastic, 2019.

Recchia, Holly E., Cecilia Wainryb, Stacia Bourne, and Monisha Pasupathi. "The Construction of Moral Agency in Mother–Child Conversations about Helping and Hurting across Childhood and Adolescence." *Developmental Psychology* 50, no. 1 (2014): 34–44. https://doi.org/10.1037/a0033492.

Remmele, Bernd, and Nicola Whitton. "Disrupting the Magic Circle: The Impact of Negative Social Gaming Behaviours." In *Psychology, Pedagogy, and Assessment in Serious Games.* Edited by Thomas M. Connolly, Elizabeth Boyle, Gavin Baxter, and Pablo Moreno-Ger. Hershey, PA: IGI Global, 2014. https://doi.org/10.4018/978-1-4666-4773-2.ch006.

"Resilience." Center on the Developing Child at Harvard University. AccessedAugust 17, 2020. https://developingchild.harvard.edu/science/key-concepts/resilience/.

Rettew, David. *Child Temperament: New Thinking about the Boundary between Traits and Illness.* New York: W.W. Norton, 2013.

Rettner, Rachael. "Are Today's Youth Less Creative & Imaginative?" LiveScience. August 12, 2011. https://www.livescience.com/15535-children-creative.html.

"The Rigorous and Regulated Learning Environment." RWJF, March 19, 2014. https://www.rwjf.org/en/library/research/2014/03/the-rigorous-and-regulated-learning-environment.html.

Rijsewijk, Loes G., Tom A.B. Snijders, Jan Kornelis Dijkstra, Christian Steglich, and René Veenstra. "The Interplay Between Adolescents' Friendships and the Exchange of Help: A Longitudinal Multiplex Social Network Study." *Journal of Research on Adolescence* 30, no. 1 (October 2019): 63–77. https://doi.org/10.1111/jora.12501.

Rittle-Johnson, Bethany, Erica L. Zippert, and Katherine L. Boice. "The Roles of Patterning and Spatial Skills in Early Mathematics Development." *Early Childhood Research Quarterly* 46 (2019): 166–78. https://doi.org/10.1016/j .ecresq.2018.03.006.

Rnic, Katerina, David J. Dozois, and Rod A. Martin. "Cognitive Distortions, Humor Styles, and Depression." *Europe's Journal of Psychology* 12, no. 3 (2016): 348–62. https://doi.org/10.5964/ejop.v12i3.1118.

Robinson, J. "Empathy and Prosocial Behavior." In *Encyclopedia of Infant and Early Childhood Development*. Edited by Marshall M. Haith and Janette B. Benson, 441–50. Cambridge: Academic Press, 2008. https://doi.org/10 .1016/b978-012370877-9.00056-6.

Robinson, Ken, and Lou Aronica. *The Element: How Finding Your Passion Changes Everything*. New York: Random House, 2009.

Rogin, Madeleine. "Seeing, Noticing, and Talking About Differences with Young Children." EmbraceRace. Accessed June 10, 2021. https://www .embracerace.org/resources/seeing-noticing-talking-about-difference-with -young-children.

Romeo, Rachel R., Joshua Segaran, Julia A. Leonard, Sydney T. Robinson, Martin R. West, Allyson P. Mackey, Anastasia Yendiki, Meredith L. Rowe, and John D.E. Gabrieli. "Language Exposure Relates to Structural Neural Connectivity in Childhood." *Journal of Neuroscience* 38, no. 36 (2018): 7870–77. https://doi.org/10.1523/jneurosci.0484-18.2018.

Romeo, Rachel R., Julia A. Leonard, Sydney T. Robinson, Martin R. West, Allyson P. Mackey, Meredith L. Rowe, and John D.E. Gabrieli. "Beyond the 30-Million-Word Gap: Children's Conversational Exposure Is Associated with Language-Related Brain Function." *Psychological Science* 29, no. 5 (2018): 700–10. https://doi.org/10.1177/0956797617742725.

Root-Bernstein, Michele M. "The Creation of Imaginary Worlds." In *The Oxford Handbook of the Development of Imagination*. Edited by Marjorie Taylor, 417–37. New York: Oxford Univ. Press, 2013. https://doi.org/10.1093 /oxfordhb/9780195395761.013.0027.

Root-Bernstein, Michele. *Inventing Imaginary Worlds: From Childhood Play to Adult Creativity across the Arts and Sciences*. Lanham, MD: Rowman & Littlefield Education, 2014.

Rose, Todd. *The End of Average: How We Succeed in a World That Values Sameness*. New York: HarperOne, 2016.

Rosenblum, Katherine L., Susan C. McDonough, Arnold J. Sameroff, and Maria Muzik. "Reflection in Thought and Action: Maternal Parenting Reflectivity Predicts Mind-Minded Comments and Interactive Behavior." *Infant Mental Health Journal* 29, no. 4 (2008): 362–76. https://doi .org/10.1002/imhj.20184.

Roser, Max, and Esteban Ortiz-Ospina. "Literacy." Our World in Data, September 20, 2018. https://ourworldindata.org/literacy.

Roth-Hanania, Ronit, Maayan Davidov, and Carolyn Zahn-Waxler. "Empathy

Development from 8 to 16 Months: Early Signs of Concern for Others." *Infant Behavior and Development* 34, no. 3 (2011): 447–58. https://doi.org/10.1016/j.infbeh.2011.04.007.

Rothbart, Mary K., and John E. Bates. "Temperament." In *Handbook of Child Psychology*. Edited by Nancy Eisenberg. New York: John Wiley & Sons, 2007. https://doi.org/10.1002/9780470147658.chpsy0303.

Rothbart, Mary K., Lesa K. Ellis, M. Rosario Rueda, and Michael I. Posner. "Developing Mechanisms of Temperamental Effortful Control." *Journal of Personality* 71, no. 6 (2003): 1113–44. https://doi.org/10.1111/1467-6494.7106009.

Rothbart, Mary Klevjord. "Measurement of Temperament in Infancy." *Child Development* 52, no. 2 (1981): 569–78. https://doi.org/10.2307/1129176.

Rowe, Meredith L. "A Longitudinal Investigation of the Role of Quantity and Quality of Child-Directed Speech in Vocabulary Development." *Child Development* 83, no. 5 (2012): 1762–74. https://doi.org/10.1111/j.1467-8624.2012.01805.x.

Rowe, Meredith L., and Kathryn A. Leech. "A Parent Intervention with a Growth Mindset Approach Improves Children's Early Gesture and Vocabulary Development." *Developmental Science* 22, no. 4 (2018). https://doi.org/10.1111/desc.12792.

Roxburgh, Susan. "Parental Time Pressures and Depression among Married Dual-Earner Parents." *Journal of Family Issues* 33, no. 8 (September 2011): 1027–53. https://doi.org/10.1177/0192513x11425324.

Ruble, Diane N., Lisa J. Taylor, Lisa Cyphers, Faith K. Greulich, Leah E. Lurye, and Patrick E. Shrout. "The Role of Gender Constancy in Early Gender Development." *Child Development* 78, no. 4 (2007): 1121–36. https://doi.org/10.1111/j.1467-8624.2007.01056.x.

Russ, Sandra W. *Pretend Play in Childhood: Foundation of Adult Creativity*. Washington, DC: American Psychological Association, 2014. https://doi.org/10.1037/14282-003.

Russ, Sandra W. "Pretend Play, Affect, and Creativity." In *New Directions in Aesthetics, Creativity, and the Arts*. Edited by Paul Locher, Colin Martindale, and Leonid Dorfman, 239–50. New York: Routledge, 2020. https://doi.org/10.4324/9781315224084-19.

Russ, Sandra, and Larissa Niec. *Play in Clinical Practice Evidence-Based Approaches*. New York: Guilford Press, 2011.

Ryan, Richard M., and Edward L. Deci. *Self-Determination Theory: Basic Psychological Needs in Motivation, Development, and Wellness*. New York: Guilford Press, 2018.

Sajaniemi, N., J. Mäkelä, T. Salokorpi, L. von Wendt, T. Hämäläinen, and L. Hakamies-Blomqvist. "Cognitive Performance and Attachment Patterns at Four Years of Age in Extremely Low Birth Weight Infants after Early Intervention." *European Child & Adolescent Psychiatry* 10, no. 2 (2001): 122–29. https://doi.org/10.1007/s007870170035.

Sajaniemi, Nina, Liisa Hakamies-Blomqvist, Jukka Mäkelä, Anne Avellan, Hannu Rita, and Lennart von Wendt. "Cognitive Development, Temperament and Behavior at 2 Years as Indicative of Language Development at 4 Years in Pre-Term Infants." *Child Psychiatry and Human Development* 31, no. 4 (2001): 329–46. https://doi.org/10.1023/a:1010238523628.

Salley, Brenda, Nancy C. Brady, Lesa Hoffman, and Kandace Fleming. "Preverbal Communication Complexity in Infants." *Infancy* 25, no. 1 (2019): 4–21. https://doi.org/10.1111/infa.12318.

Salmivalli, Christina, Antti Kärnä, and Elisa Poskiparta. "Counteracting Bullying in Finland: The KiVa Program and Its Effects on Different Forms of Being Bullied." *International Journal of Behavioral Development* 35, no. 5 (2011): 405–11. https://doi.org/10.1177/0165025411407457.

Salo, Virginia, Meredith Rowe, Natasha Cabrera, and Kathryn Leech. "Father Input and Child Vocabulary Development: The Importance of *Wh* Questions and Clarification Requests." *Seminars in Speech and Language* 34, no. 04 (February 2013). 249–59. https://doi.org/10.1055/s 0033 1353445.

Sanders, Sam, and Kenya Young. "A Black Mother Reflects on Giving Her 3 Sons 'The Talk' . . . Again and Again." NPR, June 28, 2020. https://www.npr.org/2020/06/28/882383372/a-black-mother-reflects-on-giving-her-3-sons-the-talk-again-and-again.

Sandstrom, Gillian M., and Elizabeth W. Dunn. "Social Interactions and Well-Being." *Personality and Social Psychology Bulletin* 40, no. 7 (2014): 910–22. https://doi.org/10.1177/0146167214529799.

Sansavini, Alessandra, Annalisa Guarini, and Maria Cristina Caselli. "Preterm Birth: Neuropsychological Profiles and Atypical Developmental Pathways." *Developmental Disabilities Research Reviews* 17, no. 2 (2011): 102–13. https://doi.org/10.1002/ddrr.1105.

Sansavini, Alessandra, Annalisa Guarini, Silvia Savini, Serena Broccoli, Laura Justice, Rosina Alessandroni, and Giacomo Faldella. "Longitudinal Trajectories of Gestural and Linguistic Abilities in Very Preterm Infants in the Second Year of Life." *Neuropsychologia* 49, no. 13 (2011): 3677–88. https://doi.org/10.1016/j.neuropsychologia.2011.09.023.

Sanson, Ann, Sheryl A. Hemphill, and Diana Smart. "Connections between Temperament and Social Development: A Review." *Social Development* 13, no. 1 (2004): 142–70. https://doi.org/10.1046/j.1467-9507.2004.00261.x.

Scardamalia, Marlene, and Carl Bereiter. "Child as Coinvestigator: Helping Children Gain Insight into Their Own Mental Processes." In *Learning and Motivation in the Classroom*. Edited by Scott G. Paris, Gary M. Olson, and Harold W. Stevenson, 61–82. London: Routledge, 2017. https://doi.org/10.4324/9781315188522-4.

Schonert-Reichl, Kimberly A., Veronica Smith, Anat Zaidman-Zait, and Clyde Hertzman. "Promoting Children's Prosocial Behaviors in School: Impact of the 'Roots of Empathy' Program on the Social and Emotional Competence of School-Aged Children." *School Mental Health* 4, no. 1 (April 2011): 1–21. https://doi.org/10.1007/s12310-011-9064-7.

Schultz, Stacey. "Your Child's Temperament: Finding the Right Parenting Style to Match." ParentMap, April 28, 2012. https://www.parentmap.com /article/your-childs-temperament-finding-the-right-parenting-style.

Schunk, Dale H. "Verbalization and Children's Self-Regulated Learning." *Contemporary Educational Psychology* 11, no. 4 (1986): 347–69. https://doi .org/10.1016/0361-476x(86)90030-5.

Schwab, Katharine. "Will Toys Ever Go Beyond Blue and Pink?" *The Atlantic*, May 5, 2016. https://www.theatlantic.com/entertainment/archive/2016/05 /beyond-blue-and-pink-the-rise-of-gender-neutral-toys/480624/.

Schwebel, David C., and Jodie M. Plumert. "Longitudinal and Concurrent Relations among Temperament, Ability Estimation, and Injury Proneness." *Child Development* 70, no. 3 (1999): 700–12. https://doi.org/10.1111/1467 -8624.00050.

Seigneuric, Alix, and Marie-France Ehrlich. "Contribution of Working Memory Capacity to Children's Reading Comprehension: A Longitudinal Investigation." *Reading and Writing* 18, no. 7-9 (2005): 617–56. https://doi .org/10.1007/s11145-005-2038-0.

Seja, Astrida L., and Sandra W. Russ. "Children's Fantasy Play and Emotional Understanding." *Journal of Clinical Child Psychology* 28, no. 2 (1999): 269–77. https://doi.org/10.1207/s15374424jccp2802_13.

Selman, Robert L. *The Growth of Interpersonal Understanding: Developmental and Clinical Analyses.* San Diego: Academic Press, 1980.

Senior, Jennifer. *All Joy and No Fun: The Paradox of Modern Parenthood.* New York: Ecco, 2014.

Shai, Dana, and Jay Belsky. "Parental Embodied Mentalizing: How the Nonverbal Dance between Parents and Infants Predicts Children's Socio-Emotional Functioning." *Attachment & Human Development* 19, no. 2 (2016): 191–219. https://doi.org/10.1080/14616734.2016 .1255653.

Shaw, George Bernard. *Everybody's Political What's What?* London: Constable and Company Limited, 1944.

Shechet, Ellie. "How to Do Nothing: The New Guide to Refocusing on the Real World." *The Guardian*, April 2, 2019. https://www.theguardian.com /lifeandstyle/2019/apr/02/jenny-odell-how-to-do-nothing-attention.

Shin, So Yeon, Kathryn A. Leech, and Meredith L. Rowe. "Examining Relations between Parent-Child Narrative Talk and Children's Episodic Foresight and Theory of Mind." *Cognitive Development* 55 (2020): 100910. https://doi.org/10.1016/j.cogdev.2020.100910.

Shmukler, Diana. "Preschool Imaginative Play Predisposition and Its Relationship to Subsequent Third Grade Assessment." *Imagination, Cognition and Personality* 2, no. 3 (1983): 231–40. https://doi.org/10.2190 /17cd-bkar-ybky-elew.

Shonkoff, Jack P. "Leveraging the Biology of Adversity to Address the Roots of Disparities in Health and Development." *Proceedings of the National Academy of Sciences* 109, no. Supplement_2 (August 2012): 17302–7. https://doi.org/10.1073/pnas.1121259109.

Shonkoff, Jack P., and Linda Richter. "The Powerful Reach of Early Childhood Development." In *Handbook of Early Childhood Development Research and Its Impact on Global Policy*. Edited by Pia Rebello Britto, Patrice L. Engle, and Charles M. Super. New York: Oxford Univ. Press, 2013. https://doi.org/10.1093/acprof:oso/9780199922994.003.0002.

Shumow, Lee. "Promoting Parental Attunement to Children's Mathematical Reasoning Through Parent Education." *Journal of Applied Developmental Psychology* 19, no. 1 (1998): 109–27. https://doi.org/10.1016/s0193-3973(99)80031-8.

Shutts, Kristin. "Young Children's Preferences: Gender, Race, and Social Status." *Child Development Perspectives* 9, no. 4 (2015): 262–66. https://doi.org/10.1111/cdep.12154.

Sicart, Miguel. *Play Matters*. Cambridge, MA: MIT Press, 2017.

Siegel, Daniel J. *Mindsight: The New Science of Personal Transformation*. New York: Bantam Books, 2011.

Siegel, Daniel J., and Tina Payne Bryson. *The Power of Showing Up: How Parental Presence Shapes Who Our Kids Become and How Their Brains Get Wired*. New York: Ballantine Books, 2021.

Siegel, Linda S. "Perspectives on Dyslexia." *Paediatrics & Child Health* 11, no. 9 (2006): 581–87. https://doi.org/10.1093/pch/11.9.581.

Signorella, Margaret L., Rebecca S. Bigler, and Lynn S. Liben. "Developmental Differences in Children's Gender Schemata about Others: A Meta-Analytic Review." *Developmental Review* 13, no. 2 (1993): 147–83. https://doi.org/10.1006/drev.1993.1007.

Simien, Evelyn M. "Doing Intersectionality Research: From Conceptual Issues to Practical Examples." *Politics & Gender* 3, no. 2 (2007). https://doi.org/10.1017/s1743923x07000086.

"Simple Interactions." Fred Rogers Center for Early Learning & Children's Media. Accessed June 4, 2021. https://www.fredrogerscenter.org/what-we-do/simple-interactions/.

Singer, Dorothy G., J. L. Singer, H. D'agostino, and R. DeLong. "Children's Pastimes and Play in Sixteen Nations: Is Free-Play Declining?" *American Journal of Play* 1, no. 3 (Winter 2009): 283–312. https://eric.ed.gov/?id=EJ1069041.

Singer, Dorothy G., and Jerome L. Singer. *The House of Make-Believe: Children's Play and the Developing Imagination*. Cambridge, MA: Harvard Univ. Press, 1990.

Singer, Jerome L. "Enhancing Elementary School Children's Achievement and Creativity through Imaginative Play in the Classroom." *PsycEXTRA Dataset*, 2011. https://doi.org/10.1037/e659042011-001.

Singer, Jerome L., and Dorothy G. Singer. "Preschoolers' Imaginative Play as Precursor of Narrative Consciousness." *Imagination, Cognition and Personality* 25, no. 2 (2005): 97–117. https://doi.org/10.2190/0kqu-9a2v-yam2-xd8j.

Singer, Jerome L., and Dorothy G. Singer. "Professional Paths over Six Decades Researching and Practicing Play." *International Journal of Play* 4, no. 2 (April 2015): 190–202. https://doi.org/10.1080/21594937.2015.1060570.

Singer, Judy. *Neurodiversity: The Birth of an Idea.* Lexington, KY: Judy Singer, 2017.

Sisk, Victoria F., Alexander P. Burgoyne, Jingze Sun, Jennifer L. Butler, and Brooke N. Macnamara. "To What Extent and Under Which Circumstances Are Growth Mind-Sets Important to Academic Achievement? Two Meta-Analyses." *Psychological Science* 29, no. 4 (May 2018): 549–71. https://doi.org/10.1177/0956797617739704.

Slomkowski, Cheryl, and Judy Dunn. "Young Children's Understanding of Other People's Beliefs and Feelings and Their Connected Communication with Friends." *Developmental Psychology* 32, no. 3 (1996): 442–47. https://doi.org/10.1037/0012-1649.32.3.442.

Smith, Peter K. "Children at Play: Clinical and Developmental Approaches to Meaning and Representation." *Child Psychology and Psychiatry Review* 6, no. 3 (2001): 144–47. https://doi.org/10.1017/s1360641701232699.

Snow, Catherine E. "Conversations with Children." In *Language Acquisition: Studies in First Language Development.* Edited by Paul Fletcher and Michael Garman, 69–89. Cambridge: Cambridge Univ. Press, 1986. https://doi.org/10.1017/cbo9780511620683.006.

Snow, Catherine E. "The Theoretical Basis for Relationships between Language and Literacy in Development." *Journal of Research in Childhood Education* 6, no. 1 (1991): 5–10. https://doi.org/10.1080/02568549109594817.

Snow, Catherine E., M. Susan Burns, and Peg Griffin. *Preventing Reading Difficulties in Young Children.* Washington, DC: National Academies Press, 1998.

Snowling, Margaret J., Charles Hulme, and Kate Nation. "Defining and Understanding Dyslexia: Past, Present and Future." *Oxford Review of Education* 46, no. 4 (March 2020): 501–13. https://doi.org/10.1080/03054985.2020.1765756.

Spencer, Mercedes, and Richard K. Wagner. "The Comprehension Problems of Children with Poor Reading Comprehension Despite Adequate Decoding: A Meta-Analysis." *Review of Educational Research* 88, no. 3 (March 2018): 366–400. https://doi.org/10.3102/0034654317749187.

Stafford, Mai, Diana L. Kuh, Catharine R. Gale, Gita Mishra, and Marcus Richards. "Parent–Child Relationships and Offspring's Positive Mental Wellbeing from Adolescence to Early Older Age." *Journal of Positive Psychology* 11, no. 3 (2015): 326–37. https://doi.org/10.1080/17439760.2015.1081971.

Stanovich, Keith E. "Matthew Effects in Reading: Some Consequences of Individual Differences in the Acquisition of Literacy." *Reading Research Quarterly* 21, no. 4 (1986): 360–407. https://doi.org/10.1177/0022057409189001-204.

"The State of Learning Disabilities: Understanding the 1 in 5." National Center for Learning Disabilities, February 1, 2017. https://www.ncld.org/wp -content/uploads/2017/03/1-in-5-Snapshot.Fin_.03142017.pdf.

"Statistics." National Institute of Mental Health. US Department of Health and Human Services. Accessed June 4, 2021. https://www.nimh.nih.gov /health/statistics/.

Stelmack, Robert M., and Anastasios Stalikas. "Galen and the Humour Theory of Temperament." *Personality and Individual Differences* 12, no. 3 (1991): 255–63. https://doi.org/10.1016/0191-8869(91)90111-n.

Stevens, Elizabeth A., Melodee A. Walker, and Sharon Vaughn. "The Effects of Reading Fluency Interventions on the Reading Fluency and Reading Comprehension Performance of Elementary Students with Learning Disabilities: A Synthesis of the Research from 2001 to 2014." *Journal of Learning Disabilities* 50, no. 5 (November 2016): 576–90. https://doi.org/10 .1177/0022219416638028.

Stolt, S., A. Lind, J. Matomäki, L. Haataja, H. Lapinleimu, and L. Lehtonen. "Do the Early Development of Gestures and Receptive and Expressive Language Predict Language Skills at 5;0 in Prematurely Born Very-Low-Birth-Weight Children?" *Journal of Communication Disorders* 61 (2016): 16–28. https://doi.org/10.1016/j.jcomdis.2016.03.002.

Stothard, Susan E., and Charles Hulme. "A Comparison of Phonological Skills in Children with Reading Comprehension Difficulties and Children with Decoding Difficulties." *Journal of Child Psychology and Psychiatry* 36, no. 3 (1995): 399–408. https://doi.org/10.1111/j.1469-7610.1995.tb01298.x.

Strauss, Valerie. "In a Liberal Boston Suburb, Kindergarten Teachers Say Their Students Are Learning to 'Hate' School." *Washington Post*, June 13, 2019. https://www.washingtonpost.com/education/2019/06/13/liberal -boston-suburb-kindergarten-teachers-say-their-students-are-learning -hate-school/.

Strouse, Gabrielle A., and Jennifer E. Samson. "Learning from Video: A Meta-Analysis of the Video Deficit in Children Ages 0 to 6 Years." *Child Development* 92, no. 1 (January/February 2021): e20–e38. https://doi.org /10.1111/cdev.13429.

Su, Jeb. "Why Amazon Alexa Is Always Listening to Your Conversations: Analysis." *Forbes*, May 16, 2019. https://www.forbes.com/sites/jeanbaptiste /2019/05/16/why-amazon-alexa-is-always-listening-to-your-conversations -analysis/?sh=108f020d2378.

Sundem, Garth. "Kids with Low Self-Esteem: The Parental Praise Paradox." *Wired*, March 6, 2013. https://www.wired.com/2013/03/kids-with-low-self -esteem-the-parental-praise-paradox/.

Suskind, Dana. *Thirty Million Words: Building a Child's Brain*. New York: Dutton, 2016.

Svetlova, Margarita, Sara R. Nichols, and Celia A. Brownell. "Toddlers' Prosocial Behavior: From Instrumental to Empathic to Altruistic Helping."

Child Development 81, no. 6 (2010): 1814–27. https://doi.org/10.1111/j .1467-8624.2010.01512.x.

Szycik, Gregor R., Bahram Mohammadi, Thomas F. Münte, and Bert T. te Wildt. "Lack of Evidence That Neural Empathic Responses Are Blunted in Excessive Users of Violent Video Games: An FMRI Study." *Frontiers in Psychology* 8 (August 2017). https://doi.org/10.3389/fpsyg.2017.00174.

Tatum, Beverly Daniel. *Why Are All the Black Kids Sitting Together in the Cafeteria?* Revised Edition. New York: Basic Books, 2017.

Taussig, Rebekah. *Sitting Pretty: The View from My Ordinary Resilient Disabled Body.* New York: HarperOne, 2020.

Terada, Youki. "How Metacognition Boosts Learning." Edutopia, November 21, 2017. https://www.edutopia.org/article/how-metacognition-boosts -learning.

Therrien, William J. "Fluency and Comprehension Gains as a Result of Repeated Reading." *Remedial and Special Education* 25, no. 4 (2004): 252–61. https://doi.org/10.1177/07419325040250040801.

Thomas, Alexander, Stella Chess, and Herbert G. Birch. "The Origin of Personality." *Scientific American* 223, no. 2 (1970): 102–9. https://doi.org/10 .1038/scientificamerican0870-102.

Thornberg, Robert, Laura Tenenbaum, Kris Varjas, Joel Meyers, Tomas Jungert, and Gina Vanegas. "Bystander Motivation in Bullying Incidents: To Intervene or Not to Intervene?" *Western Journal of Emergency Medicine* 13, no. 3 (January 2012): 247–52. https://doi.org/10.5811/westjem.2012.3.11792.

Torgesen, Joseph K., Richard K. Wagner, and Carol A. Rashotte. "Longitudinal Studies of Phonological Processing and Reading." *Journal of Learning Disabilities* 27, no. 5 (1994): 276–86. https://doi.org/10.1177/00222194 9402700503.

Torres, Carlos Alberto, and Emiliano Bosio. "Global Citizenship Education at the Crossroads: Globalization, Global Commons, Common Good, and Critical Consciousness." *Prospects* 48, no. 3-4 (2020): 99–113. https://doi .org/10.1007/s11125-019-09458-w.

Tough, Paul. *Helping Children Succeed: What Works and Why.* Boston: Houghton Mifflin Harcourt, 2016.

Tracy, Sarah J. "Let's Talk: Conversation as a Defining Moment for the Communication Discipline." *Health Communication* 35, no. 7 (2019): 910–16. https://doi.org/10.1080/10410236.2019.1593081.

Treiman, Rebecca. "Phonological Awareness and Its Roles in Learning to Read and Spell." In *Phonological Awareness in Reading.* Edited by Diane J. Sawyer and Barbara J. Fox, 159–89. New York: Springer, 1991. https://doi.org/10 .1007/978-1-4612-3010-6_6.

Triplett, Cheri Foster, and Mary Alice Barksdale. "Third through Sixth Graders' Perceptions of High-Stakes Testing." *Journal of Literacy Research* 37, no. 2 (2005): 237–60. https://doi.org/10.1207/s15548430jlr3702_5.

Turner, Lisa A., and Paul E. Turner. "The Relation of Behavioral Inhibition and Perceived Parenting to Maladaptive Perfectionism in College Students." *Personality and Individual Differences* 50, no. 6 (2011): 840–44. https://doi.org/10.1016/j.paid.2011.01.006.

Uccelli, Paola, Özlem Ece Demir-Lira, Meredith L. Rowe, Susan Levine, and Susan Goldin-Meadow. "Children's Early Decontextualized Talk Predicts Academic Language Proficiency in Midadolescence." *Child Development* 90, no. 5 (2018): 1650–63. https://doi.org/10.1111/cdev.13034.

Uhls, Yalda T., Minas Michikyan, Jordan Morris, Debra Garcia, Gary W. Small, Eleni Zgourou, and Patricia M. Greenfield. "Five Days at Outdoor Education Camp without Screens Improves Preteen Skills with Nonverbal Emotion Cues." *Computers in Human Behavior* 39 (2014): 387–92. https://doi.org/10.1016/j.chb.2014.05.036.

UNICEF. "Learning through Play," October 2018. https://www.unicef.org /sites/default/files/2018-12/UNICEF-Lego-Foundation-Learning-through -Play.pdf.

Vaillancourt, Tracy, Robert Faris, and Faye Mishna. "Cyberbullying in Children and Youth: Implications for Health and Clinical Practice." *Canadian Journal of Psychiatry* 62, no. 6 (2016): 368–73. https://doi.org/10 .1177/0706743716684791.

van Harmelen, A.-L., R. A. Kievit, K. Ioannidis, S. Neufeld, P.B. Jones, E. Bullmore, R. Dolan, P. Fonagy, and I. Goodyer. "Adolescent Friendships Predict Later Resilient Functioning across Psychosocial Domains in a Healthy Community Cohort." *Psychological Medicine* 47, no. 13 (November 2017): 2312–22. https://doi.org/10.1017/s0033291717000836.

Vanderbilt, Douglas, and Marilyn Augustyn. "The Effects of Bullying." *Paediatrics and Child Health* 20, no. 7 (2010): 315–20. https://doi.org/10 .1016/j.paed.2010.03.008.

Varygiannes, Dorothy. "The Impact of Open-Ended Tasks." *Teaching Children Mathematics* 20, no. 5 (2013): 277–80. https://doi.org/10.5951/teacchilmath .20.5.0277.

Vygotsky, L. S., Michael Cole, Sally Stein, and Allan Sekula. *Mind in Society: The Development of Higher Psychological Processes*. Cambridge, MA: Harvard Univ. Press, 1978.

Vygotsky, L.S. *The Collected Works of L.S. Vygotsky*. Edited by Robert W. Rieber and Aaron S. Carton. New York: Plenum Press, 1987.

Wachsmuth, Ipke, Manuela Lenzen, and Günther Knoblich. "Embodied Communication in Humans and Machines." *Oxford Scholarship Online*, March 2012. https://doi.org/10.1093/acprof:oso/9780199231751.001.0001.

Wagers, Keshia B., and Elizabeth J. Kiel. "The Influence of Parenting and Temperament on Empathy Development in Toddlers." *Journal of Family Psychology* 33, no. 4 (2019): 391–400. https://doi.org/10.1037/fam0000505.

Ware, Bronnie. *The Top Five Regrets of the Dying: A Life Transformed by the Dearly Departing*. Alexandria, NSW: Hay House Australia, 2019.

Wasik, Barbara A., and Charlene Iannone-Campbell. "Developing Vocabulary through Purposeful, Strategic Conversations." *The Reading Teacher* 66, no. 4 (2012): 321–32. https://doi.org/10.1002/trtr.01095.

Wasik, Barbara A., and Mary Alice Bond. "Beyond the Pages of a Book: Interactive Book Reading and Language Development in Preschool Classrooms." *Journal of Educational Psychology* 93, no. 2 (2001): 243–50. https://doi.org/10.1037/0022-0663.93.2.243.

Wass, Rob, and Clinton Golding. "Sharpening a Tool for Teaching: The Zone of Proximal Development." *Teaching in Higher Education* 19, no. 6 (2014): 671–84. https://doi.org/10.1080/13562517.2014.901958.

Weisberg, Deena Skolnick, Kathy Hirsh-Pasek, and Roberta Michnick Golinkoff. "Guided Play: Where Curricular Goals Meet a Playful Pedagogy." *Mind, Brain, and Education* 7, no. 2 (2013): 104–12. https://doi.org/10.1111/mbe.12015.

Weisberg, Deena Skolnick, Kathy Hirsh-Pasek, Roberta Michnick Golinkoff, Audrey K. Kittredge, and David Klahr. "Guided Play: Principles and Practices." *Current Directions in Psychological Science* 25, no. 3 (2016): 177–82. https://doi.org/10.1177/0963721416645512.

Weissbourd, Richard. *The Parents We Mean to Be: How Well-Intentioned Adults Undermine Children's Moral and Emotional Development.* Boston: Houghton Mifflin Harcourt, 2009.

Weissbourd, Richard, and Rebecca Givens Rolland. "Learning about Love: How Schools Can Better Prepare Students for Romantic Relationships." *Harvard Education Letter* 29, no. 2 (March/April 2013). https://www.hepg .org/hel-home/issues/29_2/helarticle/learning-about-love.

Wentzel, Kathryn R., Carolyn McNamara Barry, and Kathryn A. Caldwell. "Friendships in Middle School: Influences on Motivation and School Adjustment." *Journal of Educational Psychology* 96, no. 2 (2004): 195–203. https://doi.org/10.1037/0022-0663.96.2.195.

Westheimer, Joel, and Joseph Kahne. "What Kind of Citizen? The Politics of Educating for Democracy." *American Educational Research Journal* 41, no. 2 (2004): 237–69. https://doi.org/10.3102/00028312041002237.

"What Is Mindsight? An Interview with Dr. Dan Siegel." PsychAlive, September 15, 2017. https://www.psychalive.org/what-is-mindsight-an -interview-with-dr-dan-siegel/.

"Why Kids Become Bullies." Yale Medicine, February 28, 2017. https://www .yalemedicine.org/stories/understanding-bullying/.

Whyte, David. "10 Questions That Have No Right to Go Away." Oprah.com, June 15, 2011. https://www.oprah.com/oprahs-lifeclass/poet-david-whytes -questions-that-have-no-right-to-go-away_1.

Williams, Amanda, Kelly O'Driscoll, and Chris Moore. "The Influence of Empathic Concern on Prosocial Behavior in Children." *Frontiers in Psychology* 5 (December 2014). https://doi.org/10.3389/fpsyg.2014.00425.

Wingfield, Adia Harvey. "Color Blindness Is Counterproductive." *The Atlantic*, September 13, 2015. https://www.theatlantic.com/politics/archive/2015/09 /color-blindness-is-counterproductive/405037/.

Winner, Michelle Garcia, and Pamela J. Crooke. "Social Communication Strategies for Adolescents with Autism." *The ASHA Leader* 16, no. 1 (2011): 8–11. https://doi.org/10.1044/leader.ftr1.16012011.8.

Winnicott, Donald W. "Communication between Infant and Mother, and Mother and Infant, Compared and Contrasted." In *The Collected Works of D. W. Winnicott*. Edited by Lesley Caldwell and Helen Taylor Robinson, 227–38. Oxford: Univ. Press, 2016. https://doi.org/10.1093/med:psych/9780190271404 .003.0040.

Winthrop, Rebecca. "How Playful Learning Can Help Leapfrog Progress in Education." Brookings, April 2, 2019. https://www.brookings.edu/research /how-playful-learning-can-help-leapfrog-progress-in-education/.

Wolf, Maryanne. *Reader, Come Home: The Reading Brain in a Digital World*. New York: Harper, 2019.

Wright, Marguerite A. *I'm Chocolate, You're Vanilla: Raising Healthy Black and Biracial Children in a Race-Conscious World*. San Francisco: Jossey-Bass, 2000.

Wright, Michelle F., Sebastian Wachs, and Zheng Huang. "Adolescents' Popularity-Motivated Aggression and Prosocial Behaviors: The Roles of Callous-Unemotional Traits and Social Status Insecurity." *Frontiers in Psychology* 12 (2021). https://doi.org/10.3389/fpsyg.2021.606865.

Wulansari, Ossy Dwi, Johanna Pirker, Johannes Kopf, and Christian Guetl. "Video Games and Their Correlation to Empathy." *Advances in Intelligent Systems and Computing*, 2020, 151–63. https://doi.org/10.1007/978-3-030-40274-7_16.

Xi, Jiao, and James P. Lantolf. "Scaffolding and the Zone of Proximal Development: A Problematic Relationship." *Journal for the Theory of Social Behaviour* 51, no. 1 (2020): 25–48. https://doi.org/10.1111/jtsb.12260.

The Yale Center for Dyslexia & Creativity (website). Accessed May 29, 2021. https://dyslexia.yale.edu/.

Yaratan, Huseyin, and Rusen Yucesoylu. "Self-Esteem, Self-Concept, Self-Talk and Significant Others' Statements in Fifth Grade Students: Differences According to Gender and School Type." *Procedia - Social and Behavioral Sciences* 2, no. 2 (2010): 3506–18. https://doi.org/10.1016/j.sbspro.2010.03.543.

Ybarra, Oscar, Piotr Winkielman, Irene Yeh, Eugene Burnstein, and Liam Kavanagh. "Friends (and Sometimes Enemies) With Cognitive Benefits." *Social Psychological and Personality Science* 2, no. 3 (2010): 253–61. https://doi.org/10.1177/1948550610386808.

Yeager, David S., and Gregory M. Walton. "Social-Psychological Interventions in Education: They're Not Magic." *Review of Educational Research* 81, no. 2 (June 1, 2011): 267–301. https://doi.org/10.3102/0034654311405999.

Yee, Mia, and Rupert Brown. "The Development of Gender Differentiation in Young Children." *British Journal of Social Psychology* 33, no. 2 (1994): 183–96. https://doi.org/10.1111/j.2044-8309.1994.tb01017.x.

Yirmiya, Karen, Shai Motsan, Orna Zagoory-Sharon, and Ruth Feldman. "Human Attachment Triggers Different Social Buffering Mechanisms under High and Low Early Life Stress Rearing." *International Journal of*

Psychophysiology 152 (2020): 72–80. https://doi.org/10.1016/j.ijpsycho
.2020.04.001.

Yow, W. Quin, Ferninda Patrycia, and Suzanne Flynn. "Code-Switching in
Childhood." In *Bilingualism across the Lifespan: Factors Moderating Language
Proficiency.* Edited by Elena Nicoladis and Simona Montanari, 81–100.
Washington, DC: American Psychological Association, 2016. https://doi
.org/10.1037/14939-006.

Yuill, Nicola, and Alex F. Martin. "Curling Up with a Good E-Book: Mother-
Child Shared Story Reading on Screen or Paper Affects Embodied Interaction
and Warmth." *Frontiers in Psychology* 7 (2016). https://doi.org/10.3389/fpsyg
.2016.01951.

Zahn-Waxler, Carolyn, Marian Radke-Yarrow, Elizabeth Wagner, and
Michael Chapman. "Development of Concern for Others." *Developmental
Psychology* 28, no. 1 (1992): 126–36. https://doi.org/10.1037/0012-1649
.28.1.126.

Zebrowitz, Leslie A., Benjamin White, and Kristin Wieneke. "Mere Exposure
and Racial Prejudice: Exposure to Other-Race Faces Increases Liking for
Strangers of That Race." *Social Cognition* 26, no. 3 (2008): 259–75. https://
doi.org/10.1521/soco.2008.26.3.259.

Zelizer, Viviana A. *Pricing the Priceless Child: The Changing Social Value of
Children.* New York: Basic Books, 1985.

"Zone of Proximal Development." In *Encyclopedia of Evolutionary Psychological
Science.* Edited by Todd K. Shackelford and Viviana A. Weekes-Shackelford.
Cham, Switzerland: Springer, 2021. https://doi.org/10.1007/978-3-319
-19650-3_305625.

Index

NOTE: Page numbers for illustrations and notes are differentiated from those for regular text. An italicized *f* following the page number refers to illustrations and an **n** following the page number refers to notes.